Our Great Qing

Our Great Qing

The Mongols, Buddhism
and the State in
Late Imperial China

Johan Elverskog

University of Hawai'i Press   *Honolulu*

© 2006 University of Hawai'i Press

All rights reserved

Printed in the United States of America

Paperback edition 2008

13 12 11 10 09 08   6 5 4 3 2 1

Library of Congress Cataloging-In-Publication Data

Elverskog, Johan.

Our great Qing : the Mongols, Buddhism and the state in late imperial China /

Johan Elverskog.

p. cm.

Includes bibliographical references and index.

ISBN 978-0-8248-3021-2 (hbk. : alk. paper)

ISBN 978-0-8248-3330-5 (pbk. : alk. paper)

1. Mongols—History. 2. Buddhism. 3. China—History—Qing dynasty, 1644–1912.

I. Title.

DS19.E58 2006

951'.03—dc22

2006012482

Designed by University of Hawai'i Press production staff

Printed by the Maple-Vail Book Manufacturing Group

Now one of the most obscure of our institutions is that of the empire itself. In Peking, naturally, at the imperial court, there is some clarity to be found on this subject, though even that is more elusive than real. Also the teachers of political law and history in the schools of higher learning claim to be exactly informed on these matters, and to be capable of passing on their knowledge to their students. The farther one descends among the lower schools the more, naturally enough, does one find teachers' and pupils' doubts of their own knowledge vanishing, and superficial culture mounting sky-high around a few precepts that have been drilled into people's minds for centuries, precepts which, though they have lost nothing of their eternal truth, remain eternally invisible in this fog of confusion.

But it is precisely this question of the empire which in my opinion the common people should be asked to answer, since after all they are the empire's final support.

—Franz Kafka, *The Great Wall of China*

Contents

Acknowledgments / xi

Note on Transcription / xiii

Mongol Reign Periods / xv

Qing Reign Periods / xvii

Introduction / 1

1. The Mongols on the Eve of Conquest / 14

2. The Mongols and Political Authority / 40

3. Qing Ornamentalism and the Cult of Chinggis Khan / 63

4. The Poetics, Rituals and Language of Being Mongol,
   Buddhist and Qing / 90

5. The Buddhist Qing and Mongol Localization in
   the Nineteenth Century / 127

Epilogue / 166

Notes / 171

List of Tibetan Spellings / 207

Chinese Character Glossary / 209

References / 211

Index / 235

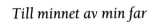

Till minnet av min far

Acknowledgments

This book is about challenging conventional narratives, thus I would like to begin by thanking my family. Nothing would have been possible without them. My mother's support through the years is beyond filial recompense; and, for inspiring me in so many ways, I dedicate this book to the memory of my father. My brothers have also always challenged me, and perhaps more important, brought me down to earth. And the wider family, from Sweden to Finland to Serbia, has always helped in putting into perspective the important things in life. Last, Liljana and Sebastian have done so much for me it is simply beyond words.

What follows, however, is a collection of words. It has appeared in many avatars. Its initial incarnation was as a dissertation; thus for their teaching, guidance and help throughout the years I thank my advisors, Christopher Atwood, György Kara, Jan Nattier, Elliot Sperling and Lynne Struve. I would also like to thank my many other teachers at Indiana University, especially Stephen Bokenkamp, Robert Campany, Larry Clark, Roger Janelli, Larry Moses, Robert Orsi and Michael Walter. Moreover, having now spent a few years on the other side of the desk and grappled with the pleasures and perils of teaching, I would like to thank my earlier teachers who helped foster my particular path: Gerald Berreman, James Carse, Alan Dundes, Robert Goldman, P. S. Jaini, Mark Juergensmeyer, Clara Sue Kidwell, Lewis Lancaster, Karen McCarthy-Brown, Jan Muhammad and Richard Payne.

Many others, some knowingly others unwittingly, have also helped me in various ways in the writing of this book. For all their help in reading through earlier drafts, raising questions at conferences, sharing with me their own work and generally helping me refine my thinking I thank Brian Baumann, Lubos Belka, Patricia Berger, Uradyn Bulag, Isabelle Charleux, Coyiji, Pamela Crossley, Mark Elliott, Caroline Humphrey, Inoue Osamu, Matthew Kapstein, Kim Songsuu, John Krueger, Peter Marsh, Ellen McGill, James Millward, Aleksandr Naymark, Peter Perdue, Sarah Schneewind, Bruce Tindall, Nikolay Tsyrempilov, Gray Tuttle, Joanna Waley-Cohen, John Wills and all my colleagues at SMU. I also thank the wonderful staff at the University of Hawai'i Press, especially Patricia Crosby and Ann Ludeman, for making the final stretch of this project such a joy.

I am also grateful to several organizations whose funding through the years has made my work possible. I thank Dwight Reynolds for arranging my stay at the Interdisciplinary Humanities Center at the University of California, Santa Barbara, in 1997–1998. I am also grateful for the funding I received from the American Council of Learned Societies that enabled me to conduct research in Inner Mongolia in 1998–1999. I also thank the University Research Council of Southern Methodist University and Felix Chen for providing funding that enabled me to return to Inner Mongolia, and to visit archives in Mongolia and Europe.

In these travels I have become indebted to a number of libraries and their staffs. I would especially like to thank all the people who helped with my work in Hohhot at the libraries of the Academy of Social Sciences, Inner Mongolia University and the Inner Mongolia Library. In Ulaanbaatar I thank the staff of the State Library for allowing me to work there while it was being renovated. I also thank Anne Buchardi at the Royal Library in Copenhagen and Håkan Wahlquist at the Ethnographic Museum in Stockholm. And finally, here at SMU, I thank Billie Stovall for patiently handling my endless interlibrary loan requests.

Needless to say, all remaining errors and erroneous interpretations are my responsibility alone.

Note on Transcription

For ease of reading, Mongolian and Tibetan words and names are transcribed according to a simplified phonetic system. I have adopted the Atwood system for transcribing Mongolian (2002: xv–xvi), which both simplifies the various philological systems and reflects dialectical differences. I have also simplified the forms of the troublesome terms *qaγan* and *qan*. Herein it is always written as khan. When there is a specific hierarchical distinction being made between *qaγan* (Manchu emperor) and *qan* (Mongol prince or lord), this is noted. In the Bibliography the philological system is used.

For Tibetan, I have adopted the THDL Simplified Phonetic system created by David Germano and Nicolas Tournadre. Written forms of Tibetan words using the Wylie transcription system are given in the word list at the end of the book.

Chinese words and names are transcribed according to the pinyin system of romanization. Manchu words are transcribed according to the system introduced by Hans Conon von der Gabelentz, also used by Möllendorff in *A Manchu Grammar* (Shanghai, 1892). All transliterations from the Sanskrit follow standard lexicographical usage. And finally, all translations are my own unless otherwise indicated.

Mongol Reign Periods

Chakhar

Dayan Khan	1480?–1517?
Bodi Alag Khan	1518?–1548?
Daraisun Küdeng Khan	1548–1557
Tümen Jasagtu Khan	1558–1592
Buyan Khangarjai	1593–1603
Ligdan Khan	1604–1636

Tümed

Altan Khan	1521–1582
Sengge Düüreng Khan	1583–1585
Namudai Sechen Khan	1586–1607
Boshugtu Khung Taiji	1608–1636

Ordos

Barsu-Bolod	d. 1521
Mergen Jinong	d. 1542
Noyandara Jinong	1543–1572
Buyan Baatur Taiji	1573–1576
Boshugtu Jinong	1577–1624
Erinchen Jinong	1624–1636

Khalkha
Tüshiyetü Khans

Abatai Khan	1567–1588
Eriyekhei Mergen Khan	1589–?
Gombodorji Khan	d. 1655
Chakhun Dorji Khan	1654–1698

Jasagtu Khans

Laikhur Khan	?
Subandai Khan	?
Norbu Bisireltü Khan	d. 1661
Wangchug Mergen Khan	1661–1662
Chambun Khan	1670?–
Zenggün	?
Shara	d. 1687

Sechen Khans

Soloi Maqasamadi Sechen Khan	1577–1652
Baba Sechen Khan	1653–?
Sechen Khan	d. 1686

Qing Reign Periods

Tianming / Tengri-yin Bosogtu	1616–1626
Tiancong / Tengri-yin Sechen	1627–1635
Chongde / Deedü Erdemtü	1636–1643
Shunhzi / Eyeber Jasagchi	1644–1661
Kangxi / Engke Amuulang	1662–1722
Yongzheng / Nairaltu Töb	1723–1735
Qianlong / Tengri Tedkügci	1736–1795
Jiaqing / Saisiyal Irügeltü	1796–1820
Daoguang / Törö Gereltü	1821–1850
Xianfeng / Tügümel Elbegtü	1851–1861
Tongzhi / Bürintü Jasagchi	1862–1874
Guangxu / Badaragultu Törö	1875–1908
Xuantong / Kebtü Yosutu	1909–1911

Introduction

"Listen, my dear Trotta!" said the Kaiser. "The whole
business is rather awkward. But neither of us comes off all
that badly. Let it be!"
   "Your Majesty," replied the captain, "it's a lie!"
                              —Joseph Roth, *The Radetzky March*

On July 15, 1779, the Sixth Panchen Lama, Lozang Penden Yeshé, rode out from Zhikatsé to attend the seventieth birthday celebrations of the Qianlong emperor. He was accompanied by a large entourage of five hundred monks, escorted by a battalion of one hundred soldiers, and nearly a thousand servants and clerks came along to help the highest-ranking incarnate lama on his travels from central Tibet to Chengde, the Manchu's summer palace north of Beijing.[1]

Before leaving Tibet the Panchen Lama and his group were feted by local Tibetan elites headed by the young Dalai Lama, whom the Panchen Lama had ordained only two years prior. After travelling together for eight days, Tibet's two supreme hierarchs parted company and the Panchen Lama proceeded eastwards, eventually arriving in Kham, where he first met the imperial envoys dispatched from Beijing. The messengers informed the lama of the emperor's great anticipation and joy at the prospect of finally meeting him. They also presented the Panchen Lama with a portrait of the emperor. The Panchen Lama was reportedly transported with joy at the sight of this representation of the imperial countenance and from then on always kept it with him.

From Kham the Panchen Lama went north to the famous Gelukpa monastery of Kumbum in Amdo, where he stayed for several months. During his stay through the winter months the Panchen Lama lived in a new opulent residence that the emperor had recently constructed at the monastery. Eventually, as the weather changed in the spring, the Panchen Lama and his entourage once again set out eastwards. This time his large entourage also included a bevy of individuals sent by the emperor, including cooks, purveyors, doctors, groomers, orderlies, key bearers, not to mention the porters carrying all the provisions needed for this convoy. These were not simply the basic sundries; they also included items specifically sent by the emperor, such as new clothes, hats and belts, as well as special foods that could not be procured in the harsh climate of Inner Asia. These delicacies included fruits, sweets and even a thirteen-foot-long fish, all of which were quite unfamiliar to the Tibetans. Nevertheless, thus girded, the procession left the plateau and proceeded slowly to the center of the Manchu state.

Along the way the court spared no expense. At each stop on the way the Qing court provided the entourage with two thousand new horses, one hundred camels, forty Mongol felt tents, one hundred cotton tents, chairs, cushions and other furniture, in addition to a large daily sum of money to pay for travelling expenses. Each stop entailed meeting local dignitaries and also other envoys sent out from Beijing, all of whom presented more lavish gifts to the Panchen Lama. Eventually, as the Panchen Lama neared the center of imperial power he was greeted by the second Jangjia Khutugtu, Rölpé Dorjé, who was an intimate of the Qianlong emperor and thus perhaps the most powerful Tibetan hierarch in the Qing Empire.

Together, the two Tibetan lamas and the emperor's sixth son, accompanied by two thousand loads of gifts presented to the Panchen Lama, proceeded to Dolonuur, the residence of the Jangjia Khutugtu and center of Manchu-sponsored Buddhism in Inner Mongolia. When he arrived, according to his hyperbolic Tibetan biography, one million Mongols came to receive his blessing. According to Mongolian sources, he also performed a purification ritual that pacified the restless demons of Mongolia.[2]

Then, after having stayed in Dolonuur for some time and met with a great number of the Manchu and Mongol banner elite, the Panchen Lama continued north to the Qing emperor's summer residence. Nestled in the hills of northwest China the lama was surprised to find that the Qianlong emperor had constructed replicas of both the Dalai Lama's residence, the Potala, and his own Trashi Lhünpo monastery at Chengde.

Nevertheless, upon settling in, on the twentieth of August 1780, the Panchen Lama was carried in a sedan chair to have an audience with the emperor on his birthday. They exchanged pleasantries and further gifts, and then over the next several days they met routinely to talk and discuss the Dharma. The relationship between the two flourished, and subsequently, when the emperor left Chengde to return to Beijing, the Panchen Lama was invited to accompany him. Upon arriving in Beijing the Panchen Lama was installed in the Yellow Temple, the famous monastery built for the Fifth Dalai Lama when he visited Beijing in 1652.

The relationship forged at Chengde continued, and the Panchen Lama visited the emperor in all his various palaces in the capital; and presumably the festivities, meetings with the emperor and high officials, Dharma teachings and blessings could have gone on for a long time. Unfortunately, however, as was often the case with dignitaries from the frontier regions who had not been previously exposed to the urban diseases of the empire, the Panchen Lama fell ill.[3] A month and a half after his arrival in Beijing, the Sixth Panchen Lama died of smallpox.

※

Although the death of the Panchen Lama was a grave loss of face, the meeting between the Manchu emperor and the Tibetan lama had certainly not been a complete failure.[4] Rather, on account of the court's extravagant expenditures and the apparently profound relationship forged between the emperor and the lama, it had once again been powerfully confirmed for the entire Inner Asian world that the Qianlong emperor was indeed the supreme ruler and patron of the unified Buddhist Qing state.

The unfortunate death of the Panchen Lama was therefore overshadowed by the broader success of this ritualized performance of religiopolitical theatre.[5] And that is indeed what it was: a form of Dharmic agitprop that secured the support of the Qing dynasty's Buddhist subjects. Or at least that is how it is generally understood, especially in the case of the Mongols.[6] By ritually confirming their rule through the symbols, myths and history of Buddhist political authority, it is assumed that the Manchus were able to ensure the undying loyalty of the Mongols.

Indeed, one of the first to make this observation was Father Amiot, a French Jesuit resident in Beijing who witnessed the preparations for the Sixth Panchen's visit. In his explanation of why the Manchu emperor expended such time and money on the barbarous idolatry of "Lamaism," rather than on the philosophically and morally superior "Confucianism,"[7] he wrote: "'By this political stroke, his Majesty foresees at once the execution of his orders, devotes the disobedient to the vengeance of the Lamas, and procures for himself more glory than ever, in their most brilliant days, had the Jenghis Khans, the Tamerlanes, and the Khubilais, who, like him, have given laws to the Tartars.'"[8] Remarkably, this view was confirmed thirteen years later by the Qianlong emperor himself in the famous "Proclamation on Lamas" (*Lama shuo*). "As the Yellow Church [i.e., Gelukpa Buddhism] inside and outside of China proper is under the supreme rule of these two men [the Dalai Lama and Panchen Lama], all the Mongol tribes bear allegiance to them. By patronizing the Yellow Church we maintain peace among the Mongols. This being an important task we cannot but protect this religion."[9]

Ever since then, virtually every source touching upon the Mongols, Buddhism and the Qing dynasty has echoed the same refrain. Be it Qing-period Mongolian histories or post-Qing Mongol nationalists and Marxists,[10] Japanese imperialists,[11] contemporary Mongolists[12] and Sinologists,[13] the *Oxford English Dictionary*,[14] or even Mongol Christians justifying their conversion,[15] they all agree: the Manchus used Buddhism to rule the Mongols. Although they all make this assertion for various discursive ends, the underlying logic is the same: the "Buddhist explanation" assumes that by promoting the Dharma the Manchus were able to ensure the loyalty of their Mongol subjects.

On one level, of course, the notion that Manchu rule was facilitated through its appropriation of Mongol discourses of Buddhist rule is entirely legitimate. Based solely on the enormous project of Buddhist cultural production carried out by the Qing court it is clear that the Dharma played a fundamental role in the Qing project of imperial consolidation.[16] And perhaps even more important, from the architectonic India-Tibet-Mongolia-Qing Buddhist narrative found in all Qing-period Mongol sources it is also clear that the Mongols themselves powerfully identified with the court's Buddhist project. Indeed, throughout the eighteenth and nineteenth centuries the Mongols were stalwart defenders of the Qing state precisely because it had become identified as a multiethnic Buddhist empire. It was the Mongol general Senggerinchen who defeated the British at

FIGURE 1. The Fifth Dalai Lama and the Shunzhi emperor. Mural in the Great Western Hall, Potala Palace, Lhasa. Photo by Liu Lizhong, in Kigell 1988: 198.

FIGURE 2. Rigzin Namgyal and Mis Ting Kha'e, *The Meeting of the General and the Monk in Kanze in 1936*, 1980. Courtesy of Per Kvaerne.

Dagu Fort in 1859.[17] Some Mongols were so loyal to the Manchu state that they even attempted an imperial restoration in 1917.[18] Clearly, Manchu Buddhist rule worked.

Yet, one may very well wonder, how in fact did it work? Did one simply have to project oneself as a Buddhist ruler, as the Qianlong emperor did by meeting the Sixth Panchen Lama, to elicit the undying loyalty of Mongol Buddhists? Can we assume that simply by fulfilling the ritualized role of a Cakravartin, the Wheel-turning king of Buddhist political theory,[19] or by being a Buddhist patron, all Inner Asian Buddhists would readily submit to Manchu domination and become loyal subjects within a Buddhist "encompassed hierarchy"?[20]

Obviously it was not that easy. If it had been, then the Shunzhi emperor's meeting with the Fifth Dalai Lama should have secured the obeisance of the Khalkha and Oirad Buddhists at that time; but it did not. Similarly, according to the logic of the "Buddhist explanation," Mao Zedong's meeting with the Fourteenth Dalai Lama and the broadcasting of its iconic representation should also have secured the Tibetans' undying loyalty, which it clearly did not. Both of these examples therefore point to an inherent flaw, or oversight, in the "Buddhist explanation." Namely, how did those on the periphery actually understand the actions of the metropole? Indeed, we may very well wonder how the Khalkhas, Oirads and Tibetans actually understood these projects of purported Buddhist rule carried out by the imperial center? In particular, we should ask ourselves, how did these Manchu projects of promoting Buddhist rule actually foster a reformulation of preexisting religious, political and communal identities?

Unfortunately, however, on account of the Buddhist explanation's static and unidirectional framework, it is precisely this process that is most often held in suspension. As a result, little in fact is known about how the Buddhists within or outside of the Qing state actually accepted, rejected, reinterpreted, deflected, or renegotiated these new narratives and rituals of political authority and state power that were assiduously broadcast by the Qing court. This study therefore aims to provide a picture of this process of engagement from the other side— from the periphery. In particular, it investigates the long process through which the politically independent "shamanists" of the Khorchin *ulus* came to be Mongol Buddhist bannermen willing to fight and die for "Our Great Qing" (*Manu Yeke Cing*).[21]

Technologies of Domination

In order to explicate this process of transformation, this study of Qing Inner Mongolia begins with several assumptions. Counter to Mongol nationalist historiography and its Western romantic counterpart, it is assumed that the Mongols were not simply the hapless victims of Manchu Buddhist imperialism.[22] Moreover, contrary to the "Buddhist explanation," the idea that the Qing simply adopted and duplicated early "age-old" Mongol traditions, rituals and narratives is rejected.[23] And finally, in contrast to the common framework of unidirectional discourses of power, this study begins with the premise that Manchu rule was an ongoing process of negotiation between the metropole and the periphery. As Struve has indeed noted, "a full comprehension of the Qing formation involves study of how that Manchurian regime transformation interacted—generatively, reactively, cybernetically, concurrently, sequentially—with other, or overlapping, contemporaneous regimes in eastern Asia, such as those of China proper, Choson Korea, the Mongolian steppe, Siberia, and the southeastern maritime sphere."[24]

The Qing conquest and subsequent Manchu rule are therefore understood less as events than continuing projects or processes.[25] Not only did the Manchus adopt and transform earlier Mongol conceptualizations of communal and religious identification as manifested through rituals and narratives of political authority, but also the Mongols in turn engaged with those new discourses emanating from the imperial center in various ways. Thus while recognizing that the Qing state employed different technologies to socialize its constituents into self-disciplining subjects, we must recognize it was also the case that there were continual counterstrategies to evade, subvert, or criticize such rationalities.[26]

Nevertheless, in the task of achieving the submission of the Mongols and ensuring their continued loyalty to the Qing state it is clear that the Manchus had recourse to a host of technologies of domination. As social historians have pointed out, they used several means, such as marriage alliances,[27] economic and social institutions, the Bureau of Colonial Affairs, legal systems and brute military force[28] to secure continued Mongol loyalty. However, while all of these factors certainly played a role in maintaining the Qing state, they will not be the focus of this study.[29]

One reason for such an approach is that this study is focused less on the activities and technologies of the center, which have been extensively studied, but rather on how these actions were actually understood or translated into reality by those on the frontier.[30] Thus, not only is the aim of this study to allow the natives to speak, but also to give them agency.[31] And in this regard it is important to note that none of the above technologies of domination are ever mentioned in Mongolian historical sources. What is talked about continually and at length in Mongol sources is what it means to be Mongol, what it means to be Buddhist, and how these relate to the Qing state.

The focus of this study is therefore precisely on how various Mongolian sources represent communal identity in relation to the state. In particular, this work investigates how Mongol narratives and rituals were transformed during the course of the Qing dynasty, and what these shifts and their intellectual and cultural context tell us about Mongol, Buddhist and Qing history.

Another reason for presenting an intellectual history of Mongol self-representation, moreover, is because it is these very transformations that have most often been occluded in the perpetuated myth of a static Buddhist rule that could simply be grafted onto the Qing "Great Enterprise." As a result, we know very little about the actual process of becoming or being Mongol or Buddhist, not only during the Qing dynasty, but also before and after as well. Yet it is precisely these processes beyond the imperial monologue that need to be explored if we are to better understand the success of the Qing, as well its collapse and lingering legacy.

Buddhist Rule in Theory and Practice

To a large degree it was this process of becoming a Qing Mongol Buddhist that was purposely subverted within the Qing's multilingual logorrhea of Buddhist state consolidation. For the Manchus themselves the process of projecting an image of continuity and tradition was greatly beneficial; and, as is well known, the Manchus had a keen sense of how to appropriate history in order to shape the legitimacy of the present. A fundamental element of their imperial enterprise was in fact the projection of themselves as the ultimate apotheosis of righteous rulers in the recurring cycles of history and myth. To achieve this project the Qing court produced and reconfirmed this new reality in a torrent of textual, visual and various performative media in order to establish a shared reality with those incorporated into the empire.[32]

Thus, long before Durkheim realized that the central focus of all human societies is the imagining of communities, the Manchus were creating such communities "by mobilizing the formal properties of such sign systems as language, poetics and ritual."[33] And perhaps nowhere was this project more successful than with the Mongols. The Qing formation, its radical social and cultural disruption, and the three centuries of Manchu domination came to be seen as simply the natural progression of Buddhist history. Thus, by drawing upon both Buddhist and Mongol history, the Qing simply became, not only a reflection of what always was, but also what in fact should be. And it was within this dynamic wherein imperial success clearly resided.

However, not only did the Mongols accept this new narrative, but, unfortunately, we also take these imaginings for granted in our own discussions of Mongol, Qing and even Tibetan history. To some extent the lama–emperor relationship even shapes the whole framework of Sino–Inner Asian cultural and political history. Yet by continuing to apply an ideal Weberian model of traditional

Buddhist rule to explain this history, we miss the very particularities that we are attempting to understand.

By appropriating a static model of Buddhist rule, be it in the Tang dynasty, the Yuan, the Ming, or the Qing, the actual processes that engendered these distinct Buddhist imperial/national/local identities are overlooked. As a result, little is known about what it meant to be Buddhist, or what the interactions between religious identities and political institutions were in the premodern period.[34] The whole process in which rituals, myths and histories were transformed in the creation of new Buddhist identities is too often displaced by the discourse of an idealized form of Buddhist imperial rule. Thus Buddhist history often reads like a laundry list of famous Asian rulers who promoted the faith.[35] However, the interrelated process of becoming both Buddhist and an imperial subject, or a national citizen, or a person within a localized community is, on account of this displacement, little understood.

In the case of the Qing these issues are not only confounded by the stunning success of the Manchu myth but, moreover, by the very absence of other voices. Until recently there were no Mongol sources from the pre-Qing period that could shed light on this process of transformation. In a sense, there was no point from which to begin reevaluating the Qing narrative, since its vision of Mongol Buddhist rule had become hegemonic. Fortunately, the recent discovery of the 1607 *Jewel Translucent Sutra* and the *Golden Summary of Chinggis Khan (Cinggis qaγan-u Altan Tobci)* affords us a new perspective. The first of these is a history of Altan Khan, his conversion to Buddhism and the lives of his two descendants. The second is pre-Qing history of Chinggis Khan that differs markedly from the later "standard" Mongol histories of the seventeenth century, especially in regard to the presentation of Buddhism and Chinggisid rule.[36] As a result, both of these works provide an important perspective, and corrective, on Mongol society, religion and the state in the late sixteenth century. Moreover, by providing a window into Mongol culture on the eve of the Manchu conquest, these two Mongolian works also provide us with a starting point from which to begin reevaluating, not only other contemporary sources such as Manchu–Mongol correspondence and imperial stelae, but also the history of the Qing formation and its impact on Mongol society.

Mongol Identity and the Qing State

Central to this project is the operative assumption that Mongol Buddhist identity was never static. Its creation and maintenance was an ongoing dialogue in which narratives and representations of identity were continually being renegotiated. Communal boundaries and notions of political authority were always being transformed within larger intellectual and cultural discourses. By revealing these changes it is hoped that a better picture of Mongol history will emerge, as well as a more nuanced understanding of what it meant to be Buddhist in late imperial China.

At the outset, however, it needs to be noted that this study is focused on "Inner Mongolia," not the Khalkha, Oirad, or Zunghars. One reason for this is that we simply do not have enough extant Khalkha and Oirad material, while for those Mongols of the area that was to become Inner Mongolia we do. Why this is the case is no doubt due to the fact that the "Inner Mongols" not only joined the Manchu project very early, but also that Inner Mongolia was the intellectual center of the Mongolian cultural area throughout the Qing period. Thus, even though this study focuses on Inner Mongolia, the term "Mongol" will be used throughout. Indeed, while the terms "Mongol," "community" and "identity" will be used, the reader is advised to "unload as much as possible of the baggage usually carried by the words 'community' and 'identity' so that these terms can travel light in the pages that follow."[37] Mongol identity was clearly multivalent and fluid during the Qing period, and I can never present it in all its complexity.[38] Thus, while I will talk about Mongol identity, the Mongols, Buddhists, Buddhism, the Qing and so on, these terms are not meant to be essentializing. If anything, this whole project is an attempt to move beyond the problems inherent in discussing "Qing" history solely in terms of "Mongol" and "Buddhist."

At the same time I do recognize that many factors shaping Mongol identity are not addressed in this book, such as gender and various other elements of identification. Some of these issues are simply not available in the sources, while others are not directly relevant to the focus of this study. Moreover, as noted above, Mongol identity was always changing. Different identities were triggered in different contexts, such as when Mongols met Europeans;[39] yet in recognizing these factors I do not believe that an elucidation of Mongol self-representation during the Qing is beyond our grasp. Rather, the available sources, produced by educated men of the elite class or the Buddhist establishment in Inner Mongolia, do provide us with a framework of how Mongol, Buddhist and Qing identities developed over the course of time.

New Qing History and Buddhist Studies

By focusing on the formation of Mongol Buddhist identity this study is also able to address two other current scholarly enterprises: the "New Qing History"[40] and the current historical turn in Buddhist studies. In regard to the expanding scholarship on late imperial China, I believe that an elucidation of Mongol intellectual history affords us a new perspective on Manchu rule and the cultural dynamics of the Qing dynasty. In particular, the case of the Mongols presents an example that focuses less on the metropole and more on the periphery.

This is important because, although there has recently been a wealth of outstanding scholarship on the Qing imperial project as envisioned in the center, little work has been done on how the projects of the imperial center were actually translated, or even understood, among the various constituents of the empire.[41] In many cases, of course, the voice of the periphery either never existed or is now lost, and we do not know how the various people of the empire understood the Qing, their ethnic conceptualizations, the court's historiographical enterprise, or their mapping projects. As a result, the case of the Mongols, with their large corpus of written materials, affords us a unique perspective on the other side of the equation, one that is beyond the "theatre of majesty" and its unidirectional power relations.

Rather, Mongol sources offer us a valuable perspective into the actual dynamics of the Qing formation in both its destructive and constructive elements. They reveal the process of deterritorialization and reterritorialization that brought the Mongols firmly within the Manchu orbit.[42] They thus provide us with a view into the "middle ground" of the seventeenth century, during which Mongol and Manchu conceptualizations of community, state formation, political authority and religion informed one another.[43] Moreover, Mongol sources reveal not only this period of engagement but also the dynamics through which these earlier conceptualizations were transformed and ultimately swept away. These sources show how this occurred, how earlier constructions were displaced by those of the center and how the idea of the Qing was actually internalized by people outside of the center.[44] And by exploring this ongoing dialogue between the metropole and the periphery in terms of an "interactional history," it is hoped that a more nuanced understanding of Manchu rule and the Qing dynasty can emerge.[45]

Investigating how Qing Buddhist rule developed also engages the growing scholarship on premodern Buddhist history. Buddhism has unfortunately often been studied outside of history,[46] and while this oversight is now being addressed, the imaginary ideal of Buddhist rule as an explanatory model still remains. Thus Buddhist rule is very often discussed and framed within the same theoretical model, whether in third-century BCE India, twelfth-century Vietnam, or eighteenth-century China.

Of course, while all of these regimes drew upon the orthodox model found in the textual sources in producing their legitimacy, this projection and the ideal should not distract us from their possible differences, or what this purported uniformity actually obscures. We need to keep in mind that religion is part of a complex process of identity creation. As Orsi has pointed out, "[a]ll religious ideas and impulses are of the moment, invented, taken, borrowed, and impro-vised at the intersections of life."[47] Thus, not only should we explore how these regimes differed from the orthodox paradigm, but also how the "imperial meta-phor" actually translated into reality on the ground. If we ignore these ques-tions, the very process that engendered a Buddhist imperial or local identity is obviated and the changes in myths, rituals and histories that actually made one a Thai Buddhist, a Tibetan Buddhist, or a Qing Buddhist are little understood.[48]

Indeed, if we are to understand how one becomes a Buddhist, or even what it means to be Buddhist, these connections are one important factor that needs to be investigated. There are certainly other factors, such as how Buddhists understand cultic practices in a transnational context; however, a fundamental component of Buddhism that transcends cultural boundaries is the saṃgha, or Buddhist community. Affiliation with this community is therefore a transcul-tural feature of being Buddhist.

As a result, Buddhist conversion has historically been enacted on a group level, as with the *ummah* in Islam, and thus narratives of this process invariably entail the production or redefinition of a new religious and often political com-munity. Histories of Buddhist conversion thus often involve reconceptualiza-tions of community ethnogenesis in order to transform the boundaries of communal identification; and in this regard Mongol histories contain the well-known apocryphal story of Chinggis Khan and his meeting with the Sakya lama Kungga Nyingpo, which supposedly introduced Buddhism to the Mon-gols.[49] No matter how historically inaccurate this episode may be, the linkage between the Mongol *Urmensch* and Buddhism generates a powerful connection between being Mongol and being Buddhist. Yet, what happens when being Mongol also means being a member of the Qing?

Since the "making and remaking of religion is a political enterprise, inti-mately linked to the imagination of new social and intellectual communities,"[50] one would assume that there would be a radical transformation between the his-torical representation of an independent Mongol Buddhist identity as opposed to one related to the Qing state. Unfortunately, as noted above, it is exactly the nature of this transformation that is glossed over in most accounts. Instead, we need to "rethink our conceptualizations of Buddhism as a translocal tradition with a long and self-consciously distinct history but which is at the same time a tradition dependent on local conditions for the production of meaning."[51] And, as noted by Kapstein, one of these important local discourses is "national" iden-tity. "When it is conversion of a nation that is at issue, the gradual transforma-tion of cosmological frameworks, or ritual, intellectual, and bureaucratic practices, and of the historical and mythic narratives through which national identity is constituted are among the key themes to which we must attend."[52]

The case of the Mongols and their shifting communal and "national" boundaries therefore provides a valuable perspective on this process, and on the connection between Buddhist identity and state formations.

More specifically, however, what follows is an intellectual history of Mongol self-representations in late imperial China. By revealing this history, which, on account of the "Buddhist explanation" has long been neglected, this study also provides a history of the Qing and the project of imperial rule. And on account of this rule being largely refracted through the prism of Buddhism, this book is also a history of Buddhism. Thus, hopefully, it may address some of the issues that have for so long kept Buddhism out of history and the Mongols within Qing history.

CHAPTER ONE

The Mongols on the Eve of Conquest

Whoever can give his people better stories than the ones they
live in is like the priest in whose hands common bread and
wine become capable of feeding the very soul.
—Hugh Kenner, *The Pound Era*

On June 28, 1626, an alliance was sealed by sacrificing a white horse and a black ox on the banks of the Hun River in Liaodong. As the blood curled into the river's current and the smoke offerings drifted skyward, Ooba Khung Taiji swore an oath of allegiance in front of God—Tengri, Eternal Heaven—to the Jurchen ruler Nurhaci.[1]

Explaining the new alliance, Ooba Khung Taiji described how peace accords among the dominant groups of the Mongol plateau had recently collapsed. Chakhar and Khalkha troops had killed seven Khorchin noblemen in the last year. Nurhaci, Ooba Khung Taiji explained, was "the even-minded Gegen Khan, who leads the unfeigning royal lineage that has descended on heaven and earth by decree of the Supreme Eternal God,"[2] so the Khorchin turned to him for protection from other Mongol groups. Phrasing their allegiance in terms of "Heaven's mandate," Ooba Khung Taiji and the gathered Khorchin nobility began their nearly three-hundred-year-long relationship with Nurhaci's Jurchen state—what was to become the Manchu Qing.

———◆———

I begin with this episode in order to problematize the common representation of the Manchus using Buddhism to rule the Mongols. Here, there are no Manchus, no Mongols and no Buddhist words or rites. The alliance is forged between the two leaders of the Khorchin and Jurchen, and is confirmed by an old Liao dynasty military ritual.[3] This fact succinctly shatters the edifice of the "Qing model" and the "Buddhist explanation." However, it also raises two important and intertwined questions: why has this reality been missed or downplayed in the standard historical narrative? Moreover, if early Manchu–Mongol relations were not based on Buddhist rule or even a notion of "Mongols" and "Manchus," what was it premised upon?

To answer these questions we need to investigate two interrelated factors: political authority and community conceptualizations. Politically, Nurhaci does not present himself as a Buddhist Cakravartin, but rather as a khan who has received Heaven's mandate to rule. Ooba Khung Taiji recognizes this, calling Nurhaci the ruler who has "descended . . . by the decree of the Supreme Eternal God." And while the Mongols readily understood the theory of divine right,[4] the epithet "by the decree of the Supreme Eternal God," also alluded directly to the reign of Chinggis Khan, the Mongol ruler Eternal God had decreed to rule the world. It was therefore not the Dharma that was defining Manchu authority, but animal sacrifice and the system of political authority shared by the Khorchin and the Jurchen.

How are we to conceive of these communities? Should we imagine them as tribes, groups, people, ethnicities, or nations? Or, in other terms, should we interpret the Khorchin–Jurchen alliance as a tribal confederation? Or perhaps it is better seen as a traditional example of an empire conquering a colony?[5] Or perhaps the Jurchens and Khorchins joined together in a kind of multiethnic state, something like a precursor to the ethnic minorities within the People's Republic of China?[6] Or perhaps the Manchus and Khorchins saw themselves more in line with "national" consciousness, and thus in joining together their alliance may have been more like France and Germany within the European Union? These comparisons, of course, parallel the development of scholarly debates within contemporary theory, and as can be expected, the history of scholarship on the early Qing can often be framed within these intellectual concerns. Early scholarship drawing upon the distinction between peoples with a state and those without (e.g., Rome and "barbarians"), as well as the radical break of modernity, talked about "tribes" and "tribal confederations."[7] More recent scholarship evaluates these same relations in terms of ethnic and national identity.[8] Such is the nature of the intellectual project as it moves forward.

Yet, at the same time as one can appreciate the value of drawing such parallels and the need for engaging with contemporary theoretical approaches, one need also be wary of how these later concerns potentially distort our understanding of the past. In particular, as with the "Buddhist explanation," what are we not only potentially missing but also misinterpreting by applying these intellectual maps onto widely different territories? Faced with the possible oversights wrought by later models, as well as the enduring "Qing model" itself, perhaps we need to go back and attempt to understand how the Khorchins and Manchus defined their community and their relations with other groups of people.

Unfortunately, on account of the common narrative and its focus on "Mongol," "Manchu," "Buddhist rule" and "conquest," the earlier realities that actually defined these steppe societies have often been occluded.[9] Indeed, if we actually look at Ooba Khung Taiji's decision to join with Nurhaci, it is clear that he is not being crushed under the boot of Manchu imperialism, but rather is grateful for the help Nurhaci provides in saving his people. On account of Nurhaci being praised as a divine ruler who saves the Khorchins from the persecution of the Khalkha and Chakhar, one may very well ask whether it is right to see this as a "conquest." Was it even a "submission"? Using such terms not only shapes but also defines our interpretation. Indeed, it is often very hard to extract ourselves from this paradigm shaping the nature of Manchu–Mongol sociopolitical power dynamics. Not only are we conditioned by nationalist and decolonization discourses, but we also know all too well what the Manchus became. Thus it is very hard to envision what the Jurchens were like in 1620. With the image of the grandiose Qing in mind it is hard to conjure forth the reality of a well-organized band of forest fishermen in the wilds northeast of China.

As an example of this cognitive dissonance we can note that, even though it is well known that the Mongols were more "advanced" than the Manchus, they are always portrayed as the inferior partner, or victim, in their relations with the Qing. Although the Mongols were a major source for Manchu political structures, military organization, legal systems and even their writing system,[10] we still readily accept the Manchus as the supreme arbiter of power in the Inner Asian world of the seventeenth century. This certainly did become the case, largely on account of the Manchus readily adopting these ideas and harnessing them to their unmatched military power. However, we need to be wary of this later reality distorting our view of these early relations, especially when we know that the Manchus were masters not only in recording the past, but more important, in transforming it to serve their present needs. Instead of projecting the "Buddhist explanation" backwards we need to reveal the sociopolitical realities that actually defined the Khorchin–Jurchen relationship.

A better understanding of how these two groups related to one another in the early period will provide a starting point from which to evaluate how the Manchus adopted and transformed early Mongol conceptualizations of community and political authority. If we ignore these transformations and continue in tautological fashion to explain Manchu rule by what it came to be, a central feature of Qing success—that the Khorchin came to accept the Qing narrative and see themselves as Mongols-of-the-Qing—will remain obscure.

The problem with elucidating this process, however, has been that it was precisely this transformation which the Qing narrative needed to forget. If the Qing was supposedly ruling the Mongols by means of a well recognized Mongol Buddhist model of rule, not only must that model of rule be well recognized, but the very idea of the Mongols themselves must also be well recognized. It would not make much sense to be ruling the "Mongols" by means of "Mongol Buddhist rule," if the people purportedly accepting this reality as their own in fact saw themselves as Khorchins, and if they saw political authority in terms of Heaven's mandate. Yet as is seen in the case of Ooba Khung Taiji, this was the reality in the early period. Qing success rested upon having these new conceptualizations appear natural to the Khorchins themselves.

Changes in Mongol self-conceptualizations came about through a continual process of negotiation between Mongol ideas and those promoted by the court. Moreover, as we will see, it was a process that was never static. Mongol communal boundaries were always fluctuating and developing in tandem with the enormous changes unfolding within the Qing dynasty itself.

State and Community in Pre-Qing Mongol History

All too often Qing rule of the Mongols has been interpreted as static. Thus, regardless of the enormous social, cultural, political and economic changes wrought during the nearly three-hundred-year period of Manchu rule, it is often refracted through the prism of Buddhist rule, or the banner system, or some other stable form of institutional control. Thus whether it is the "Qing model" itself, or its refraction in later nationalist and Marxist discourses, or contemporary academic interpretations, there is a lingering tendency to situate the Qing within a monocausal, monotheoretical frame. For the Qing itself, of course, this was valuable, since their legitimacy depended upon it. Yet, clearly, this is precisely not what the Qing was. The Qing of 1636, 1776 and 1908 are certainly wildly different realities, and not only for the court itself, but also for those on the margins who identified themselves with the Qing. Thus if the Qing and its radical changes and developments are reduced to single causes or an architectonic static narrative, not only will we not understand how the Qing functioned, but more important, we will fail to understand what made it a success. Namely, how did the independent Khorchin come to be the six Khorchin banners of the Mongol *ulus* within the Qing dynasty? To reveal how the Khorchins went from seeing themselves as an independent *ulus* within the larger Mongol world to a banner during the course of the seventeenth century, we in fact need to begin with what the Mongols meant by the term *ulus*.

It was this term, meaning "community," along with *törö*, meaning "state," that fundamentally defined, in changing ways, Mongol communal boundaries and political authority. And in all the sixteenth- and seventeenth-century Mongol sources *ulus* and *törö* mean a particular community under a state, which can be ruling one *ulus* or many communities. There is a distinct categorical divide between the community and the state. However, much as the Qing came in turn to also redefine these terms, in earlier Mongol sources the idea of the state as a separate and distinct entity from the people or country is not readily evident.

In the thirteenth century *Secret History,* for example, the term *törö* is used, not in reference to the state, but only in the sense of "principle, norm or tradition,"[11] while *ulus* is used in reference to both the people within a political entity and the ruling apparatus. The reason for not maintaining a strict distinction between people and state at this time may have arisen out of early steppe ideology, wherein a rightful charismatic ruler was chosen by God to rule a specific people and that required a uniformity, or nondistinct boundary, between ruler and people.[12] Nevertheless, when these different peoples (Merkit, Tatar, Mongoljin, etc.), or "countries" as they are defined in the fourteenth-century *Rasulid Hexaglot,*[13] began to become part of the larger Mongol *ulus* (often called the *yeke ulus,* "great *ulus*"), the boundaries begin to blur, and the term *ulus* appears to have developed a certain multivalency. It is both the parts and the totality, in that it is simultaneously the enormous land empire/state created by Chinggis, Ögedei and Möngke,[14] and the separate communities, peoples, or nations that were incorporated within it. The *Secret History* therefore speaks of "all the people" (*gür ulus*),[15] and the Great Khan's territory as the "domain of the center" (*qol-un ulus*),[16] yet all are within the Great Ulus (*Yeke Ulus*)—a term denoting both the territorial entity and the ruling apparatus. This polarity between the parts and the whole continued in the Yuan dynasty, as *ulus* became connected with Chinese *guo,* a term similarly used for both the empire/dynasty and smaller units within it,[17] though as the larger empire collapsed this multivalency began to disappear, especially as each *ulus* became an independent entity.[18] And it is at this time that the distinction between *törö* as state, separate from the *ulus,* seems to have appeared among the Mongols in both the east and the west.[19] It was also how the Mongol sociopolitical order was defined in the sixteenth and seventeenth centuries.[20]

Within this system, the community, or *ulus,* was understood as a particular group of people with a recognizable continuity of cultural practices, inhabiting a natural unit of geography. The state, on the other hand, was the governmental apparatus represented by a leader (khan, emperor, sultan) who ruled a community, or several *ulus,* by means of its form of governance, or "customs of state" (*törö yosun*). While the community was generally an immutable entity, the state and the "customs of state" could change. The framework defining this conceptualization is well captured in the description of Chinggis Khan's conquest of the Jurchen Jin dynasty found in Saghang Sechen's 1662 *Precious Summary:* "Thereupon nine generations ensued, and from the Wu Dog year (1058) it was one hundred and thirty-seven years to the Ga Tiger year (1194) when Chinggis Khan of the Mongols expelled and drove out the Manchu Altan Khan of China, seizing his State, and in the Ga Tiger year (1194) at the age of thirty-three he brought under his power the thirteen provinces of China, the Red

Ulus of eighty tümen, and became famed as the Daiming Genius Holy Chinggis Khan."[21]

In this description Chinggis Khan's conquest of the Jurchen's Jin state did not entail the destruction of China. Instead, the "Red Ulus" and its thirteen provinces survived, albeit under the Mongol state.[22] Similarly, in describing the fall of the Yuan, Mongol histories from both the pre-Qing and Qing periods present the Ming reconquest as the Chinese taking back the "Great State."[23] The Mongol "Great State" of the Yuan had therefore not destroyed "China"; it had ruled only the North Chinese, the Kitad Ulus, by means of the Mongol state.[24] The Ming reconquest and the Mongol loss of the "Great State" similarly did not entail the disappearance of the Mongols. Instead, as seen in Chinggis Khan's prophetic verse about the collapse of the Yuan found in all the chronicles, he notes that after the "shattered state" (ebderkei törö) of the Yuan, the Mongols will move to the area of Muna Mountain, namely "Inner Mongolia," and be ruled by a new "peaceful state" (engke törö).[25] Thus, a state could be conquered, and a community or peoples could be subsumed under another state, but it was assumed that this "conquered" ulus maintained its coherency even under the new state.

In both pre- and Qing Mongol histories this concept of ulus and törö did not only refer to the Yuan and Ming but also to the reign of Dayan Khan (1460–1521?).[26] Dayan Khan is often presented as a second Chinggis Khan, since he was the leader who, after the chaos of the Mongol-Oirad wars, once again united and organized the Mongols. In post-Qing seventeenth-century Mongol histories,[27] however, it is very clear that he did not unite the Mongols into a holistic entity, a Mongol ulus, or community, as it was to become during the course of the Qing. Rather, he brought the disparate and preexisting Mongol ulus, or communities, into his new state.[28] Later Qing accounts traced an eternal Mongol Buddhist nation, existing as one part of "Our Great Qing," all the way back to India and the primordial man. But seventeenth-century Mongol histories show that in the sixteenth century the Mongols were divided into long-standing independent communities, which remained intact within Dayan Khan's "Great State." As the 1607 Jewel Translucent Sutra says: "Having brought the conquered ulus into his own power, he ruled the Great State in peace."[29]

This conception also undergirds all the post-Qing seventeenth-century Mongol histories. Referring to the preexisting Mongol communities as the Six Great Ulus, or the interchangable Six Tümen, these histories argue that Dayan Khan succeeded in securing their acquiescence precisely because he was understood as being the leader who could restore order between these divided groups. This sentiment is well reflected in the deliberations of Queen Mandukhai on whether or not she should marry the seven-year-old boy Batu Möngke. She did so in order that the boy, the future Dayan Khan, could obtain legitimacy as a

Borjigid ruler in the lineage of Chinggis Khan.[30] Yet her main rationale was that the divided *ulus* needed a joint ruler and powerful state.[31]

In the post-Qing seventeenth-century histories another expression of this conception occurs when the nobility of these communities took the initiative and recognized the legitimate right of Dayan Khan's state to restore order and rule over them. The leaders of Three Western Ulus came to Dayan Khan and requested him to send one of his sons to rule over them as *jinong,* or viceroy.[32] "We have come to invite one of your descendants who will make a legitimate *jinong,* empowered to levy tribute on the Six Great Ulus."[33] In requesting a *jinong,* the leaders of these communities would cede some of their own authority and pay taxes to the new state, in return for being recognized as the local representatives of this new regime. In return, the new state system would not dismantle the preexisting communities within its control.[34]

This central conception of the theory of *ulus* and *törö* meant that, as had been the case with the Yuan and Ming, if the state of Dayan Khan were to fall, the separate communities, or *ulus,* under its control would again be able to go their own way. This is in fact what occurred. During the reign of Dayan Khan's descendants, the Six Great Ulus, which he had united within his "Great State," once again broke away and forged their own localized ruling systems. Altan Khan, most famously, rejected the authority of the Chakhar khans and asserted his right to rule over his allotted community of the Six Great Ulus, namely, the Tümed. Following his lead, other Dayan Khanid princes, who had been enfeoffed as leaders of the other preexisting *ulus,* did the same and established their own *törö,* or states, ruling over their own localized communities. Since each of these princes was a descendant of Dayan Khan, each had independent legitimacy as a "Chinggisid" nobleman. Each could choose either to join a larger state formation or, as most did, to forge his own local state government. However, as resources became scarce on account of environmental degradation,[35] and trade diminished in tandem with the collapse of the Ming,[36] these groups plunged into a fierce civil war.[37]

Thus, counter to popular narratives of eternal Mongol unity and cohesiveness, during this period these communities, the distinct sociopolitical *ulus,* boasted about killing hundreds of soldiers from other *ulus,*[38] and of "chopping to pieces the women and children and burning their homes and livestock."[39] And it was in this context of political fragmentation and social mayhem that the Manchus appeared, offering a solution that fit into the existing Mongol political theory of *ulus* and *törö.*

Indeed, what had unfolded among the Mongols during the late sixteenth and early seventeenth centuries was that the various preexisting *ulus,* the communities of the Khorchin, Kharachin, Tümed and so on, who in the post-Yuan period had recognized the authority of the Dai Yuwan (Ch. Dayuan) Khan, the recognized Chinggisid heir and ruler of all the Mongols, had come to reject this system. In particular, the leaders of these distinct *ulus,* all of whom were Dayan Khanid princes recently appointed to rule over these communities, rejected the rule of Dayan Khan's direct descendant and the Dayan Khanid state as a failed enterprise—or at least one that limited their own power. In response they asserted their right to rule their own community by means of their own state. Years later, it was these same leaders, representatives of these preexisting and now separate communities, who accepted the Manchu state, much as the Three Western Ulus had accepted Dayan Khan's state. For these groups themselves, both the initial assertion of localized political authority and the submission to the Manchu state were valid and positive responses to their own sociopolitical realities as understood in the *ulus/törö* theory.

Qing narratives, however, came to assert, as was later reasserted by modern pan-Mongolist or "nationalist" discourses, that the Mongols were an eternally unified group that moved in unison through time (but not space), although these later representations should not distract us from the realities of the sixteenth- and seventeenth-century Mongolian plateau. The fact was that various leaders and their *ulus* realized that reasserting their independence on the grounds that the Dayan Khanid state had failed no longer served their interests. Indeed, it seems as if many came to realize that, within the deteriorating situation of the civil war and its attendant socioeconomic dislocations, their own viability as functioning entities was open to doubt. Nevertheless, while there was no Mongol *ulus,* much less a "Mongol nation," as a functioning unified entity or concept at this time, one cannot suggest that the "Mongols" did not exist at this time, or that the Qing "created" the Mongols. While maintaining separate identities as Khorchin, Kharachin, Tümed and so on at one level, they also clearly identified themselves as Mongol, especially vis-à-vis the Chinese. All the Mongol sources of the seventeenth century do identify the existence of a larger, purportedly cohesive "Mongol *ulus*" that traced its origins back to Chinggis Khan. However, as seen above, the very idea of the *ulus* was malleable. Notions of community easily nested one within the other in ever-expanding circles—from the Tümed Ulus, to the Three Western Ulus, to the Mongol Ulus. Thus, during this fragmentation of the Mongols in the late sixteenth and early seventeenth centuries the larger ethnogenealogical *imaginaire* of the "Mongols" was minimized in relation to the localized community, no doubt in large part because the Dayan Khanid princes had reified these local sociopolitical entities as part of their own political machinations. At the time such a reification made sense within the theory of *ulus* and *törö,* just as later joining under the Manchus did.

Mongol sources therefore make it clear that at this time the Mongols were divided into distinct communities, namely the Six Great Ulus that had joined together within the Dayan Khanid state. However, as we have seen, the flexibility of the *ulus/törö* framework also permitted violent rejection of a particular state. As all the seventeenth-century Mongol histories reveal, several communities rejected the idea of Dayan Khan's state. The Ordos groups assassinated Dayan Khan's son Abakhai, sent to rule over the Ordos as *jinong*. They wanted to continue ruling their *ulus* themselves and rejected Abakhai, because "he has come saying he will rule our state (*törö*)."[40] As Saghang Sechen describes this affair, the local rulers did not want to cede any authority to Dayan Khan's state. "Ibarai Taishi [=regent] of the Yüngsiyebü and Mandulai Akhalakhu [=elder] of the Ordos took counsel together saying, 'What need do we have to take a prince upon ourselves? Surely we can proceed to rule ourselves? Let us slay that Abakhai now.'"[41] And they did.

In retaliation Dayan Khan launched a massive military campaign against these recalcitrant communities of the Ordos, finally defeating the Ordos and Tümed nobility in the battle of Dalan Tergün in 1510.[42] Unlike the genocidal policies of Chinggis Khan, Dayan Khan did not kill the Ordos and Tümed nobility, nor did he disassemble the various Ordos communities that had resisted him; rather, he brought them into his state. He took "the state (*törö*) of the Three Western Tümen,"[43] appointed his sons as rulers of these established communities and reorganized the Six Ulus into the Six Tümen. Central to this process was the underlying theory of *ulus* and *törö*, especially how their interrelationship was understood at the time. The fact that these preexistent communities were not dismantled or reconceptualized inevitably left open the possibility that they could later go their own way. And it was within this very logic that Altan Khan was able to challenge the hegemony of the Dayan Khanid state.

Altan could challenge the authority of the Dayan Khanid state not only because of the economic and military strength he had acquired through his trade relations with the Ming court but also because of the sociopolitical reality that defined Mongol society in the sixteenth century. Altan Khan not only rejected the authority of the Dayan Khanid state; he reaffirmed the legitimacy of his own community to run its own affairs with himself as khan. By being recognized as "Khan" himself, he asserted the legitimacy of his own government, or state (*törö*), to rule his *ulus*. In doing so he nominalized the authority of Tümen Jasagtu Khan, the Chakhar ruler of the Dayan Khanid state, much as Ibari Taishi had earlier rejected Dayan Khan himself. This development and the challenge it presented to his own authority clearly enraged Tümen Jasagtu Khan. After the Ming court had given Altan Khan a new seal and title, he wrote a letter of complaint to the emperor. "Altan-qan is Tümen Qaγan's subject, but now that he has received a princely title and a golden seal as big as a peck is it not as if he was the husband, and Tümen Qaγan has been reduced to the status of wife?"[44]

In many ways, Tümen Khan was, in this gendered discourse, accusing the

Ming of being a home-wrecker, and there may be some truth to this claim. The Ming court did provide titles of authority and economic support to the various Mongol leaders who asserted their right to rule their own community; however, whether this was a systematic policy of divide-and-rule, or simply the Ming dealing with realities on the ground is rather unclear. Most likely it was a little of both, though it is important to note that all the Mongol rulers, Altan, Laikhur and Abatai, all took the title "Khan" before receiving Ming recognition. Nevertheless, this recognition of the local authority of these Mongol princes did bolster the latters' claims to legitimacy, and it was this issue that Tümen Khan was addressing. In particular, he was confronting the problem fostered by the Ming recognition of these various Mongol princes, who were asserting their right to rule their own *ulus* by proclaiming themselves "Khan," because this was a crucial element in their claims to legitimacy, since a state can only have one khan, or more specifically, a *qayan*.

As seen in Tümen Khan's letter to the Ming court, he draws an important distinction between himself as *qayan* and Altan as *qan*. The difference was one of rank and the political order of the *ulus* and *törö* system. Technically, while a state only had one *qayan*, it could have several *qans*, or princes, who were the ones who ruled over the various communities comprising the state. Thus, when leaders of an *ulus* submitted to a new state and its reigning *qayan*, it was often the case that the *qayan* who had submitted would become *qan*. The same was true of the process in reverse; namely, if an *ulus* rejected a state and its *qayan*, the previously recognized *qan* of the *ulus* could again become its *qayan*. The use of the terms *qayan* and *qan* therefore defined the nature of the relations between communities and their various ruling elites. In using this terminology Tümen Khan articulated his superiority to Altan, a superiority that was threatened by both the Ming's actions and Altan's own proclamation.

Altan Khan rejected the rule of Tümen Khan, but not the nature of the *ulus* and *törö* system, which in fact made his independence possible. In the same manner of Dayan Khan, he forged relations with leaders of other communities, such as those of the Kyrgyz and the Muslim ruler of Hami, on a state-to-state basis.[45] When these leaders recognized the Altan Khanid state, they became *qan* to his *qayan*,[46] and their communities continued to exist as distinct *ulus* within the new state. These groups and their elites maintained their coherence, and would be free at some future point to go their own way. The same theoretical framework shaped early Manchu–Mongol relations.

State and Community in Early Manchu–Mongol Relations

When Ooba Khung Taiji forged an alliance with Nurhaci in 1626, it should be seen in the same context as the Ordos acceptance of the Dayan Khanid state, or the Hami ruler's acceptance of the Altan Khanid state. The idea that within a state the various communities retained their inherent integrity, however, had to be changed if the Qing were successfully to incorporate the disparate Mongol groups. The independent *ulus* and the Dayan Khanid elite were therefore disassembled and transformed into the banners and the Mongol nobility of the Qing dynasty.

Yet in recognizing these changes and the success they garnered in bringing the Mongols within the Qing enterprise, we cannot lose sight of how important these earlier conceptualizations were in defining early Manchu–Mongol relations. During the first twenty years of their interaction there is no mention of Mongol banners, the Qing, Buddhism, or any of the standard tropes of Manchu rule among the Mongols. Rather, the language and the framework it represents is entirely premised on the system of *ulus* and *törö*. The term "banner" (*qosiγu*), the sine qua non of Qing rule, is found only once in the Mongol histories of the seventeenth century, and then only as an imperial title bestowed upon one individual. This reveals how long and complicated the process of forging the Qing actually was. Contrary to the view of the banner system's intrinsic transformative power, the Khorchin *ulus,* for instance, did not simply become the six Khorchin Banners of the Mongol *ulus* within the Great Qing in 1626. Nor did the Mongols on a wide basis necessarily accept the idea of the banner in the late 1630s when the Manchus actually began organizing the Mongols into such units.

It is not clear exactly when, if ever, the Mongols fully accepted the idea of themselves as "bannermen." A common term for bannerman never even developed in Mongolian. The Mongolian calque of the Manchu-Chinese *Gusai niyalma-Qiren* (Mong. *qosiγun-u kümün*), was used only in legal and administrative documents; it is not found in any Mongolian history of the Qing period. This is not to say the Mongols never discussed the banner. They did, but not in these terms. The very idea of the banner as a specific category of identification is not found in Mongol histories until the eighteenth century, nearly a century after the process of reorganization into banners by the Qing court began. The Qing formation was therefore less an event than a process. Indeed, even in the central document of the Manchu's bureaucratic apparatus, the *Veritable Records of the Qing Dynasty (Qing shilu),* Mongol groups were rarely identified by their banners until the late eighteenth century.[47] During the period of the Qing formation (1620–1700) and even beyond, the two sides were slowly working out these social institutions.

In this process, both Manchus and Mongols framed their interactions within sixteenth- and seventeenth-century Mongol conceptualizations of the *ulus* and *törö*. The relationship was defined as two *ulus, gurun* in Manchu, joining together in an alliance (*ey-e*) or state (*törö*). Nurhaci specifically tells the

Naiman leader Khung Baatur in one letter that their two *ulus* will join together in a state.[48] In another letter Hong Taiji laments the distance between himself and the Tümed leaders because, until they meet, they cannot properly "discuss the state *(törö)*."[49] In another letter from 1628, Hong Taiji talks about an earlier request that several Ordos leaders had sent urging them to "form a state."[50] In using this terminology the Manchu rulers were appropriating Mongol sociopolitical concepts and using them to define the nature of their relationship with these Mongol leaders. Even though Hong Taiji shortly thereafter reconceptualized this relationship in terms of the banner, it is important to keep in mind the preceding framework. In particular, it is vital to appreciate the power encapsulated within the idea of a distinct *ulus* and its ability to both rule itself or join with other communities within a larger state formation, the *törö*.

Again, one problem in dealing with this reality is that the *ulus,* or community of identification, was itself always transforming. This was the case not only during the Qing when the *ulus* became reenvisioned as a banner, but in the pre-Qing period as well. Most often this transformation was from larger groups, such as those conceptualized in the idea of Six Great Ulus, to lesser units. Of course, in many ways such a progression is fully justified within the system of *ulus* and *törö*. If taken to its logical conclusion, any community with an ambitious prince could claim independence, were it an *ulus* or an *otog,* the "hunting camp" that was the basic unit organizing Mongol communities in the fifteenth and sixteenth centuries.[51]

Indeed, the community Altan Khan and his descendants claimed, referred to as the "Great Ulus," shrank from the entire area of Ordos within the great bend of the Yellow River under Altan Khan to only the Twelve Tümed during the reign of his grandson in the early seventeenth century. The nature or the boundaries of the *ulus* and the community it defined were malleable, yet this did not mean that it lost its legitimacy in its new configuration. The theory of *ulus* and *törö* mandated that these new formations be recognized as legitimate. A possible analogy might be the recent recognition of Bosnia and Croatia as viable entities in the modern world system of sociopolitical formations, namely nation-states, although this would have been unimaginable thirty years earlier.

As a result, even though at the time of Dayan Khan there were presumed to be six preexisting communities, the Six Great Ulus, and these were the communities he brought into his state in the early sixteenth century, a hundred years later these larger units had fragmented into an array of communities with their own ruling elite, such as the Aokhan and Five Banner Khalkha. Yet again, as with the example of Yugoslavia, this political and communal fragmentation did not imply that these new formations were any less legitimate than their predecessors had been, or that they were not able to join a new state and maintain their integrity if they so desired. Moreover, as is potentially the case with Montenegro, if the local government decides to reject the state they have joined, Serbia and Montenegro, they can justifiably do so, since the the community (*ulus*) is a viable and eternal entity no matter how recently it has been reconfigured. Montenegro as such a viable entity could thus forge its own state and potentially be recognized as such by the United Nations. Of course, Belgrade might not see it in that way, nor presumably would Hong Taiji have accepted it if the Khorchin *ulus* had decided to leave the Manchu *doro* (state) in 1632. Nevertheless, in both cases we need to understand the underlying system and logic that shape and define these relations.

Thus, returning to the case of the Mongols and their fragmentation during the early seventeenth century, it is important to recognize that these ever smaller communities, the *ulus*, were in fact understood as viable and sustainable entities. One measure of this idea is reflected in the legal arrangements stipulated by the different Mongol *ulus* when they joined the Manchus in their new state formation. What these groups asserted, no matter how small they may have been, was that their community was a distinct reality with its own unique cultural, social and even legal systems that needed to be respected. As a result, one of the stipulations of their alliance with the Manchus was that both sides would respect the laws of their own as well as those of other *ulus* within the state: "When a Manchu goes to the Khorchin and Abaga and commits a crime, [the crime] must be dealt with according to the laws of the Khorchin and Abaga. When a Khorchin and Abaga goes to the Manchus and commits a crime, [this crime] must be dealt with according to the rules of the Manchus. When one commits a crime exactly in the middle of two communities [Man. *gurun*=Mong. *ulus*], [the crime] must be dealt with according to each person's laws."[52]

Such a regulation may seem surprising on a certain level, but it well captures Mongol self-conceptualizations and the Manchu acceptance, or at least recognition, of the nature of the Mongol *ulus*. Even though it could change, the *ulus* as imagined at a particular point in time was understood as a distinct genealogically imagined group inhabiting a specific territorial area, with its own ruling elite, laws and traditions. Moreover, within the *ulus* and *törö* system, this "uniqueness" had to be respected when *ulus* joined a larger state formation. Indeed, this notion was tied into and made possible the very idea that, should a state fail, the *ulus* could reestablish itself with its nobility, culture and legal system intact.

Without any cultural or structural integration, however, the inevitable problem with this system was its centrifugal tendencies. If the *ulus* was maintained as a semiautonomous aristocratic confederation within a weak state structure, there was always the possibility it could abandon the state, go it alone, or join another state. And since the fall of the Yuan dynasty, but especially during the sixteenth century, this had been the reality of Mongol society. Indeed, as we have seen, by the early seventeenth century this reality and its inherent tensions had escalated into an open civil war. It was within the context of this turmoil that some groups decided to stay with the Dayan Khanid state, others decided to join the Manchu *ulus* in their new state, while others, such as the Khalkha and Oirad, decided to reject both of those states and continue to rule themselves.

Although all of these responses differed, all were fundamentally responding to the unfolding crisis of the early seventeenth century, and in large measure they all found their answer in a new, presumably better, state. The hope was that the new state would be able to rectify these problems and put the world back in order. However, before the Manchus none of these responses and the various states and communities they generated had really addressed the principle that played a role in creating these problems. This was certainly on account of the fact that their actions were to a large extent defined and legitimated by the underlying principle of the *ulus* and *törö*. The Khalkha and Oirad could thus claim independence because of this system, and for the same reason the Khorchin could reject Ligdan Khan and join Nurhaci. And while the Manchus themselves also conceived, or at least presented, their relations with the Mongols within this framework, they quickly understood the flaws in the system.

Early Mongol Views of the Manchus

While the political fragmentation of the Mongols had greatly helped in driving various *ulus* into the Manchu state, it would not have been beneficial for the Qing if this conceptualization had continued. The problem for the Manchus, in many regards, was less the civil war than the theory of *ulus* and *törö* and its implications. In particular, the Qing needed the Mongols to see themselves, not as semiautonomous aristocratic federations within the larger Manchu state, but as inalienable members of the Qing *ulus*. The Manchu project therefore entailed shattering the coherence of these preexistent *ulus*.

To transform Mongol conceptualizations of themselves and their place in the world, the Qing used brute military force to change Mongol social and political loyalties, and reinforced these new loyalties with traditional marriage alliances. The reordering of trade networks also brought the Mongols into the Manchu orbit, and as other scholars have pointed out, there were various other legal and social institutions that enabled the Manchu absorption of the Mongols into the Qing state.

Yet none of these strategies of imperial consolidation is ever mentioned in Mongol sources. Mongol writers themselves focus on other Qing strategies to incorporate the disparate Mongol groups: the theory of *ulus* and *törö,* and the

Manchus as the Heavenly blessed rulers of a new powerful state that could hopefully bring order back to the world. The idea of *ulus* and *törö* was accepted as the
natural sociopolitical order up through the reign of the Kangxi emperor. And
within this framework the Mongols did not consider the Manchus as radically
other: both the Manchu community and state were seen as a continuation of the
system as it had always been imagined.

As one example of the power of this conceptualization, one can look at a
letter the Tümed leader Jobiltai Khung Taiji sent to Hong Taiji in 1629.

> Sechen Khan,
>
> You presented a letter to these many noblemen: Jobiltai Khung Taiji,
> Oombo Chöökür Taiji, Aghun Sonom Taiji, and Abatai Taiji [that said:]
> "Did the Chakhar Khan seize anything from me? The well-known reason
> for my setting out on an expedition [against the Chakhar] is that the Khan
> of the Kharachin, Donui Günji, and Buyan Khung Taiji sent a messenger to
> me, asking that I avenge [them] against [their] enemy. They said that the
> evil-minded black Khan [i.e., Ligdan] killed all the noblemen of the eastern
> tümen, and [asked] that I should destroy him."
>
> When I heard that, I thought that these words were right, and swearing
> an oath to Heaven I set out on an expedition. But you did not join this alli-
> ance. Were [then] the Chakhar your ally, while they were our enemy? Now
> you do not think anything of us. I am furious at you. If you wish to cleanse
> this fault of yours, immediately find out about the people of the Black Khan,
> and send immediately a messenger here. While I was riding [against the
> Chakhar], you had gone far enough to reach the border [of Chakhar terri-
> tory]; why did you not proceed [to attack them]?
>
> Are the western tümen, headed by noblemen Boshugtu Khan, Jinong
> Khan, Yüngshiyebü, and the Kharachin Khan, not relatives of yours? Why
> do you not know your relatives?[53]

The frank and mocking tone stands in stark contrast to the obsequious puffery
demanded by later Qing etiquette. Both the tone of voice and the whole conceptual framework of the letter place it within the context of the *ulus* and *törö*
paradigm.

The Tümed leader confirms the existence of separate communities being
ruled by different khans and their states. Even though these states may have
aligned themselves with the Manchus, and even sealed this arrangement
through marriage, these entities as earlier imagined still existed. And, based on
the formulaic oath of allegiance, there is no suggestion that the Manchus challenged this system. The Mongols' oath of allegiance to the Manchu state con-

forms to this framework. "In order to form one alliance, *we two ulus, the Manchu and Kharachin,* offer a white horse to Heaven and black ox to Earth. Swearing an oath of loyalty together, we offer one bowl of araki, one bowl of meat offerings, one bowl of blood, and one bowl of dried remains!"[54] The oath establishes Manchu–Mongol relations in terms of *ulus* joining together in a union, or state, and the aim was mutual benefit.

In their letters to the Manchu rulers the Mongol leaders of these various communities always explain their situation in terms of *ulus* and *törö*. Their *ulus*, they say, is being violated by the state of Ligdan Khan, the Dayan Khanid state.[55] Or else "the evil" Ligdan Khan has ruined the unified state of Dayan Khan. The subtext of all these letters is the hope that the Manchus, the "Heavenly blessed" and militarily dominant power in the area, can resolve these problems. As the Aokhan leader explains: "Not understanding the nature of his own birth, the Chakhar [Ligdan] Khan destroyed his own state. And because he egregiously destroyed the Five Banner Khalkha, the lords of the Aokhan and Naiman despise the Chakhar Khan."[56] Erdeni Düüreng Khung Baatur Taiji also explains to Hong Taiji that he sent an envoy to the Manchu court in order to submit, "because of the great evil the Chakhar's sinful Khan has done towards the Six Great Ulus, the religion and state, the nobility, commoners and everyone and everything!"[57] Sechen Daiching of the Asud similarly informs Hong Taiji, "While ruling peacefully the Six Great Ulus the entitled Lord [Ligdan] Khan has destroyed the Great Famed State."[58] In turn, Ligdan Khan himself wrote to Nurhaci, "If I let you take an *ulus* I have conquered, what will happen to my honor?"[59] In all of these letters the framework is clearly the *ulus* and *törö* model.

Postconquest Mongol histories of the seventeenth century also treat Mongol–Manchu relations within this conceptual framework. The framework held even though the *ulus* had all been reorganized as banners. Even after they had been told repeatedly in court correspondence that they were no longer a particular *ulus* and all it entailed, but rather, for example, the six Khorchin Banners, the idea of the preexisting Khorchin *ulus* persisted. Lubsangdanjin in his *Golden Summary* of the 1650s describes the Kharachin–Manchu alliance in terms of two *ulus* forming a state.[60] Saghang Sechen in his 1662 *Precious Summary* presents the Manchus specifically in terms of a new state formation that brought various *ulus* under its control. Just as Dayan Khan had taken the *törö* of a particular community's ruler, Nurhaci first takes the *törö* of the White Jürchen, then the *törö* of the Mongols, and finally, in 1644 the *törö* of the Chinese emperor.[61]

Thus, counter to the common view of Saghang Sechen's famous work as being representative of the "Buddhist explanation," it is important to recognize that his presentation of the Qing formation is premised on the theory of *ulus* and *törö*. Writing in 1662, not only does he still draw a distinction between these communities and the state, he also makes it clear that Dayan Khan and Ligdan Khan had ultimately failed to hold the *ulus* together within the state—as he writes, "by means of the Taiping State [Ligdan Khan] could not bring into his power . . . the descendants of Dayan Khan ruling in the Six Great Ulus."[62] And thus, like a mad elephant destroying his cage, Ligdan Khan ruined the state that held these communities together.[63] As a result, the state that Dayan Khan had forged and had been ruled by his descendants for over a century came to an end.[64] However, Ligdan Khan's failure did not discredit the old system, only his own rule.

Saghang Sechen therefore explains that the Dayan Khanid state was replaced by the Manchu state, since they actually could "organize the Six Great Ulus by means of the Great Qing State."[65] Yet, for the Mongols at least, there was no fundamental transformation of the *ulus* and *törö* system. Saghang Sechen still used this model to describe the Qing, even though he himself was made to be part of a banner in 1636. This fact was forcefully reconfirmed in 1649 when the Qing court stringently confirmed the border boundaries of the six Ordos banners in the wake of Jamsu's rebellion. Thus, although Saghang Sechen had lived through all of these events and was writing about them a decade later, he and all the other Mongol historians represented the Qing state in traditional terms: as a powerful state organizing the *ulus* and ameliorating the tensions between these groups. The problem for the Mongols therefore was not the system of *ulus* and *törö*, but the civil war that had been fostered by the scorched-earth policies of Ligdan Khan. The issue at hand was thus not the existence of independent *ulus*, but the absence of a proper mediating authority.

Maintaining the *Ulus/Törö* System

In large measure the Mongols hoped that the Manchu state could restore order among the fractious Mongol groups. Rather than seeing the Mongols as inherently anti-Qing, we need to recognize that many Mongols actually welcomed the rise of the Manchu state within the parameters of the *ulus/törö* framework.

In both Manchu–Mongol correspondence and Mongol histories we find this concept as the operative paradigm. Early Mongol letters to the Manchu rulers talk about their regime in terms alluding to the glory days of Dayan Khan, and even Chinggis Khan. A Kharachin leader, preparing for a campaign with the Manchus against the Chakhar, declares in one letter that he has set out "thinking about the Great State."[66] And later, another Kharachin leader identifies the new Manchu state as the "Jade Great State,"[67] a term with direct allusions to the reign of Chinggis Khan, in particular the "Jade Jewel Seal." This was the imperial seal of government that was purportedly "discovered" in 1294. At the time it was declared to be the imperial seal of Qinshi Huangdi, the "seal transmitting the State" (Chuanguo xi) that had been used by all successive dynasties until it was lost by the Jurchens, who had seized it when they finally defeated the Song. Although Chinese scholars declared the seal a fraud, it became an important aspect of propaganda for Mongol legitimacy to rule China, and its importance only grew with time. Thus, in the Mongol chronicles of the seventeenth century the seal first actually appears to Chinggis Khan: it issued from a rock, or he was born with it in his hand, or it was given to him by the dragon kings.[68] And this story of the Jade Jewel Seal and its conflation with the Jade Great State to which the Kharachin leader alludes—drawing a direct connection between the empire of Chinggis Khan and the Manchu state—was a powerful tool in the propaganda arsenal of Hong Taiji.[69] As Weiers has shown, Hong Taiji largely promoted this connection himself, especially through his fabricated story of having acquired the seal of Chinggis Khan from the wife of the defeated Ligdan Khan.[70] Nevertheless, decades later, when Saghang Sechen wrote his history, he made similar connections by using parallel phrases in describing Chinggis Khan and the Shunzhi emperor to legitimate the Manchu state.[71]

But accepting the Manchus as a new state in the model of Dayan Khan, or even Chinggis Khan, did not change the nature of the ulus. Indeed, it was precisely this theoretical underpinning that hindered the full incorporation of the Mongols into the Qing system; and the fact that this theory and the terms conceptualizing it, rather than "banner," were used throughout the seventeenth century reveals how resistant this model was to change. On one level, this may have been irrelevant, since the ulus and the banner were virtually parallel or complementary realities; and, at least until 1675 when the larger banners were reconfigured as the Forty-Nine Banners, the terms were used interchangeably.[72] Regardless of these Qing administrative efforts, the ulus as it was earlier conceived was radically different from the banner, in that it had the "right," or at the least the potentiality, of rejecting a state formation. By no stretch of the imagination was this in the nature of the banner, which was an inalienable part of the Qing manifested through the grace of the Manchu emperor. Nevertheless, by the eighteenth century, Mongol historians had accepted the new Qing interpretation of the ulus as inalienably Qing. How did Mongol conceptualizations change?

Beyond Ulus and Törö

An important component shaping this transformation was that the Mongols themselves came to recognize the problems inherent in the ulus and törö system. However, as we have seen, the new model was not readily accepted, even with the creation of the Mongol banners. Instead, throughout the seventeenth century, Mongol sources continued to frame their reality in terms of the *ulus* and *törö*. Thirteen years after having been made a member of a well-defined banner in the wake of Mongol revolt, Saghang Sechen still talked about himself, the Mongols and the Qing in terms of the "Daiching *törö*" and the "Ordos *ulus*." And although he praises the Manchu rulers in the most flattering terms,[73] and speaks of the Qing as the Jade Great State who organized the Six Great Ulus, he uses the term "banner" only once in a fleeting reference.

Some may interpret this lack of "Qing" concepts as a subtle form of resistance. It is generally assumed within the "nationalist" paradigm, that all of the seventeenth-century chronicles are actually critiques of the new world order,[74] even though these, like the early Manchu–Mongol correspondence, all praise the Qing as a new "Great State" that ended the civil war and brought peace. Rather than expressing resistance to Manchu rule, these sources express the belief that the Manchus and their state saved the Mongols from themselves. Moreover, it was under these circumstances that the Mongols began to reevaluate the very nature of the *ulus/törö* system that had engendered the civil war.

All Mongols knew that an *ulus* seceding from a state formation was inherent to the system, but was that a positive development? In the early seventeenth century, most Dayan Khanid princes and their respective communities felt that it was. They continued to break away and forge their own "khanates." Over time, however, those within the Qing began to reevaluate such defections, while those outside the Qing state, such as the Khalkha and Oirad, continued to value the political fragmentation the system entailed. These differing views are reflected in the story of the fall of the Yuan dynasty, which is found in all the seventeenth-century histories, both those written within the Qing orbit and those outside it.

In this lengthy story of dynastic failure, the last Mongol ruler of the Yuan, Toghan Temür Khan, is, much like Ligdan Khan, blamed for not holding the *ulus* together by means of the state. Instead, he handed over control of the Yuan dynasty's various *ulus* to Zhu Yuanzhang, who in turn used this position to topple the Yuan and found the Ming dynasty. The fall of the Yuan is framed within the discourse of the *ulus/törö* model: it had failed precisely because it could no longer enforce its control over the people, groups, or nations (*ulus*) within its state. This is a commentary on state failure that is sure to follow when local elites, or in Tudor terms "over-mighty subjects," be they Zhu Yuanzhang or Altan Khan, acquire too much power.

This tension between the center and local elites, between the state and its incorporated peoples, ethnicities, groups, or nations, exists in all state formations. Yet, in the view of the seventeenth-century Mongols, a properly functioning state, like the early Yuan or Dayan Khan, would be able to unify and hierarchically orchestrate these different groups. If it failed to do so, this would enable these groups to go their own way on the basis of the *ulus* and *törö* system. The Mongols of the seventeenth century were only too familiar with this reality. According to the Mongol histories of the seventeenth century, both Toghan Temür Khan and Ligdan Khan had failed precisely because their statecraft was incapable of holding the communities within the state.

The Mongol story of Zhu Yuanzhang and the Yuan's fall was not only about the founding of the Ming. Rather it was a parable of dynastic failure and a commentary on the situation among the Mongols of this period. Like the Yuan, the power of the Dayan Khanid state and its ability to govern properly had been lost, leading to a fragmented political landscape in which various Dayan Khanid princes assumed control of their respective communities; or, as a famous refrain had it, "commoners had begun behaving like Khans."[75] This was certainly permissible within the *ulus/törö* system, but historians differed on whether or not it was good.

Curiously, the story of the Yuan's demise never fully addresses this issue. Perhaps counter to our expectations, Zhu Yuanzhang is not vilified in Mongol histories. Rather, the Mongols blame only Toghan Temür, and by extension Ligdan Khan, for the failure of their own states. Simultaneously, the story of the Yuan's demise never fully addresses the issue of what came next: was Zhu Yuanzhang good or bad? This ambiguity allows the story to be read in two ways. It can either legitimate a new powerful state, such as the Qing, that can again organize the disparate communities; or, it can legitimate a call for various *ulus* within a failed state to establish new independent states, such as the Ming, the Khorchin, or the independent Khalkha *ulus*. And it is on account of this ambiguity that the story of Zhu Yuanzhang is found in all Mongol histories of the seventeenth century. For the story of Zhu explains and justifies both the reality of the new Qing state and an independent Khalkha or Oirad state. It thus not only confirms how fundamental the theory of *ulus* and *törö* was to the Mongols of the seventeenth century, but also how it justified both acceptance and resistance to the new Qing state. It was this contradiction and the potential for revolt that needed to be resolved if the Mongols were to fully accept the Manchu state and its greater project of unification.

Through the prism of the Manchu state's resolution of the chaos of the civil war, two episodes in seventeenth-century Qing Mongol histories subtly reevaluate the very viability of the *ulus/törö* model. The first example can be found in Saghang Sechen's description of the Khalkha nobleman Abatai's enthronement as "Vajra Khan" in 1587. It was this event that established the legitimacy of an independent Khalkha *ulus* with the lineage of Abatai as its recognized representatives of state. This was entirely legitimate according to the system of *ulus* and *törö,* and in fact it was that system which enabled it. It was also the same system by which Altan had become khan of the Tümed. It is therefore presumably no co-incidence that Abatai met the Third Dalai Lama, who conducted the enthrone-ment ceremony, at the court of Altan Khan in Ordos. Nevertheless, in describing the actual enthronement of Abatai, Saghang Sechen has the Third Dalai Lama ask him, "Will this [enthronement of yourself as khan] not be an obstacle for your Mongol state?"[76] By framing the question in such a manner, Saghang Sechen is not questioning the legitimacy of Abatai's enthronement, but rather its implica-tions. Abatai being elevated to khan was certainly "legal" within the *ulus* and *törö* system; however, for the first time Saghang Sechen, or no less an authority than the Dalai Lama, raises the question of whether this is good for the state.

The immediate context clearly points to the breakdown of the Dayan Khanid state and the Mongols' descent into civil war, as well as the Manchu conquest. But, more important, this question is the first hint we have of the Mongols recog-nizing possible flaws in the system that enabled all of these events to unfold. Thus, much as the engineers of the European Union today challenge the logic of the nation-state and reinforce the need for a new suprastate by pointing to the horrors of Hitler, so the Mongols also needed to reevaluate the *ulus/törö* system that had enabled the chaotic reign of Ligdan Khan in light of Qing unity. Saghang Sechen is therefore asking whether a new powerful state built on the same edifice is truly in the best interest of all, since it could be challenged again on the same principles. He implies that the solution may not only be to accept an old or new state, but also actually to redefine the sociopolitical order that defined the nature of the relationship between the *ulus,* its leaders and the state.

To reconceptualize and reorganize the relation of state to community was clearly the aim of the Manchu project and its transformation of the various Mon-gol groups into bannermen of the Qing. And the Manchu court had not only been telling the Mongols they were now members of a banner and not an inde-pendent *ulus,* but the Qing bureaucratic apparatus had in fact been systemati-cally reorganizing the allied Mongol *ulus* into banners since the late 1630s.[77] However, even though the essential goal of this transformation was that the idea of being a bannerman had to make sense to the Mongols themselves, that in fact had not happened.

As is readily evident today, on a certain level it matters less what the center thinks it is doing, or says it is doing, than how those on the margins themselves perceive what the center is doing and their relation to it. Being told one is a Mongol bannerman is not the same as being or defining oneself as a Mongol bannerman. And as we have seen, the Mongols did not talk about themselves as bannermen re-gardless of the massive pressure to do so. Thus if we are to understand the success-ful incorporation of the Mongols, or the making of Qing Mongolia, we need to explore not only how this change actually occurred among the Mongols, but also how it related to transformations in the self-conceptualizations of the Qing itself. This shift occurred most markedly in 1635 when Hong Taiji declared that the Jurchens were henceforth to be known as "Manchus." A few months later Hong Taiji further highlighted this break by changing the dynastic title from Jin to Qing.[78] It was at this juncture that the very nature of the Qing project changed. And it is certainly not a coincidence that it was at this time that the Mongol banners were first organized (see Map 1).

Until that point both Nurhaci and Hong Taiji had modeled their rule on earlier models, the *ulus* and *törö* model in particular. Both Manchus and Mongols understood their relations as one of two distinct *ulus* joining together in a new state formation; however, in the mid-to-late 1630s the Qing project was entirely reconceptualized. The Mongols were no longer to be understood as independent *ulus* within a *törö*, but as banners within the Qing *ulus*. As a result, the very nature of the *ulus* and its relation to the state needed to be reconceptualized.

In the case of the Manchu language, the term *gurun*, which had earlier corresponded to the idea of an independent *ulus*, lost this meaning over time. *Gurun* became less the specific entities of the Khorchin, or even the Manchu and Chinese, but more and more the entirety of the Qing, both its people and the state.[79] This same categorical slippage was also to occur with the Mongol use of *ulus*, as the notion of an independent community was replaced by the idea of that same community as a banner within the larger Mongol Ulus, itself one component within the larger multi-*ulus* Qing state. This transformation took a long time. In the seventeenth century, Mongols still talked about the Khorchin *ulus*, Ordos *ulus* and so on, not the Khorchin Banner of the Mongol Ulus within the Great Qing Ulus. Yet they did eventually begin to define themselves as Mongols of particular banners, and an essential initial factor in generating this shift in communal identification was the Mongol reevaluation of their very system of the *ulus* and *törö*. In particular, the Mongols needed to see its flaws for themselves, at which point they too could see their future as being linked, not with the Khorchin *ulus*, but with the larger Manchu project itself.

As already noted, clearly a host of other factors contributed to the interweaving of Manchu–Mongol relations, including military, economic, social and legal institutions, as well as marriage relations. Yet, as Hong Taiji himself recognized, while trade and military alliances clearly brought the Mongols closer within the Manchu orbit, by themselves they did not necessarily challenge the underlying theory of communal conceptualization. Again drawing a parallel to the contemporary world, we can argue that in the same way as trade, military and suprastate alliances such as NAFTA, NATO and ASEAN clearly draw groups together, none of them challenges directly the coherence or the logic of

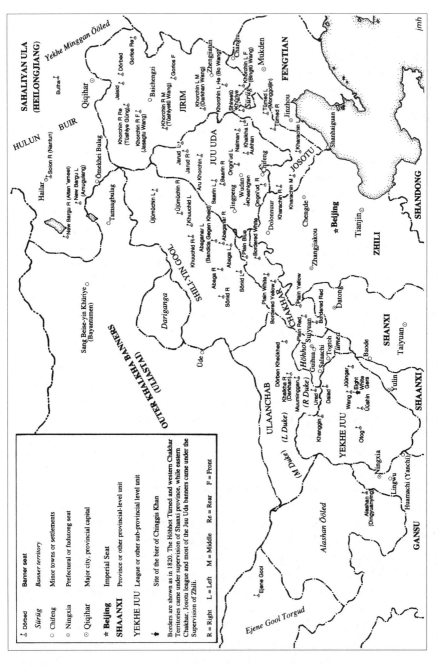

MAP 1. Inner Mongolian Banners. Courtesy of Christopher P. Atwood and Brill Publishers.

the nation-state. Similarly, the early economic and military interconnnections forged between the Manchus and Mongols did not by definition transform the logic of semiautonomous *ulus* accepting and working with a new state formation. And this was a fundamental problem for the Qing.

The future of the Qing could never be secured, nor could another civil war be averted, so long as the Mongols continued to imagine themselves as semi-autonomous communities. They needed to be transformed into inalienable members of the Qing. They needed to see themselves, not as Aokhan with their own laws and part of the Manchu *törö*, but as members of the Aokhan Banner within the Great Qing. The framework that had earlier legitimated the Manchu state also legitimated an independent Khalkha state, and the Zunghar state as well. Both used the *ulus* and *törö* model to justify and explain their rule as independent states outside of Qing control.[80] As a result, a crucial aspect of the Qing's success was not just in militarily defeating these groups, or bringing them into the economic orbit of Beijing, but transforming their boundaries of communal identification. The Mongols would come to fight and die for the Qing, not because they were Khorchin, but because they were loyal Mongols of the Qing.

The most explicit step toward reevaluating the *ulus/törö* system in the seventeenth-century Qing-period Mongol histories is found in the prophecy of Urtuukhai Ong. The title *ong*, or prince, derived from the Chinese *wang* and was a title held by the descendants of Chinggis Khan's brothers. Thus while the prophecy describes the failure of Dayan Khan's state, it should be read as a commentary on the Qing: "Urtuukhai Ong of the Khorchin says to Dayan Khan, 'Unite the whole great Yüngshiyebü of the seven otog of the Kharachin to our seven otog of the Khorchin. The eight otog of the Ordos are the middle. Unite them with the eight otog of the Chakhar. Unite the Twelve Tümed with the Twelve Khalkha.' Dayan Khan did not follow these words of the Ong . . . Urtuukhai Ong struck the head of his horse, saying, 'His posterity dies in suffering.'"[81]

What is important in this prophecy is not that it questions the system of *ulus* and *törö*, as was inherent in the question of the Dalai Lama, but that it offers a radical solution. Rather than forge a new, better and more powerful state, the solution is to dismantle the *ulus* as immutable entities, forging them together into a unified whole, as the Mongol *ulus*, the Mongol community, or the Mongol "nation" comprised of the different *otogs*. If Dayan Khan had done this, his state would have survived, for there would have been no *ulus* to challenge it. This was obviously the vision promoted by the Qing. The one *otog* of the Yüngshiyebü, the seven *otog* of the Kharachin, the seven *otog* of the Khorchin, the eight *otog* of the Ordos, the eight *otog* of the Chakhar, the Twelve Tümed and the Twelve Khalkha became the Forty-Nine Banners of Inner Mongolia within the Mongol *ulus* of the Qing state.

Nevertheless, just as the comment of the Dalai Lama can possibly be read as anti-Manchu, so can the prophecy of Urtuukhai Ong. If only the Mongols had joined together, they would not have fragmented politically, and they would then have been able to present a united front against the Manchus. Unfortunately, such a reading misses the point of how the Mongols actually understood themselves during the Qing formation. They saw themselves as Khorchin, Abaga and so on within the *ulus* and *törö* model, while the idea of a unified "Mongolia" and cohesive "Mongols" was minimized. Yet it was this concept rather than localized communities that the Qing promoted. The Qing favored a rejection of the localized Khorchin Ulus and its political ramifications, and an acceptance of a unified Mongol *ulus,* manifest in the nobility of the different banners, existing through the grace of the Manchu emperor.

Yet in order to make this shift possible, not only did the Mongol nobility need to be brought into the Qing enterprise through marriage and economic and military alliances, but also the very nature of the previous communal conceptualization needed to be questioned. And that is precisely what the prophecy of Urtuukhai Ong does. This prophecy not only critiques this earlier system but also suggests a solution—namely, the unification of these formerly disparate groups into a unified Mongol whole. Quite literally, if the Mongols are to survive they need to see themselves less as Khorchins and more as Mongols. The Borjigid nobility representing the descendants of Chinggis Khan should therefore reconceptualize themselves as members of a Mongol community, not as leaders of independent communities, which is of course the situation into which the Mongols had devolved during the pre-Qing period.

These two episodes in Mongol histories of the early Qing period show that the Mongols, or at least the Inner Mongolian nobility, had therefore begun to see their future in terms of Qing conceptualizations. The *ulus* and *törö* model had been reinterpreted, not as a positive reality, but a negative one—a system that had led inevitably to social and political chaos. The first glimpse of the Mongols accepting this new reality as well as the larger Qing enterprise as their own, with its banners and a unified Mongol community, is found in the prophecy of Urtuukhai Ong. Granted, the prophecy does not hail the banner system as a solution to the world's ills; yet none of the Mongol histories of the seventeenth century even mention the banners. Nevertheless, a first step in making the banner system natural, as well as the entire reconceptualization of Mongol social and political structures as mandated by the Qing, required that this earlier model be reevaluated. And in this regard, the prophecy of Urtuukhai Ong is a small but important step in this direction because it provides a glimpse into how the Mongols came to redefine themselves in relation to the Qing. Thus the success of the Qing resided less in brute military power and intimidation than within this process wherein they were able to redefine what it meant to be Mongol.

Unfortunately, the "Qing model" and the "Buddhist explanation" have too often subsumed this transformation, since by their very nature they demand the existence of the "Mongols," whereas the reunified Mongol *ulus* was itself largely a creation of the Qing. As a result, it is essential to recognize these changes if we are to understand the transformation and how it enabled Manchu rule. In particular, we need to understand how Mongol views of the *ulus* and *törö* system not only promoted early Manchu–Mongol relations, but also at a certain point hindered them, and thus needed to be reenvisioned.

The trajectory of these transformations therefore offers a unique window into how the Qing formation unfolded beyond the common "Qing Buddhist model." In particular, we can see how Mongol concepts of their community boundaries shifted as they were deterritorialized and reterritorialized within the larger Qing project. In particular, this process entailed the Mongols accepting themselves, not as members of semiautonomous groups such as the Khorchin, but instead as members of a particular banner within the Mongol *ulus,* which itself was only one community, along with the Chinese *ulus,* the Manchu *ulus* and Tibetan *ulus* that came to comprise the larger Qing *ulus.*[82] The nature of the *ulus* and Mongol perceptions of their community were to change again, especially in the nineteenth century. Yet in order to understand these later developments, as well as the changes wrought in the seventeenth century, we need to return to the defining features of the *ulus* and *törö* system, in particular, how the creation of social groupings was mediated through Mongol conceptualizations of political authority.

The *ulus* and *törö* system can explain Altan and the Tümeds, or Abatai and the Khalkhas' challenge to the Dayan Khanid system. But what gave Altan or Abatai the authority to be recognized as khan? This issue is central to the very construction of the legitimacy of not only the community but also the state ruling it. By turning our attention to Mongol conceptions of political authority, we can evaluate how the Manchus engaged with these ideas and transformed them in the project of legitimating themselves as the Qing. Changes in Manchu ideas of political authority in turn played a role in shifting Mongol boundaries of communal identification.

CHAPTER TWO

The Mongols and Political Authority

The new men of Empire are the ones who believe in fresh
starts, new chapters, new pages; I struggle on with the old
story, hoping that before it is finished it will reveal to me
why it was that I thought it worth the trouble.
　　　　　　　—J. M. Coetzee, *Waiting for the Barbarians*

The last independent Mongol ruler of Ordos was enthroned in the fall of 1634.
When his father passed away, Erinchen Sechen was away on campaign against
Ligdan Khan, who with his Chakhar forces had once again invaded Ordos territory. Upon hearing of his father's death, Erinchen Jinong "prayed to the bril-
liance of the Jowo Sakyamuni, his own supreme object-of-veneration." Then,
taking his men, he returned and settled down at his "own nomadic territory."

Prior to his arrival, Erinchen's younger brother had begun making the preparations for the consecration ceremony. In particular, he had ordered Sereng
Bodomal, the Jaisang of the Golden Stupa of the Chakhars, to bring the Eight
White Tents of Chinggis Khan to their encampment. When Erinchen returned,
everything was therefore ready for the enthronement to proceed. First, the older
and younger brothers rejoiced in being united with their "Great Ulus," the Ordos,
and then, "in the presence of his Holy Father [Chinggis Khan], Erinchen Jinong
ascended to the former khan's throne, as the one called Cakravartin Sechen
Jinong.

> At that time he gathered and assembled the vast, Great Ulus headed by the
> remaining greater and lesser princes of the Ordos Tümen. And saying,
> "When we had emerged from the confusion, we came together." He gave
> the title Father Lord to Bodatai Chöökür, and saying, "Having befriended
> us from the outset, he delivered us from the enemy," he bestowed on
> Saghang Sechen Khung Taiji the title Erke Sechen Khung Taiji. And for the
> sake of the *Khoshuu*[1] during great expeditions, [he] granted [Saghang
> Sechen] to be the leader in the center of the Grand Hunt.
>
> Also, each of the greater and lesser lords and officials and those who had
> in general given their effort, was granted [a title] accordingly. And thus in
> accord with previous custom, all rejoiced peacefully with hands and feet
> [resting on the ground].[2]

This description of Erinchen Jinong's enthronement as khan of the Ordos is found in Saghang Sechen's *Precious Summary* of 1662, written twenty-seven years after Erinchen Jinong had submitted to the Manchus, and thirteen years after the Ordos had been reorganized into Six Banners in the wake of Jamsu's rebellion.[3] Yet, that none of these developments are represented in this history reflects in many ways how thoroughly ingrained the logic of the *ulus* and *törö* system was within Mongol society during the seventeenth century. More important, however, Saghang Sechen's description of Erinchen Jinong's enthronement affords us an entry point into Mongol ideas of political authority.

Much like the Khorchin–Jurchen alliance of 1626, Saghang Sechen's description of the coronation challenges, or at least problematizes, the common narrative and representation of the well-recognized form of "Mongol Buddhist rule." It does this most explicitly through its inclusion of the cult of Chinggis Khan as part of the enthronement ritual. In order for the ritual to be performed, the Eight White Tents housing the relics of Chinggis Khan needed to be brought back to Ordos after Ligdan Khan had taken them to Kökenuur. Moreover, Erinchen Jinong's actual elevation as khan takes place "in the presence of his Holy Father [Chinggis Khan]."

Yet, at the same time as Saghang Sechen presents the cult of Chinggis Khan as playing a role in the ritual of enthronement, he also includes references to the discourse of Buddhist rule and the Dharma. Erinchen Jinong prays to the Buddha upon hearing the news of his father's death, and upon his enthronement he is given the iconic title "Cakravartin." One can thus conclude that Mongol notions of political authority were not solely limited to the rhetoric and rituals of the Dharma as maintained by the "Buddhist explanation."

Unfortunately, it is precisely because of the hegemonic and static nature of this explanatory model of early Qing rule that the polyvalency of both Mongol and Qing rule has often been obscured.[4] While it is clearly understandable to find an ideal vision of Buddhist rule articulated in the works of Pakpa Lama,[5] the so-called "Lamaist-Caesaropapist" model,[6] no one assumes that this imagining represented the religious and political realities of the Yuan dynasty,[7] or even of Mongol-Tibet relations.[8] In the case of Qing Mongolia, however, this separation between theory and practice has very often collapsed; and as a result, Manchu rule of the Mongols is often presented as having been defined solely within a Buddhist discourse. In many ways the whole Buddhist explanation is a tautology: the explanation of why Qing rule was both Buddhist and successful was that Mongol ideas of political authority were inherently premised upon the Buddhist model of Qing rule.

As Saghang Sechen's description of Erinchen Jinong's enthronement shows, however, such a conceptual framework is not tenable. The Dharma, or the "Lamaist-Caesaropapist" model by itself, is not sufficient to explain Mongol understandings of political authority and their attendant rituals of legitimacy. This model cannot fully explain the function of the cult of Chinggis Khan at the Ordos coronation, nor why the Khorchin–Jurchen alliance of 1626 was sealed through the ritual slaughter of animals to Heaven and Earth. Even less can it explain how and why such a sacrifice made sense to either the Khorchins or Jurchens who participated in it. Nevertheless, in all these cases there must have been some logic, theory, or conceptualization of sanctified political authority that explained or justified these acts. These were not random, ad hoc, or meaningless rituals of authority and community formation; rather, they were part of the "symbolic forms expressing the fact that [a governing elite] is in truth governing."[9]

The Symbolic Forms of Governance

Mongol and Qing political authority rested not upon the Dharma alone but upon a dual system of legitimacy: Buddhism and the will of God.[10] In many ways, of course, such a bifurcated system of imperial rule was nothing new. Rulers throughout Chinese history have appropriated a multiplicity of religiopolitical guises in their projects of imperial consolidation.[11] And since political authority was intertwined with the creation of both legitimate states and communal boundaries, it is important to pay particular attention to the "symbolic forms" that confirmed that the governing elite was "in truth governing" in order to understand better how the Manchus successfully legitimated themselves and thereby brought the Mongols into the Qing.

The starting point for such an investigation is the reign of Altan Khan, the ruler who challenged the Dayan Khanid state structure and is most often credited with reviving the traditional model of Buddhist rule by meeting with Sönam Gyatso in 1578. Both of these events are commonly understood as being premised upon the logic of the Dharma: Altan Khan was able to create a new state and challenge the authority of the Dayan Khanid lineage because he revived Khubilai Khan's traditional form of rule.[12] By meeting with the Third Dalai Lama he was therefore able to overcome his inferior position within the Mongol social and genealogical hierarchy, because, on account of the Dharma, he could claim to be more righteously "Mongol" than the other non-Buddhist rulers.

The problem with this common view, however, is twofold. It does not take into consideration the reality of the *ulus* and *törö* system, and it assumes that Buddhism was the single most fundamental element defining Mongol rule. Instead we should ask what were the "symbolic forms" confirming Altan Khan's reign and his state as politically legitimate? How did he move from being recognized as Altan *qan* within the Dayan Khanid state of Tümen *qayan,* to being Altan *qayan* of the Ordos Ulus? Furthermore, why in later Qing-period sources was he again demoted to Altan *qan* of the Tümed Tümen?

Before grappling with this specific and later historiographical development, however, it is important at this juncture to recall how Altan Khan is commonly perceived. In not only the Qing master narrative but also its refraction into contemporary scholarship, he is identified as the ruler who actually revived the Mongol Buddhist theory of rule, the theory of *qoyar yosu* forged by Khubilai Khan and Pakpa Lama. It is this model, of course, that is assumed to be the "thread [that runs] through Mongol political thought" and therefore is used as the underpinning logic to legitimize and explain Manchu rule. However, if one actually looks at pre-Qing Mongol sources regarding the *qoyar yosu* it is not that simple. To begin, the very term *qoyar yosu* is not even standardized in pre-Qing Mongolian sources.[13] And perhaps even more surprisingly, according to Saghang Sechen's *Precious Summary* of 1662, the Manchus converted to Buddhism, or adopted it for political expediency, long after the Mongols had already submitted.

This is probably rather surprising to many, especially since in both Qing and modern histories Saghang Sechen's work is held up as the archetypal source of the *qoyar yosu* model. And to some extent this is understandable, since it does contain the famous speech of Khutugtai Sechen Khung Taiji espousing the value of Buddhist rule at the meeting of Altan Khan and the Dalai Lama.[14] But in his description of the Mongol submission to the Manchus Saghang Sechen makes no allusion to Buddhist imperial rule.

> After that, as more and more decrees and documents came out profusely, his [Hong Taiji's] strength and might proceeded to become great, and on the border the Mongols became frightened. When he was nomadizing on campaign against the Western Three [Tümen] of Ligdan Khutugtu Khan, he brought into his power peacefully the Khorchin princes, and he became famed to all as Sechen Khan.
>
> Thereupon, after Ligdan Khan had been overcome by fate, his wife Sutai Taikhu (daughter of Delger Taishi, the son of Jing Taishi of the Jurchen) returned by God's own decree. While coming they were met by four princes of royal rank and their forces at a place called Toli in Ordos in the fifth month of the Yi Pig Year [1635].
>
> The Khan took the second wife [of Ligdan], Nangnang Taikhu, for himself and gave to Erke Khonggur his own daughter, Erke Gürüne Günji, who was born from the chief queen of his own *ulus.* He considerately treated as

his own the two brothers [Erke Khonggur and] his younger brother, named Abanai, born of Nangnang Taikhu in the same month in which Khutugtu Khan had died. In this way, he took the state of the Mongols' Khan when he was forty-four years old in the Yi Pig Year. He became famous as the Vastly Merciful One, the Supremely Virtuous, Peaceful, Holy Sechen Khan.[15]

Counter to the "Buddhist explanation," even in Mongol sources of the Qing period, the event that was to shape Mongol history for the next two and a half centuries was not enveloped in the warm embrace of the Dharma.

Again, this is not to assert that Altan Khan or the Manchus did not "use" the Dharma for political legitimacy. They both clearly met lamas, built temples, and sponsored translation projects. However, that is not all they did. Thus if we want to better understand not only Mongol conceptualizations of political authority, but also how the Manchus engaged and ultimately transformed them, we need to move beyond the confines of the *qoyar yosu* model.

God and Karma

The 1607 history of Altan Khan, the *Jewel Translucent Sutra,* begins with a brief history of Mongol rulers. It seems to confirm the traditional *qoyar yosu* model of Buddhist rule.

> Born by the fate of the highest God,
> From its beginning creating the supreme State and Customs,
> He caused all those of the world to enter his power.
> Temüjin became famous as the Genius Chinggis Khan.
>
> He caused the Five-Colored Nations to enter his power and state,
> Set into order the laws and state of the pleasant world,
> And invited Kungga Nyingpo the Supreme Sakya Lama,
> He was the first to propagate the Buddha's religion.
>
> Chinggis Khan's third son, Ögedei Khan,
> Invited the Powerful Sage Sakya Pandita Lama to come,
> And accordingly led the State of this world and the religion of the Buddha,
> Thus causing the important Great State to rejoice with abundant peace and order.
>
> Afterwards his grandson, born as an incarnation,
> The holy one, became famous as Khubilai Sechen Khan,

[He] invited the Holy Pakpa Lama to come,
More importantly he had all the sutras and tantras translated into Uygur.

[Khubilai Khan] richly benefacted the three foundations of Buddhism,
Greatly and immensely spread to all the world of religion,
And made all rejoice in the peace and stability of the universe.
[He] became famous like a Holy Cakravartin Khan of yore.

Born to [Khubilai's] family was the incomparable Gülüg Khan, named
    Khaisan,
Who commissioned the Omniscient monk, Chosgi Odzer Lama
To translate the Supreme Dharma into Mongolian,
And extensively spread the carved blockprints.

From the Genius Chinggis Khan, up through the reign of the fourteen
    noted Khans,
During that time Religion and State were universal.
By means of mutually supporting the naturally brilliant officials,
Thus it was that the scriptural teachings and the customs of the State were
    evenly held together.[16]

At first glance this passage seems to readily confirm the validity and continuity of the traditional Buddhist system of political authority espoused in later Qing-period sources. Indeed, that is how most scholars have read the text.

But while this introduction does dwell upon the Buddhist activities of Mongol rulers, their invitation of lamas to court and ruling by means of religion and state, it also mentions the role of the "highest God" (*degere Tengri*),[17] the deity who decreed that Chinggis Khan be born and rule the world. And this is not the only mention of the highest God in the introduction. The author of the *Jewel Translucent Sutra* also mentions this deity in relation to the collapse of the Yuan dynasty. Unlike the later Qing-period sources that contain the story of Zhu Yuanzhang's rise to power, the *Jewel Translucent Sutra* explains Toghan Temür Khan's loss of the state as attributable to two other factors. The first of these was the Buddhist theory of karma: when "former evil deeds ripened, [the khan] became foolish."[18] The second element was that Toghan Temür lost the divine right to rule: "All was lost on account of the Supreme God's fate of Ukhaatu Khan."[19]

It is evident from these passages that as with the enthronement of Erinchen Jinong, two parallel systems of political authority existed for the Mongols. One of them involved a relationship with Buddhist institutions and an acceptance of karmic effects, and the other involved the blessing of God. Indeed, this bifurcated system of legitimacy is found throughout the *Jewel Translucent Sutra.* Just as Chinggis Khan's successful reign and Toghan Temür Khan's failure are attributed to the will of God and the power of karma, so is the death of Mergen Jinong, Altan Khan's older brother.

> Thus it was, by the fate of the sovereign God, [that Mergen Jinong] changed
>   his incarnation.
> While Mergen Jinong was steering the customs of state,
> The hostile and jealous ones were put under the soles of his feet,
> And he took care of and loved his own younger brothers and the people of
>   the nation,
> [Though] the obstacles of previous deeds matured and this was the cause
>   of his passing away.

Of course, while there is inherently a logical tension between fate and karma, that does not diminish the fact that Mongol concepts of religiopolitical authority were not premised solely on the Dharma but on a dual model of legitimacy. Mergen Jinong's reign was therefore brought to an end by the forces of God *and* karma, just as had been the case with his illustrious ancestors.

This idea is found not only in the *Jewel Translucent Sutra,* but also in other Mongol sources, as well as in Chinese and Tibetan works. The opening sentence of the *History of the Yuan (Yuan Shi)* attributes the rise of Chinggis Khan to the Dharma and Heaven, as seen in his posthumous reign title "The Great Founder, the Holy Martial Emperor for whom the Dharma and Heaven opened Good Fortune."[20] Paralleling this Chinese description of Chinggis Khan's rule, Ngakwang Kungga Sönam, in his 1629 history of the Khön family, records that Köten Khan told Sakya Pandita:[21] "If I support [the world] through secular law, and you through religious law, then will not the teaching of Sakyamuni be disseminated beyond the borders of the external ocean? . . . Preach the doctrine with a tranquil mind, and I promise everything which you will need. *Your welfare depends on me, and mine on Heaven*" (italics added).[22] Thus, even though Köten Khan is conventionally credited with having initiated the ideal model of Buddhist rule by establishing a relationship with Sakya Pandita, even in Tibetan sources it was still maintained that Köten Khan's legitimacy and power to rule were contingent upon God. And the importance of this idea is well reflected in the title Köten Khan gave to Sakya Pandita. In the traditional *qoyar yosu* model, the khan and lama, as representatives of the secular and religious spheres, are usually identified as "patron and priest," or "almsmaster and object-of-veneration." Köten Khan, however, appointed Sakya Pandita to be his "head worshipper of Heaven."

The appointment of Sakya Pandita as "worshipper of Heaven" was not unique.[23] During this early period all religious specialists were made to pray to Heaven, as seen in Chinggis Khan's pronouncement concerning Chan Buddhists recorded in Nianchang's 1323 *Comprehensive Chronicle of Buddhist Patriarchs (Fozu lidai tongzai)*. "'From what your messengers have told me, it appears that the old reverend One, and the young reverend One are both true 'speakers to Heaven.' Feed and clothe them well, and if you find any others of the same sort gather them all in and let them 'speak to Heaven' as much as they will. They are not to be treated with disrespect by any one and are to rank as *darkhan*."[24] One can see from these passages that Mongol rule was understood primarily in terms of the blessing of Heaven, and secondarily in terms of the Dharma.

The power of God, moreover, did not end with the Yuan. The continuity of the Mongol bifurcated system of legitimacy is perhaps best captured in a Tibetan legal document from 1653, the *Code of the Twosome Offering [site] and Alms [master], Sun and Moon (Mchod-yon nyi zla zung-gi khrims-yig)*. This work was written explicitly to describe the ideal model of Buddhist rule between the Khoshuud Mongol Güüshi Khan and the Fifth Dalai Lama, yet it also confirms the role of Heaven in legitimating Mongol rule.

Just as formerly in India there appeared a wheel-turning king for each Buddha, [so it is] in the case of the these Victorious Ones (viz. the successive Dalai Lamas). Contemporaneously with [the third Dalai Lama] the great omniscient one bSod-nams-rgya-mtsho, there appeared in a royal family of supreme merit, might and wealth in the vast kingdom of Mongolia a person by the name of Dharma-king Altan . . . and bSod-nams-rgya-mtsho and the Dharma-king Altan were linked to one another as donee and donor, causing Buddhism to flourish in the remote land of Mongolia like the sun when it rises. The reincarnation of this Victorious One was [the fourth Dalai Lama] Yon-tan-rgya-mtsho, and this sage was born into the royal family of the Tümeds. Contemporaneously with him there appeared the powerful king 'Kho-lo-che and these two, donee and donor, caused Buddhism in general and more especially the Tantric Vajrayana (Adamantine Vehicle) to flourish extensively everywhere. The reincarnation of this victorious one, [the fifth Dalai Lama] Ngag-dbang-blo-bzang-chos-kyi-rgya-mtsho, is as renowned in name as the sun and the moon, and contemporaneously with this supremely omniscient one versed in matters spiritual and temporal . . . there appeared in fulfillment of a profound vow made in former times this [Güüshi Khan], renowned as upholder of the Buddhist teachings and Dharma-king, and *as a result of the merit he had accumulated in former times and by mandate of heaven he was conferred authority (bdang bskul ba)* as king of the snowbound land of Tibet. (italics added)[25]

Thus, even in Tibet during the reign of the Great Fifth, who forged an alliance with Güüshi Khan within the framework of Buddhist rule in imitation of Altan Khan, the power of God could not be denied.

Yet, while all of these sources confirm the bifurcated nature of Mongol political authority, they reveal little of how such legitimacy was actually conferred, confirmed, or ritualized. Buddhist rule has numerous rituals (tantric initiation, meeting Buddhist leaders, donations to the saṃgha, etc.) and activities (building temples, commissioning artwork, printing sutras, etc.) that can be performed to verify and project one's Buddhist credentials; however, what about the blessing of Heaven? Most often, actual military, political and economic success is ipso facto evidence of God's grace, while failure is proof of having lost favor. Yet, as seen in the case of Köten Khan's appointment of Sakya Pandita and all other religious specialists (be they Buddhist, Daoist, Christian, Muslim, or Confucian) as "worshippers of Heaven," for the Mongols, God was a dynamic force that demanded prayer in order to secure blessings and continued favor.[26] Thus an important question is not only how was this prayer performed, but also how was the blessing of Heaven upon a righteous ruler ritually confirmed? Chinese rulers had access to numerous Confucian, Daoist and imperial rituals to publicly confirm Heaven's continued blessing upon themselves and the dynasty, but how did Mongol rulers confirm their own God-given legitimacy?

Ritualizing God's Blessing

As has been noted in the case of Europe, since God's blessing is universal and cannot be monopolized, emerging states often sanctified their rule through local saints. The French kings thus drew upon the legend of Charlemagne, who "held France in fief from God and the holy martyr [St. Denis]—'quod a deo et a te regnum Franciae teneo' . . . [and b]y allying themselves with a saint whose principal function was the defence and protection of the French realm, Capetians emphasized the national scope as well as the religious character of their mission."[27] Among the Mongols a similar phenomenon is found; however, the rulers allied themselves not with a "national" Christian saint but with the father of the Mongol "nation," who had intially received the blessing to rule from God.

Thus, as seen in Saghang Sechen's description of Erinchen Jinong's enthronement, God's blessing was conferred and confirmed through the cult of Chinggis Khan. He was the ruler who had first received the blessing to rule, and in order for a successor to claim legitimate rule, the appropriate rites in front of the Eight White Tents and the relics of Chinggis Khan had to be performed. The legitimization of divine right to rule the Mongol "nation" within a semantic chain would be re-created only when these rituals had been performed and the blessing confirmed. In order to make sense of this ritual of legitimization and its logic, however, it is necessary to explore how Mongol conceptions of God's blessing and their relation to the Chinggis Khan rituals developed over time.

Unfortunately, the sources concerning the early nature of the Chinggis Khan cult in relation to legitimacy are scarce. However, already at the time of Güyüg Khan (r. 1246–1248), the Italian friar Giovanni Plano di Carpini recorded in his *Ystoria Mongolorum* of 1247 that the Mongols at Batu's "independent" court in southern Russia worshipped Chinggis Khan.

> They have also made an idol to the first emperor, which they have placed in a cart in a place of honour before a dwelling, as we saw before the present Emperor's court, and they offer many gifts to it, they also present horses to it and no one dare mount these till their death; they also give other animals to it, and if they slaughter these for food they do not break any of their bones but burn them in a fire. They bow to it towards the south as to a God, and they make other nobles who are visiting them do the same.[28]

Carpini's companion, Brother Benedict the Pole, also noted this worship of Chinggis Khan: "Beyond the fires there stood a chariot bearing a golden statue of the Emperor, which also it is their custom to worship."[29]

These authors note that the worship of Chinggis Khan was not only per-formed by Mongols, but that foreign dignitaries were also forced to kowtow to the image.[30] Carpini relates one episode that highlights the importance of this obeisance. He tells of Mikhail, a chief duke of Russia visiting the Mongol court. When told to bow on both knees to Chinggis Khan, he proclaimed that he would bow on one knee to Batu and his attendants, but he refused to bow to a dead man, claiming it was unchristian. The Mongols thereupon repeatedly kicked him in the "stomach against his heart until he began to weaken." Nevertheless, Duke Mikhail still refused to bow before the image of Chinggis Khan, and therefore was beheaded with a knife.[31] Over time this episode became both a tale of Christian martyrdom and of Russia's eternal "national" resistance to the "Tartar yoke."[32] Nevertheless, it also confirms the Mongols' deification of Chinggis Khan.

Yet these sources do not define in detail the significance of Chinggis Khan's sanctity in respect to legitimate rule. As Paul Pelliot first noted, though, letters of the Mongol khans contain phrases that mention Chinggis Khan as if he were still alive.[33] In particular, these letters contain passages that refer to Chinggis Khan and the current khan as ruling simultaneously. In Güyüg Khan's letter sent to Baiju in 1247, the khan describes Chinggis as the only lord on earth, *super terram Cingischam solus dominus.*[34]

Similar phrases are also found in other letters sent by the Mongols to the West. For example, in William of Rubruck's version of Möngke's letter to Louis IX, it says, "This is the order of the everlasting God. 'In Heaven there is only one eternal God; on earth there is only one lord, Chinggis Khan.'"[35] Based on the language employed, one would assume from these examples that Chinggis Khan was indeed still alive, although both letters of Güyüg and Möngke were in fact written over twenty years after his death. Another example is found in a passage from a letter of Güyüg Khan to the pope explaining why the Mongols will not convert to Christianity and why they kill so many people: "Because they did not obey the word of God and the command of Chinggis Khan and the Khan, but took council to slay our envoys."[36]

It is evident from these passages that his successors understood their rule only within a relationship between themselves and Chinggis Khan, who had the initial right to rule bestowed upon him by God. Therefore, only through the proper worship of both God and Chinggis Khan could legitimate rule be re-created. As seen in these early letters, the logic of this tripartite ritualized link was steadfastly maintained, and the present ruler's legitimacy and the Mongol state were re-created in a semantic chain purely through this sacred lineage. This idea is found not only in these imperial letters, but also in Rashiduddin Fazlullah's famous history of the world, the *Jami'u't-Tawarikh*. It begins, "Today, thanks to God and in consequence of Him, the extremities of the inhabited earth are under the dominion of the house of Cinggis Qan and . . . are united in large numbers in the service of majestic heaven."[37] The same idea is also found on coins minted in Tbilisi that were issued by Möngke Khan in the 1250s. They bear the Persian inscription, "By the power of God, by Good Fortune (*iqbal*), Universal Sovereign (*Padshahi-i Jahan* [Chinggis]), Munku Qa'an."[38]

The same idea is also found in the letters of the Yuan emperors, which all begin with a variant of this same formula, "By the Power of Eternal God, and the Fortune of the Emperor. . . ."[39] In both of these phrases the term "Good Fortune, Universal Sovereign" and "Fortune of the Emperor" are variants of the Mongol phrase (*qayan-u suu-dur*),[40] where the emperor/khan in question is not the ruling khan, but Chinggis Khan, who is called upon to transmit the initial blessing of God bestowed upon him to the contemporary ruler. And the importance of this idea and prevalence of this phrase among the Mongols was already recorded in 1237 by the Southern Song envoys to the Mongol court.[41] On account of this understanding of a linkage between God, Chinggis Khan and the contemporary ruler, one may speculate that the ritual and prayers described by Plano di Carpini for Güyüg's enthronement as khan at the Golden Palace ("Altyn Orda") incorporated a supplication to God and Chinggis Khan in order to legitimate the rule of Güyüg. While this is likely, it is only a conjecture, and we need

FIGURE 3. Rituals in honor of Chinggis Khan in 1935. Courtesy of the Lattimore family and the Peabody Museum, Harvard University.

to examine the *History of the Yuan,* which records the court's imperial rituals, in order to see how the worship of Chinggis Khan related to sanctified rule.

The *History of the Yuan* records that, already during the reign of Möngke Khan, the worship of Chinggis Khan was initiated at "Sun-Moon" Mountain.[42] Subsequently, Khubilai Khan had an ancestor-worship complex built between 1260 and 1266,[43] which consisted of eight chambers. The halls were built to house individually Chinggis Khan, his four sons and Tolui, with one for Güyüg and Möngke and one for Chinggis Khan's parents. While it may be possible to see links between this complex and Confucian imperial cults or Chinese ancestor worship,[44] the arrangement of the halls is not in accordance to prescribed neo-Confucian orthodoxy.[45] In addition, the description of the ritual precludes this conclusion.

The ritual at these ancestral halls was performed four times a year, presumably seasonally, a cycle that accords with the cult of Chinggis Khan as prescribed in the sixteenth-century *White History (Cayan teüke).* Mongol religious specialists (Ch. *menggu wuzhu*) also performed the ritual in Mongolian (Ch. *guoyu*), which entailed the recitation of the names of the deceased khans and their queens, coupled with animal and smoke offerings.[46] Not only does this echo the rituals carried out to seal the Khorchin–Jurchen alliance of 1626, but it is also possible to see a link between these imperial ancestor rites and the concept of legitimacy granted through God and Chinggis Khan. This supposition is bolstered by the fact that the imperial eight-chambered ancestral halls in Beijing are clearly reflected in the later Chinggis Khan cult, since the Eight White Tents in Ordos that preserve the relics of Chinggis Khan developed out of the spatial construction of this temple.[47]

Both the *History of the Yuan* and Marco Polo also record another ritual performed every August at the summer capital of Shangdu. The ritual itself entailed the sprinkling of mare's milk acquired from the emperor's sacred herd of white horses; and during the rite, religious specialists made two reverences and announcements to God. They also invoked the august name of the "Great Ancestor Chinggis Khan" and pronounced a wish: "Relying upon Heaven and upon the Fortune of the Emperor we shall sacrifice and hold [horse] races every year."[48] As Serruys has noted, the initial passage of this ritual pronouncement is an abbreviation of the phrase "Relying on the Force of Eternal God and the Fortune of the Emperor," which is found in other Mongol sources. And in both of these cases it must be recognized that the "Emperor" here in question is not the ruling khan, but Chinggis Khan, who is called upon to grant or transfer the initial blessing of Heaven bestowed upon him to the contemporary ruler. These small pieces thus provide evidence of the fact that, after the death of Chinggis Khan, he was transformed from founder of the empire to the sanctified holder of the right to rule. Without the proper worship of Chinggis Khan and the blessing of God, one's rule would be illegitimate and bound to collapse, as proved to be the case with Toghan Temür Khan as described in the *Jewel Translucent Sutra*.

The Cult of Chinggis Khan in the Post-Yuan Period

Although the Yuan collapsed and the Mongols were expelled from China, the rituals involving Chinggis Khan still sanctified the legitimacy of Mongol rulers. As Sagaster has noted, this apotheosis is first found within the seventeenth-century chronicle tradition expressed in the lament of Kileen Baatur after Chinggis Khan's death.[49] In particular, Kileen Baatur gave a lengthy speech when the cart carrying Chinggis Khan's corpse became stuck at Muna Mountain, and only became miraculously unstuck when Kileen Baatur confirmed for Chinggis Khan that his worship would be instituted and continued in the future.[50] The power of Chinggis Khan was then confirmed when the cart was able to proceed. Moreover, Kileen Baatur's lament explains the establishment of the Eight White Tents as the center of the rituals of Mongol political authority in the post-Yuan period.

The first "historical" mention of this ritual in Saghang Sechen's *Precious Summary* is in 1426, when Adai, who was campaigning against the Oirads, received the title "Khan" in front of the Eight White Tents. And indeed, in all post-Yuan Mongol sources, and even those of the post-Qing seventeenth century, all confirm that Mongol rulers had to be enthroned/sanctified before the Eight

White Tents.[51] The *Precious Summary* also contains a pivotal story in which Chinggis Khan supernaturally and violently refuses to sanctify an illegitimate ruler. The episode unfolds in relation to the escalating warfare between the Mongols and Oirads, each of which asserted their legitimacy by claiming Chinggisid authority. In 1438 Adai, the ruler of the Mongols, was ambushed by Toghan Temür of the Oirad. Adai Khan sought refuge in the Eight White Tents of Chinggis Khan; however, being unarmed, he was killed. The Oirad leader then rode around the tent three times, slashing the sides with his sword and boasting of his superiority:

> "You may be the White Tent personifying Genius, but I am Toghan, descendant of Sutai." Thereupon the chiefs and people of both the Forty [Mongols] and the Four [Oirad] spoke among themselves, saying, "This Holy Lord [Chinggis Khan] is not only the lord of the Mongols, but is the son of Indra, King of the Gods, and the conqueror of all the Five-colored [people] and four subjects. Something disastrous will happen to [Toghan]."
>
> They told him, "Your behaviour is wrong. You should beg the Holy Lord's pardon by making obeisance to him and asking for your own life." Still he would not listen and said, "From whom do I have to ask to for my own life? Now the whole Mongol Ulus is mine. I shall sit on the throne of the khan in accordance with the custom of earlier Mongol Khans."
>
> When he had made an offering before the Lord and turned around, the golden quiver of the Lord made a cracking noise, and the people nearby saw an arrow trembling in its middle slot. Just then Toghan Taishi fell unconscious bleeding from the nostrils and the mouth. He was undressed and found to have on [his] back what seemed to be an arrow wound. The quiver was examined and the arrow in the middle was found to be stained with blood. All the people of the Forty [Mongols] and the Four [Oirad] said amongst themselves, "The Lord did not approve of him."[52]

This episode provides clear evidence of how important the cult of Chinggis Khan was not only in confirming legitimacy but also in maintaining social and political control. The holding of the state was a sacred enterprise for the Mongols, and the privilege of rule was conferred only through the right worship and reverence of Chinggis Khan, who in turn could grant or withhold the right to rule. In the case of Toghan Taishi, a non-Borjigid leader of the Oirads who tried to usurp the throne of the Mongol khans, the sanctification was not forthcoming. Instead, Chinggis Khan killed him.

Based on this episode it is evident that Mongol political authority was legitimated within a political theology of divine right and ritualized through the cult of Chinggis Khan.[53] Yet, what happened to this system when Altan Khan reintroduced the Dharma as part of the imperial model?

The Dual Nature of Mongol Political Authority

Counter to the totalizing narrative of the "Buddhist explanation," even after Altan Khan's conversion the cult of Chinggis Khan was not displaced. Rather, as seen in the two most important pre-Qing Mongol sources, the *Jewel Translucent Sutra* and the *White History (Cayan teüke),* both of which were produced in relation to the rule of Altan Khan, Mongol political authority came to be ritualized through parallel systems of legitimacy: God's blessing and the Dharma.

The *White History,* a manual of proper imperial rule that was compiled in the late sixteenth century by Khutugtai Sechen Khung Taiji, is thus divided into two sections. The first section is a description of the requirements for the performance of the rituals toward Chinggis Khan,[54] and the second outlines the ideal model of Buddhist rule. This dual system of legitimacy also shapes the narrative of the *Jewel Translucent Sutra,* which confirms the legitimacy of Altan Khan by drawing upon both of these discourses.

Altan Khan is therefore blessed by God and is also a Cakravartin. "The Lord of the Whole World, Altan Sechen Khan, Who was born by the fate of the supreme God, remembered the State and the unparalleled Dharma."[55] He is born by the will of God, and upon his birth he is identified as a bodhisattva. As a three-year-old child he is protected from harm by God[56] but is also born with a "striped calf," one of the eighty marks of a Buddha or Cakravartin.[57] Moreover, the author informs us that many of the pivotal events in Altan Khan's life were destined by God, such as his defeat of Burkhai Taishi, his conquest of the Uriyangkhan,[58] and even the famous 1571 peace accord with the Ming.[59] All these events were caused by God.

Furthermore, the *Jewel Translucent Sutra* not only asserts the power of God as an active force within the Mongol world but also confirms the centrality of the Chinggis Khan cult as the site where this power was mediated. In particular, as noted above, it is "in front of the Lord" where all enthronements take place.[60] In addition, Altan Khan made those whom he had conquered kowtow before Chinggis Khan.

When the Six Great Ulus assembled in front of the Holy Lord's White Tent,
Altan Khan said to Bodi Khan, "With the blessing of God,
I make the evil-minded Burkhai Taishi, in front of the Lord, kowtow to
    you!"
The Six Tümen praised and eulogized the Meritorious Holy Khan thus:

"He crushed the vengeful enemies, making them become his own tax-
 paying subjects.
He made the long hostile peoples kneel in front of the Lord," they said with
 benevolence.
Then Bodi Khan with the Six Tümen in front of the Magnificent Lord, came
Forward and granted the title Supporting Wise Khan, to the truly
 courageous, sincerely pious Altan Khan.

[Everyone] heard of the fame of the Holy Lion Altan Khan.
He was born by the fate of a God in a Pure Land.
Through power and strength he made the arrogant enemies enter his own
 control,
And by compassion and kindness he made those same enemies become his
 friends.[61]

At the same time as the power of God and the cult of Chinggis Khan was
confirmed, Altan Khan was also eulogized as a great and compassionate Buddhist.
He was a "Holy Lion" of the faith, born through the wish of a Buddhist deity, who
ruled with a bodhisattva's compassion.[62] He is described elsewhere as ruling by the
power of merit acquired from the "two assemblies" of wisdom and merit.[63] Most
important, however, he was the ruler who famously brought Buddhism back to the
Mongols. He is therefore invariably identified as a "Cakravartin."[64] His Buddhist
sanctity is further confirmed through numerous miracles. His body emits rainbow
light. Upon his death natural phenomena (earthquakes, storms, meteor showers
and an eclipse) occur, and a rainbow appears when his body is cremated; it also
rains flowers, and mantras appear in the sky. Moreover, relics are retrieved from the
cremation ashes, and like those of the Buddha, Altan Khan's relics become an object
of worship for the people of the world.[65] Furthermore, the Dalai Lama saw "with his
wisdom eye, and said that Altan Khan's incarnated majestic spirit had been quickly
reborn by the side of Maitreya Buddha, in the All-rejoicing Tushita God Realm."[66]

Yet, even with these remarkable confirmations of Altan Khan's Buddha nature and Buddhist rule, the cult of Chinggis Khan was not displaced.

After Brahma Great Mighty Cakravartin Altan Khan had become a God,
His wise great son, Düüreng Sengge Khung Taiji,
Received his great title from in front of the Holy Lord's White Tent, and
Took the royal throne of his father, the powerful Altan Khan.[67]

Even in Buddhist texts such as Samdan Sengge's 1623 translation of the Ab-
hiniṣkarmaṇa Sūtra, Chinggis Khan, who as the Urmensch encapsulates Mongol

conceptualizations of religiopolitical authority, is born to rule through the agency of the Supreme God and Buddhist merit.

> Within 3,253 years after
> The founder Buddha Teacher attained Nirvana,
> Through the power of collected merit from previous births and
> By the fate of the Supreme God in the Water Horse Year [1162] Temüjin
> Chinggis Khan was born.[68]

The same idea is also found in Ligdan Khan's "White Stupa" inscription of 1626.

> Let Daiming Sechen Chinggis Khan, who was fated by Eternal God and had
> faith in and prayed to the Buddha, Dharma and those that hold the Saṃgha,
> particularly the lineage of the great Sakya lamas who are emanations of
> Mañjuśrī, be victorious over the gods and humans.[69]

Furthermore, the inscription reiterates the fact that Chinggis Khan was successful in his rule because he not only supported the Dharma but also "relied upon the protection of Eternal God."[70]

Nor did the rise of the Manchus and the Mongol submission to the Qing put an end to this bifurcated model that premised political authority upon God's blessing and the Dharma. Indeed, it is found in all the Mongol sources written in the Qing orbit throughout the seventeenth century. The anonymous author of the *Golden Summary* thus writes, "This was Temüjin Chinggis Khan, born by a command from God. More than 3,250 years after the Buddha had entered Nirvana, as twelve kings had been born, and were causing suffering to living beings, for the sake of suppressing them, an instruction was given by the Buddha, and Chinggis Khan was born."[71]

The seventeenth-century Mongol histories also reveal the interrelationship between God's blessing and the cult of Chinggis Khan. The *Golden Summary* records that when Muulikhai Ong defended himself against Molan Khan, and killed him in the mid-fifteenth century, he exclaimed, "Oh lofty Eternal God know this! And secondly, you blessed Holy One [Chinggis Khan], know this! I have done good towards your descendant. Your descendant had had evil thoughts towards me!"[72] This interconnection between God and Chinggis Khan is also found in Dayan Khan's vow made upon being told of his son Abakhai's assassination. "May you, God, and next you, Holy Lord [Chinggis Khan], know the blood which has been shed and abandoned, and the bones which lay drying!"[73] Saghang Sechen also relates that when the Ordos leaders were debating whether to kill Abakhai, one of them asks, "will the Heavenly Lord [Chinggis

Khan] approve?"[74] All these passages therefore reiterate the interrelationship between God and Chinggis Khan first seen in the death of the Oirad Toghan Taishi.

The cult of Chinggis Khan was not only a medium through which prayer was transmitted but was also central to the confirmation of God's blessing and proper rule. As a result, it is not surprising that the *Jewel Translucent Sutra* goes to inordinate lengths to confirm Altan Khan and his descendants' legitimacy in terms of God/Chinggis Khan's blessing, as well as the Dharma. It is also found in the 1583 stela of "Altan Khan's Law":

Praise to the Three Jewels that are without hindrance,
The Saṃgha complete with monks, incarnations and the seven chattels,
The Dharma of the unhindered holy supreme three vehicles
And the Buddha of the completed five wisdoms and four bodies.

Praise to the Shining Body of the blessed Buddha Teacher,
Who in the three kalpas embodies the two assemblies,
Speaks like the glorifier Brahma about the pure three vehicles OM HUNG
And whose mind knows without exception the fine and detailed Law.

Praise be to the savior who through all the sutras and tantras
Makes all the people enter the boat
On the previously incarnated's great treasury ocean,
And through the incarnated mind's instructions allows them to cross.

With the blessing of the three holy jewels,
With the great power of Eternal God,
With the blessing of the true great Genius,
Deigned by the supreme Holy One [Chinggis Khan].

Through the vastness that is Altan Khan's nature,
who was born by the fate of the Supreme God, it is granted.[75]

Altan Khan was not alone in legitimating his rule by drawing upon both of these discourses. Rather, this model was adopted by all the Mongol princes who were asserting their right to rule their own localized communities within the *ulus/törö* model. Boshugtu Jinong, a political rival of Altan Khan's descendants in Ordos, is one example of this. At the same time as Altan Khan's descendants were retelling the story of their right to rule as representatives of both the Chinggis Khan cult and the Buddhist *qoyar yosu*, Boshugtu Jinong was doing the same. Within a year of the *Jewel Translucent Sutra*'s composition, Boshugtu Ji-nong commissioned a translation of the *Ma-ṇi Bka'-'bum*.[76] In the colophon of this collection of apocryphal stories of Songtsen Gampo, Tibet's first Buddhist ruler, Boshugtu Jinong had himself identified as an incarnation of Songtsen Gampo.[77] Shortly thereafter, Boshugtu Jinong commissioned another large Tibetan history of Songtsen Gampo to be translated into Mongolian, the fourteenth-century *Clear Mirror* (*Rgyal-rabs gsal-ba'i me-long*).[78]

Based solely on this evidence and his formulaic support of Buddhism through the building of monasteries and his bringing of the Kanjur, the Buddhist canon, to Mongolia, one may assume that Boshugtu Jinong was simply re-creating himself as a Mongolian Songtsen Gampo, founding a new "Mongolian Buddhist empire" within the "Lamaist-Caesaropapist" model. However, he too followed the bifurcated religiopolitical framework used to legitimate Altan Khan. While promoting his Buddhist identity, he was simultaneously support-ing the cult of Chinggis Khan. He commissioned the *Altan Saculi*, "The Golden Aspersion," a ritual text employed at the Eight White Tents, to be copied, and had another Chinggis Khan ritual text written out in gold.[79] Thus, for Boshugtu Jinong, as for Altan Khan and his descendants, the narratives and rituals of po-litical authority incorporated both the cult of Chinggis Khan and the Dharma.

It was this system that defined and legitimated Mongol rule throughout the period of political fragmentation. Ligdan Khan therefore promoted his legiti-macy by aligning himself with the Sakya lineage and declaring himself an incar-nation of Chinggis Khan with the direct blessing of God.[80] The full title given to him by his Sakya lama was in fact: "Genius Chinggis Gegen Sechen, the Khan who turns the Golden Wheel, the Dayisun God of Gods, Indra on Earth, Van-quisher in all directions [Ligdan Khan]."[81] Unfortunately, this amplified rhetor-ical strategy was of no avail, since the various Dayan Khanid princes despised his rule and state, and in turn they adopted the same model to legitimate their own rule.

This process of political mimesis is also witnessed in the career of Abatai Khan, who founded the independent Khalkha *ulus* premised on two factors.[82] The first one was the theory of *ulus* and *törö*, which fundamentally justified the reality of a separate and distinct community. Abatai could thus reject the Dayan Khanid state and forge his own state ruling over this localized commu-nity. The second factor was legitimacy—in order to legitimate this new state, the *törö*, Abatai was confirmed within the dual discourse of legitimacy. Being blessed by God as Lord of the Khalkha, and a sanctified Buddhist ruler, Abatai was a legitimate khan ruling the state of the Khalkha *ulus*.

In many ways it was the conceptual frameworks of *ulus/törö* and the dual system of legitimacy that in fact enabled and legitimated the political fragmentation and civil war. It was these two systems that generated the possibility whereby Abatai Khan could not only forge a new "nation-state" but also be considered as legitimate ruler of that entity—no less legitimate a ruler than Ligdan Khan. Ligdan Khan and the Chakhars might have disagreed and claimed all "Mongols" were subject to his power; however, that was clearly not the case. In Abatai Khan and the Khalkha's perspective, their new state and community were equal to the Dayan Khanid state and the Chakhar *ulus*. And so was the reign and community of Sechen Khan Sholoi (r. 1633–1653), who appropriated both the discourse of divine right and Buddhism in order to claim legitimate rule over eastern "Outer Mongolia."[83] Since the ruling Dayan Khanid princes had access to these discourses of legitimacy, all they had to do was activate them. By asserting and ritualizing Chinggisid legitimacy as well as aligning with a Tibetan hierarch, all of these princes were able to assert legitimate rule over their respective localized communities.

And, much later, Mongols began to assert that this is precisely what had occurred. In his 1774 *Crystal Rosary (Bolor Erike)* Rashipungsug describes the situation as follows: "The taxes and tribute were too great and all [Ligdan Khan's] subjects were upset. All the actions taken were wrong. He expelled his own wise men. By destroying his jewel religion the imperial government became in disarray. About ten groups led by the Khalkha and Khorchin separated from the Khan, and each one willingly bestowed upon themselves the rank of Khan."[84]

Of course, as outlined in the previous chapter concerning Mongol views of the *ulus/törö* theory, it was a central concern whether such separation was a good thing. Again, it was certainly a viable possibility within the conceptual framework, but did that make it a positive development? Should all of these leaders and their respective communities have split apart? Should all of these leaders have been able to be elevated as khan? Should Tibetan hierarchs have given these lesser princes the imprimatur of Buddhist legitimacy?

As seen in the previous chapter, some leaders and communities clearly thought it was a good thing. They even followed through with their convictions. Rashipungsug writing a century later, on the other hand, did not think so. In his view it had a whiff of revolution and anarchy about it. Of course, such a view may be expected of a loyal Qing official writing in the heyday of the Qianlong emperor's reign.[85] Not only did he fill his history with the exploits of his ancestors and fellow banner members who fought valiantly against the anti-Qing Khalkha, Oirad and Zunghar, but Rashipungsug even gave his children Manchu names.[86] Thus, perhaps unsurprisingly from his point of view, this period of political fragmentation and multiple khans was a period of chaos and disorder that the Manchu rulers and the Qing state thankfully and mercifully brought to an end. Yet clearly it was not the same in the early seventeenth century when Mongol leaders actively pursued their own independence. An important question, therefore, is how did Mongol conceptualizations change so drastically from the time of Saghang Sechen's writing in 1662 to that of Rashipungsug, writing in 1774?

To understand the shift in Mongol presentations of fragmentation versus unity, we cannot simply say the Manchus used Buddhism. Not only does this ignore the fundamental importance of Chinggis Khan, but also the fact that the Mongol groups that actually were Buddhist, such as the Khalkha and Oirad, were the groups that most successfully resisted Manchu power. Moreover, it was the non-Buddhist eastern Mongol groups that actually joined the Qing. In order to resolve this contradiction we need to begin with Mongol concepts and then investigate how the Manchus actually engaged and ultimately transformed them. Just as the success of the Manchu's incorporation of the Mongols entailed a reevaluation of the *ulus* and *törö* system, so also did the Qing state transform the Mongols' intertwined understandings of political authority and the boundaries of communal identification.

Political Authority in Early Manchu–Mongol Relations

In the early period of the Qing formation the Manchus presented themselves and were understood by the Mongols within the dual system of legitimacy. Nurhaci had moved beyond his earlier title of "Wise Prince" (Man. *sure beile*) in 1616, when he had himself recognized as the "Khan Decreed by God."[87] This title and its acceptance by the Mongols was not only evident in the ritual sacrifices of the Manchu–Mongol alliances, but was also confirmed and reiterated within all the various letters and decrees issued by the Qing court. At the same time, of course, the Manchus were also representing themselves as righteous Buddhist rulers.[88]

The greatness of Manchu rule—the Manchu state, *doro*—was thereby presented within the same bifurcated religiopolitical framework as had shaped Mongol conceptualizations since the late sixteenth century. As seen in a letter of complaint Hong Taiji sent to the Khorchin leader Tüsiyetü Khan in 1628, both discourses were readily appropriated.

> "My father the Qayan, thinking about his long-term great enterprise, [sent] an envoy to talk with you, sought an agreement, and exchanged trustworthy words in [front of] Heaven and Earth; we swore an oath of allegiance and got along well. After this, you told us that you would present yourself in person and discuss political matters, and we agreed on our meeting place. My father rode there in person, but you did not go as agreed. You told a lie to a great man, and this is the first sin. . . . When you heard that my father the Qayan, who loved you, was reborn as a Buddha [i.e.,

passed away], why is it that neither you in person nor your children and ministers came? . . . This is the second sin [stemming from] your ungrateful and disgraceful actions."[89]

Hong Taiji thus scolds the Khorchin leader precisely for violating both discourses of Manchu–Mongol religiopolitical legitimacy: the power of Heaven and the Dharma.

This idea, however, is found not only in private Manchu–Mongol correspondence[90] but also in the public propaganda of imperial legitimacy. In the 1640 trilingual inscription commemorating the Manchu conquest of Korea, Hong Taiji is praised in the same terms as Chinggis Khan, Toghan Temür, Altan Khan and Ligdan Khan; he is the ruler who has both God's blessing and good karma. "The fact that he set up the high great stone on the bank of the great river, and that the land of the San qan shall enjoy peace for ten thousand years, is the might of the fortune and merit (suu buyan) of the Holy Lord."[91] And to underscore the importance and continuity of this bifurcated religiopolitical framework we can also note that the Buddhist emperor par excellence, the Qianlong emperor, began his first Buddhist proclamation, the 1737 edict commemorating the founding of the famous Amurbayaskhulangtu monastery in Outer Mongolia, by saying, "As I think, Heaven in graciously creating our Dynasty of the Great Qing has beneficently united (under the latter's powers) myriads of people."[92] Moreover, in his 1758 inscription commemorating the Qing conquest of the Zunghars, the Qianlong emperor "invoke[d] Buddhist precepts against the Zunghars, saying, 'You claim to revere the Yellow Teaching, but you are really demons who eat human flesh'; while simultaneously making it clear that 'Heaven supported the emperor; [victory] was not [a result of] human effort.'"[93]

But although Manchu use of symbolic forms understandable to the Mongols was certainly beneficial in the preliminary consolidation of power, it also presented problems in the same manner that the *ulus* and *törö* system did. Being a Heavenly-blessed Buddhist ruler did not in itself generate an "encompassed hierarchy," since it drew no distinction between the Manchu Khan, Sholoi Khan, Namudai Sechen Khan, or Boshugtu Khan. Nor did these "symbolic forms" create a single hierarchy among the *ulus* and their states.

Over time various *ulus* and their leaders were incorporated within the Qing, such as the Khorchin, Kharachin and Tümed; and it is generally assumed in this process that there was a straight, full-scale reduplicative transfer of the rituals and narratives of legitimacy. This is the underlying logic of the "Qing model" and the "Buddhist explanation," since both of them mandate the illusion of continuity. Yet one may certainly wonder—was it that simple? In order for the Qing to successfully incorporate these disparate Mongol communities, as was the case with the theory of *ulus* and *törö*, did the rituals and narratives of legitimate rule and community identification not have to change? How else can one explain the shift in viewpoint from the *Jewel Translucent Sutra* to the *Crystal Rosary* of Rashipungsug on whether political fragmentation was good or bad? Or, more to the point, why did the cult of Chinggis Khan disappear and then reappear as a seasonal rite of renewal completely shorn of its previous political power? Similarly, if Qing rule was simply a continuation of Mongol models of Buddhist rule why are there so many discontinuities in Mongol histories about the Dharma?

In the effort to make the Qing appear "natural" it was precisely these changes that needed to be forgotten. The fact that they have not been remembered is a remarkable testament to the success of the Qing. Nevertheless, as with the theory of *ulus* and *törö*, if we are to better understand Manchu rule, we need to investigate further the Qing engagement and transformation of Mongol conceptions of political authority as they related to communal identification. In particular, we need to examine how the power of the Chinggis Khan cult and Tibetan hierarchs was displaced within the framework of Qing "ornamentalism," and how the localized history of the "Mongol Buddhist nation" was reconfigured in tandem with the universalizing narrative of the Manchu Qing.

CHAPTER THREE

Qing Ornamentalism and the Cult of Chinggis Khan

[I]t is vital to the British project in India . . . his popinjay life. His lavish tours, the presents, the sightseeing, the hunt-ing. None of it, he tells them, is for him as an individual. If one were to mistake the respect one is accorded as an official for something stemming from one's own personality or talents, one would find oneself in hot water. Go off the rails. Get delusions of grandeur. No, one is simply there as a sort of projection, a magic lantern image of the Viceroy, who is himself no more than a magic lantern image of the King-Emperor.

One just puts up with it. The lavishness.

—Hari Kunzru, *The Impressionist*

In the fall of 1780, Lubsangdorji, the top official of Alashan Mountain Banner, wrote the following report for the Bureau of Colonial Affairs.

Our Banner's origin descends from Chinggis Khan's second younger brother Khabatu Khasar, and from Güüshi Chingsang there have been fifteen generations. Güüshi Chingsang's son was Obog Chingsang, his son Bubui Merze became Khan of the Four Oirad. Living in the area of Ili, in Boratala's Alimatu Sara Bel he evenly spread the religion and state. Bubui Merze's son was Khanai Noyan Khongghur, and his children were named the Five Bars [Tigers]. Khanai Noyan Khongghur's eldest son Bars Baibaghas Baatur rightly became Khan of the Oirads. The second son Bars Törö with Güüshi Khan came to the Western Eternal Land [of the] Jowo, Tibet, and established the religion and laid the foundation for all the vari-ous traditions.

Then collecting the subjects, at the time of Shizu Expanding Huangdi Kangxi, he was given a square seal and the title Sechen Güüshi Khan, the one respectful of the Dharma-nature, and made to live and rule in Tibet and Kökenuur. Then Bars Baibaghas Baatur requested, "Be compassionate upon me and give me one of your sons because your older brother has no children, though younger brother Güüshi Khan has ten sons." And being compassionate they took Güüshi Khan's third son Ayushi Dalai Ubasha Bayan.

Thereupon Bars Baibaghas Baatur had two children. The second son was Ochirtu Tsetsen Khan and the third son Abulai Noyan. Bars Baibaghas Baatur's second [son] Ochirtu Khan rightfully became Khan of the Oirads. The eldest son of compassion, Ayushi Dalai Ubasha Bayan together with the fourth son Baatur Erke Jinong Khoroli went and joined with the Zunghar's Galdan Boshugtu. There was a rebellion while they were there, and they wished for the Holy Lord's wonderful compassion.

Taking one thousand families to fight the enemy, the Holy Lord came and pursued Galdan Boshugtu's army at the pasturage. When they fought one another, by means of the Holy Lord's standard his enemies were crushed. And upon arriving at the place of the Alashan mountains, [the Holy Lord] said, "Whoever was held at the time of the Oirad Ochirtu Tsetsen Khan, now you have come to our Shizu, which is good." Saying this, in Kangxi's 29th year [1681], Baatur Erke Jinong Khoroli was lovingly granted the pasturage of the Alashan mountains.

In Kangxi's 36th year [1688] Baatur Erke Jinong Khoroli was given the rank Imperial Beile. His third son was taken compassionately and made to live in the Holy Lord's compassionate capital city [Beijing]. And with mercy on the Alashan mountain area, the city of Dingyuan Ying was bestowed and made to be occupied [by the Alashan nobility].

In Qianlong's fourth year [1740], after the death of the imperial son-in-law Jünwang, in the same year, the Holy Lord compassionately bestowed on me the rank of Imperial Beile. Living in the capital, I became an imperial son-in-law. After having returned to my native place, by imperial decree the Zunghar's many pasturages and places were attacked and destroyed. And having zealously rendered service in the actions taken against Dawachi Khan and the Khoid Khan, in Qianlong's 22nd year [1758] I was compassionately granted the title Imperial Jünwang and issued a three-eyed peacock feather and yellow button.[1]

In the two preceding chapters we have investigated Mongol conceptualizations of community and political authority as envisioned on the eve of the Manchu conquest. Moreover, we have noted how the success of the Qing resided in its ability to engage and simultaneously transform them. Lubsangdorji's *Report on the Zeal of the Alashan Mountain Banner's Khoshuud Nobility's Lineage of Princes and Lords* of 1780 not only reflects the culmination of this process but also reveals how an often overlooked element, social hierarchy—in particular, the

Qing court's bestowal of titles and ranks—can reorchestrate both notions of political authority and boundaries of communal identification.

Ornamentalism

David Cannadine calls this process of transformation "ornamentalism."[2] The term obviously counteracts the more familiar "orientalism," since in Cannadine's view the imperial discourse and practices of the British Empire were premised less on a discourse of race than on one of class. He certainly does not discount the importance of race in the empire, yet race by itself does not fully explain the creation and ultimate dissolution of the British Empire. Instead, Cannadine argues that British rule actually entailed a remapping of the subjects within an idealized version of their own class hierarchy. For example, in the settler dominions of Canada, Australia and New Zealand a new landed aristocracy was created, while the caste system was reinvigorated and legitimated by the Raj in India, and in the Middle East mandates kings were anointed within the rhetoric of the noble Bedouin hierarchical tribal culture. As a result, while the social hierarchy generally remained the same, the authority of these local elites was no longer tied to local systems of authority. It originated in, and fundamentally connected them to, the metropolis.

Far from being a problem for the British, the existence of subject elites that could be ruled through was a prerequisite. It superimposed a patina of tradition on what was in fact a radical transformation. If a suitable, preexisting, stable social hierarchy did not exist, problems ensued, for the British in parts of Africa as for the Qing in Taiwan.[3] It was not local elites that needed to be displaced, but rather the local rituals and narratives of political authority and communal identification that sustained them. In this regard, the British Empire was very successful, at least until it was challenged by an educated, urbanized and nationalized middle class.

In order to explain this unraveling, Cannadine argues that the British Empire had been based less on a discourse of race or "ethnicity," but rather a systematic project of social hierarchical mimesis. In particular, he shows how the cohesiveness of the empire was encouraged and promoted through the production of aristocratic genealogies and the bestowal of titles, awards and baubles that created one vast interconnected world, subordinated to the monarchy, between the metropolis and the peripheries. As Cannadine argues, it was through these ritualizations that "the theory and the practice of social hierarchy served to eradicate the differences, and to homogenize the heterogeneities, of empire. . . . The result was the consolidation of a pan-British, pan-imperial elite that conquered and governed, unified and ordered, the empire for the first time."[4]

An essential issue is whether or not this system can reasonably be employed in order to explain Qing rule. It is certainly problematic to suggest that the Manchus had an idea of class that paralleled that of the British aristocracy, or even to transpose European class models onto late imperial China. Yet the creation of local aristocratic genealogies as seen in the 1895 *Colonial Gentry* and the 1900 *The Golden Book of India* does parallel the late-eighteenth-century record of the Inner Asian nobility compiled by the Bureau of Colonial Affairs, the *Imperially Commissioned Record of the Mongol and Muslim Nobility*.[5] Similarly, the highly elaborate imperial honors system that tied local hierarchical structures to the British crown through a new rhetorical framework clearly parallels the Qing's bestowal of titles and ranks. And as seen in Lubsangdorji's report, the bestowal of titles such as Jünwang and the receipt of hats and buttons were clearly important to the Mongol elite and played a role in transforming earlier Mongol conceptions of political authority and communal identification. We may therefore argue that the project of consolidating the diverse constituents of the Qing lay less in the multivocality in which it indulged, and more in the creation and maintenance of an imperial elite shorn of its pre-Qing cultural logic.[6]

While it is well known that the Manchu court reveled in its cultural diversity and presented itself in a multiplicity of guises, ultimately, as with the British, the Qing project fundamentally entailed shattering these indigenous cultural, economic and political entities and superscribing them with the logic of empire. By maintaining the existing social hierarchy and engaging earlier communal conceptualizations and discourses of political legitimacy, the system maintained an aura of continuity. However, over time both of these earlier systems came to be entirely reconceptualized in terms defined by the Manchu court. Lubsangdorji therefore does not mention the *ulus*, but the banner. Moreover, counter to our expectations, he does not dwell at length on the Qing emperor's Buddhist bona fides. Rather, the Manchu rulers are the "Holy Lords" who bestow authority on local elites. Holy Lord (*Boɣda ejen*) was, of course, the title previously reserved for Chinggis Khan. In particular, it was "from in front of the Lord," where Mongol leaders received their titles of rank.

By the end of the eighteenth century, therefore, Mongol concepts of political authority and their ritualization had clearly changed. Yet how in fact did this occur? To begin unraveling these developments it is essential to recognize that this transformation was neither immediate nor wholly dictated by the imperial center. Rather, much as the British had done with, for example, the caste system and Bedouin tribal structures, the Qing first needed to engage with the sociopolitical system of the *ulus* and *törö*, and then ultimately transform it. All the while, however, the Mongols themselves also needed to accept these transformations as their own.

FIGURE 4. Cultural Uniformity. Portrait painted by the Jesuit artist Jean-Denis Attiret of the Dörbed's Beyise Gendün after his submission to the Qing (c. 1755). Courtesy of Bild-archiv Preussischer Kulturbesitz/Art Resource NY.

Granting Titles

The bestowal of titles and ranks was not a Qing innovation but had been a fundamental part of statecraft within the *ulus* and *törö* system. Every ruler of a new state incorporated its various *ulus* by bringing the preexisting aristocratic elite of these communities within the new governmental apparatus. The former *qayans*, sultans and kings of the various submitted groups were retitled as *qans*, princes, or ministers within the new state formation. In this way the preexisting local rulers were not only recognized as representatives of the new state but also maintained their positions of local authority.

It is important to recall that this practice accorded with the larger logic of the *ulus* and *törö* model, in that while it incorporated local elites it did not dismantle their local claims of authority or the communal view of the *ulus*. Otherwise it would never have been possible for those same elites either to potentially leave that state, or to reestablish their community anew. Thus, as seen in all the seventeenth-century chronicles, it was imperative that a new khan incorporate the elites of the various *ulus* within its state, so that the state would be able to properly function through those elites. Indeed, it was the bestowal of titles upon local elites that in many ways sustained the *ulus/törö* system, as can be seen in Saghang Sechen's description of Tümen Jasagtu Khan's reign: "Tümen Taiji, born in the Ga Pig year (1539), ascended the throne at the age of twenty in the Wu Yellow Horse Year (1558). In his thirty-eighth year, the Bing Mouse Year (1576), meeting together with the Sword-Girt Karma Lama he accepted the Dharma. Causing the Six Tümen to be gathered, he prescribed the Great Law. From the Six Tümen, by means of Namudai Khung Taiji of the Chakhar, Üijeng Subukhui of the Khalkha, Khutugtai Sechen Khung Taiji [of Ordos], he maintained the State through them, and became famed in all directions as Jasagtu Khan."[7]

Of course, the inevitable problem with this system of bestowing ranks upon local elites was, as with the *ulus/törö* system, its centrifugal nature. Ultimately, these constituent groups and their leaders could eventually reject the state and revert to their local structures. And that is precisely what occurred among the Mongols. It was the descendants of these local rulers and their communities, the distinct *ulus*, who challenged the authority of Tümen Khan's great-grandson, Ligdan Khan, and the Dayan Khanid state. Nevertheless, Saghang Sechen's description of Tümen Khan's rule, and the similar presentation he gives of Darayisün Khan,[8] Boshugtu Jinong[9] and even Erinchen Jinong,[10] reveals how important the incorporation of local elites through the bestowal of rank was in the minds of the seventeenth-century Mongols.

Recognition of the representatives of a khan's ruling apparatus was the distinction between successful rulers such as Dayan Khan and Tümen Jasagtu

Khan, and failed ones like Ligdan Khan. Instead of bringing the leaders of the Six Ulus into his state, Ligdan Khan alienated them by his scorched-earth policies. This development fostered the civil war, since the nobility of the various *ulus* finally rejected the authority of Ligdan Khan's state and forged their own states. Yet, even as they did so, it is important to keep in mind that the idea of ceding authority to a greater state was a valid option built into the system, especially if that state could better maintain order.

Most Mongol groups saw the Manchu state in that light, as the remedy for a further descent into chaos and warfare. However, this is not to say that the Mongols imagined that joining the Jurchens would eventually result in shattering the *ulus/törö* system and all that it entailed. Aligning with the Jurchens, of course, turned out to be a Faustian bargain.

Nevertheless, when they did first join the Manchu project it was readily understood that the new state would not only bestow titles upon the local elite, but that the same elite and their *ulus* would be recognized within the *ulus* and *törö* framework. In particular, the *ulus* and their elite would maintain their "semi-independent" status. And early Manchu–Mongol relations unfolded precisely within this system. Leaders of different Mongol *ulus,* such as the Khorchin, Kharachin and Aokhan, forged alliances with the khan of the Jurchen *ulus* in the framework of a new state, the Manchu *törö/doro.* These groups paid taxes and made offerings to the Manchu state, and in return not only did the Qing offer protection, but the emperor also bestowed titles and ranks upon the local *ulus* elite.[11]

This is the framework in which Saghang Sechen represents the Shunzhi emperor's reign:

> The Ey-e-ber Jasaghchi Khan was born in the Wu Tiger Year (1638), and at the age of seven in the Ga Ape Year (1644), sat upon the throne of the Daiming Khan of China and became famous in all directions as the "Ruler by Peace" Khan. In the south, eighty tümen of Chinese, in the western side of Adag Kham, twenty-six tümen of Tibetans, and in the north, four tümen of Oirads, and in the east, three tümen of White Koreans, and the central four provinces of Manchus, and six tümen of Mongols did he take into his power. And he bestowed such titles as Wang, Beile, Beise, Gong, etc. on the khans, princes, and officials who were in the ulus and provinces as a whole, and showed favor unto each, heavy and light, and justly ruling the vast Great Ulus, he maintained the Jade Great State in peace and tranquillity.[12]

In many regards this description of the Shunzhi emperor remarkably parallels Saghang Sechen's description of Tümen Jasaghtu Khan's reign. Both are conceptualized within the framework of various *ulus* being incorporated within a centralized state. The Manchu emperor, much like Tümen Khan, recognizes the local elite of these entities, the "khans, princes, and officials," and through the bestowal of new titles upon them, "Wang, Beile, Beise, Gong," the emperor not only brings them into the state but is also able to rule through them.

Unlike Lubsangdorji's description of the Kangxi emperor, however, Saghang Sechen's history and all the other seventeenth-century Mongol sources reveal less a new "Qing discourse" than a perpetuation of, or at least a continuity with, earlier Mongol conceptualizations, especially in terms of the theory of *ulus* and *törö*.[13] While his passage does reflect some changes, such as the Qing being identified as the Great Ulus, Saghang Sechen does not speak of the banner, or of a unified Mongol *ulus* as one part of the Great Qing. But Lubsangdorji does.

How did this happen? On one level it is easy to argue that the Manchus simply "bought off" the Mongol elite.[14] However, by itself that does not fully explain these changes. In the seventeenth century, the granting of titles certainly did not undermine the fundamental nature of the *ulus/törö* system, or generate undying loyalty to a new state formation. This is evident not only from Ming history and the court's relations with the Mongols, but also from Mongol rebellions against the Manchus throughout the Qing period. Even more important, however, is the fact that being given a title does not necessarily redefine one's communal boundaries. Mongols throughout the seventeenth century who indeed were given new titles by the Qing court continued to see themselves as members of preexisting "semi-independent" *ulus*. This only changed in the eighteenth century. Thus one may wonder what fostered this change. If it was not simply the act of being "bought off," what made Khorchins eventually identify less with their *ulus* and more with their banner as part of the Mongol *ulus* within the Great Qing?

Loyalty and Imperial Grace

Manchu rule among the Mongols was certainly facilitated in the seventeenth century by their engagement with the *ulus* and *törö* system and the bifurcated discourse of legitimacy. But for Qing rule to ultimately succeed, it was essential that these earlier frameworks be dismantled. The independent Khorchins needed to become Mongols-of-the-Qing.

One discourse that fostered this transformation and played an important role in forging an integrated and socially defined transcultural elite was the idea of imperial grace. Such a strategem was possible because the idea of the emperor bestowing "merciful and weighty grace" upon unworthy subjects, who must strive unceasingly to repay it, transcended the perceived boundaries of rulership

in the Chinese and Inner Asian worlds. In his study of this language and its practice in maintaining Qing rule, Atwood has shown how the idea of grace and loyalty became a fundamental component of Mongolian discourse in the eighteenth
and nineteenth centuries. Yet Hong Taiji was actually using this language already in the early part of the seventeenth century. As Struve has noted, Hong
Taiji "saw the need to educate his followers in more abstract concepts such as
Chinese-style 'righteous principles' and 'exhausting one's loyalty' to state and
ruler. After about 1631, this sort of ideological vocabulary increases steadily in
Qing official documents."[15]

Evidence of the incorporation of this language for a non-Chinese audience
is found in the following imperial letter from 1642 bestowing a title upon an
Üjümüchin prince for his service to the Qing.

The decree of the vastly merciful and powerful Holy Emperor, ruling by decree of God.

Upon the decree of Heaven and Earth, in each incarnation one ruler is
born and it is customary for him to give titles and ranks to the nobles who
helped the state. This is the law that began with the holy sovereigns of yore.
Now I, according to the earlier holy sovereigns intend that for everyone, in-
siders and outsiders, for each lord of the many groups who gives favor and
help, each will be established and deigned a rescript. The person who receives this rescript will have helped the state with a resolute mind, evenly
held the laws and regulations, from beginning to end not neglecting good
deeds. If this is possible it is like the loyalty of a father to a grandfather, the
blessing will reach to all the descendants. From generation to generation
there will be happiness.

Exerting yourself and not being negligent, you Dorji, descendant of the
Mongol Chakhar Khan and Lord of the Üjümüchin, did not recognize the
relatives of the Chakhar's Khan and punished that state. When that state
was destroyed, you avoided joining with your elder brothers of the
Khalkha. After I had entirely incorporated the Chakhar ulus, you understood the situation and taking your own related ulus surrendered it to me.
Therefore I grant you to become a Sechen First Rank Prince of the State.

If with a respectful mind you continue to destroy revolts, uprisings and
moral corruption, the imperial rank First Rank Prince will be inherited
indefinitely. If the government concludes that you fled the enemy, then you
will not be invited [to court] and the imperial rank of First Rank Prince will
not be inherited from descendant to descendant.

The sixth year of the Great Qing's Degedü Erdemtü, on the fourth day of
Spring's middle month.[16]

As Atwood notes, "the Qing Emperors did not always have to act as split personalities, despite the diversity of peoples within their realm. The Qing made use of
at least one language of loyalty that proved equally at home in the 'land of fish
and rice' along the Yangzi and in the rolling steppes of Khalkha Mongolia.
Among Chinese, Manchus and Mongols, they claimed and succeeded in getting
their subjects to agree, at least verbally, that their power and authority was anal-
ogous to, yet even higher than, the power and authority of parents over children,
and that any office rank, or title, held by his subjects was granted solely as a result of the immense forgiving mercy of the Emperor."[17] The language of imperial
grace therefore certainly played a fundamental role in the Qing's orchestration of
a transcultural elite ruling and regulating the vast domains of the empire.

In many ways, however, it was actually no different than the bestowal of titles
as practiced in the *ulus* and *törö* system, and therefore did not necessarily foster a
transformation in Mongol conceptualizations of communal boundaries. Indeed,
in the above imperial decree there is no mention of the banner, nor of the Mongol
ulus. The framework is still the *ulus* and *törö* model. One hundred and fifty years
later in the 1795 *Iledkil Sastir,* however, we find a marked change. The idea of a
semi-independent *ulus* and its elite as a "temporary" part of the Great Qing has
been entirely displaced. "Then Good Dayan Khan Lord ruled the various tümens,
and afterwards from his nine sons the descendants branched off and became the
Lords of the provinces. By the order of the God Buddha the Holy Taizu Taisung
Khan was born to rule the world, and all the nations united in the Great Qing. The
descendants of those who submitting previously will receive heavy weighty grace
for generations by acquiring titles and ranks, and each will be appointed [to rule]
one of the banners."[18] So, in the eighteenth century, the banner nobility of the
Mongol *ulus* existed solely through the grace of the Manchu emperor. To foster
this change it was therefore not only necessary to give out various baubles, but to
fundamentally realign communal conceptualizations and their political legitimation within the *ulus/törö* system. Only when these intertwined realities had been
dismantled could the Manchus fully incorporate the various Mongol groups and
their leaders into the new state formation of the Qing.

The court's first step in incorporating the Mongols into the Qing, and in
changing the boundaries of the many *ulus* to comprehend one single Mongol
ulus, was to reinscribe the Mongol *ulus* nobility as the banner elite through the
emperor's grace. The terms *ulus* and *qosiyu,* "banner," were used interchangeably for nearly a century, and, as noted above, they were virtually parallel phenomena in many ways. Of course, there were radical differences in the concepts
of the semi-independent Mongol *ulus* and the Manchu banner, and therefore it
was crucial for the Qing to generate a shift in the definitions of these terms.[19]

Qing ornamentalism, by redefining the *ulus* as a banner, not only tied the recognition of local authority to the imperial center, but also replaced the idea of the distinct localized *ulus* (and its local system of authority) with the logic of the single, united Mongol *ulus*. It reconnected the Mongol nobles with each other, not as representatives of separate *ulus,* but of the Mongol *ulus* in its entirety. As the *Iledkil Sastir* declares, "We all, the descendants of Chinggis Khan, greatly rejoice in the Great Qing Dynasty's Emperor's grace."[20]

Nonetheless, it required nearly a century of Manchu rule for the policy of ornamentalism to succeed. That it eventually did succeed is clear from the fact that the Khorchins, Kharachins and Tümeds became Mongols-of-the-Qing, and would in fact remain so until 1911. Moreover, the "trans-*ulus*" of the unified Mongol *ulus* of the Qing continues to sustain the modern idea, and hopes and dreams, of a pan-Mongolia. Thus, clearly, Qing rule redefined not only Mongol communal identification but also the attendant systems of political authority. But why did it take so long?

Forging the Mongol *Ulus*

Several interrelated factors can possibly explain this delay. The first is that, while the discourse of imperial grace was a powerful medium for changing Mongol society, by itself it did not necessarily challenge or redefine the *ulus/törö* system. If the Mongol nobility continued to see themselves as the elite of their *ulus* being recognized by a new state rather than as the banner elite of the Qing, these same elites could in fact revolt against the state as was their inherent right within the *ulus/törö* system. And this was precisely what occurred in Lubsangdanzin's revolt of 1722. Five years earlier, after defeating the Zunghars, the Qing had incorporated the Khoshuud Mongols through the ornamental bestowal of titles and ranks. However, after believing the court was slighting him in favor of another Khoshuud prince, Chaghan Danjin, Lubsangdanzin revolted against the Qing state.[21] And pointedly, one of his first acts of rejecting Manchu rule was to "order the revival of indigenous titles and the abolishing of the titles given by the Qing, such as wang, beile, or beise."[22] Lubsangdanzin then declared his intention of joining the Zunghar state.

Evidently, in many ways, Lubsangdanzin was still operating within the logic of the *ulus* and *törö* system. Indeed, he believed that the Qing would revive the coherent Khoshuud "khanate" after the Zunghars had been driven out of Lhasa. When the court rejected such a notion the rebellion began. The language of imperial grace had therefore not changed these earlier conceptualizations of *ulus* and state among the Khoshuud. If the Khoshuuds, or any other Mongol group or community, were to become an integral part of the Qing, they would have to accept the cultural logic of the Manchu state.[23]

At first, though, the language of imperial grace created, at most, a "middle ground": while the Manchu court saw the Mongols as part of the banner system, the Mongols, in a form of conceptual parallelism, continued to see themselves in terms of *ulus* and *törö*, as evidenced in the seventeenth-century chronicles and by the revolt of 1722. Yet, as seen with the prophecy of Urtuukhai Ong and the 1795 *Iledkil Sastir,* this parallelism was eventually shattered. Lubsangdorji, writing in 1780, presents the history of the Khoshuud Mongols as inherently culminating in the Qing. So how did this transformation occur? What forces or discourses beyond the language of imperial grace played a role in fundamentally transforming Mongol boundaries of communal identification? In order to answer these questions, we need to return to the Mongols' dual discourse of legitimacy. In particular, we must investigate how these ideas were engaged and also how they were fundamentally changed in the process of the Qing formation.

As noted above, the Manchus engaged with the Mongols' bifurcated discourses of legitimacy from the very beginning. However, merely presenting themselves as Heaven-blessed Cakravartins in multiple media did not transform Mongol conceptualizations, since much like the language of imperial grace, it allowed a conceptual parallelism to flourish. The Manchu rulers Hong Taiji and the Shunzhi emperor both took great pains to project both their receivership of God's blessing and their Buddhist bona fides. Hong Taiji went to inordinate lengths to "prove" his Mongol-Chinggisid credentials. He fabricated and extensively promoted the story of Chinggis Khan's seal; he built on the history of Yuan period Buddhism by aligning with the Sakya as opposed to the Gelukpa; he built the Mahakala temple for the statue Khubilai Khan presented to Pakpa Lama; and he received multiple tantric initiations. The Shunzhi emperor invited the Fifth Dalai Lama to Beijing and had the Yellow Temple built for him to stay in during his visit to the capital.

However, as reflected in the seventeenth-century Mongol sources, these activities in themselves did not change Mongol communal concepts. Mongols certainly remarked upon the Manchus' receipt of God's blessing and their relations with the Dharma, and indeed it was these actions that justified Manchu rule. But at the same time these actions did not fundamentally alter the underlying relationship of the *ulus* and *törö*. Nor did they necessarily distinguish the Manchus from the Khalkha and Oirad rulers. Moreover, as seen in the case of Lubsangdanzin and the Khoshuud revolt of 1722, by being Heaven-blessed Cakravartins the Manchus were no different from the Oirad Khans ruling the Zunghar state.

If the Qing project, including the creation of a Qing identity, was to be successful, the Manchus needed to make the dual discourses of legitimacy their exclusive property. If they did not do so, not only would both the Dharma and the cult of Chinggis Khan remain as viable modes of political authority beyond the control of the Manchu emperor, but also, perhaps more important, Mongol communal conceptualizations would remain the same. If the Manchu emperor could appropriate both rituals of local power, he would not only become the sole arbiter of political authority, but also the central idea of independent *ulus* within a state would be weakened, because the *ulus* elite would exist only through the emperor's grace.

The problem, however, was that throughout the seventeenth century both of these discourses remained beyond the control of the Manchu court. Throughout that century, for example, the Dalai Lama continued to bestow titles, including that of khan, upon the Mongol and Oirad elite. And the failure of the Manchu state to do anything about this state of affairs is evident in the fact that the Qing bureaucracy in turn simply reconfirmed these new titles.[24] Similarly, the cult of Chinggis Khan and its affirmation of God's blessing was external to the bureaucratic machinery of the imperial court.

For the Mongols to be fully incorporated into the Qing both of these discourses would have to become part of the Manchu project. The Manchu emperor needed to appropriate the rituals of local power conferred through both the cult of Chinggis Khan and the Dharma. The ulus elite would exist only through the grace of the Manchu emperor, and only as members of a banner representing a "pan-*ulus*" Mongol nobility of the Great Qing.[25]

Becoming a Lama, Becoming Chinggis Khan

The Kangxi emperor was the first Manchu ruler not only to emulate the earlier Mongol bifurcated system of legitimacy like Hong Taiji and the Shunzhi emperor but actually to fundamentally displace this earlier system with the logic of the Qing state. He did this by appropriating to the emperorship the rituals of both Chinggis Khan and the Tibetan hierarchs, whereby it was only through his grace that the Mongol nobility even existed. And, as such, they were recognized not only as rulers of their respective banners but also as representatives of the larger Mongol *ulus,* which itself was created and maintained through the grace of the Qing state.

The Kangxi emperor's dealings with the Khalkhas in the 1680s exemplify how the Qing engineered these changes. Before this period, the Khalkhas had remained outside of Qing control, not only on account of the theory of *ulus* and *törö,* but also because the political authority of Khalkha elite and their state and attendant community was ritualized through the Dalai Lama. Initially, the Dalai Lama had recognized the authority of a Khalkha ruler, and this confirmation was subsequently reconfirmed by the Manchu emperor and recorded by the Qing bureaucracy. But, in 1682, the emperor insisted that a recommendation be given to the court first. After the court recognized the succession, the Dalai Lama was to confirm it. In effect, Kangxi's policy was to circumvent and undermine the Dalai Lama's role in ritualizing Mongol political authority, thereby making the Manchu emperor the only medium through which local power was recognized.[26]

Of course the Kangxi emperor's aim was not solely to appropriate the ritual power of the Dalai Lama.[27] Indeed, his actions cannot be divorced from the larger aim of defeating the Zunghars, and the incorporation of the feuding Khalkha khanates into the Qing state was an important part of these power politics.[28] To this end the Kangxi emperor therefore used his position as peacemaker between two warring Khalkha groups to further consolidate his power to legitimate authority among the Khalkhas and thereby incorporate them into the hierarchy of Qing ornamentalism. A peace conference on October 3, 1686, attended by all the Khalkha khans and nobles and by representatives of the emperor and of the Dalai Lama,[29] produced an accord that the Khalkha nobility accepted, as is reflected in this letter they sent to the court in 1687:

> Letter of Khalkhas' Qan, Lords and Taijis.
>   This is to inform the Majesty of Mañjuśrī the Supreme Great Holy Lord from the two Khans and the greater and lesser lords of the Seven Banners.[30]

> On this occasion to inform the Great Khan:
>   In order to make peace in this faraway [place] you, the throne-holder of Galdan [monastery], invited to establish and set forth the [Dalai] Lama's majesty, and sent your own great official Arnai Aliga Amban. You invited the Majesty of the Jebdzundamba Khutugtu, the Great Lama of the Seven Banners, and we, all the Khalkha Khans and lords, were all assembled. When all the commands of the teaching were issued down, we received all the commands and obeyed them. The exertions of the Great Ruler cannot be compared with the rest.
>   All of us have received great joy. When the state is pacified and the religion is spreading on account of the Holy Emperor's compassion, we all greatly rejoice. This is a great kindness to us all. Therefore we wish to return this grace, a kindness that is too great to repay, with everything [we can].[31]

This act of diplomacy created the environment in which the emperor could begin to secure the power of the Qing state among the Khalkhas.

In the same year, 1687, the Khalkha's Setsen Khan died, giving the Kangxi emperor a chance to transform the legitimation of power among the Khalkhas. Drawing upon the precedents of the previous year, where actions originated from Beijing and not Lhasa, the *Veritable Records of the Qing (Qing shilu)* records that the emperor informed the leading Khalkhas that he had recognized the former Setsen Khan's son to be the new khan. Through this act the Manchu emperor appropriated the right of sanctifying the Borjigid rulers previously reserved for the Dalai Lama. The *Veritable Records of the Qing* records this transformation as follows: "The Seven Banners of the Khalkhas have sworn to a covenant of peace not long ago. It is not convenient to leave the seat of the Sechen Khan vacant. Therefore, issue an Edict to the Tüsiyetü Khan, the rJe-bTsun dam-pa Khutugtu, the Zasagtu Khan and the others, saying that the Sechen Khan Nor-bu's eldest son, Ildeng Araptan, has immediately succeeded (his father) as Khan. As usual, issue an edict to the Dalai Lama informing him."[32] Other letters sent to the Jebdzundamba Khutugtu and the Dalai Lama preserved in the Number One Historical Archive in Beijing also reflect the transformation. The letter to the Jebdzundamba Khutugtu reads as follows:

> Imperial letter sent to the Jebdzundamba Khutugtu:
> This is the Emperor's command proclaimed to the Khalkha's Jebdzundamba Khutugtu.
>
> I have been thinking: From before until now, to establish and unite into one the great kings of the world, one must be compassionate to both the inner and outer, have no distinction between those near and far, [as if] all were one, and bestow grace upon the 10,000 nations. When the wise teaching has spread in the world, tribute will be given yearly. I have zealously perfected my mind and always regard with favor and compassion upon seeing those praiseworthy. You, from generation to generation have served as a firm, stable and zealous envoy, offering weighty tribute every year, having shown a zealous peaceful mind. This is very great praise.
>
> Unexpectedly I have heard the Setsen Khan has passed away. I am greatly saddened and have sent an official to transmit blessings. Previously when your Khalkhas were antagonistically slandering each other, I with compassion issued an order, sending an official to make harmony and accord. Therefore, it is not permissible, in the land of Setsen Khan, to have the throne vacant. Because in your Khalkha customs the eldest son inherits it, Yeldeng Arabtan Taiji the eldest son whom I hear is a good person, should inherit it and take the throne. For this reason the letter has been beneficially dispatched; quickly enthrone him as Khan.[33]

The letter from the emperor to the Dalai Lama simultaneously reflects the change in status of the Dalai Lama vis-à-vis the Khalkha:

> Written decree sent to the Dalai Lama. The Emperor's decree.

Sent to the majesty of the All-knowing Vajradhara Dalai Lama, who leads the Buddha's teaching in the world, the very good rejoicing Buddha of the Buddhas.

Before we were compassionate to the Khalkhas as they were disagreeing and antagonistic among themselves, and had an official and lama sent to restore [peace]. Now I hear Setsen Khan has died, and I am greatly upset. I have sent an official to grant blessings. Because you previously regulated [the Khalkhas] well, it is not permissible in the territory of Setsen Khan to have the throne vacant. According to Khalkha customs, because the eldest son is to inherit it, Yeldeng Arabdan Taiji, the eldest son whom I hear is well-known as a good person, should become Khan. I have immediately informed the Tüshiyetü Khan, the Jasagtu Khan and the Jebdzundamba Khutugtu. In addition to the letter sent of the decree saying install the accepted Khan, this letter is sent to inform the [Dalai] Lama [of these actions].[34]

This appropriation of the power of the Dharma by the emperorship was not restricted to the recognition of the nobility, but as is well known, the recognition of Buddhist hierarchs themselves was eventually brought under the control of the emperor and the Bureau of Colonial Affairs.[35] The Qing emperors therefore became the sole arbiters of local authority, including in the realm of the Dharma. This imperial authority was even projected anachronistically into the past. The 1737 inscription at Amurbayaskhulangtu monastery credits the Kangxi emperor with having appointed the Jebdzundamba Khutugtu,[36] when in fact it was the Khalkha who had done it themselves.[37] Moreover, in a 1713 colophon to a new Mongolian translation of the twelve volume *Yum* section of the Kanjur, the Kangxi emperor, the "Mañjuśrī Khan," is praised for his compassion and bestowal of rank upon the Khalkha nobleman who had commissioned the translation.[38] The elite of the preexisting and distinct Khalkha *ulus* now existed, and were only legitimated as the nobility of the Mongol *ulus,* through the Buddhist emperor Kangxi.

Another essential factor in fostering this transformation was the displacement of the symbolic power of the blessing of Chinggis Khan. As noted above, the Chinggis Khan cult had been a fundamental component of legitimate Mongol rule; however, at the same time it had also played a powerful role in ritualizing the Mongol community. As Chiodo has noted in her study of the pre-Qing cult of Chinggis Khan: "The offerings performed by the qaγan to the hearth of Chinggis Khan are private offerings to the ancestor, but they also express an idea of nation. Worshipping the hearth of Chinggis Khan, the qaγan ensures the continuity of the Mongolian nation and of the Mongolian people."[39] Yet, as is evident in the ritual texts of the Chinggis Khan cult from the Qing period, the concept of Chinggis Khan granting the authority to rule and ritualizing the entirety of the Mongol *ulus* has been displaced.[40] Instead, the rituals are simply seasonal rites of renewal.

Parallel to this demotion in the realm of sacred power there is also a large-scale interpenetration of Buddhist concepts into the structure and language of the rituals. Many scholars have previously taken this fact as evidence of the inherent "shamanic" nature of the Mongols, who could never accept "true" Buddhism, thus only a Buddhist patina concealed a truly "shamanic" worldview. However, as is now known, this idea is based on dubious methodological approaches, particularly nineteenth-century constructions of Buddhism and the Humean two-tier model of religion.[41] Nevertheless, this view of the Chinggis Khan cult and its focus on the problem of "Buddhicization" also avoids the very real transformation wrought in the cultural logic of this cult that occurred in the process of creating the Qing. Namely, how did the cult of Chinggis Khan change from one aspect of the dual legitimacy of the Mongols in the pre-Qing period into a seasonal ritual incorporating Buddhist language and symbols performed by the Ordos Mongols?

The function of the Chinggis Khan cult to re-create the Mongol elite and *ulus* was appropriated by the Manchu emperorship during the course of the seventeenth century. Indeed, as seen above in the letter of Lubsangdorji, by the end of the eighteenth century the Manchu emperor was not only a Heavenly-blessed Cakravartin, but had in fact become Chinggis Khan. Unlike seventeenth-century Mongol sources, which simply confirm the Heavenly-blessed nature of the Manchu emperors, Lubsangdorji actually identifies the Kangxi emperor as the "Holy Lord." This epithet, Bogda Ejen, "Holy Lord," was used in the pre-Qing period exclusively in reference to Chinggis Khan. Lubsangdorji also specifically describes the Kangxi emperor as defeating his enemies through the power of his "standard" (*sülde*), the martial emblem that was a central component of the Chinggisid myth and the cult of Chinggis Khan.[42] Thus by the end of the eighteenth century the Qing rulers were not simply blessed by God, they also functioned as Chinggis Khan.

The Qing, Chinggis Khan and the Mongol Ulus

Between the time of the *Precious Summary* and the late eighteenth century, the Mongol conception of the *ulus* had changed from that of a local, separable, temporary part of one *törö* or another to being a single Mongol *ulus*, existing in time as a single people predestined to find rest in the protection of the Qing. One important component in fostering this transformation was the increasing Mongol identification of the Qing emperorship with Chinggis Khan, particularly in his role of ritualizing the Mongol community.

To understand this development we need to begin with Rashipungsug's *Crystal Rosary* of 1774, wherein he goes so far as to say that the Qing state was in fact a direct blessing of Chinggis Khan himself.

> In my, Rashipungsug's, opinion, when some say that the descendants of the sons, younger brothers, and princesses of the holy Chinggis Khan have become rulers of the Mongolian multitudes and have been entitled as taijis [nobility] and tabunangs [noble-affines], and as guests of the Great Qing empire have been granted titles and ranks of their own with a most desirable situation; under examination it is truly the wondrous genius and might and the power of the good merit of Holy Chinggis Khan, and in addition their worship of weighty, supportive, and merciful supreme grace of the Holy Chinggis, the Lord.[43]

In this rather remarkable passage Rashipungsug readily asserts that not only are the Mongols a unified entity, but they should inherently be a part of the Qing; that is the natural order. Moreover, his assertion also confirms the fact that it is through the blessing of Chinggis Khan, or more specifically through the grace of the Manchu emperor, that the Mongol nobility and *ulus* exist at all. As Rashipungsug writes, "In brief, the descendants of First Rank Prince Alchu Bolod, the lords of the four Jarud Banners of the Baarin, they submitted with zeal to the compassionate established order of the Great Qing Dynasty's Holy Lords. They each held a government office and from generation to generation without interruption they relied on the weighty grace [of the emperor]."[44]

This is clearly a profound development, not only in terms of the discourse of political authority, but also in terms of communal conceptualizations. And an important component fostering this transformation was the Manchu emperorship's appropriation of the dual role that the cult of Chinggis Khan performed. The emperor not only bestowed local authority upon the Mongol elite, but this relationship also generated the Mongol *ulus*. The Qing state therefore legitimated not only the Khorchin or Ordos elite and their distinctive *ulus* but the banner elite who, as descendants of Chinggis Khan, represented the "pan-*ulus*" Mongol "nation."

This was achieved by building upon the religious nature of the language of imperial grace. As Atwood has noted, this discourse resulted in the "Qing emperor . . . becom[ing] the object of reverence by his Mongolian, Manchu, and Chinese servitors that was undeniably religious in quality."[45] And this phenomenon parallels the cult of monarchy that Cannadine argues was central to the creation and maintenance of the British Empire,[46] especially the need to inspire "awe and submission."[47] Indeed, the sacred nature of the emperor is readily confirmed in the "pilgrimages" to Beijing for imperial audiences with the Bogda Khan, (Holy Khan), which the Mongol nobility had to undertake yearly.[48] "Failure to attend would incur punishment—in the case of a banner prince, a fine of three years' salary. The purpose of such audiences was 'to inculcate awe and veneration in the heart' (*xing sheng jing wei*) among the Mongol nobles."[49] The Qing emperors were thus clearly understood in religious terms; indeed, they were the rulers blessed by God. Yet Manchu rule was not only legitimated by the idea of divine right; it also engaged with its manifestation in the cult of Chinggis Khan.

In his *Precious Summary* Saghang Sechen therefore makes the connection between the Manchu rulers and Chinggis Khan explicit by having a man from Ordos (the site of the Eight White Tents) initially identify Nurhaci with the semantically resonant term *suu* (fortune [of the emperor]), which was used only in reference to Chinggis Khan.[50] Yet even though Saghang Sechen makes this connection between Nurhaci and Chinggis Khan, he does not make explicit the *identification* of the Manchu ruler as Chinggis Khan, as does Lubsangdorji writing over a century later. Even in Gombojab's early-eighteenth-century *Flow of the Ganges* (*Ganγ-a-yin Urusqal*) the author does not make this connection.

Instead, according to Gombojab, the Mongols accepted Qing rule on account of God having blessed the Manchus. "At that time God's weighty grace and powerful blessing aided the Qing state. On account of this blessing the main descendants of the nomadizing Mongols' Holy Chinggis Khan, the nobility and in-laws of the [Mongol] ulus believed in the Great Qing's Great State and rejoiced greatly for a long time in peace and quiet."[51] Gombojab, who lived in Beijing and taught at the Tibetan school, was a staunch supporter of the Qing. He was also an imperial son-in-law. Even so, he too does not identify the Manchu rulers as Chinggis Khan. Indeed, his work in large measure is still framed within the discourse of the *ulus* and *törö*; nonetheless, it reflects an important shift.

This shift represents the recognition that there are no longer distinct Mongol *ulus* such as the Khorchin or Tümed within the Manchu *törö*, but simply one Mongol *ulus* within the Qing. Unlike Saghang Sechen and the other chroniclers of the seventeenth century, Gombojab recognizes the unity of the Mongols—the pan-*ulus* Chinggisid nobility. Thus, rather than princes ruling independent *ulus* within the Manchu state, they have all become the "ethnonational" descendants of Chinggis Khan recognized through the grace of the Manchu emperor. As with the pre-Qing cult of Chinggis Khan, the Manchu emperor therefore not only legitimated the Mongol elite but also the Mongol *ulus*. Both the Mongol nobility and the *ulus* they represented were created and maintained through the rituals of ornamentalism.

The same idea is also found in Dharma's 1739 *Golden Wheel with a Thousand Spokes* (*Altan Kürdün Mingγan Kegesütü*). In his introduction to the history of the

Mongol nobility descended from Dayan Khan, who are to become the Manchu-recognized banner rulers, he explains: "On account of various actions the [Mongol] descendants submitted at different times and received titles and ranks. From generation to generation they have received weighty great grace [from the emperor], and each has been delegated their own banner."[52] And at the end of his long genealogy of these various descendants and their banner histories, Dharma goes further in amalgamating the power of Chinggis Khan with the grace of the Manchu emperor.

> All those who from Batu-Möngke Dayan Khan's
> Nine sons have been confirmed as chiefs
> Over the nomadic folk of six tümens west and east,
> Are the descendants of Lord Chinggis and equally
>
> Rejoice greatly in the grace of the Great Qing empire.
> Growing and flourishing by merit from a single man
> Happy in the peace under the Lord's wonderful and weighty grace
> Ruling as one over the folk in the land.
>
> Both sovereigns and commoners have become the best of all.
> How wonderful the powerful grace of the man
> To those for more than five hundred years ruling their folk
> Since their birth in the supreme golden clan
> Of Chinggis Khan, born by the protection of God.[53]

It is evident in this presentation, as with Rashipungsug's work and Lubsang-dorji's report, that both the Mongol nobility and the Mongol *ulus* that were once ritualized through Chinggis Khan are now manifested and maintained on account of the emperor's grace.

Rituals of Local Authority

The Qing court's appropriation of Tibetan hierarchs' power to bestow titles and ranks, and of the Chinggis Khan cult's power to create Mongol political authority and community, is well confirmed in the annual bestowal of seals. The emperor granted these seals and they confirmed the local authority of the Mongol elite. The seal was therefore a powerful symbol in Mongol society, as noted by Antoine Mostaert, who had lived in Ordos from 1906 to 1925.

> Let me here say a few words regarding the great seal of the banner. The inscription of the seal is in Manchu and Mongolian. It says: "Seal of the Jasagh

who governs such and such banner." The seal is the same one that the first Jasagh received from the Manchu emperor at the founding of the banner. The Mongols consider it a sacred object. It is always in the immediate vicinity of the prince and a lamp burns night and day in front of the chest holding it. When the Jasagh undertakes a trip to the interior of his banner, he will take the seal with him, and it is then transported on [its own] horse, which a cavalier leads by the hand. When the prince spends a night on the road, the seal rests in a little tent that is guarded by a functionary.

The great seal is only used for important documents and the important official correspondence. On documents and letters of lesser importance one applies the little seal of the *jamu* [Ch. *yamen*].[54]

The seal was therefore not only a "sacred" item bestowed by the emperor but, more important, its bestowal was also a vehicle whereby local rituals of authority were transformed.[55] And in a collection of political addresses from Ordos one can see how Qing ornamentalism fostered this change.

The first address is pronounced upon the return of a banner prince from an imperial audience where he was given a new "order," which refers to a new rank.

Born in the exalted family of the Virtuous Qans because of the excellent merits accumulated from early times, at a time when you were still young like a new moon by (imperial) command you obtained an eminent title rank; now suddenly at a time when you have perfected the magical gift of long life, during an audience with the Lord Emperor, Esrua-Tengri [i.e., the God Brahma], you have received an order; and now that you have come back and settled in your golden palace you have placed your seal made with assorted jewels upon a broad white silk, the possession of the powerful gods.

As a present (for this occasion when) you offer and hand over (your seal) together with the (imperial) decree, in (this) Golden Tent, we fill (the goblet) with brandy having the qualities of a rasayana, and offer it (to you) and give this speech.[56]

What is important to note in this address is not simply how the Manchu emperor employs the language of the bifurcated discourse of legitimacy, but how it reflects the changes already discussed. The Mongol prince is a *qan* of his banner, not a *qayan* of his independent *ulus*. Moreover, it is the Manchu emperor, a Buddhist god, not Tibetan hierarchs, who bestows rank.

In addition, the fact that this ritual takes place or is visualized as taking place in the *chomchog,* the "Golden Tent," reveals how the creation of local authority previously mediated through the cult of Chinggis Khan was now maintained by

FIGURE 5. A Chomchog Tent. Courtesy of the Lattimore family and the Peabody Museum, Harvard University.

the power of the Manchu emperor. A *chomchog* is a particular style of tent with a pointed roof, which in the Ordos refers only to the ritual tents of Chinggis Khan.[57]

The performance of this ritual of local power within this actual or visualized space reflects a symbolic linkage with the pre-Qing Chinggis Khan ritual, where a ruler received the right to rule "from in front of the Lord" *(ejen emün-e-ece)*. However, the transmission of power now emanates from the Heavenly-blessed Buddhist Manchu emperor.

In addition, just as Mongol rulers once ritualized the "Mongol nation" through the cult of Chinggis Khan, with the imperial seal granted through imperial grace to a banner prince, so this prince in a semantic chain transmits this grace to his subjects, who are in turn incorporated into the banner of the Qing Empire. This ritualization of the Mongols as part of the Qing, based on the relationship between the emperor and the local Mongol nobleman, is reflected in the following address to a local leader upon receiving his seal.

> Holding your incomparable seal made with assorted jewels and granted by your saintly Lord and Emperor who turns the Golden Wheel, you strengthen the law of a vast great nation and government which is like a jade-rock, and govern your vast and a numerous myriad (of subjects). You share (with us) a banquet and manifold favors resembling the abundant great and timely rain.

As a present (for this occasion when we) enjoy happiness (equal to that) of Vast Heaven, we offer brandy having the qualities of a *rasayana* and deliver this address.[58]

One consequence of this development was that the exalted cult of Chinggis Khan and its ritualization of Mongol rulership and the Mongol "nation" lost much of its political meaning. The cult, which previously had been the exclusive sanctifier of a Mongol ruler, and through synecdoche of the Mongol community as a whole, was no longer feasible. As a result of the incorporation of this power into the institution of the Manchu state, it is not surprising to discover that there was a hiatus in the cult of Chinggis Khan after the Manchu conquest. In fact it was only through an imperial decree that the cult of Chinggis Khan at the Eight White Tents was reinstituted, albeit with an irrevocably transformed social and ritual logic. Shorn of its previous political force after the Manchu throne had usurped its power of political legitimacy and community creation, the cult of Chinggis Khan became solely a seasonal rite.

The Fate of the Chinggis Khan Cult

In its new manifestation, the entire ritual complex was divorced from its previous ritualization of a Mongol ruler, his state and the *ulus* it represented. Instead, the Qing court appointed the five hundred families of Darkhads, one clan of Mongols, to be the sole caretakers and practitioners of the cult of Chinggis Khan.[59] In this way not only were the initial structure and ritual logic transformed, but the entire ritual complex was removed from exclusive Mongol control and brought under imperial surveillance. As was the case with other diverse religious practices in the Qing state, the cult of Chinggis Khan was placed under the authority of the Bureau of Colonial Affairs.

The extent of the bureau's control over the remnants of the cult is evident from laws and administrative correspondence. In 1696 the Kangxi emperor ordered a compilation of all the ordinances and edicts issued since 1627 that bore on Qing rule in Inner Asia.[60] This compilation, which prescribed "the treatment of local elites, in particular the Mongol aristocracy and the powers to be granted them. Ranks, posts, promotions, and demotions, salaries, visits to court, ceremonies, banquets . . . ,"[61] also came to contain a law concerning the cult of Chinggis Khan.

A law has been made pertaining especially to the remains of Chinggis Khan. From the beginning the remains of Chinggis Khan have been within the borders of Yeke Juu. From the beginning the Five Hundred Darkhads were made to be in charge, make offerings and guard the remains within the

Seven Banners of Ordos. Each year 500 taels of silver are issued that are to be used for the worship of the remains and supplying what is needed. On this affair the subjects are not under the rule of the princes, and the League is to select one good and able official who will especially rule over, direct and take care of [the worship of the remains]. After arriving, the League leader needs to arrange in order all the League government's titles and inform the Yamen. The Yamen will then issue a memo informing of their consent. Afterwards the government should meet and rule on this matter. The Darkhads are not to be imposed upon with unnecessary taxes, and furthermore, they are exempt from the taking of relay horses. The same as the League's princes and officials also comply with. The League leader has to count and carefully check the one year's issued silver and inform the Yamen.[62]

And there is a large corpus of correspondence extant between the Yeke Juu leaders and the Bureau of Colonial Affairs concerning the administration of the Eight White Tents. A typical example of these annual letters from 1767 reflects well how the cult had been incorporated into the ritual economy of the Qing:

Letter of the Ordos' Beise of the Third rank Namjildorji and the Administration's Taijis submitted to the Bureau of Colonial Affairs.

To inform you that we have taken from the people who guard Chinggis' White Palace and examined and counted how the 500 taels of silver intended for the four rituals per year at the Eight White Tents and the repair of the palaces was used: 4 horses, 40 taels; 175 sheep, 5 castrated goats, 180 taels; the felt covering the palaces, 64 taels; 4 spotted oxen, 20 taels; the dried meat of 2 oxen, 10 taels; sandalwood incense burned in the eight palaces, 12 taels; lamp oil, 7 taels 2 qing; offering fruit, 5 taels; 14 white [bolts?], 4 tael 9 qing; offering tea, 4 taels; interior felt, 5 taels. Thus we inform you that we examined and that 352 taels 1 qing was used for horse, oxen, sheep and other necessities. In addition, of the remaining 147 taels 9 qing we have counted and let it be known that 130 taels was used for 12 white silk [bolts] used this year to wrap two small palaces and 12 tael 9 qing was used for four red brocades to be used next year. We, the League leaders, have taken this and presented it to the Great Ministry.
Therefore will you please respond whether you agree or disagree?
The 10th of the last winter month of the 31st year of Qianlong.[63]

As evidenced in the law code of the Bureau of Colonial Affairs and the above letter, it is clear that both the Mongol *ulus* and the remnants of its previous central religious and political institution had come under pervasive and detailed imperial supervision.

The impact of this incorporation into the Qing bureaucracy is reflected in the language used concerning the Eight White Tents. When the Bureau of Colonial Affairs took control of the ritual, the name of the Eight White Tents, *naiman cayan ger,* found in all the seventeenth-century Mongol works, was changed to the Eight White Palaces, *naiman cayan ordu.* This phrase could be seen as reflecting a greater symbolic power, but it also hides the reality of its transformation. It is not surprising that this later term is found in all the works of eighteenth-century Mongols. These authors systematically glorify Chinggis Khan and his descendants who, as the banner elite, represent the Mongol community, which is now ritualized, not through the cult of Chinggis Khan, but through the Qing emperor.

Similarly, there is a cultural amnesia about the cult of Chinggis Khan in Mongol histories. Although all these histories identify the cult as the site where Mongol khans and *ulus* were ritualized prior to the Qing, following the Manchu conquest it is no longer mentioned at all. Only in the mid-eighteenth century does there appear a standard historical interpretation of the transformation of the cult of Chinggis Khan. In the 1757 *Light of Wisdom (Bilig-ün jula),* the destruction of the cult is attributed to Ligdan Khan, who destroyed it while retreating to Tibet in 1632.[64] Why this account appears when it does is an interesting question, and one can only conjecture whether or not there was a recognition between what the cult had once entailed and the one enacted under the auspices of Qing authority. Nevertheless, this history does offer us a powerful narrative concerning the relationship between the cult of Chinggis Khan and the Manchu Qing.

The appropriation of the Chinggis Khan cult within the Qing state also transformed the nature of Mongol boundaries of communal identification. The pre-Qing reality of independent Mongol *ulus* ruled by Borjigid rulers recognized through the power of the Chinggis Khan cult had been destroyed by the evil Ligdan Khan. In its place the Mongol nobility, and thus by extension the Mongol *ulus* in its entirety that they represented, were now created and maintained through the grace of the Manchu emperor. This is an idea that is eloquently noted by the Mongol bannerman Lomi in his 1732–1735 *History of the Mongolian Borjigid Lineage (Mongyol-un Borjigid oboy-un teüke):*

> In conclusion, that our Mongolia rose again having almost fallen and was reborn having nearly been cut off, is well and truly all the grace of the Holy Lord. It is also Supreme God secretly assisting, and in recompense to the achievements and wisdom of the early ancestors, joining its forces to that.

Had it not been so, it has been almost one hundred years from Ligden Khutugtu Khan's rebellion to the year of Nairaltu Töb [Yongzheng, 1735], and
amongst the many aimags the strong would have oppressed the weak, flesh
and blood would be killing each other, and sufferings would have become
unbearable. Recalling the weighty beneficence repeatedly broadcast with
pity and mercy from the time of Emperor Taizong [Hong Taiji] to Emperor
Shengzu [Kangxi], it is truly deep. Therefore, when children and grand-
children carefully read these three volumes, they should distinguish clearly
trunks from leaves. And should they moreover recall in perpetuity the
weighty grace of the Emperors, guard their own station, pity their subject
peoples, and live rejoicing in peace and tranquillity, will it not be their merit
forever?[65]

As a result, by the end of the eighteenth century Mongol historians presented
their history in terms not of the *ulus* of Chinggis Khan, or in regard to the independent *ulus* of the sixteenth and seventeenth centuries, but in terms of the
Mongol *ulus* and the banner.

Mongol history had indeed become redefined within the social realities of
the Qing.

> To summarize the birth of Chinggis Khan and his descendants in the world,
> it was called the Great Yuan Dynasty. After creating the state it lasted 162
> years. Then, from Wuyin, the Chinese Ming's Zhu Hongwu came and
> pacified the confusion and established the [Ming] state. Although it was
> named the Great Ming, Chinggis Khan's descendant Biligtü Khan ruled
> what is now the Mongols of the Six Leagues and the Four Aimags of the
> Khalkhas. The descendants continued for about three hundred years until
> the time of Ligdan Khutugtu Khan. When the Mongol states were in disar-
> ray, the Great Qing State was founded and continued for about 180 years.
> This book is written as a summary of the clans, descendants, names and
> places of the Eight submitted Banners, sums and regions in today's Great
> State.
>
> It was written and prepared by the official seal holder, Meiren Wu Sai
> Liu, in the second year of Sayisiyaltu Irügeltü [Jiaqing, 1797].[66]

In the subsequent chapters we will explore in detail how these conceptualizations
further developed, especially in relation to the Dharma; however, we first need to
return to the impact that the appropriation of the Chinggis Khan cult by the Manchu emperorship actually had on these rituals, and its broader implications.

In this regard one can fruitfully compare this earlier development with the transformation of the cult of Chinggis Khan in a more recent ideology emanating from Beijing.

> We devoutly request [our wish] to you [Chinggis Khan], that we will be loyal to the Party and State, that we will support the masses, that the red flag with five stars will flutter in the sky, that the badge of the five-pointed star will gleam on our chests. Thereby, through confessing in you our wish, likewise, take it under your protection and make it our contribution to the Four Modernisations.[67]

Thus we see that in both the Qing and the People's Republic of China, the cult of Chinggis Khan had been appropriated and reconceptualized within the new logic of empire.[68] In both cases the cult survived, yet it was entirely changed. Not only did it reflect new political realities, it also confirmed new communal conceptualizations. In the case of the People's Republic of China, the cult remains a powerful medium for ritualizing and asserting Mongol ethnic identity. Yet precisely because it confirms the *minzu*—the "national, ethnic, minority" identity mandated by the state—the contemporary cult of Chinggis Khan and its narratives and rituals are stripped of any political power and simply reconfirm the reality of the "multiethnic China."[69]

Similarly, in the case of the Qing, the usurping of the Chinggisid cult by the Manchu emperorship not only redefined the dynamics of ritualizing and understanding political authority but also transformed Mongol communal boundaries. Much as the Capetian kings' appropriation of the cult of Saint Denis resulted in the formation of "France" and "Frenchmen" from the disparate local communities incorporated into the expanding French state,[70] the Qing similarly forged the "Mongol Ulus" from the distinct *ulus* through the cult of Chinggis Khan. Yet, as we have seen throughout this book thus far, these relationships were always intertwined with the Dharma. The forging of a pan-*ulus* Mongol identity was not generated solely by the Manchu emperorship's takeover of the ritual authority of the Chinggis Khan cult; the Dharma was also instrumental in this process. In fact, Buddhism, with its embedded power of creating communities, played a fundamental role in forging a new pan-*ulus* Mongol identity. Indeed, it went further to help create a new Qing Buddhist identity. This transformation will be explored in the next chapter.

CHAPTER FOUR

The Poetics, Rituals and Language of Being Mongol, Buddhist and Qing

The British had entered the country's bloodstream like
a malady which proves so resistant that the host organism
adapts itself to accommodate it.
　　　　　—Michelle de Kretser, *The Hamilton Case*

In the early nineteenth century an anonymous Mongol author wrote a brief history entitled *How It Came About That the Mongol Royal Family Descended from the Indian Kings*.[1] The genealogical connection between the Mongol and Indian royalty had been a part of the Mongol historiographical *imaginaire* since the seventeenth century, and thus the author of this particular work paid it little heed. Rather, after summarizing the lineage from India's first king, Mahāsammata, to Chinggis Khan in two short pages, the author begins with the main part of his narrative—a history of the Manchus.

> The occasion of the first appearance of the Manchu Khan. Long ago there lived a blessed nation called the Niu Ching at the place called the Mukden River. At that place there was a Great Mountain called Ki yi ya where wild animals and beasts roamed. It was surrounded by a sky like leather skin bags that rumbled, and there were also clouds and fog. It was there, on the top of one Tangsug Mountain at a cool, pure, and beautiful lake that the Eight Banners were established.
>
> Into that lake the Son of Heaven descended and bathed himself and played games. Then on one occasion, one of the God's Ḍākinīs came and while she was bathing herself a white goose flew by and dropped on her breast a fruit he had taken from the ocean's shore. The Ḍākinī took it, ate it and became pregnant. She stayed there until the pregnancy was complete and one son was born, which she covered in the leaves of the Ebsu tree and then abandoned it, returning to her realm.
>
> The Lord of the Nāgas protected the child, and all the animals helped in raising him. When he descended from the mountain and found one person of the Niu Ching *ulus*, they said to one another, "We all need a Ruler." Thus he was bestowed with the title Boshugtu Khan. That Khan stayed on the

Mukden throne for eleven years, ruling the Niu Ching community until the Tenth Rabjung cycle's female black pig year [1623].

At the time, in that place no trees grew, and one fortune-teller pronounced the prophecy: "Because it seems as if there are too few trees to shade 10,000 people, the Khan has said [to wait] till the lineage has multiplied to 100,000. Then when the Mukden River floods, in your lineage a great Khan will rise up and rule many nations!"

That [Boshughtu] Khan had great faith in the Buddhist religion and invited one great Lama from the Buddhist direction. That Lama was given the title Ba Erdeni Lama. That Erdeni Lama asked the Dalai Lama for a title for the Khan, who bestowed on him the title Mañjuśrī Khan. By the sound of this name the Ching nation was given the name Manchu. The Khan and the Lama were in agreement, and taking the Mongol and Tangut scripts and stories the Manchu script was created.

That Khan's son Gegen Sechen Khan sat on the Mukden Throne for ten years until the Eleventh Rabjung's blue dog year [1634]. At that time our Mongols, the forty-nine separate titled nobility of their own banners, *aimags* and *ulus* were living together suffering under the taxes of Ligdan Khan. Because of Ligdan Khan's violence, great requisitions upon the people and his lack of love and compassion, the Mongols broke away [from Ligdan] for the great mercy and great peace of that [Gegen Sechen] Khan. They joined Gegen Sechen Khan and presented their requisitions [to the Qing].

When Gegen Sechen Khan was a seven-year-old child, the Mukden River flooded and all the soldiers and farmers who witnessed it knew it was a wonderful and auspicious sign. At the time Wu Sangui of the inner lands was thinking to join [with the Manchus] in order to seize the state of Li Zicheng Khan, and requested troops from the Manchu Khan. Upon this request he gave one thousand cavalry troops, saying, "You will succeed if to the tail of each horse you tie a broom." Li Zicheng Khan's fortune-teller saw that army coming and said, "If we look at the numbers, they are a hundred thousand soldiers, we cannot win. We should flee!"

Li Zicheng Khan took his gold and crystal seal and fled through the front gate of Beijing. Thus it was that Wu Sangui's army pursued him, and that afterwards the Manchus' Gegen Sechen Khan, at the age of seven, rode out toward Beijing. At the age of seven he was placed on the Imperial Throne, and Wu Sangui became a subject.

"Because it is written that in every *saṃsāra* cycle there should be one ruler, and that there should never not be a ruler, your son shall take the imperial throne. Because you and I shall act as officials of our thirteen provinces, you can rule seven, which shall be given as an offering." When this was said, Wu Sangui was very happy. He rejoiced and consented, and although he praised this offering [eventually he] changed his mind.

That gold and crystal seal had been given to Chinggis Khan by the Nāga [king] and Li Zicheng took it and was planning to throw it into an outer ocean. However, when he was going along the road, he put it down and the ground opened up, as is clearly told in stories. . . . Later, a careless person was going along and fell down a dried-up well . . . where he saw the gold and crystal seal. He presented it to the Khan and he received great favor.

At that time, when the three violent nations, the Ööled, Khalkha and Chakhar, were made to enter into the peaceful realm, the Khan was given the title Shunzhi. By this Khan's command laws were established and the leaders of many leagues were appointed after inspectors were sent to inspect each one of these areas. And according to his command the hierarchy of the Wangs, Beile, Beise and Güng were established and bequeathed. The foundation and order of Qan, Taiji and Tabunang also began at the time of Shunzhi Khan. Afterwards, by means of power the people of many nations submitted, and the state was stabilized. This Khan's power was spreading the people's good society by establishing laws and customs, and spreading the Dharma.[2]

I begin with this passage not to confirm the prevalent idea that the Manchus somehow "used" Buddhism to rule the Mongols. Rather, I present this history in order to bring to the fore the reality of change. In particular, what is intriguing about this passage is how radically different it is from the passages of Saghang Sechen's history. Indeed, there is virtually no correspondence between the 1662 *Precious Summary* and *How It Came About That the Mongol Royal Family Descended from the Indian Kings,* written 150 years later.

Instead of *ulus* and *törö*, there are Mongol banners and a Qing ruling elite. Instead of the bifurcated discourse of legitimacy, the Aisin Gioro lineage actually descends from an orally impregnated Ḍākinī.[3] The Manchus are born to rule as Cakravartins over a Buddhist realm. Moreover, even the concept of time has changed. Instead of the Sino-Mongolian calendrical system found in Saghang Sechen's *Precious Summary,* the author of the nineteenth-century history uses the Tibetan Rabjung cycle.[4] And perhaps most remarkable, this Mongolian history has virtually nothing to say about the Mongols. Instead of being a reiteration of the insular genealogical narrative of the Mongol nobility that shaped Mongol historiography through the eighteenth century, it focuses on the Manchus and the founding of the Qing state, of which the Mongols are only one, albeit proud, component.

This development, or progression, from independent Khorchins to Mongols-of-the-Qing has been the central focus of the preceding chapters. We have seen how the Qing was less an event than a process—an ongoing negotiation between the metropole and the periphery in which Mongol conceptualizations of political authority and communal boundaries were not only engaged but also ultimately transformed. By the eighteenth century the Mongols were thus not simply a part of the Qing, or loyal subjects of the emperor; it was their Great Qing. They had in fact become Mongols-of-the-Qing.

However, we have not yet fully explored the role that Buddhism actually played in forging this development. The Dharma was clearly a fundamental element within the discourse of Manchu rule, and indeed it is the only continuous element between Saghang Sechen's 1662 *Precious Summary* and the above-cited nineteenth-century history. The Qing is Buddhist, and thus since the Mongols are Buddhist they support the Qing. This rather glib summary is, of course, the underlying logic of the "Buddhist explanation," which as noted above was aptly summarized by the French Jesuit Father Amiot in 1799 and continues still today. This interpretation may even be true.

Unfortunately, however, this theoretical framework really tells us nothing about the process through which the Khorchins actually came to see themselves as Mongols, Buddhists and integral members of the Qing dynasty. Indeed, on account of Buddhist rule being framed as inherently static in both theory and practice, these important changes are the ones most often subverted. It is therefore not surprising to find that the same ideas and rhetorical tropes are employed in the proclamations, edicts, paintings and histories projecting the Buddhist rule of Mao Zedong in Tibet, the Qianlong emperor in Mongolia and Altan Khan among the Tümed. They all claimed to be manifesting the righteous model of Buddhist rule; however, clearly the People's Republic of China (PRC), the Qing, and the Tümed *ulus* are very different realities—communities with different boundaries, rituals of political authority, as well as notions of what it means to be Buddhist.

Of course, it is precisely these transformations that are required to be ignored in order to maintain the illusion of continuity. The PRC is therefore imagined to be just like the Qing vis-à-vis Tibet, just as the Qing is the same as Altan Khan's Tümeds. Yet clearly they are not the same. However, it is this illusion of continuity that gives the "Buddhist explanation" such power; that is its logic and how it functions. Indeed, the legitimacy and explanation for the reality of a new state formation, its political authority and communal boundaries reside within the displacement of change. Thus the problem is not whether Mao or Qianlong projected themselves as Khubilai Khan in their projects of state consolidation, or whether this was simply cynical political manipulation, but rather what is

occluded when we frame our own interpretations within the very same tautological reasoning that undergirds the discourse of Buddhist rule.

If we are actually to understand the success of the Manchus in making the
Mongols proud members of the Qing, or the failure of Mao in securing the undying loyalty of Tibetans, we need to investigate precisely those changes in the
narratives and rituals of political and communal identity that made the Mongols
part of the Qing or kept the Tibetans resisting the PRC. Thus, rather than as-
suming that there was a straight, reduplicative transfer of rituals and narratives
of legitimacy from either the Qing to the PRC, or from the independent Mongol
ulus to the Qing imperial state, we need to recognize that the "Buddhist rule" of
each of these enterprises was a contemporary creation. The "Buddhism" that the
Manchus are thought to have adopted from the Mongols was actually being created as the Mongols submitted.

Until recently this process of transformation has been hard to recognize because the sources that have shaped our understanding of this development were
all written during the Qing. And Qing-period sources all present a linear history
that conforms with the narratives and rituals of the Qing. In the same way as we
have used pre-Qing sources in the previous chapters to explore how the theory
of *ulus* and *törö*, and the bifurcated discourse of legitimacy, were engaged and
transformed within the Qing project, we now need to investigate how the rituals
and narratives of Mongol Buddhist identity were also being transformed to coincide with the Buddhist Qing's mythic structures of legitimacy. In particular, we
need to explore how the Dharma helped to map new communal boundaries, especially a new Mongol identity that was tied less to an independent Mongol
community than to the larger reality of the Buddhist Qing.

Sanctifying the Starting Point

Histories written after the advent of the Qing—or more precisely, since the
Mongol *ulus'* acceptance of the Qing state—were intended to generate a cohesive narrative that held in suspense the Mongols' previous independent history
and what in fact had been their submission to the Manchus. In particular, these
histories moved beyond specific localized *ulus,* as in the *Jewel Translucent Sutra*
and its focus on the Tümed, to a broader conceptualization of the Mongols
within the Qing. This project entailed creating shared realities that transcended the immediate context "by mobilizing the formal properties of such
sign systems as language, poetics and ritual."[5] Such shared realities, or totalizing
representations, created an identity through narratives and rituals of community,
usually in the medium of political authority. We therefore need to reevaluate
the dominant narrative as found in Qing-period sources in order to enhance

our understanding of this transformation. In particular, we need to explore the dynamics of the process that made the Mongols a part of the Qing by examining the different Buddhist narratives deployed between the period of the independent Mongol *ulus* and that of the Qing.

A logical place to start this excavation is, to borrow Hastings' phrase from his study of Christianity's effects on national formations, "the sanctification of the starting point."[6] Because histories of conversion are produced to define the newness of a religious community, a fundamental aspect of these narratives is the representation of the group's ethnogenesis. Most often there is a fusion of the legendary founder of the group with the new religion, as in the case of the well-known link made between Chinggis Khan and the Sakya Lama Kungga Nyingpo. Although modern scholarship has shown that Kungga Nyingpo died before Chinggis Khan was born, the fiction played a vital role in creating a powerfully linear narrative of the Mongols as Buddhist. And as is clear in the rhetorical structure of all pre-Qing Mongol sources, the vision of the Mongols as Buddhist was always stressed.

Both pre-Qing and post-conquest Mongolian sources are the same in this regard—both are pervasively Buddhist. However, if one looks closer it becomes evident that the sanctification of the starting point of the Mongols' Buddhist history shifted during the course of the Qing formation. In the earlier sources this history begins with Chinggis Khan, but in Qing sources the Mongols imagine their genealogy stretching all the way back to India. Now this idea is generally taken for granted; however, such a connection is not made in any of the pre-Qing sources. Rather, the sanctified community is understood solely to be tied to specific *ulus* and their leaders, all of whom descended from Chinggis Khan.

Thus, counter to the Qing and later narratives, Mongol history in pre-Qing sources begins, calendrically as well as narratively, with Chinggis Khan, and not with Mahāsammata in India. This can be seen not only in the *Jewel Translucent Sutra* but also in Tsogtu Taiji's 1624 inscription. Not only does it praise Ligdan Khan, Tsogtu Taiji's ally and the nominal ruler of all the Mongols, but it also defines this community in terms of the Buddhist pantheon and the divinely blessed Borjigid lineage.

Homage to Samantabhadra and Amitābha and the Buddha Sakyamuni.
Homage to Hevajra and Mother Vārāhī and Vajrapāṇi.
Homage to God Above, to the Emperor and Empress, and to all benevolent people . . .

By the order of Tsogtu, Prince of Khalkha, offspring of Chinggis Khan and grandson of Vajra Khan, this was, for the case of the Holy Khan of the Mongols [Ligdan], written on the rock like a gem of jade by Page Daiching and Güyeng the Valiant on the great white day, the fifteenth of the month of the fire tiger, which is the first of the months, in the wood mouse year [1624], which is the first of the years, when four hundred and sixty-four years had elapsed since the water ox year [1160] in which Chinggis Khan was born.[7]

For the pre-Qing Mongols, therefore, "year zero" was the birth of Chinggis Khan. By situating themselves in such a calendrical framework the Mongols did not link themselves to anything beyond the temporal and ethnospatial boundaries of Chinggis Khan's initial formation of the Mongol *ulus*.

The same temporal structure is also found in a recently published early history of Chinggis Khan, the *Golden Summary of Chinggis Khan,* from which the standard Qing-period Buddhist genealogy is absent.[8] This early source recognizes the history of the Mongols as originating with Chinggis Khan. Similarly, a 1594 stela inscription from Olon Süme in Inner Mongolia also begins with Chinggis Khan. "From among the descendants of the Genius Chinggis Khan for fifteen generations the Buddha Dharma was built. After the enlightenment, the ocean of Chinese subjects destroyed the jewel of the peaceful Great Yuan . . . [then] Supreme Altan Khan invited the Majesty of Sodnam Gyatsho."[9] No connections are drawn to either India or Tibet. This also occurs in the opening passage of the 1607 *Jewel Translucent Sutra,* wherein Chinggis Khan, the founder of the Mongol *ulus,* is also the first propagator of the Mongol Buddhist community.[10] In none of these presentations is a genealogical link made with the larger Buddhist continuum. Rather, all of these histories affirm solely the Buddhist history of the Mongol *ulus.*

A similar format is found in the Chaghan Baishing (White House) inscription commemorating the building of monasteries at Tsogtu Taiji's city. "Having accumulated an enormous amount of merit, through endless Kalpas, [Chinggis Khan] was born miraculously in this great Mongol land, and became the Khan of the ten directions."[11] In this inscription there is again no appropriation of other genealogies; Mongol history begins with this narrative of Buddhist ethnogenesis. The same conceptualization is also found in the famous colophon of the *Five Treatises (Pañcarakṣā),* which also makes no allusions to the India-Tibet-Mongolia genealogy[12] but begins Mongol Buddhist history with Chinggis Khan, as is the case with other pre-Qing Buddhist translations.[13]

The genealogical link between India, Tibet and Mongolia, however, is found in all the seventeenth-century Mongol chronicles written after the Manchu conquest. In these works, the "ancestral figure of Börte Chino—the 'blue-grey wolf' named as Chinggis Khan's first ancestor in the thirteenth-century *Secret History*— was transformed into a Tibetan prince with [genealogical] links to the sacred centers of Buddhism in India."[14] This historiographical development continued throughout the Qing period, as is well captured in Gonchugjab's 1836 *Pearl Rosary (Subud Erike)*.

Long ago in the Holy Land of India, and the Northern Snowy Land of Tibet, and the very great Mongol Land, from the three with the custom of the Dharmarāja appearing in succession; shortly after the world was established, in this Jambudvīpa living beings originated, and then a person with great beauty, a straight and honest heart and scintillating intelligence appeared. He loved the correct ones, instructed the mistaken ones, and nourished everyone equally. Everyone said, "Don't leave us outside your decrees," and mutually they made an oath and they enthroned him as emperor. In this good *kalpa* he was the first to appear, and became famous as Mahāsammata, the "one raised up by the many."

Then there were five great emperors in this same *kalpa*, who followed in succession; Splendid Beautiful Khan, Meritorious Khan, Supreme Meritorious Khan, Greatly Nourishing Protector Khan. Then there were the five Cakravartin khans, who had all the seven jewels of state, the seven important jewels, and the seven good jewels, they were "I am Blue" Emperor, Splendid Emperor, Important Splendid Emperor, Completely Splendid Emperor, and Important Completely Splendid Emperor. They ruled from the time of immortals till the age when people lived to the age of eight thousand years.

Then in those ages when humans lived for forty thousand years, the first of this good *kalpa*'s thousand Buddhas, the World Destroyer Buddha named Krakucchanda, came hither to this Jambudvīpa. At the time that he turned the Wheel of the Dharma, the above-mentioned Important Completely Splendid Cakravartin was emperor. Then from Important Completely Splendid Emperor's son named Bhadra, down to the Bright Emperor there were thirty khans; and in succession from Bright Emperor there were a hundred emperors that came to the Vessel Holding Land called Potala . . .

Secondly, this is how the Great Dharmarājas of the northern snowy land of Tibet descended. Although there are many things not taught by Wise Men and the Sastra literature, [this is actually how it happened]. The Buddha Teacher made a prophecy and said, "From within the lineage of Mañjuśrī, in the religion of the Sugata, the Doer-of-many-Deeds worshipping the north, at that time will appear. He will appear in the lineage of the Licivis, and be named God of the People, the emperor who lives on top of a snowy mountain called Land of the Complete Buddha." And in that way in the lineage of the Emperor Raised-by-the-Many, long ago in India, from the lineage of Emperor Ten-Carts, there were three lineages of Sakyas. The Tibetan emperors certainly descended from the Licivis of the Middle Sakya.

Long ago in India to Sharba, the son of Emperor 100-Soldiers of Kusambi, a son was born. [Because the son had] the signs of a leading man, like turquoise eyebrows, conch-like teeth, drawings of a wheel on the palm of the hand, and a web joining the lower part of the fingers, [the father] was fearful and dubious and said, "Is it another kind of god or demon?" Subsequently, there were several opinions of what to do: some said "put him in a box and abandon him at the Ganges River"; others wanted to exile him to another place. Nevertheless, no matter what home he had [the son] came to the northern snowy Tibet and became great. He went to the summit of Yereltei Shambu, Yarlung's snowy mountain. Then, descending to the four doors of Cha-tang, he met twelve people who worshipped the land. When they asked him, "Where do you come from?" he said, "I am Jambu," and because he pointed with his index finger to the sky, the people said, "He has descended from the sky and we should elevate him as emperor." Dressing a chair, they made him sit on it, and by raising it up on their necks, he became famous as the Neck-Chair Emperor, Nihri Jambu. This emperor resided in the palace named Yambu Lhakhang . . .

Thirdly, this is how great Dharmarājas appeared in succession in this great land of the Mongols. Long ago in India, the Land of Saints, from Mahāsammata till the 1,121,574th Emperor, at that time in the Red Horse Year Buddha Sakyamuni came to this Jampudvipa, did the twelve deeds and then in the Red Tiger Year showed the nature of Nirvana. After 417 years in Tibet, Rigumja Emperor of the In-Between-Two Tings, descended in the lineage of the original Neck-Chair Emperors, was seized by the bad-minded official named Luo. At the time when he took and established the state, Emperor Rigumja had three sons, all of whom were malefactors.

The eldest son, Jardi, went to Ningbu. The middle son, Sardi, went to Buubu. The youngest son, Nardi, went to Kongbo and took one wife. Afterwards, Jardi returned and ruled as emperor in the Pure Tibet. He became famous as Bodi Kongjil. Nardi lived in Kongbu and never acclimated. [Thus] he took his wife, Ghowa Maral, and arrived at the mountain named Burkhan Khaldun on the banks of Baikal in Mongolia.

They met the Bede people. When he clearly spoke of his relation in lineage to the long ago Mahāsammata, and the reason for his land and family, etc., then all the tribe of the Bede people consulted. Saying, "He is the son of a lineage descended from God," they raised him up to become a lord. Then to the Mongols he became famous as Börte Chino-a.[15]

I cite this lengthy passage not only to give readers a familiarity with this historiographical development and reveal its parallelism to the history of the Manchus heretofore cited, but, more important, to highlight again the difference between this description and those of the pre-Qing period. While in both cases the Dharma is presented as a central component of Mongol conceptualizations of communal identity, in the pre-Qing sources the Dharma is engaged solely in terms of the Mongol *ulus*. In Qing period sources, in contrast, the history of Buddhism and its relation to the Mongols is situated within a world historical continuum—one that inevitably culminates in the totality of Mongols conceived as simply one part of the Buddhist Qing.

Buddhism, History and the Unified Mongol *Ulus*

From examining the developments in the presentation of history during the Qing formation it is evident that Mongol views had changed. Not only had the boundaries and nature of the Mongol *ulus* been transformed, but so too how the Mongols presented the Dharma. An important question the static "Buddhist explanation" has held in abeyance is therefore not only this change but how these shifts were interrelated. In particular, how did the Buddhist discourses of the Manchu state play a role in transforming Mongol communal conceptualizations?

Before investigating the dynamics of this process, however, let us first look at the consequences of this discourse. The first was the reaffirmation of the Mongols as a unified community. As seen in Gonchugjab's *Pearl Rosary*, the community is not the distinct independent *ulus* of the seventeenth century. The *Pearl Rosary* does not culminate in the reality of the Tümed *ulus*, as does the *Jewel Translucent Sutra*. It does not speak of the exclusive legal rights of the Aokhan and Abaga that need to be respected by the Manchu state. Rather, it proudly affirms the linear history of all the Mongols as a coherent community through time and space, which on account of the Dharma can even trace its origins back to the primordial community of humans in India.

Of course, in order for this narrative of the eternal Mongol *ulus* to make sense the pre-Qing reality of distinct independent *ulus* had to be forgotten. The sociopolitical fragmentation instigated by the Dayan Khanid princes, which defined early Manchu–Mongol relations, needed to be suppressed. Even though these realities had contributed positively to the Qing formation, their perpetuation was not beneficial to the unification of the Qing state. Nor were their relations with Tibetan lamas of various lineages outside of Qing control. As a result, much as the discourse of ornamentalism had fostered the creation of an entitled Mongol nobility descended from Chinggis Khan, the uniform and orthodox narratives of the Dharma also helped to forge a pan-*ulus* Mongol identity. This identity was defined less in terms of the localized *ulus* and its social and political networks and was based more upon the narrative of a unified Mongol community —a community that, moreover, was inherently Gelukpa Buddhist, and thus a part of the penultimate Dharma realm, the Manchu Qing.

What had therefore occurred in the process of the Manchus' promotion of a distinctive Buddhist discourse was that being Mongol and being Buddhist were dissociated from any earlier identifications with local communities and their religiopolitical boundaries. Rather, being Mongol and being Buddhist became inherently incorporated in a Buddhist Qing identity. The three had become intertwined: being Mongol and being Buddhist also entailed being Qing.

It was this linkage, along with ornamentalism and the Qing's dismantling of local systems of political authority, that played a crucial role in weakening the Mongols' earlier boundaries of identification. The Dharma therefore became a powerful discourse of deterritorialization and reterritorialization. Mongol Buddhist identity became not necessarily a mark of distinction, as was the case with Altan Khan and the Tümed Ulus, but actually its inverse, one of integration.

And, as previously noted, a central element that fostered this shift was the dissociation of Chinggis Khan from the Mongol Buddhist community. Rather than being considered the founder of the Mongol Buddhist "nation," as is found in all pre-Qing sources, Chinggis Khan was seen as a Buddhist ruler within the universal continuum. Chinggis Khan was thus only one of many rulers within the mythic cycles of Buddhist world history—a "denationalized" history that, of course, reached its summit with the Manchu khans, of whose Buddhist state the Mongols were one integral part.

As a result of this narrative shift, it is possible to argue that the creation of the Qing and its absorption of the Mongols worked in a reverse manner to the collapse of the Holy Roman Empire. The emperor's legitimacy to rule over a multiethnic Christian world rested on links to Constantine and the ideal of universal Christian rule. However, with the empire's collapse, different groups appropriated the same discourse while producing distinct narratives to affirm the reality of their new religiopolitical communities. Thus, the French traced their descent as a collectivity from the baptism of Clovis at Reims by Saint Regimus in 496. In the case of the Qing, this process occurred in the opposite direction. In the pre-Qing period the different *ulus,* were they Chakhar, Tümed, or Ordos, all traced their religious and genealogical origins to Chinggis Khan and his conversion in the early thirteenth century. Within the discourse of the Buddhist Qing, however, Chinggis Khan was no longer the founder of the Mongol Buddhist community; rather, he became just one transnational avatar of a Buddhist ideal within a Buddhist cosmological continuum.

The origin of this transformation is unclear, but it undoubtedly draws on the Tibetan historical tradition wherein the three Buddhist groups—Indians, Tibetans and Mongols—are presented consecutively but not actually genealogically. This can be seen in Pakpa Lama's *What Is to Be Known (Shes bya rab gsal)*, written in 1275 for Zhenjin, Khubilai Khan's heir to the throne.[16] This format also appeared among the Mongols in the pre-Qing period, as is seen in Shireetü Güüshi's early-seventeenth-century compilation, also titled the *What Is to Be Known (Ciqula kerelegci)*.[17] Yet, just like its predecessor, it also does not make explicit the genealogical links that were to become standard in Qing-period works. Thus, although this universalizing Buddhist discourse may seem to be inherent to the "Buddhist explanation" and the Weberian ideal-type of Buddhist rule, it is important to recognize that this transformation in the origins of Mongol Buddhist history was historically tied to the discourse of the Buddhist Qing, and to the creation of new communal boundaries that were not related to the independent *ulus*, but the Mongol *ulus* within the Manchu-Buddhist empire.

Being Buddhist, History and Qing Orthodoxy

Since being Buddhist was becoming a fundamental element of Qing imperial discourse, one would imagine that the second conversion would be one of the most highlighted and expanded aspects of Mongol history, yet this was not the case. Instead, paradoxically, the Buddhist conversion of the Mongols, in particular of the Mongol ruler who initiated it—namely Altan Khan—is minimized in Qing-period sources. One possible reason for this may have been to draw attention away from the realities of the pre-Qing period, such as independence and the theory of *ulus/törö*, and instead highlight the universal and eternal links that the Mongols had maintained with the Dharma. Buddhism was thus tied, less to the specific individual who initiated the "second conversion" and his independent Tümed *ulus*, and more to the eternalized categories of Buddhist rule. While this is certainly possible, a more important factor in the transformation of Mongol Buddhist history was the reality of Qing orthodoxy. In particular, the elevation of the Dalai Lama's Gelukpa lineage as the sole legitimate tradition of the Buddhist Qing was instrumental in fostering this historiographical transformation. Much in the same way as the Qing's successful incorporation of the Mongols entailed changing the theory of *ulus* and *törö* and its discourses of political legitimacy, so it also entailed a reconceptualization of Mongol notions of "being Buddhist."

Nowadays it is generally taken for granted that the Mongols are followers of Gelukpa Buddhism, but Mongol, Tibetan and Chinese sources antedating the Qing demonstrate that it is not that simple. All Qing-period works assert that, ever since Altan Khan's meeting with the Third Dalai Lama in 1578, the Mongols have been loyal followers of the Gelukpa tradition; all other traditions are entirely excluded. But pre-Qing sources make it clear that Altan Khan's conversion, or incorporation of Buddhist legitimacy into the emperorship, did not proceed as the Qing chronicles have led us to believe.

Of course, what it meant to "be Buddhist" for the Mongols of the sixteenth century is perhaps impossible to fully unravel. From contemporary Chinese sources we do know that the Mongols were sincere in their beliefs.[18] Unfortunately, the same sources do not tell us much about the details of these beliefs and practices. From Mongolian sources, however, we can infer that the power and ability of Tibetan lamas to heal both the microcosm of the body and the macrocosm of the world through ritual cosmologies played an important role in the early Buddhist conversion of the Mongols. Yet again, how Mongols of different social levels actually understood or partook of these new ideas and practices is rather unclear. Nevertheless, while keeping this in mind we can compare how the Mongols wrote about the Dharma in the pre-Qing and Qing periods.

Contrary to Qing-period representations of Mongol Gelukpa orthodoxy, the *Jewel Translucent Sutra* depicts Buddhist identity and practices at the court of Altan Khan as having malleable boundaries. Indeed, this source does not even mention the iconic phrase "Yellow Religion" (*sira sasin*), that is, the Gelukpa, as a distinct entity. Later Qing sources, on the other hand, mention only the Yellow Religion as the religion adopted by the Mongols. On the other hand, the *Jewel Translucent Sutra*'s only reference to the Gelukpa is in an account of a gathering of "Yellow and Red Hats" presided over, not by a Gelukpa hierarch, but by the abbot of the Kagyü Taglung tradition:

> Afterwards in the incarnated month of the White Rabbit Year [1591] at Bull
> River,
> The Supreme Taglung Chöje and the Yellow and Red Hat Saṃghas
> gathered.
> They were extensively presented with an infinite merit *pāramitā*,
> Thus they all made great and immense merit and prayers.[19]

In his 1776 book on the Mongols, the explorer P. S. Pallas also noted that at the court of Altan Khan there were monks with "yellow and red hats"—namely, Gelukpa and Kagyü.[20] Altan Khan, however, not only had relations with numerous Tibetan lineages but also with the Chinese White Lotus. Indeed, as confirmed in the *Jewel Translucent Sutra* and contemporary Chinese sources, there was in fact a diversity of religious practitioners and practices at the court of Altan Khan.[21] This is not found in Qing-period sources.

Pre-Qing and Qing era sources also differ in describing the role of Altan Khan in the conversion process. In the standard Qing narrative, Altan is presented as a passive agent acting solely within the dictates of the idealized and "well-established" form of Buddhist rule. But the *Jewel Translucent Sutra* makes it clear that he was not only engaged in this process, but was also dictating the parameters. He exercised his right as the most powerful ruler on the Mongolian plateau in order to foster multiple Buddhist relationships in the ritualization of Buddhist emperorship.[22]

For example, Altan Khan's relationship with the Tibetan Taglung order developed in tandem with those of the Gelukpa. The initial contact between Altan and the Taglung was made in 1576. At that time "Altan Khan and the Stag-lung official in charge of offerings, Grags-'od-pa, came together, and Altan Khan made 'inconceivable' offerings of gold, silver, silk and cotton cloth, tea, horses, mules and camels. These men were met by Rje-dpon Kun-dga' dpal-bzang-pa and listened to his Buddhist teachings."[23] The Taglung abbot did not attend these meetings because he was ill, but in 1578 he left central Tibet and in the fourth month met Altan Khan's envoys at the headwaters of the Yangzi. He was then brought to Altan Khan's encampment at Kökenuur, where he performed miracles, taught the Dharma and received gifts. This meeting was held in the fourth month of 1578, meaning that Altan Khan actually met the Taglung abbot prior to his meeting with Sönam Gyatso in the fifth month. And then, even after having met with the Dalai Lama, Altan Khan continued to meet with the Taglung. In 1579 Altan bestowed on the Taglung abbot the title "Tathāgata," the same title that the Yongle Emperor had bestowed on the sixth Black Hat Karmapa. He also gave him a silver seal, along with official documents, hats and clothing, as well as a large amount of silver.[24]

The Mongols' simultaneous relations with the Taglung and Gelukpa continued after the death of the Dalai Lama. Namudai Sechen Khan invited a Taglung hierarch to come to Kökenuur,[25] where, as seen in the passage cited above, he presided over an ecumenical prayer session convened during the politically charged New Year's celebrations.[26] Such an ecumenical gathering of Tibetan lineages is not found in any of the later Qing-period Gelukpa or Mongol histories, much less the idea that a group of Gelukpa monks would be led by the leader of a different lineage. Yet this was the reality at the court of Altan Khan.

At first glance the inclusion of these different Buddhist groups within the conversion narrative might be perceived as the standard conversion foil whereby they are included only to be eventually rejected, thus confirming the validity and correctness of the Mongols' acceptance of Gelukpa Buddhism. In the *Jewel Translucent Sutra,* however, this does not appear to be the case, as evidenced by the continuing presence and joint ritual celebration by a diversity of traditions after the death of the Dalai Lama.

Unfortunately, these facts have largely gone unnoticed—largely because the Qing narrative concealed this reality. During the Qing, being Buddhist came to be identified solely with the Gelukpa. The religious "pluralism" of the pre-Qing period therefore had to be forgotten—and it was.[27] Yet how did it happen? To explain this fact we need to begin with the 1652 meeting between the Shun-zhi emperor and the Fifth Dalai Lama.

It was at this meeting that Qing rule not only became tied to the Dharma but also the court specifically aligned itself with only one tradition. Rather than continuing the "pluralistic" policies of Altan Khan as Nurhaci and Hong Taiji had done, at this time the new state was formed to manifest the ideal model: one lama, one ruler.[28] It is therefore not surprising that Qing-period Mongol sources do not dwell on Altan Khan's affiliation with various Buddhist schools or his alliances with the Ming court—much less on other inconvenient facts, such as Nurhaci and Hong Taiji's alliance with Ligdan Khan's Sakya lamas, that potentially challenged the trajectory of the Qing's founding and its legitimate rule through its affiliation with the Gelukpa order.

The Manchus' decision to ally themselves with the Gelukpa and not the Sakya was clearly tied to the rising political fortunes of the Great Fifth Dalai Lama.[29] As a result of his increasing power and influence, especially his intimate relations with Mongols, Khalkhas and Oirads still outside Manchu control, the Dalai Lama was of pivotal importance to the Qing court. The Shunzhi emperor's invitation for the Great Fifth to visit Beijing was thus the beginning of a process to both engage and subvert this reality. And while this invitation was to have numerous consequences for the subsequent history of Inner Asia,[30] one of its impacts was on what it meant to be Mongol and Buddhist.

The Dalai Lama and the Manchu Court

The emperor's meeting with the Dalai Lama in many ways codified the ideal of "Buddhist rule," the "Lamaist-Caesaropapist" relationship that was to define the Buddhist Qing, since it confirmed the essential component of this vision: that indeed there was only one "priest" and one "patron." Both the Manchu court and the Dalai Lama were well aware of the potential dangers of religiopolitical fragmentation resulting from multiple Buddhist schools being allied with local rulers. They were well aware of the civil wars in Tibet, where Mongols like Tsogtu Taiji aligned themselves with the Kagyü. They also knew that within the *ulus/törö* model new Buddhist states could be forged, as was the case with the Khalkhas and Oirads. The Khalkhas even went so far as to create their own "priest" in contradistinction to the Dalai Lama, the Jebdzundamba Khutugtu. The Qing engagement with the Gelukpa was thus aimed not only at bringing the Great Fifth into the Manchu orbit, but also at fostering a unifying religious discourse among the fractious Mongols. And the first evidence we have of this process of unification is from the 1652 meeting itself, in which the Dalai Lama was recognized as the supreme teacher of the Dharma during his audience with the Shunzhi emperor.

It is important to keep in mind that before this 1652 meeting the Dalai Lama's power had been far from secure.[31] Indeed, the Dalai Lama was well aware of the fickle nature of political alliances and the consequences they might have had within the idealized model of Buddhist rule. Thus this meeting created the perfect forum wherein to confirm his own authority.[32]

The Dalai Lama's authority was affirmed not only in their ritualized meeting but also, more important, in the Great Fifth's purging of the Mongol Buddhist missionary Neichi Toin, the most prominent local Buddhist teacher among the Inner Mongols. He had not only been active among the Dayan Khanid princes of Ordos, but more recently had also been converting the "shamanist" Mongol groups of the east.[33] In many ways, one would imagine these actions would have been considered positive developments for both the Buddhist Qing and the Gelukpa hierarchy, as it promoted their influence in these areas; however, that was not the case.

Neichi Toin was instead deemed "unorthodox." He wore blue-and-green-colored robes. He took money given to the monasteries and returned it to the poor. Most radically, he was bestowing upon the uninitiated the Yamāntaka tantric ritual cycle empowerment, and in addition proclaiming himself to be the reincarnation of Tsongkhapa.[34] As the Fifth Dalai makes clear in his autobiography, these actions clearly deviated from Gelukpa orthodoxy. However, more significant is the fact that they also had the potential to undermine the influence of both the Lhasa-based Gelukpa order and the Buddhist Qing among the ever-increasing Mongol followers of Neichi Toin. Thus, much as the Khalkhas, who had both drawn on the theory of *ulus* and *töro* and created their own Buddhist hierarch, these Mongol *ulus* could clearly do the same, rejecting both the Qing state and the Gelukpa order.

While Buddhist rule was a powerful element in imperial consolidation, it could also be easily appropriated by competing communities, as had occurred during the Mongol and Tibetan civil wars and was to become the case with the Manchu state and the Zunghars. Indeed, as many other scholars have noted, all centralizing states have reacted against local religious specialists because they derive their "'charisma independently of the imperially dominated hierarchy' and [are thus] 'potentially a subversive weapon in the hands of ambitious princes of the blood.'"[35]

The activities of Neichi Toin among the "shamanist" Mongols bordering the Manchu homeland was therefore volatile and needed to be dealt with. Moreover, the manner in which they were defused also revealed the beginnings of the Qing–Gelukpa discourse of orthodoxy that would once again reunite the disparate Mongol Buddhists within the Manchu state. In particular, it initiated the process wherein what it meant to be a "Mongol Buddhist" was defined by the Tibeto-Manchu religiopolitical authorities.

This transformation is well captured in the events surrounding Neichi Toin, which began when a formal complaint about his activities was brought before the imperial authorities. According to the 1739 *Biography of Neichi Toin,* upon hearing these accusations the Shunzhi emperor declared, "Because I am the Emperor of the laws of the world, I do not know the laws of the Dharma. After the Dalai Lama arrives, the Dalai Lama will know what to do."[36] And upon arriving the Great Fifth did state that, although Neichi Toin did not in fact fully understand the Dharma, his actions were not a threat to the established order— that is, Qing-Gelukpa orthodoxy—but he did need to be purged nonetheless. In his autobiography the Fifth Dalai Lama writes, "In my opinion, Neichi Toin truly wants to spread Tsongkhapa's teaching and he has a pure heart, but he must know the limits. He does not have the qualifications of a high lama's guidance; thus from this perspective one can say that what the complainant has charged is fundamentally correct. Although Neichi Toin is not able to change the nature of the Dharma, we cannot endure his influence and power."[37]

The later Mongolian biography of Neichi Toin, in accord with the logic of the Buddhist Qing, places the blame on the duplicity of Neichi Toin's Mongol accusers, not on the Fifth Dalai Lama or the Shunzhi emperor.

> Then after the Fifth Dalai Lama arrived, by [imperial] decree all the Dalai Lama's affairs and Sakya Dharma Lord's accusation were handled by Gabala Gong. However, Gabala Gong and Sakya Dharma Lord were good [friends] from before and also took great bribes, [thus] because the words were handled carelessly for the Dalai Lama's envoy, being distorted and mistranslated, the monk [Neichi Toin] was punished. It was decided that the thirty monks, who had previously met the Holy One [Neichi Toin] and at that time taken vows, along with thirty other younger disciples, were ordered to live in Hohhot. Also the remaining sixty saṃgha [members] were ordered to live in the Bai Chi Mañjuśrī Monastery.[38]

In purging Neichi Toin the Dalai Lama and Shunzhi emperor accomplished three goals: Neichi Toin's activities and his potential role in forging new religiopolitical communities were dismantled; the power of the Dalai Lama as the ultimate arbiter of Buddhist theory was confirmed in an audience with the Manchu emperor; and, most important, as a result of this meeting the Manchu state became intimately involved in defining and regulating the realities of Mongolian Buddhism. Altan Khan's "Buddhism with Mongolian characteristics" of the late sixteenth and early seventeenth centuries, as evidenced in the Tümeds' identification of one of their own descendants as the Fourth Dalai Lama and then questioning whether he should even be allowed to return to Tibet, was no longer tenable. Instead, this earlier "Mongolian Buddhism" was replaced by the narratives, rituals and authority of the Buddhist Qing and its new vision of the Dharma.

Central to this vision was the promotion of Gelukpa orthodoxy. Thus not only do post-Qing Mongolian histories of the seventeenth century focus exclusively on the Gelukpa, but in accord with the Neichi Toin episode they also greatly amplify the power of the Dalai Lama. Unlike the *Jewel Translucent Sutra,* in which the Dalai Lama is not only just one of various Buddhist leaders but is also described as only the holder of religious authority at Ganden Monastery,[39] all the Qing period sources highlight the unique glory of the Dalai Lama.

The Dalai Lama's transformation is most evident in the extensive incorporation in the Mongols' own conversion narrative of the Third Dalai Lama's magical abilities. These episodes can be found already in Lubsangdanzin's *Golden Summary* of the 1650s[40] and are drawn mainly from the Great Fifth's own hagiographical accounts of his two previous incarnations,[41] which perhaps not coincidentally were written enroute to meet with the Manchu emperor. Clearly the reason why these episodes are included in the narrative is, as with the Great Fifth's own hagiographies, to highlight the power of the Dalai Lama, and by extension the Gelukpa. Moreover, as found in Mongolian sources, both of these in turn also confirm the orthodox narrative of the Buddhist Qing.

This presentation of the wondrous power of the Dalai Lama is elaborated most extensively in Saghang Sechen's *Precious Summary.* The crucial ninth chapter that describes Altan Khan's conversion focuses almost exclusively on the activities and magical abilities of the Dalai Lama. Thus on the way to the meeting with Altan Khan the Dalai Lama makes a river run backwards by means of a *mudrā.* In a barren wasteland he makes a spring appear, and he himself appears as an emanation of the Four-armed Avalokiteśvara. Even the Dalai Lama's horse leaves hoofprints inscribed with *Om Maṇi Padme Hum.* Most important, as is also described in Lubsangdanzin's *Golden Summary,* Saghang Sechen tells of Begtse and the Dalai Lama's conversion of Mongolian sacred deities to protectors of the Dharma. Moreover, when Altan Khan and the Dalai Lama meet, Altan Khan relates that previously, when he had placed his gout-ridden feet in the chest cavity of a horse, a white man had appeared, saying this was not good. This man was the Dalai Lama. Khung Taiji then relates that when he had attempted to eat horseflesh, a man in a black robe had asked him why he would eat that. The Dalai Lama confirms that that was he as well.

The *Precious Summary* then goes on to relate in extenso the Dalai Lama's activities after his meeting with Altan Khan, all of which highlight the Dalai Lama's great power. He gives a prophecy of Hāyagriva, the Jang King of the Naxi who after desecrating a Dalai Lama statue realizes his mistake, makes a new one and then lives happily ever after, and so on. These stories are further reinforced by the events surrounding the Dalai Lama's trip to Mongolia after the death of Altan Khan. On his way he converts the Chinese of Gansu by performing an act of spirit writing. Upon arriving in Hohhot, he tells the Mongols that their "Shamano-Buddhist" funeral rites for Altan Khan are incorrect and that he must be exhumed and cremated. The Dalai Lama also performed a powerful exorcism:

> Altan Khan himself had, according to pagan custom, inherited one of his father's wives at the former's death, and had had a son by her. When the boy died, the mother arranged for the children of a hundred families and the foals of a hundred camels to be slaughtered to provide him with a death escort on his last journey. Though this must have been a familiar custom, uproar broke out amongst the families of the victims, and a *taiji,* or a member of the imperial family, stopped the whole affair by threatening to get himself killed to go and plague the dead child. Even after this rebuff the queen did not abandon her evil ways, and at her death her body became a *vetala,* or "living corpse," and had to be exorcised by the Dalai Lama, who was in Tumet at the time (1585). The superior rituals of which he was master got the better of the *vetala,* which turned into a lizard and was consumed by holy fire.[42]

This ritual and the other miraculous episodes therefore all confirm the religious power of the Dalai Lama. Yet the fact that none of these lengthy episodes are found in earlier sources shows that they are not simply part of the standard conversion narrative, whereby the power of the Dalai Lama confirms that the Mongols made the right choice. Rather, it is an affirmation of the larger narrative of Gelukpa orthodoxy that defines the Buddhist Qing.

The narrative focus on the power of the Dalai Lama, however, not only justifies the Qing's Gelukpa orthodoxy, but also diminishes the power of Altan Khan and reverses the actual dynamics of the relationship that he had with the Gelukpa.[43] Altan Khan is therefore not aligned with numerous schools, nor is he shaping and defining the characteristics of his rule. Instead, he wants solely to bolster his genealogically inferior position through the power and prestige of the Dalai Lama. The notion of a powerful independent Tümed Ulus whose ruler produced a different form of the Almsmaster-Offering-site relationship was counter to the Qing narrative and is not found in any of the Qing-period Mongolian histories. On the contrary, these works promote the vision of the universal "Lamaist-Caesaropapist" model of Buddhist rule and its manifestation within the Manchu Qing. And what is most important in this regard is that the Qing state truly does re-create and manifest a model of Buddhist rule that allegedly harks back to the glorious days of the Yuan.

Using the Yuan as a model, of course, raises the problem of the "rightful ruler." If Manchu rule was supposed to be premised upon the precedent of "Mongol Buddhist rule," one may wonder why were the Mongols in fact not ruling? Be it Altan Khan, Abatai Khan, or Ligdan Khan, they all promoted the idea of a Buddhist restoration. In the sources relevant to each of these rulers, all are praised in terms of reviving the Buddhist rule of the Yuan period (itself, of course, a reimagining). Nevertheless, for the Manchus one solution was to universalize Buddhist history. Another was to situate Mongol history within the larger framework of chaos—from the Mongol-Oirad war to the chaos of Ligdan Khan's reign. Mongol history was thus not one of revitalization, but of decay. Moreover, Buddhist rule by its very own logic mandates that a ruler provide peace and stability for his subjects, a requirement the Mongol rulers had clearly failed to fulfill. Furthermore, the Qing representation of Ligdan Khan as a good Buddhist who somehow went astray (through his bad karma, drinking evil-inducing poisoned wine, ending five hundred years of the Dharma, etc.),[44] amply set the stage for the Manchus to claim to be the legitimate rulers over the Buddhist ecumene.

Mongol history thus came to be written within the parameters of the Qing and its logic of Buddhist rule. One consequence of this process was that Mongol Buddhist identity was dislodged from previous religious, political and communal identities. As reflected in the changes found in pre- to post-Qing Mongolian histories, being Mongol and Buddhist had become conflated with being part of the Buddhist Qing. Nevertheless, while these later histories reflect the discourse of the Buddhist Qing and in fact legitimate Manchu rule, they also reveal a certain ambiguity about the actual submission of the Mongols to Manchu power. Although all the narratives do incorporate this framework and culminate in the recognition of Qing authority over the Mongols, the actual loss of independence still required explanation. Why had the powerful Mongols, the heirs of Chinggis Khan, the rulers of independent *ulus,* the ones who had reestablished Khubilai Khan's system of Buddhist rule, actually been conquered?

Buddhism and History in the Eighteenth Century

There were clearly numerous answers to the question of why the Mongols submitted to the Manchus. Political, economic and social historians can readily point to the civil war, military weakness, economic collapse, Manchu bribes and so on; however, in all the seventeenth-century Mongolian histories the most powerful explanatory model advanced is the Dharma. Buddhist history provided a world historical framework within which to explain the Qing. Mongol history was thus subsumed by the universalist continuum of Buddhist rule. In this way, not only was the Buddhist Qing narrative legitimated, but also the actual details of the incorporation of the Mongols into the Qing ignored the negative aspect of the actual loss of Mongol independence. As a result, at the same time as the appropriation of an ideal Buddhist rule necessarily distorted the past relationships between Mongol rulers and Tibetan hierarchs and Mongol history, it also made sense of the Mongol submission and justified Manchu rule.

However, this transformation of what "being Buddhist" meant was not accepted lightly. The very need to include these extensive transformative elements thus far described confirms this fact. The incorporation of the India-Tibet-Mongolia genealogy, the highlighting of the Dalai Lama's greatness, and the extensive elaboration on the Buddhist bona fides of the Manchu Qing were integral aspects in the formation of a new Mongol Buddhist identity that linked the Mongols to the Buddhist Qing. These elements were thus fundamental to the process of both creating and justifying the new religious and political community, the Buddhist Qing, since they dissociated Buddhism from the independent Mongol *ulus* thereby shifting the religious community of identification to themselves.

Nevertheless, as in the case of other conversion narratives, these earlier elements of justification eventually lost their relevance over time.[45] In particular, as the new community became simply taken for granted there no longer was any need to marshal these powerful transformative narratives. By the eighteenth century, when the Mongols readily identified themselves as part of, if not the vanguard of, the Buddhist Qing, these elements began to disappear. In these works, the extensive discussions on Buddhist rule are simply taken for granted and are absent. The Buddhist Qing had become the natural order.

Yet curiously, not only are those aspects less important, but the whole Buddhist conversion is minimized. For example, in Dharma Güüshi's lengthy 1739 work, the *Golden Wheel with a Thousand Spokes*, the entire conversion and actions of Altan Khan are compressed into a few lines.

[Altan Khan] took the Amdowas and the Yellow Uygurs into his power and collected tribute. He built Kökekhota on the southern side of Onggon Dabaan [Pass] and lived there assisting the fractured state. In order to continue the religion that [the Mongols] had been cut off from, he invited the incarnation of the Bodhisattva Avalokiteśvara, the All-knowing Sodnam Gyatsho the Third Dalai Lama, Tongkhor Yontan Jamsu, Mañjuśrī Khutugtu, and Chamdo Jedrung Khutugtu. [Thus] the Holy Tsongkhapa's religion was enlightening anew. He built the Yellow Roofed Monastery and had made out of silver a twelve-span-tall Jowo Sakyamuni statue and many others. He greatly established the saṃgha and aided the Dharma. The All-knowing Dalai Lama was presented with the title Vajradhara. The khan was bestowed with the title King of the Dharma, Great Brahma, Khan God.[46]

Dharma Güüshi's history confirms the naturalness of the Qing in two ways. First, being Buddhist is simply taken for granted and the conversion no longer needs to be reaffirmed. Second, Altan Khan is presented as helping the "fractured state." Thus, like Altan Khan, all Mongol nobles should also help the state, namely the Buddhist Qing.

Dharma's history, however, goes even further in naturalizing the Qing by making the Manchu rulers, not the Mongols, the prime actors in Mongol Buddhist history. He does this by identifying the monastery founded by Altan Khan, not as the Yeke Juu, but as the Yellow-Roofed Monastery. This later title had been given to the monastery by the Kangxi emperor. After defeating Galdan Khan and on his way back to the capital, the emperor had stayed overnight in the monastery, and thereupon had ordered that its roof receive the imperial yellow tiles.[47] Thus, in this early-eighteenth-century history, not only is the Qing accepted as natural but history is defined by the Qing and its Buddhist activities.

As the colophon of Gombojab's 1725 *Flow of Ganges* declares, "Let the imperial rule of the Qing Empire be firm and expand, Let spread to the minds of all those of various customs the religion of the Vanquishing Lion [i.e., Buddhism]."[48] In many ways this passage highlights the relation between the Qing and Buddhism as found in eighteenth-century Mongol sources—they have become synonymous. Indeed, the earlier vision of "ethnic" and "religious" multiplicity has in a sense been replaced with Buddhist orthodox imperialism. And in order to maintain this vision the conversion of Altan Khan, its relation to the independent *ulus* and its "plurality" are no longer relevant—a fact that is made evident in the 1757 *Light of Wisdom (Bilig-ün Jula).*[49]

This history of Buddhism ignores Altan Khan's conversion almost entirely. It begins with an outline of the history of Buddhism in India and Tibet until 1750, then describes the history of the Mongols and Chinggis Khan's adoption of Buddhism, and it ends with Ligdan Khan. The final section then highlights the key episodes in the Mongols' Buddhist history: Köten Khan's meeting with Sakya Pandita, Khubilai Khan and Pakpa, Ligdan Khan's Kanjur translation. Then, finally, as almost an afterthought, just before the text elaborates at length on the history of the Manchu emperors and their Buddhist activities, Altan Khan and his meeting with the Dalai Lama are described. "At the time of the Tümed's

Altan Qan, Dalai Lama Sodnamjamsu was invited, spreading the religion. . . ."[50] As this truncation reflects, the importance of Altan Khan and the conversion of the Mongols had become irrelevant to the concerns of the Mongols of the Buddhist Qing in the eighteenth century. Indeed, the most striking evidence for this fact is that even the whereabouts of Altan Khan's "tomb/stupa" that was famously prepared by the Third Dalai Lama and is lauded in all the histories was lost. Still today no one knows where Altan Khan is buried.[51]

From this overview it is clear that the narrative of the Buddhist Qing had by the eighteenth century displaced earlier conceptualizations. The idea of Mongol Buddhist identity being linked to a distinct independent *ulus,* so evident in the *Jewel Translucent Sutra,* had changed to its being related solely to the Qing state. Qing-period Mongol authors recognized themselves, and presumably all Mongols, as being situated firmly within the Qing narrative, and their identity as bound to the Manchu empire.

Reclaiming the Past

At the same time as an independent Mongol Buddhist identity was dispersed throughout the structures of the Manchu state, a new representation arose that did maintain boundaries of differentiation for the Mongol *ulus* within the multiethnic Qing. Although it is unclear whether or not this new appropriation of a primordial Mongol Buddhist identity arose in relation to the eighteenth-century imperially sanctioned Manchu ethnicity project, the remythologization produced a new narrative for Mongol identity that originated, not in relation to the Mongol community but to a lengthy history of pure Buddhism.[52]

The first example of this is found in the well-known *History of Buddhism in China (Rgya-nag chos-'byung),* written by Qing loyalist and Beijing resident Gombojab around 1740.[53] In this work the primordial nature of Mongol Buddhist history is reaffirmed through the use of Chinese historical materials. In this endeavor, Gombojab made a historiographical supposition that still resonates today in both nationalist discourse and academic inquiry: all the nomadic peoples north of the Great Wall are identified historically as Mongol; more important, since the Han dynasty they have been Buddhist.

The first evidence used to support this claim came from the *History of the Former Han (Hanshu),* which records that a Chinese general saw at the court of the Xiongnu khan a statue of a "gold man" that is interpreted as having been a Buddha statue.[54] This observation is followed by information culled from Tang dynasty sources, which record that an Indian monk, Prabhakaramitra, with ten companions, spread the Dharma in the north during the era of the Turk empires. The Turk ruler of Prabhakaramitra's day is identified in the Chinese sources as Tong Yehu Kehan, which enables Gombojab to argue that Yehu is a Chinese distortion of the Mongolian term *yeke,* "great," and that Kehan is "khan."[55] Using these suppositions, Gombojab brought plausibility to etymologies that showed the Turk empire as in fact being Mongol. He also used the same idea in his later work on Xuanzang's travels to India, based on Xuanzang's own *Xiyu ji,*[56] wherein he similarly argued that the nomadic inhabitants of Inner Asia whom Xuanzang met were actually Mongols.[57] In this way Gombojab, through historical and philological studies of Chinese sources,[58] was able to generate a mythology of Mongol Buddhist identity, which in turn was adopted in the *Crystal Rosary* by Rashipungsug, who went so far as to say that the Mongols had existed and had fought the Chinese since the Zhou dynasty.[59]

While this new narrative entailed prestige within the narrative of the multiethnic Buddhist Qing in that the Mongols could claim the longest Buddhist history, it did not challenge the current state of Mongol integration with the Qing.[60] By obscuring the past reality of independent Mongol Buddhist *ulus* and its implications for what could be in the present, this vision reaffirmed Mongol Buddhist identity through a new historical genealogy, one that did not challenge the multiethnic Buddhist Qing narrative.

A similar phenomenon is found in Mergen Gegen's *Golden Summary (Altan Tobciya)* of 1765, which uses material from the Tibetan historical tradition rather than from Chinese sources. In two works on which the author drew, the *Blue Annals (Deb ther Sngon po)* and the *Clear Mirror (Rgyal rabs Gsal ba'i Me long),* it is recorded that during the reign of Langdarma in the mid-ninth century, three monks fled Tibet with scriptures in order to preserve the Dharma from the king's persecution. While in neither of these sources do they flee to Mongolia, this idea is presented in Mergen Gegen's work.

> At the time when Tibet's [Lang]darma was destroying the religion, three monks, Sakyamuni Gelong with the clan name Mar, Buyandalai Gelong with the clan name Wi and Geigülügchi Gelong with the clan name Chang, fled from Tibet. When they came, [the Mongols'] Tamaji Khan became a disciple, and was named Shakya Sherab. Tamaji's twenty-first son, Khurcha Mergen, became khan and received initiations and teachings from those lamas. While he was still on the throne he became fully accomplished and attained magical powers. Finally, because he abandoned his body and flew into the sky, he became famous as an emanation of Padmasambhava. After having gone to and stayed in Mongolia, those three lamas went to a place called Sergüleng in Amdo.[61]

At the same time as these new historical narratives were being produced, ritual texts that mirrored this shift were also created, thus further shaping this new conceptualization. At the request of the Üjümüchin First Rank Prince, Sedendondub, the First Jangjia Khutugtu wrote one such text. The aim of the ritual was the protection and propitiation of the Chinggisid lineage through the power of the Buddhist deity Brahma, identified in the text as the White God holding the white conch and riding Brahma's steed, Ajinai.

> Namu Guru Buddha Bodhisattva. This a written summary of how to do offerings and purification to the White God, the male protector with the white conch, who protects the lineage of Chinggis, the earth's Brahma, fated here by God, together with the Earth Gods and Lords of the Ground. Yourself being complete, bless first the visible objects, the offerings and food offerings, then through the six *dhāraṇīs* and six *mudrās* the various necessary affairs.
>
> Samantabhadra, with a Dharma body of spontaneously complete great joy, Sakyamuni, an incarnation of Vajrasattva with a complete joyous body, the Dhāraṇī-holder Padmasambhava, Tsongkhapa with the power of victory, and the auspicious assemblies of the three Buddha lineages, show compassion!
>
> The Supreme White God Conch Protector, who propagates the root lineage of the God's great powerful Chinggis [Khan originating] from the palace with the true nature of great joy, deign to come together with the Earth Gods and Lords of the Ground!
>
> [The Supreme White God who] is in the sky and holds the power of the incarnated *ridis* rides on the wise horse Ajinai, which moves like the clouds. He is the Great Khan of the white-mountain-like Hostile God. In his left hand he holds a spear to crush the lives of the enemies and in his right hand he holds a sword to kill the evil ones. He wears a purifying scarf and is decorated with ornaments, and he is united with the Nāgas and Ground Lords and all the others and rules in a state of rejoicing.[62]

The text next describes at length the attributes of the White God and then, in accordance with Buddhist ritual texts, concludes with requests for the protection of the Mongol nobility, their long life, increased wealth and influence and so on. Nevertheless, what is important to note is that the power of the Mongol *ulus* as represented by the Mongol nobility does not reside in the ritualization of Chinggis Khan as the protector and propitiator of the Mongol community, as had been the case in the earlier cult of Chinggis Khan. Rather, within the Buddhist Qing, the Chinggisid lineage and in turn the Mongol *ulus* are formed and protected through Buddhist rituals prepared by lamas affiliated with the Qing court.

A similar phenomenon is also found in a large percentage of the extant ritual texts for the performance of the cult of Chinggis Khan, in which he is incorporated into the Buddhist pantheon. What is interesting to note in these works is that, as time goes on, and the Mongols identify more with the Buddhist Qing in contradistinction to the independent Mongols, Chinggis Khan's status decreases as his Buddhicization increases. In early works, such as the *White History,* Chinggis Khan is identified as an incarnation of Vajrapāṇi, placing him and the Mongols in relation to Mañjuśrī and China, and Avalokiteśvara and Tibet. Although this idea was supported by the Great Fifth and weaves its way through various histories of the Qing period, in Rashipungsug's seminal *Crystal Rosary* he is identified as the king of the Nāgas, a marked demotion in the Buddhist pantheon. Moreover, this demotion also confirms the reality that, by the end of the eighteenth century, Mongolia, Tibet and China were no longer independent entities, much less equal. Instead all were under the control of the incarnation of Mañjuśrī, the Qianlong emperor.

Yet, more important, in the extant corpus of Qing-period texts involving the worship of Chinggis Khan, there is a radical dissociation from the exclusive ritualization of the Mongol *ulus* as envisioned in the earlier texts described in Chapter 2. Instead, Chinggis Khan is always situated within a Buddhist framework—a framework wherein Chinggis Khan, previously the one who had ritualized the Mongol community and its ruling elite through the grace of God, is superseded by the Buddhist pantheon and the Buddhist saṃgha. The two examples that follow clearly illustrate this transformation. The first is a ritual performed toward the standard of Chinggis Khan.

> Incense offering to the Flag of the Holy Lord.
> Praying, I worship at the indestructible vajra feet of the Superior Saint of the pure jewel [the Buddha], by whose favour we receive great happiness and who make us certain to acquire in one moment (great riches).
> Om maṇi hum! (three times)
> I worship the many lamas, I worship the Buddha, I worship the Dharma, I worship the Saṃgha.
> Making an offering I worship You, Holy Golden Flag . . .[63]

The second example is from a *julag* ceremony text:

> In the midst of the mass of a very beautifully blazing fire, the smoke of the burning odoriferous *arca* (juniperus), white and green sandalwood, and various incense substances, billows like a massive cloud: through it we worship the lamas with a purificatory sacrifice. The bodhisattvas and the

śravakas, we worship with a purificatory sacrifice. The pratyekabuddhas and the heroes, we worship with a purificatory sacrifice. The assembly of the rakinis, we worship with a purificatory sacrifice. The protectors of the religion, we worship with a purificatory sacrifice. Esrua [Brahma] and Qormusta [Indra], we worship with a purificatory sacrifice. The Lord Chinggis Khan, we worship with a purificatory sacrifice.[64]

From both of these texts it is clear that Chinggis Khan is dissociated from the exclusivity of the Mongols and has become, instead, merely one aspect in the larger story of Mongol Buddhist mythology. His role as founder of the Mongol *ulus* is marginalized, and his power now resides solely in his incorporation into the Buddhist pantheon.

This appropriation of a Buddhist discourse and its superscription of Chinggis Khan in relation to the Mongol *ulus* is clearly reflected in the ritual text "Offerings to the Holy Lord" (*Ejen boyda-yin serjim*), written by the Ordos reincarnation Lhundub Bandita at the instigation of Mergen Gegen. In this work Chinggis Khan's rise to power was not a result of God's blessing, but solely attributed to the lamas: "'By order of the gracious lamas, [You] became famous by the name Holy Lord Chinggis.'"[65] In these three works, and in the large corpus of other Chinggis Khan ritual texts, it is evident that within the new Buddhist genealogical mythology the ritualization of Chinggis Khan had been transformed. It must therefore be recognized that, instead of describing an original "shamanist" ritual "contaminated" by Buddhist elements, all these works existed in the context of the larger narrative of Buddhism utilized by the Mongols during the Qing; and as it operated within the larger structure of the Buddhist Qing, it simultaneously produced a narrative of differentiation vis-à-vis the Manchu Buddhist Qing by fostering a new primordial narrative of Mongol Buddhist genealogy. Thus, as Mongol identity was dissociated from the independent Mongol *ulus,* a new narrative and ritual structure of the Mongols within the Buddhist Qing was produced.

Sacred Space, Local Power and the Qing State

An essential question, of course, is how these radical changes in Mongol conceptualizations and boundaries of identification were actually generated or maintained. As seen in the preceding chapters, the Manchu project was one of engagement and transformation. And in this dynamic one important feature was the Gelukpa establishment itself, since "what a clergy with some education and status did in most medieval and early modern societies was to mediate identity between rulers and ruled."[66] As is seen in the transformation in the cult of Chinggis Khan, sacred power was ultimately subordinated to the authority of the lamas. Thus, through their relationship with the imperial court, the Gelukpa became an integral part of the Qing ideological and bureaucratic framework of control.

Many scholars have already outlined the incorporation of the Gelukpa into the Qing bureaucracy, most notably the handling of Buddhist affairs through the Bureau of Colonial Affairs, the political appointment of reincarnations, and the large-scale building of monasteries and temples. Nevertheless, underlying the analysis of these phenomena is the idea that the Mongols readily accepted this Qing political superstructure because it accorded with their own understanding of Buddhist rule. Yet, as we have seen, the reality of the Qing state was not simply a continuation of earlier models; rather, it was itself a religiopolitical construct of the Qing. As a result, an important question is how this historical retelling and its attendant reconceptualizations were created in the process of both "Buddhicization" and "Qingification."

Qing sources and modern studies represent the institutionalization of Tibeto-Manchu hegemony over the Mongols through Tibetan Buddhism as a natural progression of Buddhist rule. In particular, the full-scale incorporation of Gelukpa Buddhism into the religious, social and cultural lives of the Mongols is seen as a natural development from the 1578 meeting of Altan Khan and the Dalai Lama. As a result, while the Manchu "use" of Gelukpa Buddhism is seen as a political issue, its cultural and religious impact is often ignored.

In a way it is somehow readily accepted that the Mongols should be Gelukpa Buddhists. Thus, it is often noted without comment that the Mongols during the Qing used Tibetan as a liturgical language, on the analogy of the Catholic use of Latin, but without any further inquiry into the massive dislocations inherent in this dramatic development. Instead, the Qing narrative of Buddhist rule and its modern scholarly refraction readily assumes that the Mongols ought not only to have accepted the Qing state but also ought to be Lhasa-based Tibetan-style Gelukpa Buddhists. I have argued that the first was not the case, and hinted that the second was not either. Given this radical rupture between the period of independence and that of Manchu rule, the second part of this equation, the cultural impact of the process of becoming Gelukpa Buddhist must also be reevaluated.

In doing so, it is vital to accept the fact that Manchu rule was not only premised on the Mongol acceptance of the Buddhist Qing but that this project was also a stunning success. The Qing-period Mongolian histories outlined so far are evidence of this process, as is the incorporation of the Mongol elites into the Qing bureaucratic system through the discourse of ornamentalism. Thus while these discourses were certainly intertwined, we need to explore how the court's political support of the Lhasa-based Gelukpa justified the Qing ideologically,

since it was this development—the institutionalization of Gelukpa orthodoxy—
that mandated the Mongols to become Lhasa-oriented Qing Buddhists. As a
result, the incorporation of the Mongols into the Buddhist Qing entailed the
thorough transformation of their culture to a Tibetan-style Gelukpa one and the
suppression of locally produced Buddhisms, which potentially created competing centers of authority.

The strategies employed to achieve this goal differed; however, one important element in this process was the appropriation by the Tibeto-Manchu bureaucratic apparatus of the mediation of the sacred, especially the spatial
embodiment of the Buddhist Qing.[67] Thus the court and its lamas were intimately
involved in transforming and redefining the Mongols' sacred space and its attendant ritualizations of identity.[68] Mongol histories of the Qing period therefore
highlight the power of Tibetan lamas, who are able to convert the local hostile
Mongol deities into protectors of the Dharma.[69] Of course, such conversions and
mandalizations of sacred space are also found in pre-Qing sources; however, during the Qing by definition this process became part of the imperial process.

The sacred realm was thus solely mediated through the Tibeto-Manchu bureaucracy. Not only was the Mongol landscape reinscribed, but simultaneously
the Buddhist Qing was spatially embodied among the Mongols. And it was
through this process that Mongol identification with local cults and communal
networks were shattered and taken over by the ritualization of the Buddhist
Qing. This mandalization of the Mongol world produced ritual and social networks based on new orders of space and time linked to Beijing and Lhasa.

Through the replacement of these earlier practices with ones bound to the
imperial and Buddhist ritual calendars and sacred sites, the Mongols were ritualized as members of the Buddhist Qing.[70] The most striking example that fused
both of these together was the Mongols' religious fervor surrounding Wutai
Shan in Shanxi, the mountain revered for its connection with Mañjuśrī, who
was none other than the Manchu ruler. In the end, the Mongols' desire to be
buried at the mountain reached such epic proportions that in the nineteenth
century the Qing court eventually forbade all Mongols other than those resident
at Wutai Shan to be buried on the mountain.[71]

Thus, ironically, even though the Manchu ruler Hong Taiji was privately
contemptuous of the Mongols' adoption of Buddhism because it "vitiated their
cultural identity,"[72] in order for the rhetoric of the Buddhist Qing to be employed, Mongolian culture needed to be fully reengineered within the Buddhist
structure mandated by Qing rule. And indeed, as all the evidence makes abun-
dantly clear, a Tibetan-style Gelukpa Buddhism became a fundamental feature
of Mongol religion and culture during the Qing.

While it is clear that the Qing generated and institutionalized Buddhism

within the ideological apparatus of their rule, why Mongol elites readily appropriated it and promoted the often brutal transformation of their own historical
and cultural traditions is another question. A dramatic example is that of Norbusangbu of the Khorchin Right Flank Middle Banner, who rounded up all the
shamans in the ten banners of the Jirim League and burned them alive on a
wooden pyre.[73] Of course, such tactics are also well known among the pre-Qing
Mongols, and all pre-Qing Mongol law codes do outlaw "shamanizing"; yet, in
this case, the actions of Norbusangbu affirmed, not a localized concept, but
rather the narrative of the Buddhist Qing and its Gelukpa orthodoxy. It was by
means of this ideological construct that Manchu rule and the actions of Norbusangbu were both legitimated and produced. Thus a relationship had been created between the elites and the rulers in which local authority was legimated
only through the enforcement of this construct.

Local Mongols ritualized not only their own but also the state's authority
through their Buddhist activity as was mandated by the orthodoxy of the Buddhist
Qing. This symbiotic relationship in turn strengthened the legitimacy of both
ruler and local elite. A parallel is offered in the Christianization of Imperial Rome.

> It assumed a chain of command drawn as starkly on earth as it was in heaven.
> An emperor, hailed by Ambrose as *militans pro Deo,* on active service for the
> Christian God, was linked to his upper-class subjects, and through these, to
> all inhabitants of the empire. . . . Service of the church could extend to all
> places and situations. For an imperial administration and a landed aristocracy
> which now faced, in heightened form—at a time of political dislocation asso-
> ciated with the barbarian invasions—the perennial problem of how to make
> their presence felt at a distance, to ally with a more exclusive and universalist
> notion of monotheism was to gain a strong sense of agency on the local level.
> It was to believe that actions pleasing to God could be microcosmic re-enact-
> ments, in one's own region, of a universal order. The presence of a pagan
> temple, of an altar, of a schismatic conventicle on a faraway estate became,
> even for a relatively minor representative of the Roman order, an opportunity
> to show, in its destruction, paternal authority over others, rendered active
> and majestic by the service of the one God. Churches set up on estates, gifts
> to the local clergy, the support of local zealots in the destruction of shrines,
> such as that enjoyed by Saint Martin in Gaul from landowning families, en-
> sured a more prominent role for the Christian lay persons as *filii ecclesiae,*
> loyal and visible "sons of the church" in their own city and region.[74]

It was in this manner of an inverted loop that Qing hegemony, through the discourse of Buddhist rule, was maintained.

As a result the Manchu rulers were recognized as the rightful rulers through the authority of the Gelukpa, and the continuance of Manchu power was thus predicated on the continued existence and support of Lhasa-oriented Gelukpa Buddhism in its imperial form. The legitimacy of local Mongol Buddhist elites was based on the authority of the Buddhist Qing, and it was in turn maintained through their support of the Tibetan-style Gelukpa order. Thus, in order to produce legitimacy, Mongol elites had to support the Lhasa-based Gelukpa order, which entailed the destruction of local religious practices and their related local community identifications, and replace them with the relations to the Gelukpa, the banner and the Mongol *ulus,* all of which defined Qing rule and the new Buddhist identity of the Mongols to which it was bound.

On account of these interrelationships and political dynamics the process of "Tibetanizing" Mongolian Buddhism proceeded unhindered. Indeed, as evidenced in Qing-period histories, Mongol elites, whose own power rested on this system, appropriated the discourse of the Buddhist Qing and facilitated the incorporation of Lhasa-based Gelukpa Buddhism into the religious and cultural life of the Mongols. Moreover, the linkage of Gelukpa Buddhism with state power, and vice versa, generated the environment wherein the conversion and practice of Buddhism by the Mongols only reaffirmed the narratives and rituals of the Buddhist Qing. In effect, the process of producing the Buddhist Qing undermined the conventional assimilation policies of Buddhist missionary activity, fundamentally nullifying the production of a "Mongolian Buddhism" in contradistinction to a "Qing Buddhism."

Tibetan Buddhism and the Qing State

The loss of an independent, or non-Qing Buddhism, was a reality not lost on several leading Mongol lamas. They realized that the production and maintenance of the Buddhist Qing had a profound impact on the development of an autochthonous "Mongolian Buddhism." The first and most dramatic figure in this regard was the Inner Mongol reincarnation, Mergen Gegen (1717–1766), who venerated, and perhaps emulated, the famous and subsequently purged Mongol missionary Neichi Toin. Thus, following in his footsteps, Mergen Gegen attempted to "reconstruct the model of Buddhism's relation to Mongolia, first, by providing a rich array of services in Mongolian language, and second, by reinterpreting the relation of the Buddhist church with native religious powers."[75] This was an important first step toward reorienting the Mongols' relation to Buddhism outside of the discursive framework of the Buddhist Qing and its Gelukpa orthodoxy. It may also explain why in late-nineteenth-century Urad folklore Mergen Gegen was hailed as a rebel against the Manchu state.[76]

Yet, be that as it may, Mergen Gegen's vision of a Mongolia-oriented or local-ized Buddhism beyond the dictates of the Buddhist Qing as manifested in his Mongolian liturgical ritual cycle did not have a lasting impact.[77]

Instead, the use of Tibetan language ritual materials and their affirmation of the Buddhist Qing continued to be the accepted practice among the Mongols. One invariable result of this development was an inevitable dissociation of the Mongols from Mongol ritual and culture. Thus within the framework of the im-perial Buddhist Qing, Mongol monks performed rituals in Tibetan for protector deities in Drepung monastery in Lhasa, or hierarchs in Beijing, not any local deities. Rather, earlier ritual practices and their social networks were displaced by the narratives and practices of the Buddhist Qing.

The most evident manifestation of this phenomenon can be seen in Tibetan-language ritual texts concerning the cult of mountain and local deities written for Mongol use, in which Mongolia's local sacred beings are merely subordinate to Tibet's. Unlike the works of Mergen Gegen, which promoted the engagement of a dialogue between native Mongol religious practices and Buddhism, these other works simply projected the Tibetan sacred landscape writ large. These Tibetan-language rituals make no attempt to add legitimacy to the new repre-sentational agenda through creating an interpretive arena wherein the old engages with the new reencoding. Unlike in Tibet, where powerful spirits are overcome in fierce battle and nailed down with stupas and temples, the names of Mongol mountains and deities were simply included in the larger and more im-portant litany of Tibetan sacred mountains and deities. In this way, the ritual "recitation acts as the means of ritual integration of the otherwise foreign deity into the constituted groups within the pantheon."[78] In this reencoding both Mongolia and its local sacred beings are subordinated to the power of Tibet, its sacred beings and its religious specialists.

As a result, the reinscription of Mongol sacred space was never engaged or transformed through local agency, or when it was, as was the case with Neichi Toin, it was eventually displaced by Gelukpa orthodoxy and the narratives and rituals of the Buddhist Qing. An example of this synergistic process is found in Rashipungsug's *History of Shireetü Güüshi:*

> In our own Banner [Baarin West Banner] to the east of the Black River, there was a mountain called Khalagchin. After successive generations of the mountain's local inhabitants had informed *the State* of sometimes hearing cymbals, drums and music [in the area], that Lama, saying it was "pos-sessed," in the Yellow Ox Year went to the mountain and circumambulated it. And while going through and looking at that mountain's large and small areas, he arrived at a valley on the south side of the mountain,[79] and said, "If

a monastery is built on this valley it will become good!" Thus Gurban Jalan Monastery was built.[80]

As a result, one of the most powerful discourses in the cultural transformation of Tibet into a Buddhist realm, the mandalization of geography,[81] was denied in the historical development of Buddhism in Mongolia. Instead, the appropriation of space and the definition of categories of place came to be handled through the agency of the Tibeto-Manchu Buddhist political structure.

Another example of state definition of sacred space is recorded in the memoirs of the prominent Mongol hierarch the Kanjurwa Khutugtu (1914–1978), who tells of an episode that occurred when his previous incarnation went to visit the Qianlong emperor in Beijing:

> The emperor, it is reported, seemed to see a person standing behind him [the Second Kanjurwa Khutugtu] and inquired who he was. Turning to see for himself, the incarnation replied that the *ejen,* the spirit of the Serku region in Kokonor, was standing there. This pleased the emperor who then conferred upon the *ejen* a yellow jacket and a red button, the headdress of special rank, denoting the second rank in the hierarchy of the imperial bureaucracy. Such bestowals from an emperor were rare and greatly prized. . . . This tradition was [the emperor's] means of demonstrating that they regarded themselves as supreme not only over local rulers but even over regional gods. The bestowal of recognition was not limited to a particular spirit but was also upon the place where the deity was customarily believed to reside. Because of this incident, my previous incarnations over the centuries were always searched for and found in this Serku area.[82]

This form of "spiritual ornamentalism"—or "enfeoffments"[83] —therefore demythologized local beliefs in early divine mediators, and instead tied these sacred networks and conceptualizations to the narrative of the state. Pilgrimage thus became a cult of empire.

Still, certain Mongol lamas, as seen in the work of Mergen Gegen, realized that the imposition of Tibetan-style Gelukpa Buddhism and its ritualization of the Qing state was problematic. The Choiji Lama Agwangdorji, for example, critiqued directly the Gelukpa-Qing manner of reencoding Mongolia's sacred space in the colophon to his nineteenth-century ritual text for local deities in Mongolia.[84] While he recognized that the original ritualization of Tibet within a lengthy discourse of mandalization was effective, its simple imposition upon Mongolia without engaging in a new Mongolian discourse/mandalization was not only a mistake, but also ineffective.

The books written in general, by our ancestors to offer for sacrifices to the lords of the earth are very blissful. They have long proved to be blissful, this is how we inherited them, but as most were written in Tibetan and some of the lords of the earth did not understand them, (the prayers) failed to reach their goal and the common Mongols did not know them. And since, translated into Mongolian word for word from the Tibetan, they were difficult to understand in Mongolian, they were ill-fitted to Mongolian, it was difficult to understand their original meanings, really well and exactly. In my mind if we prepare Mongolian food for the lords of the Mongolian world and say our reasons and wishes in Mongolian that cannot be but favorable for our *qan* Mongol land. Besides, my intention was to make the contents (of the text) available for common Mongols, thus turning them into believers.[85]

Writing in the nineteenth century, Agwangdorji provides a valuable perspective on what had unfolded in the production of the Buddhist Qing. He realized that the imposition of state-sponsored Gelukpa orthodoxy had mandated the shattering of local traditions. Indeed, the power of the Buddhist Qing was only enhanced by distancing itself from Mongol religious culture, further breaking earlier bonds of community and ritual practice, and culminating with all of these becoming centered upon Gelukpa lamas and their institutions, which were intrinsically tied to the Qing state.

Language, Buddhist Identity and the Third Conversion

While Agwangdorji, like Mergen Gegen, did recognize that this state-sponsored imposition was problematic, he did not challenge it. Neither of these famous Mongol lamas rejected the system of either Lhasa-based Gelukpa Buddhism or the Manchu state. Rather, much as the creation of a "longer" or more "pure" Buddhist past generated a mode of distinction for the Mongols within the Qing, these authors similarly also only promoted a new liturgy in Mongolian. They therefore did not challenge the Qing state but actually enabled a better understanding of its logic in their native language. Yet, the work of these authors not only reveals the success of the Buddhist Manchu state, but also highlights the importance of language and its role in the process of creating the Qing.

As noted above, the Mongol use of Tibetan is often compared benignly with the use of Latin in Catholic Europe. However, as was the case in Europe, the process of Latinization was a powerful tool in reinscribing religiopolitical discourses, as witnessed in the displacement of Anglo-Saxon, Saxon and Slavic liturgies.[86] Thus even though within the structure of the Buddhist Qing the Mongols themselves adopted Tibetan instead of its being imposed through some sort of Beijing-mandated program, their acceptance of the language was not a natural progression. As Tibetan became the medium of Buddhist authority, Mongol Buddhist elites invariably began to accept and elevate it as the sacred language of the church. This trend was no doubt reinforced through the expansion of Mongols receiving religious training in the large Gelukpa monasteries of Tibet and the Qing policy of appointing Tibetans, particularly those from Amdo, as leading reincarnations in Mongol areas. All these factors acted synergistically within the institutionalized Tibetanization of Mongolia in the same inverted loop of authority already described to lead to the abandonment of Mongolian as a viable language of Buddhist authority. Yet, as was the case with the reformulation of the historical narratives between the pre-Qing and post-conquest periods, the switch to a Tibetanized Buddhism was not natural. There was an apparent discord between the two phases of Buddhist conversion.

In particular, it is clear that, for Altan and Ligdan Khan, the production of Mongolian Buddhist literature was tied to the creation of independent communities premised upon a distinctive "Mongolian Buddhism." This was not only in terms of narratives and rituals confirming local Buddhist identities, but also the explicit production of a vernacular Buddhist literature. Both Ligdan Khan and the descendants of Altan Khan therefore ordered the production of a Mongolian translation of the 108-volume Tibetan Buddhist canon, the Kanjur. While the Manchus also prepared new editions of the Mongolian Kanjur during the Qing, in this earlier period it is clear that these works and the other translation projects of the time were intended to be used. They were not simply merit-making exercises, printed and stored, as was to be the case during the Qing.

In fact, in contrast to what occurred during the Qing, there is no evidence to suggest that Tibetan was ever considered as a possible church language in the pre-Qing period.[87] In 1587 the Third Dalai Lama even helped the Mongol lama Ayushi create a new Mongolian script for the exact transcription of Sanskrit and Tibetan words. However, in the course of producing Qing Buddhists, or Qing Buddhism, not only did history and rituals become an issue, but language as well. During the Qing, therefore, Tibetan and its relation to the power of the Lhasa-based Gelukpa reinforced the narrative of the Buddhist Qing.

The elevation of Tibetan as the "church language" must therefore be seen in the same light as the radical gap in the presentations of Mongol Buddhist history between the pre-Qing and Qing periods. In all the pre-Qing sources the production of a vernacular Buddhist literature was of paramount importance to ritualizing and confirming the Buddhist community. The most likely source for this tradition is the history of Songtsen Gampo, credited with creating an organized Tibetan Buddhist state through the creation of a Tibetan script that could be used to produce a vernacular canon and a secular law code. By producing these, Songtsen Gampo was thus able to forge the "Tibetan Buddhist nation." And it is not surprising that other Inner Asian groups followed the same model when producing Buddhist states, most notably the Uygurs and Tanguts.[88]

During the late sixteenth century the Mongols followed the same strategy. One component fostering an independent Mongol Buddhist community was the creation of a Mongolian Buddhist canon and a secular law, as is explicitly stated in the *Jewel Translucent Sutra*.[89] Moreover, an inscription from Olon Süme wherein Altan Khan is praised for his leadership and his support for the production of Buddhist literature confirms the importance of creating a vernacular Buddhist literature in the pre-Qing period.

> Supreme Altan Khan, who invited the Limitless Ocean Majesty,
> and thus aided the many leaderless people,
> and was often leading and powerful, who
> established the rare poems, sutras and texts that are the greatness of the
> Three Jewels.[90]

And in fact Altan Khan did initiate the translation of Buddhist sutras during his reign, as seen in the colophon to the *Golden Beam Sutra (Suvarṇaprabhāsa Sūtra)* he commissioned.[91] In addition, during the reign of his grandson, the project of translating the entire Kanjur into Mongolian was also begun[92]—a project that Ligdan Khan also undertook in 1628–1629. As a result, it is clear that for the Mongols there was a powerful connection between a Buddhist community and a vernacular canon;[93] and it was precisely this relationship that was shattered in the course of shaping a new Mongol identity bound to the Qing state.[94]

The adoption of Tibetan as the church language of Mongolia was therefore the culmination of the Mongols' conversion experience. It was an important part of the process that inherently bound the Mongols to the Tibeto-Manchu political structure. Nevertheless, except in parts of Kökenuur, Mongolian was never entirely eclipsed, as was the case with the Arabization of Aramaic- and Coptic-speaking countries. Yet as a result of its dissociation from Buddhism, the key element in Mongol narratives of historical identity, there was a radical break with the past; and, as with pre-Qing narratives of the Mongol community, Buddhism was disconnected from pre-Qing communal identities such as the *ulus*. This fact not only enabled the new Qing communal boundaries to be established, but also allowed the virtually complete Tibetanization of Mongolian Buddhism to proceed unhindered. Thus Buddhism, which had first shaped the independent Mongol Buddhist *ulus* such as the Tümed, Chakhar and Khalkha, had been irrevocably dissociated from the exclusivity of a Mongol Buddhist identity and instead entailed only belonging to the Buddhist Qing.

If we return to where we began this chapter, the changing nature of Mongol narratives of Buddhist identity, it is clear that during the Mongol incorporation into the Buddhist Qing a radical transformation did take place. Indeed, counter to the "Buddhist explanation," which functions within the logic of stasis and continuity, we need to recognize that the success of the Qing was premised precisely on this process of transforming Mongol conceptualizations of political authority and communal boundaries. And within this process one of the most powerful discourses was the Dharma.

With the Manchu appropriation of Buddhist rule and its promotion of Gelukpa orthodoxy, Mongol narratives of communal ethnogenesis changed dramatically. New Mongol rituals were created in accord with these narratives, and all these projects culminated in the abandonment of the Mongolian language in favor of Tibetan, signaling the end of the Mongols' process of Buddhicization and the incorporation of the Mongols into the Tibeto-Manchu ritualized Buddhist Qing.

On a certain level perhaps we therefore need to speak of a "third conversion." Much as we identify Altan Khan's conversion as the "second" in relation to the first that unfolded during the empire period, the developments during the Qing should perhaps be seen as a third conversion. This is especially the case as the process of Buddhicization, or what it meant to be a Buddhist, did not end with the "second conversion" initiated by Altan Khan in 1578. Rather, as we have seen, the transition from the pre-Qing to the Qing period entailed radical transformations in how the Mongols understood the Dharma. What had initially been a fundamental element in the formation of independent Mongol and pluralistic Buddhist identities and communities ended with Buddhism being the discourse that dissociated the Mongols from those very possibilities. Being Mongol and being Buddhist became intrinsically intertwined with being part of the Manchu state. Unfortunately, however, it has most often been this process of transformation that has been held in suspension by various discursive frames. Yet it is precisely within this realm of engagement and transformation where new meanings were produced. An entirely different question, though, is what happened to all of these notions during the upheavals of the nineteenth century.

CHAPTER FIVE

The Buddhist Qing
and Mongol Localization
in the Nineteenth Century

The bones of my beloved mother,
The ashes of my holy lama,
The plain of my Daichingtala,
What of these will be cut off by the pawning
Of our Da Wang, who rules us as master?
—Khorchin folksong

During the Muslim Hui uprisings of the 1860s the banner of Otog of the Yeke Juu League in Ordos suffered greatly.[1] Not only did Muslim rebels attack its citizens and ransack Buddhist monasteries, but the people of Otog were also victims of their own local government. In particular, they chafed under the despotic rule of the regent Rashinamjil. He was ruling because Chagdurjab (1862–1881), the rightful Chinggisid heir and banner prince, was still a child. Nevertheless, both of these problems eventually passed.

The Hui uprising was suppressed by Qing forces, and the reign of the regent Rashinamjil was challenged by the people of Otog Banner through a petition sent to Beligbadarkhu, the Bureau of Colonial Affairs' appointed chairman of the Yeke Juu League. Unfortunately, Beligbadarkhu was not interested in resolving the peoples' grievances with Rashinamjil; rather, he was more concerned with resolving a long-simmering land dispute between the neighboring Otog and Üüshin banners.[2] Beligbadarakhu wanted the government of Otog finally to relinquish all claims to the land that his own Üüshin banner had been offered in 1827 by Otog banner in exchange for money, so that the Otog monastery of Shine Usun Juu could afford to join the new craze for masked *cham* dances. To this end, he rejected the people's complaints, and in turn he supported Rashinamjil as long as he agreed to confirm Üüshin's claims to this contested territory with a letter bearing the imperially bestowed official seal of Otog Banner. Rashinamjil concurred, and shortly thereafter the Üüshin government, which was short of funds, sold a part of this territory to the Belgian Scheut missionaries so they could build their community of Borobalgasu.

The government of Otog was appalled at this turn of events. At first it sent troops into the area and demanded that, not only the Catholic Church and its followers, but also that all the people living in this disputed territory pay taxes to Otog and not Üüshin Banner. It eventually went to court in Ningxia, and with the support of the church, Otog won the court case and the residents of Borobalgasu were to pay taxes to Otog. At the same time, however, people in the area continued to pay taxes to Üüshin. Thus the dispute over the land and who was to pay taxes continued.

The problem was only further exacerbated when Otog Banner was ordered to pay huge indemnities as reparations for the Boxer Rebellion. During the rebellion Borobalgasu had been burned to the ground, and its Christian converts killed. Unfortunately, the Otog government was very poor, so it took a loan of silver from the Scheut mission in order to pay its debts, and when it was unable to pay this loan back, the government offered the church a piece of land adjacent to the Üüshin border. When the government of Üüshin heard of this arrangement they felt that Otog had given land to missionaries that was not rightfully theirs.

In order to resolve this dispute, the church fathers dispatched a group from Borobalgasu to discuss it with Arbinbayar, the prince of Khanggin Banner, who then held the rotating position of Yeke Juu League chairman. But members of Üüshin Banner kidnapped these representatives. Wanting to finally resolve the dispute and confirm their actual territorial holdings, the Scheut missionaries set up a new meeting. Yet at the same time as these proceedings were going forward, the Manchu resident general of Suiyuan, Yigu, was pressing the banner princes of Yeke Juu League to open up their territory to Chinese colonization. Thus, in order to curry favor with Yigu, the prince of Üüshin offered up the disputed territory for Chinese cultivation, and it was in this atmosphere that the following letter was composed.

> Letter from Arbinbayar, Chairman of the Yeke Juu League with the privilege of walking in the Emperor's presence, ruling prince of an Ordos banner, with the rank of Banner Beise, with four additional honorary ranks and registered three times, holding the title Jinong; sent to Yan Mingzhi [Edmund Vereenooghe] priest of the Catholic religion, with a view to making a communication.

> If we examine the files: the banner administration of the Beile of Otog claims that the banner of Üüshin has taken advantage of its power to steal a piece of land given to the foreign church for "repayment of silver," and in order to adjudicate this affair which has resulted in a law suit and quarrel, the office of us, League Chairman, . . . sent and delegated the scribe with rank Jakirugchi, Rinchendorji, and the Taiji and Jalan-u janggi with the

rank of Meyiren, Mergen. These subordinate functionaries whom we have sent, have presented to us the following report:

"With a view to making a report.

We, insignificant functionaries, following our instructions, on the sixteenth of the first winter month of this year [December 4, 1903], reached such designated placed as the Khargantu-yin Monastery, and as we arrived, we convened with the delegates Ochirbatu, a taiji holding the office of Gatekeeper Meyiren, with the rank of Jakirugchi, and one additional rank, and the Jalan-u janggi Garmasiddi, Taiji with the rank of Meyiren, sent by the office of the League's vice-chairman with the privilege of walking through the Qianqing Gate, ruling prince of Üüshin Banner, with the rank of Beise and the honorary rank of Beile; with the delegates Öljeibatu, Taiji of the fourth rank, and who has been awarded the peacock feather, whose former commission was Jakirugchi, Janggi with one additional rank, and others, sent by the office of Cimeddorji, Taiji with one additional rank, minister judging banner affairs of the Otog banner prince with the title Imperial Beile, and with the delegates sent by the office of the Catholic priest, Yan Mingzhi, Bandar, holding the rank of Jakirugchi, Masidelger, holding the rank of Jakirughci, and Chogdüüreng, holding the rank of Jakirugchi.

"Sonomyarpil, Jarguchi and Meyiren, with the rank of Jakirugchi, and Tümen, with the rank of Janggi, and others from Üüshin banner, stated that the banner of Otog relying on its power previously had without proof, secretly and stealthily, sold land of our banner, namely the one piece of land given to the foreign church for 'payment-silver.' The office of Ming Yuqing, Catholic Bishop with the honorary rank of Güng, by Papal command in charge of the administration of Mongol and Chinese Christians, has reported thereon in detail.

"When we arrived at the place and took out the maps of the string of border marks between the two banners Üüshin and Otog, and inspected them, we found that within the territory of Otog banner they mentioned the landmarks of Bayan-deresü, Tabunang Ubasi-yin Usu, Amasar-un Sübe. When on this occasion we asked Seringdongron, Jakirugchi with the rank of Meyiren of Otog Banner, and other guardians of the borders, they stated as follows:

'Previously in the fourth year of Badaragultu Törö [1878] our two banners delegated officials who set up new landmarks starting from Aguljar-un Eriyen Tologai to the border of the sand northwest of

Boro-Tologai, namely erected seven landmarks, and then peacefully separated. But the remaining old frontier landmarks; Bayan-deresü, Tabunang Ubasi-yin Usu, as far as Chagan Düise and Amasar-un Sübe, we Janggi Duruga have been guarding as before, and it is absolutely not true that we have "hooked" that section from Üüshin territory and given it illegally to the church.'

Moreover, if we inspect the old records of both banners Üüshin and Otog we find that on the sixteenth of the middle month of the winter of Tengriin Tedkügsen's fourth year [December 16, 1739], Liu Bayar, imperial official regulating Sino-Mongol Affairs, and Ciwangbaljur, with the rank of Beise, and Chairman of the Yeke Juu League, came together at Nangsu Monastery. They drew up a map of the banner boundaries with the seals of the seven banner princes on it and in a letter presented to the proper Bureau [of Colonial Affairs] they stated that the boundary is at Bayan-deresü and from there to Tabunang Ubasiin Usu, and from there to Amasar-un Sübe. So if we functionaries carefully reflect upon this, the present row of boundary marks between the two banners of Üüshin and Otog, and the old archives, perfectly agree with each other, and it is not true that the land previously given by Otog banner to the foreign church was "hooked" away from Üüshin; since it is land really belonging to Otog banner, the church must be allowed to take possession as before.

"And we officials from the various parties together with the Jarguchis, Meyirens and Jalans from both banners Üüshin and Otog have re-established the one old landmark of Bayan-deresü, and entrusted it as before to those responsible for surveillance of the landmarks; but as soon as we said that from there to the two remaining landmarks Tabunang Ubasi-yin Usu and Amasar-un Sübe, cairns and landmarks would be repaired, a hundred or so Taijis, functionaries, and common people, evil companions of Sonomyarpil, Jarguchi and Meyiren, with the rank of Jakirugchi of Üüshin banner, assembled and came over to take him [i.e., Sonomyarpil] forcibly away, and as we were thus unable to re-establish the two landmarks we made a sketch of the configuration of the terrain, and peacefully dispersed, and we reported this.

"In addition, when we functionaries carefully consider the situation, there is this to be said: claiming that Sonomyarpil, Jarguchi with the rank of Jakirugchi of Üüshin Banner had been fighting with Otog Banner for a piece of land, more than a hundred men united into a crowd, called duguilang, and feeling strong in their great numbers, made a point of as-suming a threatening pose, and with great shouts repeatedly came and confined us officials who had come from the League Chairman, and from the ruling banner princes to decide this issue. And they never let us explain the matter at all; with many and various sorts of words, they conceived the plan to cause disorder, and attack and oppress us. Then they wrecked the quarters of responsible functionaries, and plundered the tent where the Five Milk products were kept; then they even laid hands upon their own functionaries, dragged them off, mistreated them and took them forcibly away. Indeed it came to this paroxysm of lawlessness. And if we did not report these actions in detail to have them judged, these evil officials and common people, relying on prestige and power, were sure to raise again and again grave affairs.

We report this, and in addition: Tümen-delger with the rank of Jakirugchi, being an official who had come on orders from his responsible office, without knowledge of the border, straightaway erected two earthen marks; but since these do not coincide with the original emplacement we report herewith that we have decided to summon those functionaries and commoners to make them obey law and rules, and show them that they must observe prohibitions, and this in order to cut off the root of future evil. And apart from our report at the end of our petition, we list the names of those recalcitrant taijis, functionaries, and commoners, and present the list together with this report. When you receive it, from your exalted position examine and consider it and, please, make a decision. For this reason we present this."

So it says. On that occasion, the Catholic priest Yan Mingzhi presented the following letter:

"We, insignificant persons have reported that we have been oppressed by Üüshin, and from your exalted position, consider the issue, you have decided to do us a favor of sending Jakirugchi Rinchendorji and others on a special mission, with orders to find the right and wrong of the entangled troubles between our three parties, Otog, Üüshin, and ourselves; to decide according to the law and justice, cut off the roots of trouble and clear away the suffering borne by all of us. The Jakirugchi and dignitaries who had come with such orders convoked us, the three parties; they examined the situation according to the essence of the truth and came to a decision: according to the original rulings they ordered to set up one landmark at the border of our church-land named Bayan-Chagan-Deresü. But with regard to the issue of the two remaining landmarks, the yamen employees, and commoners of Üüshin banner alone congregated in large numbers, stirred up trouble like bandits and refused to obey orders from above.

"For this reason, several of our problems have not been solved, and apart from reporting this there is another question: with the higher officials of Üüshin banner in the lead, the Taijis, yamen employees, and commoners of Üüshin have conceived evil plans and by and by are organizing duguilangs. And also, during the last month of fall of this year [1903], among other news heard in the church there was this: Chinese and Mongols have conspired and decided to kill to a man and utterly root out all priests and Christians of our several churches. They prepared flags, vests with distinctive markings, arrows of command, letters with seals affixed, swords and other weapons; they forwarded their letters to both Otog and Üüshin Banner. And after we had gathered information regarding their mutual relations, we seized one man from among those evil-minded Chinese, and we interrogated him, this Chinese among other things said:

'We have gone to the Meyiren-ü Janggi of Üüshin banner, Öljei's house, and asked him: "are your soldiers ready?" Whereupon he declared, "in our banner are a thousand soldiers ready!" And from there we went to the meeting in Otog banner, but when we inquired about troops, Otog replied, "our troops are not ready!"'

"If we carefully consider this confession, it is clear that Üüshin, conceiving evil intentions toward us, has conspired with inimical Chinese, and has plans to do away with all of us without reason and to lay hands on all our possessions; and the fact of their oppression and mistreatment of the poor banner of Otog is also evident.

"Moreover, this year when the church sent forty plow teams to cultivate our land, around forty men led by the Jarguchi, Meyiren with the rank of Jakirugchi Sonomyarpil and Tümen with the rank of Janggi, came from Üüshin banner and held them away from the land we wanted to cultivate; and by usurping the land which they claimed as theirs, they made us lose 1,200 large bushels of grain which we would definitely have harvested.

"Also Üüshin not only by various means wants to suppress us, insignificant persons, but now it is clear that they have conspired with inimical Chinese to kill us. Therefore, putting our lives under your protection, we priests and Christians all together report true facts and present this letter.

When your highness, the Great Superior Prince, receives it, from your exalted position reflect and consider: take the side of us, insignificant persons, and as fast as possible grant us your favor, namely a compassionate means to let us save our lives; do away with the misfortunes the numerous people are suffering; judge and inflict a salutary punishment upon the evil-intentioned men. If you wish to cut off once and for all the evil root, a thousand times we wish that it be a ten-thousand fold good for the people.

"We present this; when it arrives, we petition that you deign to send us as fast as possible a reply to all these facts"

When I consider the situation, I find that all those grave affairs are true, and seeing what the situation demands: whereas it is necessary to pass judgement in accord with law and custom, the many taijis such as Sonomyarpil, Jarguchi with the rank of Jakirugchi of Üüshin Banner and the commoners who have together to protect each other, and acted irresponsibly, and have not accepted and obeyed the decision rendered in the matter; indeed they have gone to an extreme degree of illegality in contravention of law and ordinances.

Therefore, I dispatch this to inform uniformly Üüshin, Otog, and the foreign church, and hand each party a copy. When this letter arrives, the priest will examine its contents, and until next year when we render a decision regarding this matter, you will keep under orders and control your proper individual functionaries and people and not allow them to cause trouble.

It is not allowed to disobey. Besides the dispatch of this command, I write out the list of names of the recalcitrant Taijis, functionaries, and commoners of Üüshin Banner at the end of the letter to that same banner, and forward it together.

Therefore I send this letter.

On the thirteenth of the last month of winter of the twenty-ninth year of Badaragultu Törö [January 29, 1904].[3]

On the basis of the above historical sketch and the Yeke Juu chairman Arbinbayar's letter of 1904, it is clear that the situation among the Mongols had undergone enormous changes during the course of the nineteenth century. In this regard the Mongols were clearly not alone. Everyone within the Qing had to grapple with the social, religious, political and economic changes transforming the realities of the Manchu state during this turbulent period. This chapter will explore how the Mongols dealt with some of these enormous changes. In particular, it examines how the eighteenth-century conceptualizations of being a Qing Buddhist were transformed within the cauldron of nineteenth-century China.

Of course, as seen in the above letter, not everything had changed. Qing ornamentalism and social hierarchy were still of fundamental importance. Similarly, the holding of the negotiations to settle this land dispute at Khargantu-yin monastery makes it evident that the Tibeto-Manchu religiopolitical structure still prevailed. Yet, at the same time as there were these continuities within the structures of Qing rule, the letter also reveals dramatic changes. Most striking in this regard is the radical break between the holistic concept of the Mongols as one community within the Qing that was so powerfully promoted during the eighteenth century.

Counter to the vision of an eternally unified Mongol *ulus* manifested in the Mongol nobility, we find instead the elite and commoners of one banner attacking and kidnapping members of another banner over a territorial dispute. Thus Mongol communal boundaries had shifted yet again. Indeed, to a certain extent Mongol communal conceptualizations had come full circle—namely, back to the distinct "independent" *ulus* that had defined the realities of the civil war period during the seventeenth century. Yet in the nineteenth century these entities were no longer the independent *ulus*, but instead were the immutable banners of the Qing.

At the same time as this process of "relocalization" was taking place, which was also happening elsewhere in the Qing at the time,[4] the letter sent by Father Edmund Vereenooghe also reveals a complementary and seemingly contradictory phenomenon wherein the communal boundaries have actually expanded. In particular, Father Vereenooghe warns of the dangers posed by Mongols and Chinese working together against the Christian community of Borobalgasu. While this Sino-Mongol unity was clearly triggered by the presence of Western missionaries and native converts in their midst, it is also important to keep in mind that this is the first time that such a unity is in fact confirmed. Although these two groups had clearly been part of the Qing dynasty since 1644, Mongol histories generally made no mention of this fact. Rather, in producing a Buddhist Qing identity, Mongol narratives were situated within a historical arc that excluded China and the Chinese. Yet in the nineteenth century these two groups apparently worked arm-in-arm against the foreigners who were seen as threatening not only the local order but the Qing order as well.

These events in Ordos, as reiterated in the above letter, reveal that the lived realities of the Qing were always changing. As a result, if we are to better understand both Qing and Mongol history, we need to pay closer attention to these transformations. In particular, we should investigate how Mongol concepts were both engaged and transformed by the forces unleashed during the nineteenth century. I would therefore now like to turn to these two noted shifts: the apparent universalizing, or expansion, of the community in Mongol conceptualizations and the simultaneous creation of localized banner identities. In particular, I would like to clarify how these two apparently contradictory concepts—a transethnic community and a localized banner identity—actually developed.

At first glance, the two concepts may seem incompatible. However, it is more likely that they were intertwined, since they were both grappling with what it meant to be Mongol within the discursive framework of the Qing. Thus, while all the earlier Mongolian histories had presented the idea of the Mongols as a distinct entity under the Qing through the narrative arc of India-Tibet-Mongol-Manchu Buddhist history, in the nineteenth century this presentation began to change.

Mongol histories of this period do not focus exclusively on the Mongols within the Qing, but rather, on the entire Buddhist Qing, of which the Mongols, along with the Manchus, Chinese and Tibetans, were only one part. And in tandem with, or in reaction to, this dispersal of the distinctive Mongol community within a transethnic Buddhist Qing, the Mongols' boundaries of differentiation began to concentrate on localized Buddhist narratives of communal identification. This implies that, as the Mongols began increasingly to identify with the larger Buddhist Qing, not only was a distinctive Mongol identity founded upon a pure primordialized Buddhist identity, but it came to focus again on the localized community of the banner. So, as a result of its having been subsumed by the Buddhist Qing, in the course of the nineteenth century Mongol identity came to manifest itself through local identifications, in particular the banner and its land. And although this phenomenon seemed to be occurring among the majority of Mongols, as reflected in the explosion of local histories in the nineteenth century,[5] this study will focus exclusively on Ordos.

Transethnic Buddhism and Mongol History

Although the localization of Mongol identity began to play a large role in the nineteenth century, this tradition began with the seventeenth-century idea of distinctive *ulus*. Saghang Sechen's *Precious Summary* therefore focuses largely on Ordos and in particular the activities of his own ancestors. Lubsangdanzin's *Golden Summary* describes how the Kharachins submitted to the Manchus.[6] He also has material on the Three Deeds of the Khorchins and how the Khasarid descendants helped the Chinggisids. The Khalkha historian Byamba Erke Daiching details the history and genealogy of Dayan Khan's son, Geresanje, who is the ancestor of the Khalkha nobility. Even in the eighteenth century, when Mongol histories came to dwell less on these distinct *ulus* and more on the totality of the Mongol *ulus,* the authors, perhaps understandably, continued to elaborate more upon their own communities, or lineages, than others. Rashipungsug, for example, has an extensive and detailed history and genealogy of his own ancestors and the nobility of the Baarin banner, especially their valiant fighting with Qing forces against the Zunghars.[7]

None of these histories, however, went so far in terms of localization as the Kharachin bannerman Lomi's 1732–1735 *History of the Mongolian Borjigid Lineage,* which is the first work that focuses explicitly on the author's family history. It was originally written in Chinese and Manchu (Lomi was a member of the internal garrison banners and eventually became lieutenant general of the Mongol Bordered White Banner), and it was not actually translated into Mongolian until 1839. Nevertheless, this history set a precedent for narratives localized through genealogy. This approach is first found in a Mongolian work in Mergen Gegen's 1765 *Golden Summary,* which, in contradistinction to the Mongol historiographical focus on the Chinggisid lineage, explores the history and genealogical descendants of Chinggis Khan's brother, Khabatu Khasar, who were the nobility of Mergen Gegen's own Urad Banner.

Perhaps more important than the role these localized Mongolian histories of the eighteenth century played in forging a transethnic Buddhist Qing narrative was the growing Mongolian literature influenced by Tibetan *chos-'byung* (history of the Dharma) literature, which focused especially on Buddhist history. These works shifted away from the predominantly historical-genealogical narratives of the Mongol *ulus* found in earlier histories and in their place offered stories revolving around the transmission of the Dharma. One of the most important works of this genre was Gombojab's *History of Buddhism in China* (1740), a history of China and Chinese Buddhism, and an analysis of the Chinese Buddhist canon.[8] Gombojab's history opened up a whole new field in Mongol historiography, since rather than focusing exclusively on the Mongols, the narrative situated the Mongols within a transethnic Buddhist discourse. The first work of this genre written in Mongolian was the 1757 *Light of Wisdom.*[9]

Even though these two new narrative forms, localized and the transethnic Buddhist histories, developed individually and continued to do so throughout the rest of the Qing, they both also came to shape the discourses of the nineteenth century. The Buddhist works contributed to the idea of the Qing as transethnic Buddhist community, and the earlier histories that focused on specific genealogies and localized groups helped foster the localization of Mongol identity.

Nevertheless, although these two conceptions differed, similar underlying suppositions ask to be explored. The first and most evident one is that both of these representations maintained the fundamental notion that the Mongols were an integral part of the Qing state. None of the authors of either the Buddhist works or localized histories questioned or critiqued this reality. The framing of the discourse is entirely encapsulated within the Qing, and this does not change in the nineteenth century. However, these later works are also unlike the earlier histories of the seventeenth and eighteenth centuries that were so important in initially shaping the conceptualization of the Mongols as part of the Qing. Most notably, the later works mirror the historical Buddhist ones, which, in focusing on Buddhism as the defined community, actually transgress previously distinct "ethnonational" boundaries, a framework that is found in all the Mongol works of the nineteenth century.

As we have seen, in the seventeenth and eighteenth centuries the Mongols represented Buddhism as part of a specifically Mongolian identity. It helped to define the Mongol *ulus,* both as an independent entity and as a part of the Qing. However, under the influence of *chos-'byung* literature, Buddhism became for the Mongols in the nineteenth century no longer an element of cultural production that signaled differentiation, but its opposite. The Dharma was now the element that undergirded the structural framework of transethnic unification within the Qing.

In Gombowangjil's[10] 1817 *Golden Rosary (Altan Erike)* Buddhism is thus no longer related exclusively to the Mongols. Rather, he envisions the Dharma as a shared cultural element of various communities within the Qing. This realignment is reflected through the author's seamless interweaving of the history of the Chinese, Manchus and Mongols, and their relations with the Tibetans. Other Mongol sources of this period also include the history of the Ming dynasty, in particular that of the Yongle emperor's invitation of Tsongkhapa and his student's visit to Beijing.[11] Others relate the well-known story of the Bodhisattva Mañjuśrī having appeared long ago on Wutai Shan in order to teach the Dharma to the Chinese.[12] And, perhaps most remarkably, in the 1835 *Pearl Rosary* the author overturned two hundred years of historiographical precedent and noted that Chinggis Khan actually did not meet with the Tibetan lama Kungga Nyingpo.[13] Moreover, he even notes that Chinggis Khan's first encounter with the Dharma was through a meeting with a Chinese Chan master.[14] While this meeting may also never have taken place in fact, it is important to recognize that none of Chinggis Khan's well-known meetings with Chinese religious teachers had ever been part of Qing-period Mongolian historiography.[15] Only in the transethnic Buddhist discourses of the nineteenth century was it possible to once again imagine that "Mongolian Buddhism" had begun with a meeting between Chinggis Khan and Haiyun.

In these representations Mongol communal boundaries are therefore dissociated from both the earlier distinctive *ulus* and the holistic Mongol *ulus,* and instead are united with all the other Buddhist groups living within the Qing. And this idea of unity, or a transethnic Buddhist ecumene, is vividly evident in a ritual text focusing on Buddhist sites that incorporates all areas in the Qing domains.

> I make pure offerings to all the mountains, earth and water led by the Female Gods of earth and water. I make pure offerings to all the mountains, earth and water of India, the Vajra-dwelling-place of the Wise. I make pure offerings to all the mountains, earth and water of the eight continents on the four sides of Mount Sumeru. I make pure offerings to all the mountains, earth and water of Tibet headed by Lhasa's Samye Monastery. I make pure offerings to all the mountains, earth and water of Tibet headed by the brotherly three Great Ones [Sera, Ganden, Drepung]. I make pure offerings to the twelve great sacred sites led by Semid Kengskiri [Kailash].
> I make pure offerings to the entire atmosphere headed by the blue dome of the sky. I make pure offerings to all the mountains, earth and water of China led by Wutai Shan. I make pure offerings to all the mountains, earth and water of this side headed by Kharbuglasa. I make pure offerings to all the mountains, earth and water headed by the Khangai [in Outer Mongolia]. I make pure offerings to all the mountains, earth and water led by rounded Jalaman [Mountain, the Oirad homeland]. I make pure offerings to all the mountains, earth and water headed by the Muna Jedkhü Khan Khatun Ekhe [Mountain, in Inner Mongolia]. . . . I make pure offerings to all the mountains, earth and water headed by Shangdu, Kaifengfu, Daidu [Beijing] and the Andai River. I make pure offerings to all the mountains, earth and water headed by the hidden Jinjin Stupa. I make pure offerings to all the mountains, earth and water headed by the three great places with many waterfalls. I make pure offerings to all the mountains, earth and water headed by Burkhan Tung, Khonggorai Khan, Saikhan Khan and Gerel-ün Eke. I make pure offerings to those being the Lord of the Mountain and Mountain Queen headed by the blessedness of this settled nomadic camp. OM A HUU.[16]

Here, Buddhism does not act as a specific agent in the reification of Mongol history, community, or identity, but as its inverse. Buddhism is the element that transcends these previous ethnic, cultural and national boundaries, and in turn it unites them within the Qing.

Another text, a ritual offering to the fox spirit,[17] even declares that, in the mythic past, "Tibetans, Chinese and Mongols . . . those three were born from one mother."[18] As a result, Mongol Buddhist history, particularly that of Altan

Khan as found in the lengthy passages devoted to him in nineteenth-century histories,[19] no longer potentially challenged Qing authority but reinforced it through the reaffirmation of Mongol Buddhist identity within the transethnic context.

Buddhism and the Muslim Other

Along with the conceptualization of a transethnic religious community encompassed by the Qing state, new boundaries of communal identification also arose. In accord with the Buddhist historical tradition, the author of the *Golden Rosary* interwove the histories of the Chinese, Manchus and Mongols as a unified whole in terms of their relations to the Dharma. A similar presentation of a mutual multiethnic history is found in Jimbadorji's 1848 *Crystal Mirror (Bolor Toli)*. Jimbadorji, however, not only employs the narrative strategy of Buddhism as an element of unity in order to generate a holistic narrative for the community of Buddhists within the Qing, but he also generates a node of distinction with another religious group: the Muslims.[20] Thus, rather than employing a discourse of "ethnonational" differentiation as represented in the Mongols vis-à-vis the Chinese, Manchus and Tibetans, when these groups are united through Buddhism, this unity is formed through the discourse of religious boundaries.

The affirmation of a Buddhist narrative implied exclusion by religious affiliation. The highlighting of this differentiation is seen in Jimbadorji's analysis of the world. He begins with those closest to home, the Oirads to the west and the Kazakhs and other Turks who also live there; he then goes further afield, describing the Russians and Swedes. This is followed by the fantastical groups drawn from Chinese literature such as the dog-headed people, horse-headed people and so on. So, as they are located farther from the center, groups become more and more fantastic and beyond the pale. Nevertheless, whereas great narrative attention is devoted to these faraway peoples, closer to home and about whom more is known are succinctly reduced to the bare essentials.

Concerning the Turkic Muslims of Inner Asia, Jimbadorji provides only a cursory description, and unlike earlier sources, he does not mention the fact that the rulers of Turkestan were supposed to be descendants of Chaghadai, Chinggis Khan's third son.[21] Instead of trying to produce a genealogical link with Chinggis Khan and the Mongols, however thin or dubious, he summarily dismisses the Turks of Inner Asia with the concluding comment, "As for the Turkestanis, they are a people without the majestic pure Dharma."[22] In this way, although the Turks of Inner Asia were a part of the Qing state, and perhaps even part of the Mongol genealogical imagination, they were not considered part of the constructed transethnic Buddhist Qing.

The division between these two religious groups is also heightened through Jimbadorji's inclusion of a lengthy description and history of Shambhala, just prior to his history of the Mongols.[23] Shambhala is the mythic Buddhist kingdom that preserves the Buddhist teachings, particularly the *Kālacakratantra,* while barbarians, most often identified as Muslims, overrun the world. After these barbarians are ultimately victorious and the Dharma has become extinct, the twenty-fifth king of Shambhala, Kalkin Raudra Cakrin, will ride forth with his Buddhist army, annihilate the enemies and usher in a new age of pure Buddhism.[24] While the Shambhala legend has had a long history outside of Mongolia, it is only during the beginning of the nineteenth century that it appears within Mongolian histories.

Invariably one must wonder why the Mongols began appropriating this myth during the early nineteenth century. It is likely that its adoption was fueled in part by the work of the Sixth Panchen Lama Lozang Penden Yeshé (1738–1780), who popularized the myth of Shambhala through a poem expressing the wish to be born there,[25] as well as by writing the most famous guidebook to Shambhala *(Sambha-la'i lam yig).*[26] And one measure of the Mongol enthusiasm for this work is reflected in the fact that three of the Sixth Panchen Lama's poems are known to have been translated into Mongolian,[27] and a Mongolian work paralleling his guidebook was prepared as early as 1828.[28] Moreover, in this Mongolian version of the Shambhala legend, and in Jimbadorji's work, the enemies threatening the Dharma are clearly identified as the Muslims who live in the city of Mecca,[29] whence the Muslims threaten not only particular people, nations, or states, but the Dharma as a whole: "From that time [of Muhammad] till now those Muslims' false view has gradually spread. Of the people of Jambudvīpa the majority are [now] Muslim."[30]

Of course, in such texts what being Muslim entails is never fully explained. The only specific example of their evilness is the manner in which they prepared meat products, reflecting a dispute that existed already in the Empire period. According to Mongol slaughtering practices, an animal's blood was not permitted to be spilled on the ground, which produced the Mongol practice of killing animals by rupturing the aorta. This practice is the complete opposite of *halal* regulations, where the blood is supposed to pour out of the severed neck. One dire consequence of this dispute occurred when a group of Muslims refused to eat the meat offered at a Mongol banquet, in response to which Khubilai Khan issued an edict in January 1280 prohibiting *halal* practices and imposing the death sentence on violators.[31]

It was therefore in regard to the part played by food rituals in religiocultural identification that gave rise to the differentiation between Islam and Buddhism.[32] This representation is the one employed to highlight the distinction between these two groups: "According to those Muslims, they say that you cannot eat the meat of animals that die naturally. To kill an animal according to their own wrong view, one will be saved if, while cutting the neck with a knife, you recite once the Lord's *dhāraṇī*, Bismillah."[33]

Although the ritualization of food is one form of differentiation,[34] in Buddhist works it is also common to find Muslims represented as the antithesis of civilized Buddhism. This attitude is first found in Buddhist works in India, especially the *Kālacakratantra,* which was composed at a time of increased conflict between Muslims, Hindus and Buddhists.[35] Nevertheless, it continued within the Buddhist tradition, as is evident in the Fifth Dalai Lama's *History of Tibet,* wherein he describes the situation in Inner Asia just before the introduction of Buddhism to Mongolia: "At that time, those countries which had become more barbaric than even barbarian (countries), were like the kingdoms of the Muslims."[36] While we may ironically note in this passage the presence of "oriental orientalism," it is important also to see in the Great Fifth's representation that the Muslims, as a community, are considered the epitome of barbarism and backwardness, an implied evil that potentially threatens the Dharma.[37]

Of course, this representation reflects the fate of Buddhism in the course of the Islamization of India and central Asia, a process of conversion that was no doubt lengthy and complex, yet one that certainly colored Buddhist representations of Islam. One such representation is already found in the eschatology of the eleventh-century *Kālacakratantra:* "Adam, Noah and Abraham; there are also five others endowed with tamas in the family of demons and snake: Moses, Jesus, the White-Clad One, Muhammad and Mathanī—the eighth—who will belong to the darkness. The seventh will clearly be born in the city of Baghdad in the land of Mecca, where the mighty, ferocious idol of the barbarian, the demonic incarnation, lives in the world."[38] Indeed, this view was probably reinforced through Islamic polemics and attacks against Buddhism, which are succinctly summarized in a Turkic folk song about the Karakhanid attack on the Uygur Buddhist kingdom of Turfan, recorded in Al-Kashgari's twelfth-century dictionary.

> We came down on them like a flood,
> We went among their cities,
> We tore down the Buddha temples,
> We shat on the Buddha's head![39]

And indeed, this song reverberates through the ages to our own time, as attested in the Taliban's recent destruction of the two large Buddha statues at Bamiyan.

Nevertheless, the appearance of these references to Islam and its growing threat in relation to the Buddhist Qing must be placed within an appropriate historical context. In particular, we need to look at some of the possible socio-political influences that inspired the Panchen Lama in the 1770s to begin drawing upon the deep reservoir of Shambhala mythology in the Tibetan tradition, as well as its subsequent resonance among not only the Mongols but also the larger Buddhist Qing community.

The Qing conquest of East Turkestan in 1759 might appear to be the most obvious factor in this regard. It was the last piece of territory incorporated into the Manchu's imperial project and was given the name Xinjiang, meaning "New Dominion." The conquest had taken nearly a century. In 1757 the Qing finally defeated the Oirad Zunghars, and two years later crushed the final resistance of Muslim leaders of Altishahr. Thus for the first time the Qing found itself the rulers of an enormous territory inhabited mainly by Turkic Muslims. In general, however, the Qianlong emperor took a rather hands-off approach to this buffer region, allowing Islam to be practiced while the state set about to maintain an orderly society in order to promote trade.[40] This policy was rather successful, and Turkic Muslim resistance to the Qing was minimal.[41] So initially the conquest and subsequent rule of Xinjiang does not seem to be the most important element in resurrecting the Shambhala myth and its specter of fear and Muslim hordes. Rather, its appearance is more likely linked to another event, one perhaps more pertinent for both the Mongols and the Qing—the appearance of a new revivalist strain of Naqshabandi Sufism in northwest China among the Hui in the 1760s.[42]

Islam and the Qing State

The Hui had long since transformed their religious practices and community into a localized Sino-Islamic one[43] and had for centuries worked within the shifting political winds emanating from Beijing. In the 1760s, however, a *shaikh* named Ma Mingxin (1719–1781) returned from studying in Mecca and Yemen, where, at the time, an intellectual revolution was taking place. This was the time of *tajdid,* or renewal movements such as that of Muhammad b. 'Abd al-Wahhab, the founder of the Salafist movement, which stretched from western Africa to China and focused primarily on a return to a "pure Islam." This involved not only purging the tradition of perceived "cultural accretions," but also creating a righteous Islamic state ruled by *shar'ia* law. Thus, when Ma Mingxin returned to the Qing domains in 1761, the goal of his form of Naqshabandi Sufism was purification and revitalization on Middle Eastern models.

Upon his return, Ma Mingxin was successful in enlisting converts in the local community, not least because of his zeal and ideas, but also because he carried the legitimacy of having studied in the West. He knew both Arabic and

Persian, unlike many local religious leaders, who had forgotten it long ago. Thanks to such academic credentials and to old grievances in the Muslim community concerning the power of hereditary *shaikh* lineages, monetary disputes and other matters, Ma Mingxin's following continued to expand. For a while, the tensions within the community remained internal. Debates over doctrinal and ritual minutiae led to local violence between the traditional community and the new converts of Ma Mingxin. However, in reaction to the growing militarization of these groups and the escalating violence, the Qing eventually became involved with this essentially theological dispute between the Khafiya ("Silentists") and Jahriya ("Aloudists").

As the names make clear, the dispute between these two groups began over whether *dhikr* recitation should be done aloud or silently to oneself. When this specific dispute over Islamic ritual, and others such as the veneration of saints and tombs, became embroiled in other economic, social and political issues, the violence escalated. In assessing the situation the Qing court deemed Ma Mingxin and his followers heterodox and a threat to the state; and it was in this context that the Qing policy of universalism was put to its greatest test.

Prior to the 1760s, although Chinese officials had repeatedly petitioned the court to outlaw Islam entirely in the empire, the Manchu emperors had maintained that Islam fell within the bounds of civilization and that Muslims should receive the same treatment as all imperial subjects. However, as the Qing became more involved on one side of this internal theological dispute, the imperial rhetoric did not necessarily accord with actions on the ground. This resulted in an upward spiral of communal and state violence and the subsequent or tandem growth of the supposedly "anti-Qing" Jahriya. Moreover, on account of Qing bureaucratic malfeasance the local economies of Muslim areas were devastated, and this further spurred the escalating spiral of communal and state violence. Tensions were further exacerbated when in violation of Qing universalist theory the court began implementing laws that discriminated against Muslims based solely on their religion.

The Board of Punishments passed the first of these laws in 1762. It mandated that all Muslim leaders had to report any inappropriate behavior within their community to the authorities, and local officials had to report Muslim criminal acts to the state authorities. As might have been expected, court records began to fill with Muslim acts of criminality, and local officials inundated the court with reports of Muslim bandits and their intrinsic propensity for violence. In response, the Qing authorities became more suspicious and drafted further regulations concerning Muslims. Thus Muslims found in groups of three or more with any weapon were immediately considered criminals. In the 1770s, the Qing court even created a new criminal act/category, *dou'ou* (brawling) that

could be used as a pretence to arrest Muslims specifically. As an inevitable result, Muslims who initially might not have sided with the Jahriya teachings
joined them in protesting Qing policy, thus further reinforcing the Qing's fear of
a growing Islamic anti-Qing movement. The burgeoning mutual animosity
reached a climax in 1781, when a Qing official, sent to quell a local disturbance
between Khafiya and Jahriya groups, informed one group whom he thought
were Khafiya that the Qing would exterminate all followers of the Jahriya tradition. To his dismay, his audience turned out to be Jahriya followers, and they
summarily executed him.

With the death of a Qing official at the hands of the Jahriya, the internecine
violence moved to a new level, that of "rebellion." In official discourse such a categorization mandated a swift and brutal response by the Qing state. What ensued
was a systematic "pacification" campaign to restore social order; and because it
was directed by local leaders who, in trying to impress the court, were overly
zealous in killing perceived enemies of the state, the violence again spiraled out
of control, and a new Muslim rebellion was launched in 1784.

At this turn of events the Qianlong emperor was baffled, and he wrote in a
letter to one of his ministers: "Why would Muslims from far and near join up
and follow them like sheep? . . . did news of Li Shiyao's investigations of Muslims leak out, so rebels could start rumors flying of [a government campaign to]
'exterminate Muslims' as an excuse to incite riots? I have thought of all these
things, but none seems to be the true reason. In the end, why did they rebel? We
must get to the bottom of this!"[44] Whether they got to the bottom of it is unknown. What is clear is that the 1784 rebellion was suppressed, and as an in-
terim solution the Qing instituted a virtual military occupation of the northwest.
And although it held the peace for the next half-century, when Qing forces had
to move south in the 1850s to fight the growing Christian Taiping rebellion, internal and external violence later erupted again in the northwest, culminating in
the devastating Muslim rebellions of the 1860s and 1870s.

It is within the context of this course of events—the introduction of a revivalist Islam, the official categorization of Muslims as violent and anti-Qing, the
subsequent spiraling cycle of violence and the militarization of northwest
China—that the appearance of the Shambhala myth in Mongol sources should
be situated.[45] On account of these events and the tensions created along the
boundaries of these two religious communities, it is understandable that Buddhists identified Muslims as the hard boundary of group identification.[46] The
Mongol "othering" of Islam in this context opened the door to a transethnic formation of a Buddhist Qing that was reinforced through their mutual animosity
toward the Muslims, who were threatening the very stability of the Buddhist
Qing.[47]

While we have seen that this conceptualization exists in Jimbadorji's *Crystal Mirror,* this development can also be found in the 1835 *Pearl Rosary.* The author even asserts for the first time that Chinggis Khan was born in a time of many Muslims.

> Thus Temüjin grew up and spread in the great way prophesied by the Buddha Teacher and [as found] at the end of *Mañjuśrī's Root Tantra,*[48] which says [it will happen] when there are various types of Muslims. And [he would] become famous as an Incarnation of Vajrapāṇi, Lord of the Secret, as decreed by the All-knowing Panchen Jewel, "He is the leader of this good Kalpa, Because the Secret Lord, for all time, has supported this world, and becoming an imperial body with completed great power, and being named Chinggis Tengri, Vajrapāṇi, Glorious Secret Lord, came and took an emperor's form. As a result he is a trustworthy and worshipful object of worship.[49]

What is important to note in this passage is that there is no reference to the Mongol *ulus.* Chinggis Khan is only represented within a Buddhist discourse, as Vajrapāṇi, who will invariably crush the Muslim heathens.[50]

This narrative form already alludes to a link between the Mongols and Shambhala, but this affiliation is further advanced through the prophecy being made by the Panchen Lama, as he was a pivotal figure in the Shambhala legend. Not only was the Sixth Panchen Lama integral to the revival of the Shambhala myth, but the second incarnation in the long line of Panchen Lamas was Mañjuśrīkīrti, the ruler of Shambhala who organized the disparate teachings of the *Kālacakratantra* into a systematic whole and was thus the first Kulika, "Holder of the castes," ruler of Shambhala.[51]

Through this prophecy, and the birth of Chinggis Khan at the time of many Muslims, an overt connection is made between the Mongols and Shambhala. Other texts take this idea even further by creating a genealogical link between Chinggis Khan and the Shambhala kings, all of whom are identified as incarnations of Vajrapāṇi.[52] Either way, however, what is important to note here is that both of these representations obviate Chinggis Khan's exclusive relation to the Mongol community; he is instead associated with the greater Buddhist community as a protector of the faith. In this way, the Mongols are not only ineluctably part of the larger transethnic Buddhist world but are also differentiated within the Buddhist ecumene, not through being Mongols, but as being affiliated with Shambhala.

The Mongols are thus the vanguard of the multiethnic Qing in the duty of protecting the Buddhist community—which was none other than the multiethnic Buddhist Qing. And, indeed, the historical record shows that the Mongols remained steadily loyal in the face of the Taiping and Muslim uprisings against the Qing. Mongols such as the general Senggerinchen also fought valiantly against Western military threats to the Qing. Many others, as previously seen, also participated in the Boxer Rebellion and other anti-Christian movements.[53]

In nationalist historiography this loyalty to the Qing has invariably been interpreted as a sign of passivity and social degeneration. But it can also be viewed as an active response to threats directed toward the Buddhist ecumene. As we have seen, ever since the seventeenth century the Mongols had identified themselves with the Buddhist Qing. Thus, when it was under attack from both internal and external forces it is not surprising that they fought to the death to preserve what they understood to be the natural order.

Localization within Universalization

The transformation of Buddhism from a mere element in the distinct ethnonational conceptualization of the Mongols to a component in forging the transethnic Qing reflects a shift in communal boundaries. In particular, the boundaries of the distinct ethnonational unit, the Mongol *ulus,* begin to blur. There is a slippage in the representation of the Mongol *ulus* to the point where its distinctiveness is dispersed and superseded by the multiethnic Buddhist community of the Qing. However, it is in tandem with, or in relation to, the weakening cohesion of the imagined Mongol community that we also find Mongol identity once again identifying with localized communities.

Although these two developments may seem incongruous—the simultaneous adoption of a larger community and a localized one—they were in fact intertwined responses to the dispersal of a Mongol identity within the empire of the Buddhist Qing. Indeed, as Appadurai has shown, localization in the form of the constructing of local identities is a common response to globalization and transnationalization.[54] This is not to suggest that we can draw direct parallels between these two historical developments, but rather to highlight the fact that these two apparently contradictory phenomena—universalization and localization—can and do in fact occur simultaneously. As in the case of the Mongols, when the distinct Mongol *ulus* began to disperse within the larger Buddhist Qing, Mongol identity was preserved in terms of local identification.

Again, this was not an entirely new development, as Mongol histories had always focused on the local. Yet while doing so, earlier authors had always maintained the superstructural framework that recognized only the history of the elites, the descendants of Chinggis Khan, who ultimately represented the cohesive reality of the Mongol *ulus.* What happened in the nineteenth century is that this cohesiveness was challenged. In particular, these ruling elites became more and more dissociated from the whole, and less identified as representatives of the Mongol *ulus* than of the specific banner they ruled. Even more remarkable, however, was the fact that this transformation included not only the Mongol nobility but all the inhabitants of the local banner, including the commoners.

To understand the full import of this development it is vital to recall that Mongol society was rigidly stratified between the hereditary Chinggisid aristocracy and the tax-paying commoners under their control.[55] These were the people who, according to Qing law, were identified as the "black people" (kharachins). It was only the pure, "white"-colored aristocracy, the Taijis, who were ever understood as actually being representatives of the Mongol *ulus*. Even though this social stratification had clearly long been a part of Mongol society, it certainly gained new impetus from the Qing project of ornamentalism. It was also legitimated by the standard Qing-period Buddhist ethnogenesis narrative, wherein the "original" people, the Bede,[56] only became fully formed after they were ruled by a descendant of the Mahāsammata lineage. This Buddhist narrative therefore mythologized the strict social stratification of Mongol society whereby only the Taijis, the descendants of Börte Chino-a and Chinggis Khan, were full members of the Mongol community who rightfully ruled over the lesser commoners, the amorphous, rulerless and thus senseless Bede (or Kharachin).

As a result, we need to keep in mind that the very idea of "the Mongols" as we have been using it referred only to the hereditary nobility. The rest were the tax-paying subjects and commoners, the "black people." What happened in the nineteenth century, however, is that this distinction began to weaken as everyone began to identify with the local banner regardless of class. Indeed, as can be seen in the above quoted letter, it was a union of noblemen and commoners from Üüshin banner who attacked members of Otog banner.

This newfound unity between the social classes of the banner was in no small part due to the Qing institution of the banner. Not only had the banner earlier been a powerful tool in redefining Mongol communal boundaries, but later in the nineteenth century it also became the fixed unit of identification. That this later development occurred was clearly the result of Qing policy, which maintained the banners as distinct geopolitical units. The Bureau of Colonial Affairs thus compiled genealogical records based on the structure of the banner system. Moreover, the conceptualization of the banner as a distinct and identifiable unit was reinforced through the Qing project of mapping and ordering the Mongols into these geographically defined units, as seen in the letter quoted above.[57]

And thus, with the Qing institutionalization of the banner as a defined and bounded community, it is necessary to explore how this entity came to be understood and represented by the Mongols themselves.

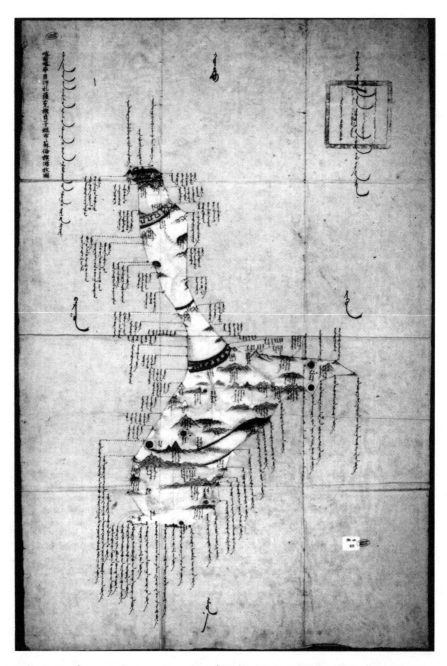

MAP 2. Gombosurun Banner. Courtesy of Bildarchiv Preussischer Kulturbesitz/Art Resource NY.

Banner Narratives and Rituals

One work that sheds light on the strategies employed in the production of new banner identities is a collection of addresses, used almost as a toastmaster's guide, for specific rituals within the Ordos' political calendar. These include addresses made to the prince of the banner after returning from Beijing or a Buddhist pilgrimage; speeches while he is reviewing the troops of his banner; or ritual pronouncements for the yearly ceremony of "opening the seal." In all of these, there is a rather standard panegyric opening passage that captures well the transformation toward localization. In particular, it reflects a shift away from the genealogical connection with the Mongol Buddhist *ulus* of the ruling lineages to that of the geopolitical unit of the banner.

The addresses all begin by praising the respective banner prince, identifying him as a deity who, out of his compassion, came to this world in order to guide the wayward individuals of his banner. The prince is then identified within the descent lineage of all the great Buddhist rulers beginning with the original ruler, Mahāsammata, followed by the great kings of Tibet, then Chinggis Khan. The prince is also clearly identified as inferior to the Manchu emperor, who is an incarnation of Mañjuśrī, the Bodhisattva of Wisdom. Yet what is relevant to note is that, within this mythic representation of the Buddhist community and Buddhist rule, there is a transformation in the representation of the history of Buddhism in regard to localized rule.

> Contents of an address spoken to His Highness the Prince of Government, who while residing in the region of the Perfectly Rejoicing, was born and especially incarnated in the region of this revolving existence in order to protect and unite the living beings of the stable world:
>
> Taking his roots from the Holy Chinggis Khan who had great glory and who strongly flourished with splendor, there came Batu Möngke Dayan Khan: from that period rose (one) incarnation of the flamboyant White God, known as Barsubolod Sayin Alag Jinong: sitting (on his throne) he ruled over the Ordos Tümen known as the Western Three; the rebellious and the wicked he assembled under his control and made them walk by the law of the Holis, and greatly expanded the Religion of the Buddha. Your Highness, our Lord, descendent of that Holy One [Chinggis], has propagated in all Ten Quarters the Religion of the second great Victor, the Holy Tsongkhapa perfectly adorned by the dance of the Golden Yellow [sect of the Gelugpa]; in accordance with the Law, strengthening your vast laws and regulations, you let all your people enjoy a full measure of peace. As a present for (this occasion when) we rejoice with a happiness (equal to that)

of a Blessed Heaven, we offer our brandy having the qualities of rasayana
and deliver this address . . .[58]

In the narrative of this ritual in honor of the banner prince, who as the head of
the ruling lineage represents the banner as a whole, Buddhist history is framed
only in relation to the formation of a localized identity.

This presentation, while operating in the production of the larger Buddhist
Qing as manifested in all the ruling bodhisattva lineages of the Mongol nobility,
also dissociates these lineages from the Mongol community and instead incar-
nates them in terms of the localized unit of rule. The banner prince is thus not
portrayed as a representative of the Mongol community, but as a deity who
deigned to return to earth in order to rule over his banner within the Buddhist
realm of the Manchu emperor. Thus, although this ritual confirms the Buddhist
Qing framework, the power of the prince is still shaped within the local context.
In addition, by the power of the prince being linked to the genealogical imagination of the Mongol *ulus,* the ritual reaffirms the reality of the local community.

It does this by initiating the community's history with the Buddhist rule of
Barsubolod Jinong, the third son of Dayan Khan and first ruler of Ordos. It is irrelevant that no evidence supports the notion that Barsubolod had any relations
with Buddhism; what matters is that this is the narrative adopted at this time.[59]
With the dispersal of the Mongol *ulus* throughout the transethnic Buddhist Qing,
Mongol identity was no longer bound solely to the Mongol *ulus,* but was nonetheless shaped in terms of the local. Moreover, within the Buddhist Qing, differentiation is indicated by an intermediate identification with the localized Ordos,
as seen in the representation of Buddhist rule beginning with Barsubolod Jinong's reign over the Yeke Juu League. No attempt is made to reconstruct the exclusive Mongol Buddhist *ulus* by tracing the genealogical links through Chinggis
Khan and Khubilai Khan, much less Altan and Ligdan Khan. Instead, the narrative and its ritualization of power are based solely on the local community.[60]

Another ritual pronouncement offers the same narrative:

Contents of an address spoken to His Highness the Prince and Lord resem-
bling Esrua-Tengri [i.e., the god Brahma], who while residing in the region
of the Pure Tuṣita, in order to govern and protect all his living beings, came
down as an incarnation upon the region of the Jambuling where the vast
precious Religion has established itself: Through eminently perfect merits
excellently accumulated ever since early and incomparable times, (some-
one) acquired magical power and majesty of manifaceted [sic] and unhindered intelligence, and in the era of the very first kalpa became born as an
incarnation in the central region of India known as Magadha; he became fa-

mous as Menggurbi Khan with the vast and perfect glory; he governed and guided all his living beings and gave them harmony according to a pure and just law. After he had let the noble race of the very virtuous qans spread out, coming by the region of vast Snowy Tibet he became famous as the first Universal Ruler "Having the Necks (of his bearers) as his Throne," and administered in a superior manner Religion and Government.

After (a series of successors) had come shining with full perfection, there came Batu Möngke Dayan Khan taking his root from the Holy Chinggis Khan who strongly flourished with splendor and had great glory; after that period arose one incarnation of Flamboyant White God known as Barsu-bolod Sayin Alag Jinong: sitting (on his throne) he was lord over the Ordos tümen known as the Western Three; the rebellious and the wicked he assembled under his control and made them walk by the law of the Saints; and he greatly propagated and raised the Religion of Buddha. Your Highness, our Lord, descendant of that Holy One [Cinggis], has propagated and raised the religion of the Sutras and the tantras of the great second victor the Saintly Tsongkhapa perfectly adorned through the dance of the Golden Yellow [sect of the Gelugpa].[61]

In this text, the local Mongol ruler is again represented as a divine emanation ruling a bounded local community—namely Ordos, or the Yeke Juu League of Inner Mongolia, "founded" by Barsubolod Jinong. In this way, the Mongol *ulus,* as represented in the Qing-appointed ruling lineages, became diffused as the narratives and rituals of these ruling lineages were transformed in terms of localization.

One result of this development was that, within the rhetorical matrix of community ethnogenesis, there was a move away from the representation of the Mongols as a whole, and toward the local. And while this new local identity may still have been identified as the microcosm of the larger Mongolian community through synecdoche (where the part stands for and functions as the whole), there was nevertheless a growing shift from the larger Mongol community to that of the localized banner. As reflected in the letter of 1904 quoted above, these new conceptualizations were not only symbolic but also played a role, along with the fact of diminishing resources and Chinese colonization, in generating violence between these new communities of identification.

Of course, the fact that the banners became the new boundaries of communal identification is not surprising, as this development was certainly promoted through the bureaucratic structure of the Qing. Not only did the court maintain the genealogical imagination of the banner through its record keeping, but the banner was in fact the recognized unit within the governmental framework. As a result, a growing sense of community in terms of the banner developed among the Inner Mongols. One aspect of this shift is seen in the nineteenth-century histories that avoid the repetition of the endless Mongol genealogies that represent the Mongol community in its entirety and instead record only the history of their own distinct banner. This move displaced not only the Mongol *ulus* as represented by all the ruling lineages, but also created the foundation for a new dual Mongol representation between the larger transethnic Buddhist Qing and the banner.

Banners, Geography and Buddhist History

Although the Manchu court's division of the Mongols into different banners is found in earlier works, the banners in those works were only political divisions within the more important genealogical lineages of the Mongol *ulus*. The banners, as represented by the genealogical descendants of the Borjigid nobility, did not impinge upon the perceived unity of the Mongols as represented in these local banner rulers. However, in the nineteenth century, the ruling Chinggisid lineages that were seen previously as a measure of Mongol cohesion became instead the medium for which localization at the banner level was produced. As seen in the ritual exhortations cited above, the appropriation of historical elements was dissociated from the totality of the Mongol *ulus* that was critical to earlier Mongol historians, and the histories instead revolve around the formation of a localized Buddhist history, in this case, Ordos.

In addition to the Qing's mapping projects and the institutionalization of the banner as a political unit, a further factor that fostered this identification with specific localities was the Mongols' growing awareness of both their own and world geography.[62] While this awareness greatly expanded the horizon of Mongol histories so that they included Xinjiang, Russia and even Sweden, it also generated a conceptual disconnect between land and people. As described above, *ulus* had earlier been understood as a systematic whole, a natural ethnoterritorial space. In the nineteenth century this changed as a distinction arose between the people and the actual land they inhabited.

Nineteenth-century Mongol histories therefore adopt the term *oron*, "land," as opposed to *ulus*. Buddhist histories thus begin to interpret the history of the Dharma in terms of when it came to the Tibet *oron*, the Mongol *oron*, and not necessarily to the Mongols and Tibetans.[63] This may be seen as a minor linguistic detail, but it in fact betokens a profound shift in Mongol conceptualizations of space and place.[64]

In particular, the dissociation of "ethnicity" from geography not only fostered the idea of a multiethnic Qing but also enabled Mongol identity to be localized to the specific territory of residence.[65] These shifts in ideas about space were presumably both influenced by the new geographical discourses of the eighteenth century and greatly fostered by Qing policies of land rights and taxation policies that reinforced the distinction between land and people. Nevertheless, both of these realities acted in tandem to generate this new Mongol concept of community that was focused on both the larger Qing community and the banner.

However, since the above example focused on Ordos, which was not a banner but a league consisting of seven banners, it is necessary to look at how the narratives and rituals of a specific banner manifested themselves. In the two previous ritual texts, the focus was on Ordos as evidenced in the reification of the Buddhist rule of Barsubolod Jinong, the first appointed Dayan Khanid ruler of Ordos. After his elder brother, Abakhai, had been assassinated, Barsubolod was appointed *jinong* in 1512 over the Three Western Ulus consisting of the Ordos, Tümed, and the Yüngshiyebü. After Barsubolod's death, his eldest son, Gün Bilig Mergen, was made *jinong,* though his power did not include all three *ulus,* but only the Ordos. In the fragmented political landscape of the sixteenth century, Altan Khan and his descendants controlled the Tümed, and the Yüngshiyebü were under the control of Bayaskhal Kündüli Khan, Altan Khan's younger brother. Yet, be that as it may, Gün Bilig had nine sons. The eldest, Noyandara, became *jinong* upon his father's death in 1544, and the other brothers were given appanages of their own within the Ordos *ulus.* The title "jinong" was then handed down in primogeniture to Boshugtu Jinong (1565–1624) and Erinchen Jinong (d. 1656), who as leader of Ordos submitted to the Manchus in 1635. After their submission, the Mongols of these Three Western Tümen were reorganized into six banners, each of which was headed by the descendants of Gün Bilig's nine sons.[66]

As a result of Qing ornamentalism and its elevation of the Dayan Khanid lineage, all of the ruling lineages of the banners in Yeke Juu League therefore traced their descent from their ancestor and the original ruler of Ordos, Barsubolod. Moreover, in accord with the discourse of the Buddhist Qing, he was lionized as a great Buddhist ruler. This is the representation found in all of the ritual exhortations in the extant collection of political addresses from Ordos. Since this manual was apparently used for all the ruling lineages of the Yeke Juu League, the historical narrative and the identification with Barsubolod is the same. However, there is one exception to this narrative frame—a wedding manual for a member of the nobility from Üüshin banner.

Coming before you with an auspicious speech in verse to express (our wishes) namely: as, upon the command of His Highness the Omniscient

Holy Jangjia, the blessings of the deceitless Lama Buddhas, the devotion and belief of us all, and the power of an exceedingly good thought have come together: by the power of the marriage alliance, may happiness of a long life and an occurence of glory expand:

Teacher Khanpo who lead us all, (your) son the Minister (with the rank of) Duke, and others, present (the following) request in the hope (that you will consider it):

At a certain time of this kalpa, when the living beings came to conceive such desires as greed and evil, and for the first time sinful deeds occurred, those with correct understanding deliberated saying that it would be advisable to make qayan one man able to punish the wicked and encourage the righteous, and they installed the Khan "Elevated by the Many." Thereafter in order to pacify the living beings of the region of Tibet and make religion prosper, the Bodhisattva Avalokitesvara became (the one) "with the necks (of his bearers) as his seat," and successors: in the region of the Chinese, Mañjuśrī took the appearance of the Emperor, but especially in the region of the Mongols, Vajrapāṇi became incarnated as Chinggis Khan: he repressed those who walked evilly and encouraged the righteous; in order not to let the manner by which they had made the Religion of the Buddha rise like the sun come to an end, the root like the constant flow of the Ganges River, uninterrupted, came (to us).

In the midst (of these developments) many came forth in the form of unusual (personalities) with power over men such as Batu Möngke Dayan Khan, Chogchas-un Jirüken[67] Khutugtai Sechen Khung-taiji and Sagang Sechen Khung-[taiji], who protected the Religion and the living beings and led (them) in a pure and just way.

Through sucession coming to the present time, Your Highness, too, with extraordinarily excellent intelligence and power expanded with an incomparable great perfection; where the Religion had previously flourished in this Banner, you have made it rise even higher, and where it had not yet flourished you have increased its splendor; following the rules you have cared for the eminently important Government (of the Banner), and have on many occasions brought peace and delivered the multitude from all sufferings and harassments which in the present era have from time to time cropped up.[68]

While this text reaffirms the transethnic Buddhist community of the Qing through the Bodhisattva trinity, Avalokiteśvara (Tibet), Mañjuśrī (China) and

Vajrapāṇi (Mongolia), it also simultaneously presents a localized narrative bound exclusively to Üüshin banner.

Üüshin Banner beyond Social Hierarchies

The localized focus on Üüshin Banner is reflected in this text by its inclusion of a history that is different from both the larger Mongol narrative and that of Ordos. In particular, this Üüshin text ignores Barsubolod and instead glorifies the Buddhist activities of Khutugtai Sechen Khung Taiji and Saghang Sechen. On account of the genealogical connection between these two and the southern Üüshin nobility,[69] headed by Baljur and Ragbajamsan, it may be possible to surmise that this strategy may have arisen out of sympathetic connections and was limited only to these noble descendants.[70] While this may be true for this particular ritual text, there is evidence to suggest that the appropriation of Khutugtai and Saghang Sechen was not limited to their direct descendants. Rather, this appropriation transcended these class boundaries. These two individuals were invoked by all the inhabitants of southern Üüshin in both histories and rituals as a confirmation of their localized identity.

One piece of evidence in this regard is found in a *julag* ritual text that was used at a public horse race held at the banner level. In his work on these rituals, Serruys published two texts from Ordos, one from Jungar banner, and another from Üüshin banner. Although the ritual contents of the two texts are essentially identical, the personages incorporated into the pantheon receiving libations vary. Most notably, the Jungar text makes no mention of Khutugtai and Saghang Sechen, while on the other hand the Üüshin text has several references to them.[71] All of the references place them within the pantheon just below Chinggis Khan, as is seen in the text's opening call for the deities to manifest themselves to receive their offerings.

> Invitation. Hey! Lamas perfect in benevolence, and titulary deities and assembly of the Buddha, all bodhisattvas with the Buddhas of the ten quarters, from your great peaceful palace in the Continent of Religion: on this day repair to the southernly sky! Śravakas and Pratyekabuddhas, heroes, Ḍākinī protectors of the Religion and the gods of possessions and treasures, gods of the horses and gods of the harvest: on this day repair all here to (this) place! Brahma and Indra; the eight great kings of the Nāgas; Lord Chinggis Khan, (his) queen, sons, and ministers; gZugs-can-sñin-po [Khutugtai] Sechen Noyan; Sagang Sechen Noyan; together with (your) retinue, repair all here to (this) place; all eight classes with the deities of (all) quarters of the earth, the assembly of the *ada* and *todqar* (demons), the ghosts

and the bodinar, and all those entitled to govern the offerings, on this day repair all to (this) place here.[72]

In this public ritual performed in Üüshin there is again the remembrance of these two individuals. They are not mentioned in the work from Jungar banner. It is possible to argue on the basis of this that Khutugtai and Saghang Sechen were not incorporated into the narratives and rituals of a certain Üüshin noble lineage, but were instead represented as the forebears of Üüshin banner as a whole, and were thus used to establish a localized identity, one that was in contradistinction to the other banners of Ordos.

The utilization of Khutugtai and Saghang Sechen in forming a localized Üüshin narrative is also evident in the unique folklore of Üüshin concerning these two, which portrays them as rebels against the Manchu state. This portrayal is based on two factors: during the Qianlong emperor's literary inquisition, Saghang Sechen's *Precious Summary* was prepared in an imperial edition, and several sections were deemed anti-Manchu and deleted;[73] in addition, nothing is known about Saghang Sechen after the completion of his work. These two facts provided fuel for the creation of stories representing Saghang Sechen as one who resisted the Qing and whose literary critique of Manchu power resulted in his extermination at the hands of the authorities. This representation, and its relation to the differentiation of Üüshin in regard to the other banners of Ordos, is found in one story that Mostaert recorded during his residence there.

In this tale, Saghang Sechen is identified as a good friend and relative of Erinchen Jinong. The *jinong* is portrayed as a powerful military chief who did not submit to Manchu rule (though of course he actually did in 1635), only to then be betrayed by his six sons (who are understood to be the six other banners of Ordos) and thus executed upon the order of the Manchu emperor. Later, Saghang Sechen, who continued the struggle of Erinchen Jinong, told his sons that when he died they were to surround his body with the roots of roses, and he would thereby be resuscitated and continue the struggle. Yet, in Beijing a court diviner informed the emperor of these events and the consequences of Saghang Sechen reviving, since he was both a friend of Erinchen Jinong and a rebel against the Qing state. As a result, they sent a lama to Üüshin to help with the burial ceremonies, and he convinced the sons not to put roses in the grave, but to surround the corpse with a copy of the Buddhist canon written in gold. The sons agreed and followed his advice, and as a result of this sacrilege, Saghang Sechen did not revive, and since then the people of Ordos have been born stupid, unhappy and under Manchu domination. A similar tale is also told about Khutugtai, who was supposed to be buried surrounded by the chaff of millet, but a Tibetan lama recommended in its place to use the wooden covers that protect volumes of the Kanjur, and as a result there was no reincarnation of Khutugtai.[74]

While these stories represent a powerful critique of the Mongols' submission to the Qing as a whole and the duplicitous role played by Gelukpa monks in this enterprise, it is important to note that they were found only among the Mongols of Üüshin. On the basis of this representation of Saghang Sechen and Khutugtai in Üüshin folklore, it is clear that the remembrance of these two individuals was not restricted to their genealogical descendants, but that the stories were diffused and part of the process of forging cross-class communal ties in Üüshin.

The first piece of evidence in this regard is a history, the *Shining Mirror (Gegen Toli)*, which describes exclusively the life of Khutugtai Sechen Khung Taiji and his Buddhist activities. The work is based largely on Saghang Sechen's *Precious Summary* and is thus not important in shedding new light on the history of Khutugtai, but it is significant as the first history to focus exclusively on him and his descendants. And although the colophon of this work does not inform us who created it or when, there is some evidence to suggest that the Üüshin official Gonchugjab wrote it in the 1830s. This supposition is based on mutual cross-referencing. In the *Shining Mirror* the reader is told to read the *Pearl Rosary,*[75] which no doubt refers to Gonchugjab's own *Pearl Rosary*. It, in turn, informs the reader that the activities of Khutugtai are elaborated in the *Shining Mirror*.[76] On the basis of these two passages, it is possible to conjecture that the author was the same, and similarly, that the two works were composed at approximately the same time in the 1830s to allow for this cross-referencing.

With this in mind, it is important to note that, shortly thereafter, a ritual text appeared that brought Khutugtai and Saghang Sechen into the pantheon of Buddhist deities. The text was for the worship of Chinggis Khan, and it was commissioned by an Üüshin nobleman and written by an Üüshin lama, Lubsangchoirag. In this work, a tantric visualization text, Khutugtai and Saghang Sechen, along with Chinggis Khan, are incorporated into the hierarchy of fierce protector deities of the Dharma.

> Upon a triangular precious throne in the middle of the billowing waves of the sea of blood surrounded by awesome mountains of red shale, [evoked] in front of oneself out of emptiness, and upon a carpet [adorned] with various lotus [flowers] and moons [stands] the heavenly lay disciple [Chinggis Khan] who originated from [the letter] *barim [bhrim]* and the spear [?]: the color of his body is red, with one face and two hands. [His face] perfected with three round eyes is shining; he has a yellow beard and brows. He bares his canine teeth; with the right hand he brandishes a red spear; his left, together with a threatening gesture, holds a lasso in front of his heart. They

have plaited his hair in a tress [hanging down] his back; on his head he is wearing a big helmet of turquoise; he is wearing a vest of green silk and hanging [from his shoulders], a long cape of flowered silk; he stands in a position with his right foot set back and his left set forward, he is installed in the middle of a blazing fiery hale.

For his companions, there are the gods, and the assembly of the eight classes of demons who are countless; to the southwest is *Chogchas-un jirüken Khutugtai Sechin Khung-taiji,* and to the south-east *Sagang Erke Sechin Khung-taiji:* the color of both is red, and their brows are joined. Their beards are green and beautiful. In their right hand they turn from left to right a prayer wheel filled with relics of the *Dharmakaya,* and in their left they hold in front of their hearts a rosary of white glass [beads] to count the six syllables. Their clothes are of the silk of the god. On their right side they carry a quiver of tiger [skin], and on their left, a bowcase of leopard skin. With both feet together they stand in a whirl of fire and wind. On top of the heads of their eminent followers there is a white [letter] *om;* on their throats there is a red *a,* and on their hearts a blue *hum,* and they bear the mark of the letter *barim.*[77]

This tantric representation is not only mentioned in the *Pearl Rosary*[78] but also parallels the narrative in the publicly performed *julag* ceremony. It can therefore be surmised that, at this time, there was a growing interest in appropriating Khutugtai and Saghang Sechen for the local narratives and rituals.

This idea is supported by the request of Baljur, a descendant of Khutugtai and head of the ruling family of southern Üüshin, to have the same lama, Lubsangchoirag, compose a ritual for the veneration of Saghang Sechen sometime after 1835.[79] In his edition of this work, Mostaert claims that this text was not produced ex nihilo, but was a reworking of a ritual that had long been practiced by the descendants of Khutugtai Sechen and Saghang Sechen. At present, this cannot be disproved, yet Mostaert presents no positive evidence for its earlier form. Moreover, the earliest evidence we have for such a ritual is 1821. In that year Tusalagchi Todai, a descendant of Saghang Sechen, had gone to Kumbum Monastery in Amdo and, after making an offering to the Panchen Lama, had a ritual text prepared for the worship of his ancestors Khutugtai and Saghang Sechen.[80]

As a result, it is important to note that the creation of this work coincided with the other works described above, all of which similarly incorporated Khutugtai and Saghang Sechen in producing a localized Buddhist history of Üüshin. It is therefore feasible to argue that at this time, the 1820s to 1840s, members of the southern Üüshin nobility, who were in fact genealogical descendants of these two individuals, began the affirmation of this particular narrative. Nevertheless, while this representation can be understood through sympathetic connections of the genealogical imagination of the nobility, it does not explain the public aspects of identifying with Khutugtai and Saghang Sechen as seen in the *julag* ritual and Üüshin folklore. Indeed, for the first time, the shift to localization included commoners. Earlier they had had virtually nothing to do with the Mongol *ulus,* since as it was imagined and represented by the Qing state and the elite themselves, it entailed only the Chinggisid nobility. However, as seen in these public ritual performances during the nineteenth century, the commoners actually came to be included in the new localized community.

This unification of the nobility and commoners within a new banner community was clearly fostered by the Qing bureaucratic system.[81] Not only were the nobility appointed to rule individual banners through the grace of the emperor, but the commoners themselves were also in turn bound to these entities through their affiliation with the prince. This relationship not only subjugated the commoners as tax-paying subjects of the banner prince, but by the dictates of the Qing state they were also bound to the geospatial community of the banner by birth. Qing authorities actually forbade movement from one banner to another.[82] The banner was indeed their geographically bounded community.[83] Thus, as the discourse of the nobility shifted its own boundaries toward the local, the commoners who shared the same geographic space were incorporated into the same narrative and communal conceptualization. In the case of southern Üüshin, one of the important factors that contributed to the creation of this localized identity was the production of narratives and rituals that appropriated Khutugtai Sechen and Saghang Sechen.

Social Hierarchy and the New Mongols

Although the process of employing Khutugtai and Saghang Sechen in the production of a local identity originated with the noble lineages and was ritually performed exclusively by them, over time the ritualization included the Üüshin population at large. This development is reflected in the two different versions of the ritual texts for the cult of Khutugtai, which Mostaert has identified as the "official" and the "popular." The official version was older and in the final part of the text, where the worshippers' requests for long life, prosperity, wealth and so on are expressed, those who receive these blessings are restricted to the nobility, the *taijis.* On the other hand, the more recent "popular" ritual text requests Khutugtai, who is represented as Vaiśravaṇa, the Buddhist Protector King of the North and God of Wealth, to bestow these blessings upon the commoners, the tax-paying subjects, *albatu irgen.*[84] Another ritual text for the worship of Saghang Sechen also includes this request for both the nobility and the commoners: "We together, the great and small, all, request the pacification of demons and ill-nesses. Make our lives longer!"[85]

As a result, the ritualization of Khutugtai and Saghang Sechen transcended Mongol social hierarchies, and instead operated as a "social cement" that was integral to the production of a local Üüshin solidarity.[86] A similar phenomenon has been noted in the construction of identities in a Japanese city, wherein present-day descendants of both elite and ordinary settlers have in common a "nativeness" "that now transcends historical status inequities and has been reified as a type of primordial solidarity."[87] In the case of Üüshin, this nativeness was reified through the symbolization of Khutugtai and Saghang Sechen as Üüshin's Buddhist "ancestors."

It was through such means that a localized narrative of communal affiliation was both produced and maintained by the people of Üüshin. This identity was confirmed particularly through the annual rituals performed for these two ancestors at their respective grave sites, during which all "citizens" of southern Üüshin were enabled to participate in remembering these two individuals within their own historical awareness. The importance of these sacred sites for the people of Üüshin is evident in references to them in the letters written in the early twentieth century by the *duguilang*, or "revolutionary circle" movement.[88]

The *duguilangs* originated in the 1820s for a variety of reasons, though in Ordos the main issue that fueled popular discontent and the activities of the movements were the issues of land and Chinese colonization, which were being facilitated by the perpetually bankrupt ruling nobility, who sold or rented land to Chinese settlers in order to pay their debts.[89] Nevertheless, as seen in the league chairman's letter, the *duguilang* groups were composed of a spectrum of social levels. Mostly their members were commoners, along with some low-ranking lamas and impoverished noblemen, who worked in unison in an attempt to protect their native pasturelands from Chinese immigration. As one letter to the Qing authorities declares: "This year, we, the numerous (subjects) of our banner have repeatedly declared that we have absolutely no other intention but to protect our land [ɣajar] and native country [nutuɣ oron-iyan]. We have also asked that you, please, kindly do us, insignificant populace, the grace not to be separated from our native land."[90] And it is in this context of Chinese colonization and issues of native land that two letters written by southern Üüshin *duguilangs* mention specifically the potential threat that settlers posed to the "graves and human remains venerated from early days."[91]

This reference is not found in the letters from the *duguilang* of other banners. The graves and human remains certainly refer to the Khutugtai and Saghang Sechen cult sites, and this fact provides evidence of how important these sites had become for the people of Üüshin. These sites and the ritualization of Üüshin's "ancestors" were integral to the creation of this new local identity. Thus it is clear that by the early twentieth century Üüshin local identity was no longer based solely on genealogy, but rather was linked to geography, in terms of the bounded administrative entity of the banner.[92]

It was therefore the geopolitical unit of the banner that became the framework for the Mongols' localized narratives of identification. Moreover, the representation of community ethnogenesis transcended the genealogical imagination of the nobility and instead was forged through the spatial orientation maintained by the Qing bureaucracy. As seen in the case of southern Üüshin and the appropriation of Khutugtai and Saghang Sechen for their communal narrative, the boundaries were drawn, not between the levels of Mongol society or different lineages, but between the geographical units of the banner. This shift is eloquently displayed in the work of the famous southern Üüshin writer Kheshigbatu (1849–1916).

In his prose and verse history of the Mongols, the *Precious Summary of the Past and Present,* Kheshigbatu's description of the Mongols during the Qing begins with their separation into banners.[93] Moreover, he dispenses entirely with the "standard" format of describing all the noble lineages that represent the Mongol *ulus* and focuses only on the descendants of Barsubolod and Gün Bilig Mergen Jinong—that is, the Ordos nobility.[94] In addition, when he does describe important personages, in particular those who helped to fight in uprisings against the Qing such as Senggerinchin, they are identified not by their genealogical lineages but as members of particular leagues and banners.[95]

The same phenomenon is also found in Jigmed-Rigbi-Dorji's 1819 *History of Buddhism in Mongolia (Hor chos-'byung)*[96] in which the author

> always speaks about himself as belonging to the Tümed Wing. In the colophon we also find: rang-re'i Thu-med sog "our Thu-med Banner." He calls the Thu-med "our banner" in the text, and we quote a few examples from among the many occurrences: rang-re'i Har-cher Thu-med sog. "Our Banner of the Har-cher Thu-med" (f. 116a 5; H I 208, II 328); Thu-med sog 'dir "to this Thu-med banner" (f. 129b; H I 230; II 363); sog 'di dang Mongol-cin dang Har-chen dang Nas-man "this (i.e., our) Banner and that of Mongolchin [the east wing of the Banner] and Har-chen and Nasman (=Naiman)" (H ibid.); Thu-med sog 'dir "in this Thu-med Banner" (f. 135b; H I 239, II 376); Thu-med sog 'di dang Mon-gol-cin gnis-su "In this Thu-med Banner and in that of Mongolchin both" (f. 144b: H I 254, II 400).[97]

Other histories, such as the *Ancient Dynasties and the Organization of Mongol Banners and Leagues,* focus less on the author's identification with his own banner than on simply confirming the contemporary reality of the banners within China's long dynastic history.[98] In this way, it is evident that, for Kheshigbatu, Jigmed-Rigbi-Dorji and other Mongols at the time, the main unit of identification for all levels of society was the banner, a tradition that indeed continues today in Inner Mongolia.[99]

Localized Identities and the Writing of History

On account of localization being based on the banner, new histories were written that confirmed this new reality. As seen in the case of Üüshin, a Buddhist history focusing on Khutugtai and Saghang Sechen was created. And this transformation is also found in another of Kheshigbatu's works, which was written on the occasion of the rebuilding of an Üüshin monastery that Hui Muslim rebels had burned down in 1868. The poem, "Praise of Yellow Monastery," dispenses entirely with the Mongol history of Buddhism and instead outlines the history of Buddhism solely in terms of Üüshin banner. At the same time, however, Üüshin Buddhism encapsulates the whole history of Mongolian Buddhism.

> As for Buddhism in this, our Üüshin,
> It was begun by the foremost holy Chinggis Khan.
> The benefit of this was great, and that Holy One is now
> Truly, Vajrapāṇi, the protector of the Dharma.

> Taizu Holy Chinggis Khan, Lord of the Worlds,
> Said to the marvelous supreme Kungga-Nyingbo of U-Dzang,
> "Let us be friends in the pleasing Dharma."
> Then the fifth Shizu Khubilai Sechen Khan implored

> To invite Pakpa Lama [to come] from the land of U-Dzang,
> Thus the traditional Dharma spread.
> However, [according] to true nature it gradually changed and was stopped
> By Toghan Temür Khan who was once full of meritorious deeds.

> Then Altan Khan, the Genius Holy Chinggis Khan's descendant,
> With Tsugchanningbo Sechen Noyan Baatur and the wise
> Sodnamjamsu, the Dharma Lord and Third Dalai Lama,
> Illuminated like the sun the yellow religion.

> Spreading ever more the Great Qing State rose to power,
> And firmly united the State and Religion.

Toghon Temür who was full of faith and merit
Built an immeasurable number of shrines and monasteries.
The Lords of the government, full of the wonderful standard's power,
Controlled the opposition and supported the Dharma.

Ordos Üüshin Banner's original lords,
In the center of a golden bowl of hazy prajñā,
As deigned by the government they built a wonderful
Monastery to house the Ganjuur.[100]

This shift in the history of Buddhism solely in regard to the banner reveals the radical effect of localization in the late nineteenth century. Buddhism was no longer employed as a distinct element of Mongol identity, but instead solely in terms of the banner. And this transformation captures well how the Mongols' adoption of localized identities developed in tandem with the dispersal of the Mongol *ulus* within the transethnic Buddhist Qing.

Moreover, the fact that the *duguilang* movements developed along these same lines further confirms these processes. Thus, although Chinese colonization threatened large areas of Inner Mongolia, in the earliest periods of resistance there was no concerted effort to protect the lands of the Mongol *ulus* in its entirety. Some of this may have been the result of the diverse actions of certain banner princes in relation to Chinese colonization. For example, the prince of West Baarin Banner refused to allow any of his banner's land to be sold for Chinese immigration.[101] On the other hand, Chagdursereng, the head of Üüshin banner and vice-chairman of the Yeke Juu League, proposed opening up all of Üüshin for Chinese colonization in order to ingratiate himself with the Manchu official Yigu at Suiyuan.[102] Even though these opposite responses were predicated on different circumstances, it is clear from the available material that the *duguilang*s were in fact concerned only with the fate of their own "native lands" of the banner, even to the extent that those of different banners feuded over claims to territory.[103]

The importance of the banner as the key unit of identification for the *duguilang*s is found in another of Kheshigbatu's poems that recounts the efforts of the Üüshin *duguilang*.

Living all time in the land of the banner of Üüshin,
(we) with other banners and friends and companions
murmured and made much noise around the "circles."
The name of their fame became a legend, celebrated.

But the whole banner suffered and the profit gained
in ten years, twenty-five thousand ounces,

was flippantly lost, it is sure, wasted without a proof,
and (I) was arrested in Barsukhai and suffered a stupid affair.

When the harassed people kindled firebrands,
Commander Tong Lin arrived with ten thousand soldiers.
His Lordship the ruling viceroy announced a merciful policy
and with harmonious means he let (them) return withdrawing.

The Jinong, the head of the government, investigated the case,
the Viceroy with the top [dignitaries?] calmly agreed [with him].
Seeing what happened, those at the Rich Hill and the Moist Land stopped.
The three circles of the south complained and shouted.

They clamored and mourned over losing earth and land.
A single affair arranged, (but even that became) funny and foul and pitiful!
Harshly blaming the benevolent superiors,
everybody recklessly grinds those who are helpful.

While the noble order (commands) to serve one's own master,
(they) say: This is a flatterer, and (they) slander [me].
Those who follow the right and pure order always have one (and the same)
    manner,
but the instigators of extremities, these villains of (mis)deeds

created the whole affair by the mercy of the leader of the banner of
    Khanggin.
The circle at the Monastery of Khali'utu resigned, dispersed and collapsed.
The many respectable circles, alas, (became) foul and funny!
To this lonely man, (to me), there happened various (unpleasant) things.

This is why the whole world laughed and back home
(people) told (this) to their wives and, enjoying peace, shared pleasure.

While Khesigbatu notes the existence of *duguilangs* in other banners, the focus
of the poem is the events and their consequences in Üüshin. This local focus on
the struggles of the Üüshin *duguilangs* therefore is a vivid example of the divide
between the idea of the Mongol *ulus* in its entirety and the more recent local
identities that transcended previous social boundaries.

The trajectory of Mongol concepts in the nineteenth century Qing must
therefore be placed within this framework. While in the eighteenth century

there had been a clear attempt to maintain the integrity of the Mongol *ulus* as represented in the ever-expanding noble lineages, over time this ideal began to disintegrate. In its place, Mongol identity came to be represented in the two directions allowed by the structure of the Qing state. One direction was toward the transethnic Buddhist Qing, wherein the Mongols constituted one group within the Buddhist Qing ecumene; and the other was toward the localized geopolitical entity of the banner. While both of these identities continued to operate within a Buddhist discourse, they were also dealing with the radical changes and upheavals of the nineteenth century. And it was these developments that explain why it was that in 1903 armed bands of noblemen and commoners of Üüshin and Otog banners were fighting one another over territorial claims, and simultaneously why Mongols fought together with Chinese and the Qing state against Muslim, Christian and Western imperialist threats to the Buddhist Qing.

Epilogue

*History often repeats itself. Before history repeats itself,
we need to investigate the true historical facts to find ways
out of the fate concocted by the distorted history.*
                    —Wu Cho-liu, *The Orphan of Asia*

Manchu policies in Mongol areas changed dramatically during the first decade of the twentieth century. This was especially the case with the 1906 reform of the Qing bureaucracy, which had far-reaching consequences for the Mongols of Outer Mongolia. These policies not only reformed and strengthened the administrative structure of Outer Mongolia, they also called for the deployment of large military forces to the northern border in order to halt Russian encroachment. Most important, however, was the Qing court's decision to open up Outer Mongolia to Han Chinese agricultural settlers. It was in regard to all these events and the pursuant feeling of impending doom that a group of Khalkha religious hierarchs and secular elites met in the summer of 1911.

The point of their meeting was to discuss the future—the "what ifs" and "then what" questions that were arising not only because of these policy changes but also the possibility of the impending fall of the Manchu Qing. The Mongol elite knew the dynasty was under enormous internal and external pressures and that it was slowly but surely coming apart; they had to prepare for the inevitable. In doing so they decided to write a letter to the Russian czar, Nicholas II, describing the situation as well as expressing their grievances against the Manchu Qing. The Eighth Jebdzundamba Khutugtu and the four Mongol khans of Outer Mongolia signed the letter.

The letter states that the Mongols, "submitting to the Manchu Emperor," have "dwelt in peace" for more than 200 years, but that "recently the Han Chinese bureaucrats have grabbed the political power [of the Qing] and have brought confusion and discord to the affairs of state." In particular, the letter goes on to say, "we cannot bear" the new policy of the government which was designed to "search out ways to turn Mongol land into farmland, which, if accomplished, will inevitably destroy our traditional way of life." "We followed the Manchu Emperor because he was a believer in Lamaism and a man of great compassion, but this turned out to be all talk

166

and no substance, with the result that our suffering has only increased over the years."[1]

Five months after sending this letter and two months after the anti-Qing uprising in Wuchang, the leaders of Outer Mongolia declared their independence. Mongolia entered the modern world as an independent theocratic Buddhist nation-state—the Mongol *ulus* being ruled by the Jebdzundamba Khutugtu, the incarnation of the first Indian ruler, "Elevated-by-the-Many," Mahāsammata.[2]

———◆———

History had apparently come full circle. Or had it? Perhaps it might be more accurate to say that it had spiraled back though it had changed its orbit. Thus, although the Khalkha nobility and the Gelukpa establishment invariably built their modern enterprise upon essentialized and primordial myths, in point of fact its very conceptualization partook of radically new ideas, such as race, ethnicity, anti-imperialism and the modern nation-state.[3] However, at the same time, much of what defined the new Mongol *ulus,* its communal boundaries, social structure, political framework and culture, did in fact derive from the discourses of late imperial China. The formation of modern Mongolia was thus, like the forging of the Qing, a process of engagement and transformation, deterritorialization and reterritorialization. And as was the case with the civil war of the early seventeenth century, the fall of the Qing resulted in reconceptualizations of what it meant to be Mongol and Buddhist, and how these concepts related to the various new competing states and their political formations.

Yet as had also occurred in the seventeenth century, there were differences of opinion on these matters. They involved not only the territorial boundaries of "Mongolia" and who was actually "Mongol," but also what role, if any, the Dharma should play in defining these entities. Thus, in contradistinction to the Khalkha religious and secular elites' call for a Buddhist theocracy, the Mongols of Eastern Inner Mongolia responded differently to the fall of the Qing and to the question of what it meant to be a Mongol in the modern world. Drawing upon the anticlericalism of the nineteenth century, they began to openly criticize the Dharma.[4] Some even began calling for its complete rejection, an idea that gained greater currency when the Japanese-educated Kharachin Lubsangchoidan (1874?–1929) published for the first time the fact that the *Urmongol* Chinggis Khan had, in fact, not been a Buddhist.

On the other hand, some, like Rinchinkhorlo, continued to support the Dharma but advocated the need for secular education in order to build a better future for the Mongols. Others rejected such modern ideas entirely and continued to support the defining role of religion in the public sphere. Some even supported a Qing imperial restoration. Others had more complex visions, such as the Ordos members of the People's Revolutionary Party of Inner Mongolia, whose manifesto declared that "the aim of the [revolutionary] party is to be the support of Gelukpa Buddhism. Two treaties signed by the Central Committee with local party activists and the governments of Üüshin and Otog Banners both proclaim the party's goal as [to] 'make our Mongolian race (ugsaatan) great, spread its religion and Buddha, protect our land, and let the people live peacefully and in freedom.'"[5]

Thus, while many of the Mongols' varied ideas came from elsewhere, such as Japan and the West, many of their concepts derived directly from the intellectual environment of late imperial China. The manifesto of the People's Revolutionary Party of Inner Mongolia therefore not only adopted modern theories of race and liberation but also drew upon the ideas and bureaucratic institutions of the Qing period. Of course, to find such elements of continuity and transformation in this period of enormous upheaval is to be expected. Yet, as we have seen, it has been precisely this dynamic process of engagement and transformation that has too often been overlooked in the study of Qing, Mongol and Buddhist history.

Of course, to explain the origins of the "Buddhist explanation" and its model of stasis one can point to various discourses, among them the modern secular teleology of both Mongolian Marxist and nationalist historiography.[6] Both of these historiographical models, which are not only the twin engines that have driven Mongol sociopolitical culture for nearly a century, but have also greatly influenced Western scholarship, regularly equate the Qing and its Buddhist rule with backwardness and cultural stagnation.[7] Moreover, another element that shaped this model of stasis is the tradition of "Buddhology" itself, with its legacy of rationalizing, deritualizing and dehistoricizing the Buddhist tradition.[8] Buddhist scholars, of course, were not the only ones with such a methodology; this approach fit rather well with the larger ahistorical and sui generis phenomenological approach to the study of the religion.[9] Nevertheless, in the case of the Qing the impact of these methodologies was also heightened by the popular view of Asian rule as mere spectacle. This model also facilitated the historiographical focus on the center, as well as its embedded unidirectional manifestations of power. Nevertheless, while all of these discourses have in various ways played a role in shaping modern representations of Qing Inner Mongolia, all of them are invariably based upon the master narrative of the Qing dynasty itself, which was also premised on the idea of continuity and stasis.

This book has therefore attempted to provide a counternarrative, or at least a more nuanced interpretation of Qing Inner Mongolia. Of course, to explain fully the history of this period and the success of the Qing state one needs to explore numerous other technologies of domination, such as economic, legal, social and military institutions. Yet while recognizing the importance of these factors, this work has focused on the actual issues reflected in the available Mongolian sources. It has attempted to reveal how the Mongols themselves defined their own reality over this course of time in terms of their communal identity and how it interrelated with the overarching elements of Buddhism and the state.

In order to do so, this study has presented an intellectual history of Mongol self-representations, and in doing so it has been necessary to turn around some of the standard theoretical frames. Rather than stasis, the focus has been upon change. Instead of investigating how the center utilized particular discourses to create an empire, we have investigated how the projections of the center and the process of imperial consolidation was actually an ongoing dialogue between the metropole and the periphery. The success of the Qing, especially the Mongol acceptance of the Manchu state, must therefore be seen as having developed within a sphere of mutual symbolizations. The Mongols were not simply hapless victims of Manchu imperialism, but rather active participants in the dynamic process that was the Qing dynasty.

The success of the Buddhist Qing should thus be attributed less to the court's adoption of a static Buddhist idiom than to the Mongols' continual renegotiation of their identity, communal boundaries and political structures in relation to the historical development of the Qing state. Manchu rule was thus successful, not through its appropriation and projection of ideological frameworks directed to specific constituents within the empire, but through the recognition and reconfirmation of those continually evolving representations in the empire's inhabitants' own narratives of self-identification. Contrary to received wisdom, therefore, being Mongol came to mean being a Buddhist Qing Mongol. As the Mongols themselves declared, it was "Our Great Qing."

To recognize this fact, however, is not to bolster the contemporary positive reevaluations of imperialism. Clearly, the profound disruption and cultural impact of the nearly three-centuries-long Qing enterprise upon the Mongols cannot be underestimated. Yet, was it all exploitative and marked by cultural inertia? By asking such a question we can, not only perhaps better reevaluate the history of the Qing, but also grapple with its enduring legacy.

In doing so, however, we also need to keep in mind that, although Buddhism was employed in the formation of the Manchu state and its attendant identities, it was also a part of the narratives defining Mongol identity in the pre- and post-Qing periods. Thus, while the boundaries of Mongol communal/ethnic/national identification in relation to political superstructures were continually changing during these periods, Buddhism as part of the communal narrative remained constant.

The fact that Manchu rule was premised on Gelukpa orthodoxy and the creation of a Buddhist Qing identity should therefore not distort the fact that the Mongols continued to see themselves as Mongol and Buddhist. In this sense, the Mongols' relation to the Dharma must not be seen solely as a tool of oppression, but quite its reverse. As in the case of Tibet, Buddhism should be regarded as an essential factor within the matrix of Mongol narratives of communal representation. We may therefore even truly speak of a Mongolian Buddhism, recognition of the historical existence of which is essential to a better understanding of the dynamics shaping Qing, Mongol and Buddhist history. In addition, it is an idea that is essential for all those who continue to grapple with the legacy of the Qing and the long shadow it casts over what it means to be Mongol and Buddhist in the contemporary world.

Notes

Abbreviations Used in Notes

AE   Na-ta. Ed. Coyiji. *Altan Erike*. Kökeqota: Öbör Mongɣol-un arad-un keblel-ün qoriy-a, 1989.

AKMK   Dharm-a. Ed. Coyiji. *Altan kürdün mingɣan kegesütü*. Kökeqota: Öbör Mongɣol-un arad-un keblel-ün qoriy-a, 1987.

ANT   Kämpfe, Hans-Rainer. *Das Asarayci neretü-yin teüke des Byamba Erke Daicing alias Samba Jasay (Eine mongolische Chronik des 17. Jahrhunderts)*. Wiesbaden: Harrassowitz, 1983.

AQMBD Li Baowen. *Arban doloduɣar jaɣun-u emün-e qayas-tu qolbuɣdaɣu Mongɣol üsüg-ün bicig debter. Shiqi shiji menggu wen wenshu dang'an (1600–1650)*. Tongliao: Obör Mongɣol-un baɣacud keüked-ün keblel-ün qoriy-a, 1997.

ATA   Bawden, Charles. *The Mongol Chronicle Altan Tobci*. Wiesbaden: Harrassowitz, 1955.

ATL   Lubsangdanjin. Ed. Coyiji. *Altan Tobci*. Kökeqota: Öbör Mongɣol-un arad-un keblel-ün qoriy-a, 1983.

ATMG   Lubsangdambijalsan. Ed. Cimeddorji, Möngkebuyan and Gerel. *Altan Tobci*. Kökeqota: Öbör mongɣol-un soyul-un keblel-ün qoriy-a, 1998.

BA   Roerich. George N. *The Blue Annals*. Delhi: Motilal Banarsidass, 1976.

BE   Rasipungsuɣ. Ed. Kökeöndür. *Bolor Erike*. Kökeqota: Öbör Mongɣol-un arad-un keblel-ün qoriy-a, 1985.

BT   Jimbadorji. Ed. Liu Jinsuo. *Bolor Toli*. Beijing: Ündüsüten-ü keblel-ün qoriy-a, 1984.

CB   Obermiller, E. *History of Buddhism (Chos-'byung)*. Heidelberg, 1931–1932.

CT   Sagaster, Klaus. *Die Weisse Geschichte. Eine mongolische Quelle zur Lehre von den Beiden Ordnungen Religion und Staat in Tibet und der Mongolei*. Wiesbaden: Harrassowitz, 1976.

CMBX   Heissig, Walther. *Catalogue of Mongol Books, Manuscripts and Xylographs*. Copenhagen: The Royal Library, 1971.

CMC   *Dumdadu ulus-un erten-ü mongɣol nom bicig-ün yerüngkei ɣarcaɣ. Catalogue of Ancient Mongolian Books and Documents of China*. Beijing: Beijing Tushuguan Chubanshe, 2000.

CQO   *Cinggis qaɣan-u naiman caɣan ordo*. Qayilar: Öbör Mongɣol-un soyul-un keblel-ün qoriy-a, 1988.

DL3   Ngag-dbang blo-bzang rgya-mtsho. *Rje-btsun thams-cad mkhyen-pa bsod-nams rgya-mtsho'i rnam-thar dngos-grub rgya-mtsho'i shing-rta*. Dolanji, H.P.: 1982.

DL5   Awang luosang jiacou. *Wu shi Dalai Lama Zhuan* [Biography of the Fifth Dalai

171

Lama]. Trans. Chen Qingying, Ma Lianlong. Beijing: Zhongguo Zangxue Chubanshe, 1997.

DMB Goodrich, L. C., and Chaoyang Fang, eds. *Dictionary of Ming Biography 1368–1644*. New York: Columbia University Press, 1976.

EEET Kesigbatu. Ed. C. Altansümbür and L. Qurcabayatur. *Erten ba edüge-yin erdeni-yin tobci*. Kökeqota: Öbör Mongγol-un soyul-un keblel-ün qoriy-a, 1997.

EM Atwood, Christopher P. *Encyclopedia of Mongolia and the Mongol Empire*. New York: Facts on File, 2004.

ET Sayang Secen. Ed. M. Go, I. de Rachewiltz, J. R. Krueger and B. Ulaan. *Erdeni-yin Tobci ('Precious Summary'). A Mongolian Chronicle of 1662, vol. I*. Canberra: The Australian National University, 1990.

GC Mgon-po-skyabs. *Rgya-nags chos-'byung*. Si-khron mi-rigs dpe-skrun khang, 1983.

GT Sonam, ed. *Gegen Toli. Ordos-un tuqai temdeglel*, 4–35. Beijing: Ündüsüten keblel-ün qoriy-a, 1995.

GU Gombojab. Ed. Coyiji. *Γangγ-a-yin urusqal*. Kökeqota: Öbör Mongγol-un arad-un keblel-ün qoriy-a, 1984.

H Aalto, Pentti. "A Catalogue of the Hedin Collection of Mongolian Literature." *Contributions to Ethnography, Linguistics and History of Religions, VIII. 6*. Stockholm: Statens Etnografiska Museum, 1954.

ISK de Rachewiltz, Igor, et al. *In the Service of the Khan: Eminent Personalities of the Early Mongol-Yüan Period (1200–1300)*. Wiesbaden: Harrassowitz, 1993.

JMZD *Jiu Manzhou Dang*. 10 vols. Taipei: Kuo-li ku-kung, 1969.

JTS Elverskog, Johan. *The Jewel Translucent Sutra: Altan Khan and the Mongols in the Sixteenth Century*. Leiden: Brill Publishers, 2003.

KS Hangin, John Gombojab. *Köke Sudur (The Blue Chronicle): A Study of the First Mongolian Historical Novel by Injannasi*. Wiesbaden: Otto Harrassowitz, 1973.

MBOT Lomi. Ed. Naγusayinküü and Ardajab. *Mongγol-un Borjigid oboγ-un teüke*. Kökeqota: Öbör Mongγol-un arad-un keblel-ün qoriy-a, 1989.

QSL *Qing shilu*. Beijing: Zhonghua shuju, 1985.

RWL Damchø Gyatsho Dharmatala. *Rosary of White Lotuses, Being the Clear Account of How the Precious Teaching of Buddha Appeared and Spread in the Great Hor Country*. Trans. Piotr Klafkowski. Wiesbaden: Harrassowitz, 1987.

SE Elverskog, Johan. *The Pearl Rosary: Mongol Historiography in Early Nineteenth Century Ordos*. Bloomington: The Mongolia Society, 2006.

SH de Rachewiltz, Igor. *The Secret History of the Mongols: A Mongolian Epic Chronicle of the Thirteenth Century*. Leiden: Brill, 2004.

ST Shastina, N. P. *'Shara tudzhi' mongol'skaya letopis' XVII veka*. Moscow-Leningrad: Akademiya NAUK, 1957.

T Takakusu Junjirō and Watanabe Kaigyoku, eds. *Taishō shinshū daizōkyō*. 100 vols. Tokyo: Taisho issaikyo kankokai, 1924–1932.

TFSHD *Tongki Fuka Sindaha Hergen i Dangse: 'The Secret Chronicles of the Manchu Dynasty' 1607–1637 AD*. 7 vols. Trans. and annot. Kanda Nobuo et al. Tokyo: The Toyo Bunko, 1955–1963.

TH   Martin, Dan, with Yael Bentor. *Tibetan Histories. A Bibliography of Tibetan-Language Historical Works*. London: Serindia Publications, 1997.
YS   *Yuan Shi* [History of the Yuan]. Beijing: Zhonghua Shuju Chuban, 1995.

Introduction

1. On this important meeting between the Qianlong emperor and the Sixth Panchen Lama, see Cammann 1949; Hevia 1995: 46–49; Wang 2000: 152–160; Berger 2003: 167–197; and Ragnubs 2004.

2. *Tngri tedkügsen qayan bancin boyda-yi jalaysan tuqai jarliy* (MS. p. 20).

3. On the problem of smallpox and Qing policies to control it, see Serruys 1980: 41–63, and Perdue 2005: 42–50.

4. On the impact of this death, see Berger 2003: 187–197. On its lingering influence into the twentieth century, see Tuttle 2005: 21.

5. Many scholars have presented Asian state formations as "religio-political theatre," in the sense that the state is forged and represented through ritual practices. As noted in Toni Huber's study of the Tibetan state, which draws upon Geertz's "theatre state," Tambiah's "galactic polity" and Inden's "imperial formation," he argues that the state is represented through ritualization for three reasons: "first, because ritual and ceremony themselves were the arena in which the dynamic constitution of complex political formations was worked out, in the form of 'ongoing dialectical and eristical relations'; second, because on the ground there was often little actual political control or ability to enforce order in the local affairs of daily life; and third, because . . . the interests of the polity lay ultimately in the control of persons rather than in the land" (Huber 1999: 154).

6. One of the most important studies of this phenomenon was Farquhar's seminal 1978 article, "Emperor as Bodhisattva in the Governance of the Ch'ing Empire." For a bibliography and overview of the scholarship on the Manchu court's use of Buddhism, see Henss 2001a and 2001b, as well as Berger 2003.

7. While the Jesuit "construction" of Confucianism as a moral philosophy compatible with Western thought has been the focus of extensive scholarship (most recently, Jensen 1997), the implications of this discourse in simultaneously shaping Western conceptualizations of Buddhism have been less explored, especially in terms of Western views of Buddhist rule. Of particular interest in this regard are the consequences of the Jesuit model that conflated Confucianism with imperial China. Thus the fact that the Manchus became "Sinicized," or "Confucianized," is fully understandable within this model, and this was really never questioned. Yet, in the Jesuit view, since the emperors were followers of the one true religion like themselves, the Manchu engagement with Tibetan Buddhism, a well-known form of "idolatry," "superstition" and "devil dancing," could only have been interpreted as a form of political manipulation. In other words, for rational Confucian emperors and their philosophical brethren the Jesuits, there could be no other explanation for Buddhism at the court than as a political tool to ameliorate the "Tartar barbarians." However, as Western views of China began to change in the seventeenth century from positive to negative, the linkage became reversed and Manchu rule became

more closely identified with "debased Buddhism." This later representation can be clearly seen in the early-eighteenth-century Beauvais tapestries, which confirm that the Qing was "the degraded antithesis of legitimate authority in the religious and political spheres" (Porter 2001: 151).

8. Quoted in Cammann 1949: 16.

9. Lessing 1942: 59. For critical studies of this inscription, see Hevia 1993: 243–278; and Berger 2003: 35–36, 196.

10. A Communist pamphlet published in Dolonuur in July 1929 warning the Mongols of the danger posed by the Panchen Lama captures the idea of Manchu Buddhist imperialism very well: "From the latter period of our Mongolia's great Yuan dynasty, Buddhism began to penetrate. About five hundred years ago, at the same time as Altan Khan of the Tümeds had spread Buddhism widely among the Mongols, the Manchu Qing dynasty arose. Seeing it as a fine-tuned way to decrease the unparalleled brave and heroic nature of the Mongols, they turned towards affairs of emptiness like mercy and merit, sin and future incarnations, and then fell completely behind in political knowledge and economic development. The might and glory of the ancient Mongols was already covered over and we preserved a gentleness like sheep, thus becoming food for the wolves" (quoted in Atwood 1994b: 128). A more recent Communist interpretation of the Mongols' Buddhist conversion is found in Natsagdorj's 1963 History of the Khalkhas (Xalxiin tüüx): "The Mongol feudalists strove to cause the Yellow Sect to expand into the conquered territory under them, beginning with the second half of the sixteenth century. As for suddenly having a liking for the religion on the part of the Mongol feudalists, that was not directed solely by religious belief, but was motivated mainly from the goal they had of exploiting the influence of the Yellow Sect. The propagation of the Yellow Sect was directly related to the use of the religion by the feudalists to subdue the anger of the masses who had become mindless with suffering in the uninterrupted wars of the feudalists" (quoted in Moses 1977: 111).

11. On the imperial Japanese use of Buddhism in Mongolia as defined by the Qing model, see Li 1998 and 2003.

12. In the study of Qing Mongolia most Mongolists agree with the assessment of the Qianlong emperor: Qing rule was maintained through a Buddhist discourse. See, for example, Bawden 1989: 86–88; Jagchid 1974 and 1976; Jagchid and Hyer 1979: 177; Moses 1977; and Bira 2002.

13. The view expressed by Father Amiot that the Qing court used Buddhism to rule the Mongols is also echoed in contemporary Sinological scholarship: "The Manchu rulers had to compete with Mongol khans for regional hegemony and they too turned to Tibetan Buddhism for legitimacy. The history of Tibetan Buddhist patronage by the Qing court is thus closely intertwined with the successful Manchu campaigns to extend their control over the Mongols, who constituted their greatest potential threat" (Rawski 1998: 244). For similar presentations of Manchu Buddhist rule of the Mongols, see Crossley 1997: 113; Zito 1997: 23; Naquin 2000: 308–309; and Hostetler 2001: 35.

14. Under "Lamaism" the following sentence is given: "It is with this view [of enfeebling the strength of the Mongol princes] that the emperors patronise lamanism" (quoted in Lopez 1998: 41).

15. One Mongol convert to Christianity explained his decision as follows: "'If my father had not been forced out of the monastery [during the 1930s], I would never have been born. If Mongolia had not been a nation of celibate monks, following a religion forced on us by the Manchus to keep us weak, we would be a strong nation of 40 million people today'" (O'Donnell 1999).

16. On the Qing court's use of Buddhism as a tool of political legitimacy, see Grupper 1984: 51; Dabringhaus 1997: 122; and Kam 2000: 161–173. On the importance of the Mahakala cult at the earlier Manchu court, see Grupper 1979; Yao 1994; and Gimm 2000/1. On the various Buddhist projects carried out by the court during the dynasty, see, for example, Heissig 1954b; Chayet 1984; Charleux 1998; Foret 2000; Berger 2003; and Millward et al. 2004.

17. Hevia 2003: 40–48. For an overview of Qing rule in the nineteenth century, see Fletcher 1978: 352–360.

18. See van Hecken 1977 and Serruys 1985a.

19. On the two myths of the Buddhist *cakravartin,* see Strong 1983: 44–46.

20. "Encompassed hierarchy" is the term Zito uses to explain the ritualized process through which the Qing emperorship "include[d] them [the people] in a whole that embodied simultaneously his [the emperor's] own power and their relative importance vis-à-vis that power. What interests us here about this mode of social engagement is how it acts not to overcome Others by force but to include them in its own project of rulership" (1997: 29).

21. Counter to the common narrative, many Mongols, especially those in eastern Inner Mongolia, were not Buddhist during the period of the Qing formation. On this topic see Kam 2000.

22. On the impact of Mongol nationalist historiography on the study of Qing Mongolia see Elverskog 2004.

23. Elverskog 2005.

24. Struve 2004: 11.

25. "Gramsci's notion of hegemony is generally understood as political and cultural domination and popular acceptance of ideologies of domination. William Rosebury, extending Gramsci, suggests that we 'explore hegemony not as a finished and monolithic ideological formation but as a problematic, contested, political *process* of domination and struggle' (1996: 77; original emphasis). He further argues that formations of particular regional, religious, ethnic, national, or class communities and identities involve languages of contention and opposition to other groups that vie for dominance" (Bulag 2002: 12–13).

26. Ong 2003: 5–7.

27. On Manchu–Mongol marriage alliances, see Jagchid 1986 and Weiers 1989–1991. On the institution of the banner system among the Mongols, see Aberle 1953: 1–53; Farquhar 1960; Legrand 1976; and Atwood 2002: 23–42. On the Lifan Yuan, see Chia 1992, 1993; and Di Cosmo 1998. On Qing legal institutions among the Mongols, see Heuschert 1998a, 1998b. For detailed studies of how the legal system actually worked in Mongolia, see Bawden 1969a, 1969b, and 1969c.

28. Di Cosmo 2002.

29. For an overview of recent scholarship on Qing Mongolia, see Tatsuo 1996.

30. As recently noted by Millward, if we are to advance our understanding of the Qing dynasty we need to face the "challenging agenda" of conducting "empirical research into societies of mobile people who left few indigenous records" (2004: 113).

31. In Crossley's recent book on the Qing court's transformation of historical narratives in shaping the different "constituencies" of the Manchu state, she writes, "Given the history of Mongolia and Turkestan before the coming of the Qing, and the complex story of why the Qing called certain people 'Mongols,' it is not very surprising one finds few informative statements of Mongol sentiments in the Qing period" (Crossley 1999: 322). It is hoped the following study will reveal some of the "Mongol sentiments" during the Qing period.

32. For an overview of these practices, see Perdue 2005: 409–494.

33. Comaroff 1994: 303.

34. Blackburn 2001: 7–8. There are two intertwined issues that have fostered this reality. The first is the legacy of scholars like Heinz Bechert, Stanley Tambiah, George Bond, Richard Gombrich and Gananath Obeyesekere who "have divided the history of Buddhism into three periods: (1) canonical or early Buddhism, (2) traditional or historical Buddhism, and (3) reformist, protestant, or modern Buddhism" (Baumann 2002: 55). This temporal categorization that compresses more than two thousand years of history into one eternalized model has also been fostered by the idea that Buddhism was rational and politically powerful, much like the West (Inden 1990: 85–130). Both of these factors have contributed to the occlusion of studies on the particularities of imperial Buddhist formations or the process that engendered a Buddhist imperial identity. It is therefore often taken for granted that Buddhist rule works, be it in Tibet, Thailand, or Korea; however, the actual processes or reasons that made it work are less understood.

35. On the preconceptualizations and meanings of the genealogical hermeneutic in Buddhist history, as well as its embedded problems, see McRae 2003: 1–21.

36. This manuscript was discovered in 1958 in a cave in Darkhan Muuminggan Banner of Ulaanchab League and recently published (Durungy-a 1998: 21–67).

37. Naquin 2000: xxx.

38. As one example of this fluidity and multivalency see Sperling's 1997 study of the Chi-kya in Amdo, whose "ethnicity" shifted in different contexts between Mongol and Tibetan.

39. On the difficulties of defining Mongol identity during the Qing, see Atwood 2002: 37–38.

40. Millward summarized this scholarship as that which "seek[s a] greater understanding of the dynasty in Inner Asian history and traditions and consult[s] sources in Inner Asian languages. Most make ethnic or cultural difference an important concern of their work. All attempt to move beyond the Sinocentric model and other paradigms discussed above in order to reconfigure the historian's approach to the Qing and, by implication, to modern China" (1998: 15). For an overview of this scholarship, see the review essays by Guy (2002) and Sen (2002).

41. On the larger problem of studies on China being focused on the center at the exclusion of the periphery, see Gladney 2004.

42. Deleuze and Guattari argue that as capitalism spreads it not only deterritorializes but also reterritorializes earlier or local systems into the new system, namely the "capitalist machine." "The more capitalism 'deterritorializes,' they argue, 'decoding and axiomating [material] flows in order to extract surplus value from them, the more its ancillary apparatuses, such as government bureaucracies and the forces of law and order, do their utmost to reterritorialize,' to recode that which had been decoded. The ancillary apparatuses may be understood as the recovery and redeployment of a host of European cultural, social, and political forms that provided a kind of life-support system for further acts of imperialist deterritorialization" (Hevia 2003: 21–22).

43. I use the idea of "middle ground" from White's study of the intellectual engagement and mutual understandings created when Indians and colonial settlers first met (1991). On the existence of an "intermediate political space" in Qing relations with Inner Asia, see Di Cosmo 2003. A similar process of negotiation is also described by Ching in his study of the Taiwanese response to, and negotiation with, the realities of the imperial Japanese state (2001).

44. For a similar progression, see Meyer-Fong's study of elite views of Yangzhou, which over time also shifted from local conceptualizations to those of the imperial center (2003).

45. "Interactional history is precisely an attempt to go beyond the national story and get at some of the fragments without losing coherence in the telling of the tale" (van der Veer 2001: 8).

46. Buddhist modernism's decontextualization of the tradition is well known, and one unfortunate by-product of this development has been the study of Buddhism outside of Asian intellectual and cultural history. As noted by Lopez, "Historians of India, China and Japan, for example, generally regard Buddhism as an esoteric domain entered only by the initiate, and Buddhologists are often regarded . . . as woefully ignorant of Asian history" (1995: 8). On the trepidation of non-Buddhologists dealing with Buddhist materials, see Teiser's comments on Sinological readings of the *Heart Sutra* (2000). For an overview of the sui generis study of Buddhism and its implications, see Cohen 2002.

47. Orsi 1997: 8.

48. In some regards my approach parallels H. L. Seneviratne's "liberation anthropology," especially his call for a need to approach Buddhism within a larger theoretical field. "Stated differently, I contend that the anthropological categories such as Thai Buddhism, Burmese Buddhism, and Sinhalese Buddhism need to be expanded beyond their present connotation of syncretism between doctrinal Buddhism and folk Buddhism, great or little traditions of mystical beliefs and practices and so forth, to embrace the broader array of religiously grounded phenomena like 'fundamentalism' and 'ideology.' Such an expanded definition would cover the political, economic and cultural activities of diverse religious personalities . . ." (1999: 7). Moreover, I agree with Steven Wasserstrom's conclusion that "the history of religions . . . must end up being a historical study or it may be no study at all" (1999: 238). Indeed, if we are to better understand the

history of the Dharma it is essential that we situate Buddhism within the larger forces shaping history.

49. Although later Mongol and Tibetan sources claim that Chinggis Khan was the first propagator of Tibetan Buddhism, this has long been recognized as a later historical fabrication; see Ratchnevsky 1954, and Wylie 1977. Yet this is not to deny any early relations between the Mongols and Tibetan Buddhists, which began at the time of Chinggis Khan's invasion of the Tanguts; see Petech 1983; and Sperling 1987, 1994.

50. Peterson and Walhof 2002: 6.

51. Hallisey 1995: 51.

52. Kapstein 2000: 65.

Chapter 1. The Mongols on the Eve of Conquest

1. The Mongolian oath of Ooba Khung Taiji is preserved in the JMZD (fol. 2081–2082), and AQMBD: 32–34. For a study of this oath and its various versions, see Weiers 1983.

2. Weiers 1983: 420.

3. Wittfogel and Feng 1949: 561.

4. Sárközi 1993.

5. On whether the Qing was an empire or engaged in "European-style" colonialism, see the special issue on "Manchu Colonialism" of the *International History Review* 20 (1998). On the theoretical implications of the Qing as an "Asian empire," see Teng 2004.

6. On this issue see Hostetler 2001: 25–30; and Perdue 2005: 506–517.

7. On the scholarly and popular revival of the notion of "tribes" in response to postsocialist ethnic nationalisms, see Gladney 2004: 175–181.

8. The idea of ethnicity has been a focal point of discussion within the work of the New Qing historians and their reevaluations of Manchu rule. On the issue of "ethnicity" in the study of the Qing, the debates and some of the lingering problems, see Atwill 2003.

9. Similarly to the way Lamarre (2000) reveals how the "national imagination" has distorted the real ethnic, territorial and linguistic diversities of Heian Japan, we need to realize that a similar phenomenon has occurred in the case of the Mongols.

10. On the Mongol origins of Manchu policies, see Farquhar 1968 and 1971.

11. de Rachewiltz 1972: l. 3135, 6018, 8116, 8507, 8625, 10823.

12. For surveys of early steppe ideology, see de Rachewiltz 1973; Fletcher 1979–1980; and Golden 1982.

13. Golden 2000: 248.

14. See, for example, *ulus bayi'ulucaqsat,* SH, pars. 224, 227; see also Cleaves 1952: 70, 80.

15. de Rachewiltz 1972: l. 7821, 7823, 7826, 10325.

16. SH, par. 269; see Buell 1980: 43–44.

17. See, for example, the "Uighur *guo,*" in Cleaves 1949: 30, 83.

18. Jackson 1999.

19. The fragmentation of the Golden Horde of southern Russian into distinct *ulus*, their civil war and their eventual submission to the Russian state, parallels remarkably the processes of the Qing formation. See Khodarkovsky 2002: 76–125.

20. As will be shown in detail below, a central feature of Qing rule was the transformation of Mongol conceptualizations of the *ulus*, and one consequence of this transformation, as *ulus* again became both state and people, was that the meaning of *törö* reverted to its earlier meaning of custom or tradition. It was even used to translate Confucian "propriety" (Ch. *li*); see Cleaves 1995: 44, and 1996: 27n197.

21. ET: 35r.

22. The same idea is also reflected in Nurhaci's letter sent to the Khalkhas in 1620, wherein Chinggis Khan is described as taking the Jin state [Man. *doro*]. "Thinking the worst, [the Jin] attacked, but Heaven favored Temüjin, and so the Mongol Chinggis Khan took the state from the Jin Khan." JMZD I, 540–541, quoted in Elliott 2004: 31.

23. JTS 69. In the ATL, the fall of the Yuan is also described as a loss of the "state," and not the defeat or obliteration of the nation: "The empire of the Mongols was taken by the Daiming emperor" (quoted in Cleaves 1986: 190). The ATA similarly describes the Ming conquest as "when that government [the Yuan] was taken over" (67, 154).

24. In this regard it is also relevant to note that the Kitad Ulus did not include the former Song territories, which was the "Southern" Nanggiyad Ulus.

25. ET: 39v; ATA: 137; ATL: 489; ANT: 74.

26. On the problems related to Dayan Khan's dates, see JTS: 49–53.

27. The post-Qing seventeenth-century Mongol histories are often identified together as the Mongol chronicles. They are Lubsangdanjin's *Golden Summary* (*Altan Tobci*, ATL), the undated and anonymous *Golden Summary* (*Altan Tobci*, ATA), Saghang Sechen's 1662 *Precious Summary* (*Erdeni-yin Tobci*, ET), the anonymous *Yellow History* (*Sira Tuyuji*, ST) and Byamba Erke Daiching's late-seventeenth-century *Asaragchi's History* (*Asaragci neretü-yin teüke*, ANT). While these sources follow the same theory of world history in a similar structural format and contain many of the same episodes, poems, and stories drawn from the *Secret History*, oral lore and Buddhist historiography, there are also differences based on regional orientations. For an introduction and overview of these works, see Heissig 1959 and Bira 2002.

28. Examples of the use of *ulus* as a separate entity within the larger Mongol world can be found in all three early-seventeenth-century chronicles; for example, in the ATA, *ulus cin-u Caqar mayu bileü*, 186, *qoyina Dayan Qayan caqar Tümed ulus abcu*, 187. Lubsangdanjin uses *ulus* in the same manner: *Mongyol jiryuyan yeke ulus ergüce terigüten yeke ed nayurasun caylasi ügei egüjüküi* ATL: 644; *Mdowa ulus sirayiyur ulus-i erke dür-a-iyan oroyulju* ATL: 638; *Caqar Qaracin qoyar ulus jokis ügei bülüge* ATL: 659; *Qaracin-u noyad ulus-iyan abcu* ATL: 660. *Ulus* is also used by Mongol princes in their early correspondence with the Manchus to identify their respective nations, *mani Aru-yin ulus-tu mordaba* (AQMBD: 121). It is also found in early Buddhist translatations, as in Ligdan Khan's colophon of the *Arya bhadra-kalpika nama mahayana sutra*, which notes the *Caqar ulus* (MS 24v, H 3517).

29. JTS: 81.

30. On the historiographical problems of this story, see JTS: 50–52.

31. ATA: 183.

32. After conquering the Six Great Ulus which made up the Eastern Mongols, Dayan Khan organized his state into six sociomilitary tribal units, called the Six Tümens. The six groups were divided into two wings: the Western Tümen were comprised of the Ordos, Tümed and Yüngshiyebü (with the Asud and Kharachin); and the Eastern Tümen of the Chakhar, Khalkha and Khorchin (previously it had included the Uriyangkhan; however, they were dismantled as a *tümen* after their 1538 revolt). After Dayan Khan reunited the Six Tümen in 1510, he divided them among his sons. In particular, he made his son Barsubolod the *jinong,* or viceroy, of the Three Western Tümen, who not only ruled over these three *tümen,* or *ulus,* but also administered the cult of Chinggis Khan in Ordos (JTS: 76–77).

33. ET: 63r.

34. On the continuity of this idea see, for example, Lubsangdanjin's description of Darayisün Khan: "In the time of that Khan the State was organized and united, and he tranquillized the Six Great Ulus" (ATL: 648).

35. On the issue of environmental problems on the Mongolian plateau and their impact, see Okada 1972; Fisher 1988; Geiss 1988; and Robinson 1999: 95.

36. Trade between the Mongols and the Ming court was essential for the functioning of their economic, military and political systems; however, with the chaos of the early seventeenth century these trade networks collapsed. A telling example of this disruption is found in the horse trade: in the early fifteenth century the Ming army received 1,700,000 horses from the Mongols, but during the rise of the Qing they could barely maintain 100,000 regular mounts for its cavalry (Wakeman 1985: 202–203). This deficit clearly not only affected how the Ming could respond to Qing encroachments but also the socioeconomic environment among the Mongols and their decisions regarding their relations with the Manchus. For detailed studies on Mongol–Ming trade relations, see Serruys 1967 and 1975.

37. On the ferocity of this war and its implications, see Di Cosmo 2002.

38. AQMBD: 143.

39. Ibid.: 62.

40. ATA: 188.

41. ET: 63v.

42. On the battle of Dalan Tergün, see Okada 1989.

43. ATA: 190.

44. Quoted in Serruys 1967: 104.

45. When Altan Khan created relations with other rulers it is framed as state-to-state relations: "By speaking together of the state, the long separated nations [Kirgud and Ordos] were in harmony" (JTS: 113). Similarly, when 'Abd al-Karim Khan of Hami submits to Altan Khan, he proclaims "Let us unify our states!" (JTS: 169).

46. How these same leaders presented themselves, and this new situation, to their own community is, of course, an entirely other issue and unfortunately beyond the scope of this study.

47. I thank Ellen McGill for this information.

48. AQMBD: 11.

49. Ibid.: 42.

50. Ibid.: 80.

51. The *otog*, meaning "hunting camp" or "hearth," frequently combined or divided various Mongol clans, though all the *otog*s were ideally to be of the same size. During the reign of Dayan Khan the fifty-four *otog*s were divided into the Six Tümen, and each *otog* was bestowed upon one of Dayan Khan's grandsons. Subsequently, as we have seen, during the period of fragmentation these two entities, the *tümen/ulus* and *otog*, both become viable communal and political entities. In turn, these groups, namely, the *otog*, became the foundation for the Qing's Forty-Nine Banners of Inner Mongolia.

52. TFSHD, 5:505–507, quoted in Di Cosmo 2002: 345.

53. AQMBD 137–139, translated in Di Cosmo 2002: 341.

54. AQMBD: 12; for parallel passages, see pp. 3, 7–8, 32 and 44.

55. On Ligdan Khan's reign, see Weiers 1973.

56. AQMBD: 20.

57. Ibid.: 58.

58. Ibid.: 69.

59. Okada 1991: 167.

60. Manju qaracin bida qoyar ulus nigen ey-e-ber yabuju törö jasaγ nigetuy-a, ATL: 660.

61. tendece Yekege Caγan Jürcid-ün Jing Tayisi-yin törö-yi abuγad (ET: 92r), tere metü Mongγol-un qaγan-u törö-yi abuγad (ET: 92v), ga becin jile Kitad-un qaγan-u törö-yi abubai (ET: 93v). The same format is also found later in the text, after Saghang Sechen's summary of the Ming emperors: Manju-yin Ey-e-ber jasaγci Qaγan törö-yi anu abubai (ET: 95r).

62. ET: 68r–68v.

63. Qaγan kilingbesü törö-yügen ebdemüi . jaγan kilinglebesü qota-yügen ebdemüi kemegsen metü, ET: 68v.

64. Ene ber Dayan qaγan-u nigedüger köbegün Töröbolad-aca saluγsan qad-un törö yabudal bolai, ET: 68v.

65. jirγuγan yeke ulus-i Dayicing törö-ber quriyaγad, ET: 68v.

66. AQMBD: 84.

67. Ibid.: 111.

68. Aalto 1961; Franke 1978: 42–46.

69. Okada 1992.

70. Weiers 2000.

71. The Manchu ruler thus "justly ruled the vast great nation, and maintained the jade great state in peace and tranquillity" (kür yeke ulus-i tulγurca jasan qas yeke törö-yi esen tayibing bolγabai, ET: 95v); which parallels remarkably Saghang Sechen's description of Chinggis Khan's reign (kür yeke ulus-iyan toγtaγan jasaju qas yeke törö-ben tulγurca bayiγuluγad, ET: 39r8).

72. Farquhar 1968: 204.

73. ET: 95r–95v, 96r.

74. One of the most explicit examples of this view is found in Bira: "At the very end of his work Saghang Secen gives a very brief survey of the history of the first Manchu emperors. We may regard this as a *sui generis* tribute of the time. But this survey stands in isolation, it is not organically linked with the basic part of the work" (2002: 211).

75. The importance of this idea and the reality of the political fragmentation during the seventeenth century that it reflects is evidenced in the fact that this phrase is incorporated into Chinggis Khan's *biligs*. On the history of these "wise sayings," see de Rachewiltz 1982; and on how they were compiled during the late sixteenth–early seventeenth century, see Okada 1995: 459. In addition, it is relevant to note that this same phrase is found in Toghon Temür's lament, which is also contained in all the seventeenth-century chronicles (Okada 1967).

76. tanu Mongγol-un törö-dür qarsi ele boluγujin, ET: 83r. On the Dalai Lama's role as arbiter of political authority in Inner Asia during the seventeenth century, see Ishihama 1992.

77. For examples of this transformation of *ulus* into banner, see ATL: 655.

78. On this shift and its historiographical implications, see Elliott 2004.

79. On this development, see Elliott 1996: 46–78.

80. As seen in the letters published by Krueger (1969), these ideas continued to be used among the Oirads.

81. ATA: 191. This prophecy is found in both the ATL (631–632) and ET (66v–67r).

82. It is important to stress that this conceptualization was how the "Inner Mongols" understood the Qing and their place within it at this period of time. How other Mongols and "Chinese" in different areas, much less the "Tibetans" in the distinct areas of Amdo, Kham and Central Tibet (none of which was incorporated into the Qing at this time), saw or understood the Qing and their relation to it is an entirely different issue.

Chapter 2. The Mongols and Political Authority

1. As noted above, this is the only time Saghang Sechen uses the term Khoshuu (*qosiγu*), the Qing-period term for banner. In this case, however, it is used for the military force of the *otog*.

2. ET: 91v–92r.

3. Erinchen Jinong submitted to the Qing in 1635, and in 1649 the Ordos was divided into two wings. The right wing contained the Üüshin, Otog and Khanggin banners, and the left wing included the Junggar, Wang and Dalad banners. In 1736 a seventh banner was created out of Üüsin named Jasag. After 1949, Otog was split into two and Wang and Jasag were merged into one (van Hecken 1972: 132–155). For more on the history of the Ordos nobility, see Veit 1999.

4. On the polyvalency of Qing imperial ritual, see Waley-Cohen 2002.

5. The theory of the *qoyar yosu* as envisioned by Pakpa Lama is found in several of his works, but particularly in the *Shes-bya rab-gsal* and the *Rgyal-bu ji-big-de-mur-la gdam-du-byas nor-bu'i phren-ba*; see Bira 1999.

6. According to this view, the two syncretic spheres are mutually dichotomous, one being secular and the other religious, though each one provides legitimation to the other. It is premised on the idea "that secular and spiritual salvation are something that all living beings try to obtain. Spiritual salvation consists in complete deliverance from suffering, and worldly welfare is secular salvation. Both depend on a dual order, the order of Religion *(nom-un yosun)* and the order of the State, or worldly rule *(törö-yin yosun)*. Just as the religious order is based on the sutras and magic formulae *(dhāraṇī)*, the secular order rests on peace and quietness. The order of Religion is presided over by the Lama, and the state by the Ruler. The priest has to teach religion, and the Ruler has to guarantee a rule which enables everyone to live in peace. Religion and State are thus mutually dependent. The heads of religion and state are equal, although each has different functions. The Lama corresponds to the Buddha, and the Ruler to the cakravartin" (Franke 1981: 308). For a detailed study of the *qoyar yosu/yon mchod* theory of rule, see Ruegg 1995.

7. On Mongol rule in China, its various policies and its impact, see Langlois 1981; Chan and de Bary 1982; Rossabi 1988; Endicott-West 1989; Chan 1999; Smith and von Glahn 2003.

8. On Mongol–Tibet relations during the Yuan, see Schuh 1976 and 1977; Tsering, 1978; Franke 1981; Szerb 1985; Petech 1990; Ruegg 1991 and 1997; and Dunnell 1992.

9. Geertz 1983: 124.

10. The use of the word "God," or the phrase "will of God" may seem jarring; however, drawing upon the scholarly corpus challenging Western presuppositions in the study of religion (e.g., Smith 1990; Masuzawa 2005), I believe this is the best translation of the Mongolian term *tngri/tengri*. A term that heretofore has much like the Chinese *tian* most often been unfortunately relegated to a lower order through its translation as "Heaven" (Kirkland 2004: 32).

11. There is a wealth of scholarship on the polyvalency of Chinese imperial rule; on the role of Buddhism at the court, see Janoush 1999; Orzech 1998; and Yao 1995.

12. See, for example, Bawden's description of Altan Khan's adoption of Buddhism in *The Modern History of Mongolia:* "Growing dissatisfaction was making itself felt with the barbaric notions of shamanism, its bloody sacrifices, its primitive cosmology, its unattractive revelations of the world beyond, and its complete lack of organization which made it useless as an instrument of political power . . . Khungtaiji [was] making a conscious appeal to an unforgotten Mongol tradition of the alliance of the Buddhist Church with the secular power, which ran like a thread through Mongol political thought at the time of the Yüan dynasty" (Bawden 1989: 28–30). The prevalence, or commonality, of this view is seen in the similar presentation in Rossabi 1995: 38.

13. In Shireetü Güüsi's 1612 translation of the *Diamond Sutra* he speaks of the *qoyar törö yosun* being lost. In his translation of the history of Padmasambhava, the *Badma Gatang,* Sakya Dondub speaks of the *qoyar jüil nom-un törö,* while an inscription from Olon Süme does not even mention the "two realms" in any form, simply that the Yuan was lost on account of losing Buddhism. See Heissig 1984: 206–207.

14. "Now, on account of the previous good blessings, the Offering-site Lama, and

the Almsmaster Khan, dwell like the sun and moon which have risen in the blue sky. Now, in this time, as the command having been given by the ancient powerful Khan Indra, the grandsons of the Genius Holy Chinggis Khan who brought into his power the Five Colored [nations] and the Four Foreign [peoples], the bodhisattva incarnation, Köden Khan, and the Wheel-turner Khubilai Sechen Khan, both met Sakya Pandita who has arrived at the place where all is known, and Pakpa Lama, the people's blessing and Lord of the Dharma. When the faithful princes of Mongolia and the wise lamas of the Sakya met, by means of the two realms all sentient beings were excessively joyous. Because the State and the Religion have been in disarray since Ukhaatu Sechen Khan, we have practiced sin and wickedness. When we ate, we made use of flesh and blood in our food. Now the holy lama, Sakyamuni of today's time of strife [the Third Dalai Lama], and the great mighty Khan Indra of these lands [Altan Khan] have met. Beginning on such a fine and auspicious day, when the great stream moving with waves of blood transforms and converts into a transparent sea eddying with milk, when one proceeds on that white path of Dharma as traversed by the Holies of yore [Khubilai and Pakpa], this surely will be the grace of our having relied on the Khan and the Lama" (ET: 76v–77r).

15. ET: 92v–93r.

16. JTS: 63–68.

17. The "highest God" is the highest heavenly power or deity of the Mongolian pantheon that is engaged in regulating the powers and events of the world; see Banzarov 1981–1982; Heissig 1980: 47–59; and Humphrey and Onon 1996: 78–84. The role of Heavenly God and Mother Earth in recognizing the authority of Chinggis Khan's reign is found throughout the *Secret History*. In later Mongol sources the role of Mother Earth is omitted, and instead his legitimacy derives from the blessing of God and a relationship with Tibetan Buddhism.

18. JTS: 68.

19. Ibid.: 70.

20. YS 1: 1.

21. 'Jam-mgon A-myes-zhabs Nga-dbang kun-dga' bsod-nams (1597–1662), *Sa-skya gdung-rabs chen-mo,* see TH no. 210.

22. Translated in Bira 2002: 57.

23. As Franke has noted, in the tax exemption orders from the Yuan dynasty, the phrase "they shall give prayers for religious merit" is "normally preceded by *denriyi jalbariju* ('pray to Heaven')" (1977: 36).

24. *Fozu lidai tongzai* (T 2036, 49: 702), quoted in Waley 1976: 8. Moreover, according to Pakpa Lama, the Mongol khans not only ordered the monks to pray to Heaven, but they were also ordered to pray for the khan's long life; see Szerb 1985: 172.

25. Translated in Ishihama 1993: 40–41.

26. For a study of Mongol conceptualizations of Heaven during the Yuan dynasty and how they shaped the court's policies toward other religions, see Atwood 2004.

27. Spiegel 1983: 155, 159.

28. Dawson 1955: 9.

29. Ibid.: 80.

30. On the ritual significance of the kowtow (Ch. *koutou*) in East–West relations, see Hevia 1995: 232–237.

31. Dawson 1955: 10.

32. The martyrdom of Knyaz Mikhail is found in *The Chronicle of Novgorod* (Mitchell and Forbes 1914: 88–92). On the role of the Mongols in Russia's imagination, see Figes 2002: 358–429.

33. Pelliot's observation in *Les mongols et la Papauté* is noted by Franke 1978: 24.

34. Franke 1978: 17.

35. Jackson and Morgan 1990: 248. See also Vogelin 1940–1941: 391.

36. Dawson 1955: 83.

37. Quoted in Allsen 2001: 83.

38. Allsen 1987: 43.

39. This phrase, "monka denri-yin kücün-dür yeke su jali-yin 'ihen-dur," is the standard opening phrase of imperial letters written in Pakpa script during the Yuan; see Poppe 1957; and Sgrol-dkar 1995: nos. 1, 2, 5, 6. A slightly different form is found in the Pakpa script letter published by Pelliot ("Monkha denri-yin khuchun-dur kha'an u su-dur") in Tucci 1949: 623.

40. On this phrase and the important term "Fortune of the Emperor" (*qayan-u suu-dur*), see Mostaert and Cleaves 1952: 485–486, and 1962: 18–22.

41. Haenisch and Yao 1980: 141.

42. YS 72: 1780.

43. Ratchnevsky 1970: 423–424.

44. See, for example, ibid.: 425.

45. Ebrey 1991: 105, 160–161.

46. YS 77: 1923–1924; translated in Ratchnevsky 1970: 418–421.

47. Ratchnevsky 1970: 424–425.

48. Serruys 1974a: 3. Ratchnevsky (1970: 426–427) translates the phrase "Im Ver-trauen auf den Himmel wie auf dad glückliche Geschick und die Hilfe des Kaisers sollen von Jahr zu Jahr immerdar Dankopfer dargebracht!" The phrase in the YS 77:1924 re-volves around the reading of *sai,* and it seems that Serruy's translation is more plausible.

49. Sagaster 1970.

50. "Arriving at Kööbür of Muna [Mountain], the wheel of the cart became mired down and did not move. When, after hitching the steeds of the Five-Colored Nations, they were still unable to move it, the vast great people were in distress, and Kileen Baatur of the Sönid spoke once more respectfully: "My heavenly Holy Lord, Lion of Men, Born by the fate of eternal blue Heaven! You have gone, attaining your supreme rebirth, Though abandoned your extensive great empire. Your queens whom you met and mar-ried, Your evenly established state, The laws made as you desired, Your people gathered by the myriads, they are there. . . . Have you truly abandoned your old Mongols, my Lord? Although for your warm golden life there is [no longer] protection, Bringing your jade jewel-like illumined body, Should we not display it to your wife, Queen Börte Jusin, Should we not gratify your whole great people?" He said respectfully. The Khan lovingly granted [this wish], The Kazakh-cart moved squeaking, The amassed great people be-

came joyous, They brought it to the place called the 'Khan's Great Land.' Thereupon, led by his queens and sons, everyone weeped and wailed. Unable to bring out his imperial body, they were despairing. Erecting the eternal grave here they established the Eight White Tents of general veneration" (ET: 41v–42r).

51. All of these ritual enthronements at the Eight White Tents as they are found in the seventeenth-century Mongol histories are excerpted in CQO: 13–27.

52. ET: 53v–54r; translation based on Miyawaki 1997: 49–50. This same episode is also found in the ATA: 171. For a further discussion of this episode, see Okada 1984: 158.

53. For a study of how these rituals were performed in the pre-Qing period, see Chiodo 1989–1991, 1992–1993.

54. The Paris manuscript published by Sagaster also concludes with a list of donors and their gifts to the Chinggis Khan shrine.

55. JTS: 129.

56. "And it was heard that harm was to be done [to Altan Khan] by the depraved and evil Ibari of the Uiguds. . . . While guarding him in fear and trembling, by the fate of God, they were not harmed" (JTS: 80).

57. "The brilliant body of the powerful Holy Altan Khan became wounded in the middle of his striped calf, but did not suffer" (JTS: 94).

58. "As presaged, and as God deigned and approved, The feuding enemies were suppressed without hindrance" (JTS: 89).

59. "To speak of the reason, of how after this, by the decree of the supreme God, a fine time arose for the Chinese and Mongols to bring an equal harmony between the States" (JTS: 117). Furthermore, in order to ritually confirm the peace accord "they repeatedly sprinkled libations to the Eternal God, and took an oath" (JTS: 127).

60. "As Abakhai and Babakhai were sitting, having worshipped before the White Tents," (JTS: 79); "The loyal Six Tümens assembled in front of the Lord" (JTS: 88); "Afterwards, in front of the White Tent of the Sovereign Genius, the Six Tümen assembled. Praying to the sable holy thing and beside a larch tree, from in front of the Lord, The entire Great Nation gave Bodi Khan the title Küdeng Khan" (JTS: 89–90).

61. JTS: 94–95. The power of Chinggis Khan is also confirmed in another passage, "After the vengeful enemies had been weakened, the Lords begged their lives from the Holy Lord [Chinggis Khan]" (JTS: 91).

62. Acting with compassion is the central trait of a bodhisattva, and Altan Khan is presented as such in several episodes, especially when he saves the lives of the defeated Uriyangkhan chieftains, as well as those of captured Tibetan monks (JTS: 97, 108). On these episodes and Altan Khan's portrayal as a bodhisattva, see Kollmar-Paulenz 2001: 139–140.

63. "[Altan Khan], by the power of the merit acquired from the two assemblies, He suppressed all enemies, and made them his companions" (JTS: 77).

64. Altan Khan is not only confirmed as a Cakravartin in the *Jewel Translucent Sutra* but also in the colophon to his commissioned translation of the *Suvarṇaprabhāsa Sūtra* (CMBX 204–206), which is itself a work centrally concerned with Buddhist rule (see Orzech 1998: 116–117).

65. "From the Holy Khan's majestic remains, Peaceful, Expansive, Powerful and Fearsome Buddhas, Bodhisattva Avalokiteśvara's white seed syllable, Hri, And other, worship objects of body, speech and mind were repeatedly and rapidly produced. Immediately the Sugatas' seed syllables, The unparalleled syllables, Om hum tram hrih ah, Distinctly appeared strung as a five-colored pearl rosary. When an unfathomable variety of relics including a relic like a wishing jewel, a white conch shell with whorls turning to the right, and other uncountable five-colored relics, were seen by everyone, together with other innumerable signs, they venerated in faith. The Five Colored Nations, each individually, took them as a site of worship. Then the wonderful shining remains were inhumed in a great [stupa], made by a Nepalese craftsman of jewels, gold and silver, In the fashion of the ancient Sugata's reliquary stupas, named Bodhicitta" (JTS: 192–193).

66. Ibid.: 181.

67. Ibid.

68. Heissig 1959: 48. For a similar presentation of Chinggis Khan's bifurcated legitimacy, see also the colophon of the late Ming history of Avalokiteśvara, the *Qutuγtu yeke nigülesügci qomsim bodi sadu-yin cadig gegen toli neretü sastir orosiba*, MSS p. 51, CMC no. 4616.

69. Based on the text in Pozdneyev (1977: vol. 2, pp. 240–262). The English translation incorrectly reads "long-life tengri" instead of "Eternal Tengri/God." This is a result of a back translation from Tibetan. The Mongolian phrase *möngke tengri-yin* is translated into Tibetan as *tshe-ring gnam-kyi* and then retranslated back into Mongolian as *urtu nasutu tngri-yin*. This distortion can already be found during the Yuan; see Coyiji 1998: 248–249n2.

70. The Tibetan text reads *tse-ring gnams-gyi she-mong-la bsten-nas* (p. 244), which Pozdneyev reconstructed in Mongol as *urtu nasutu tengri-yin sülde-dü sitüjü* (1977: vol. 2, p. 254).

71. ATA: 128.

72. Ibid.: 176.

73. Ibid.: 189.

74. ET: 63v.

75. Altan'orgil 1989: 5–6.

76. On this work, see Kapstein 1992: 79–93; and TH no. 16. On the importance of this work as a narrative for Tibetan national identity, see Dreyfus 1994.

77. Heissig 1961–1962: 575n68; and Kara 1972: 36–37n35.

78. Heissig 1959: 34–36. On this work, see TH no. 94, and for an English translation of the Tibetan, see Sørensen 1994.

79. Heissig 1961–1962: 576.

80. It is unclear whether Ligdan Khan ever received the title "Khan" in front of the Eight White Tents; see Hagiwara 1969. Nevertheless, it is clear from all the evidence in the Kanjur colophons and letters to the Manchu court that Ligdan presented himself as sanctified by Heaven (see Ligeti 1942; Heissig 1962). For example, in a letter he wrote to the Manchu ruler in 1619, Ligdan even went so far as to project himself as a reincarnation of Chinggis Khan, and therefore titled himself "Lord-Hero Chinggis Khan of the Forty Tümen Mongols"; quoted in Serruys 1959: 50.

81. ATL: 648.

82. JTS: 188–190.

83. Weiers 1987: 111; and Weiers 1994: 129.

84. BE: 852.

85. Mostaert 1959: 31–32.

86. Ibid.: 7.

87. Mong. *Tengri bosug-iyar qayan;* see Zito 1997: 21.

88. Nurhaci (1559–1626), the founder of the Manchu state, had already received tantric initiation and appointed his "guru," Olug Darkhan Nangso, as Dharma-master of the Manchu realm in 1621 (Grupper 1984: 51). Nurhaci also had seven large monasteries built near his residence of Hetu Ala (i.e., Yenden, the old capital) in the 1620s (Dabringhaus 1997: 122). These building projects were then followed by those of his successor, Hong Taiji (1592–1643), who had the famous Mahakala Temple constructed in 1635, which was a paragon of Manchu imbrication with Mongol Buddhism. Not only was the temple to house a copy of the Buddhist canon in Mongolian but also the remains of Ligdan Khan's guru, Sharba Khutugtu, and most important, the famous Mahakala statue. Khubilai Khan had given this statue to Pakpa Lama during the Yuan dynasty, and when Ligdan Khan's family submitted to the Manchus they presented it as tribute. The importance of this statue, with its historical linkages and ritual significations, was profound in order for the Manchu claim to be seen as the rightful heirs of Mongol Buddhist rule; and thus, in 1643, Hong Taiji initiated an extension of this important temple complex. In 1645 this project was complete, with four temples and adjoining stupas having been built to encircle the Mahakala Temple, the imperial palace and the Manchu capital of Mukden within a mandala. As Grupper notes, "this architectonic representation of the Buddhist cosmological order (an arrangement reminiscent of the ensemble of Bsam yas at the old Tibetan imperial precinct of Brag mar) celebrated [Hong Taiji's] succession as cakravartin, defined Manchu dynastic right, and set the Manchu capital and realm under the protection of Mahakala" (Grupper 1984: 53.). The Manchus were therefore clearly involved in the project of appropriating and projecting the narratives and rituals of Mongol Buddhist political authority.

89. Di Cosmo and Bao 2003: 56–57.

90. See, for example, the early letter from the Tümeds to Hong Taiji in which proper rule is described precisely in terms of this bifurcated discourse, even quoting a passage from the *White History (Cayan teüke),* AQMBD: 127.

91. Cleaves 1995: 47. See also his commentary on the phrase *suu buyan* in 1996: 48.

92. Quoted in Berger 2003: 32.

93. Perdue 2005: 434.

Chapter 3. Qing Ornamentalism and the Cult of Chinggis Khan

1. *Alasan ayulan-yin qosiyun-u qosud wang güng-ner-ün uy oboy jidkülge-yin casa jisa,* MS pp. 1–6, CMC no. 9334.

2. Cannadine 2001. On the role of class and social heirarchy in the British Empire, see also Jayawardena 2002; Mukherjee 2003; and Carroll 2005.

3. See, for example, the debates about whether or not to use the *tusi* (native chieftain) system in Taiwan. Ultimately, the court decided against it, because there did not appear to be any kind of native structure giving overlordship over multiple tribes or regions. See Shepard 1993.

4. Cannadine 2001: 10, 21.

5. The *Jarliγ-iyar toγtaγaγsan mongγol qotong ayimaγ-un wang güng-üd-ün iledkil sastir* (Ch. *Qinding waifan menggu huibu wanggong biaozhuan*) was first compiled in 1795, and printed in 1802 in 120 volumes. It was later revised and reissued in 1814 in 24 volumes, which edition was then reprinted in 1839. A new edition was prepared in 1849 and was again reprinted in 1859 (Veit 1990: 74–104).

6. The idea of the multiple guises (Wu 1995) and even the "multiculturalism" of the Manchu emperor has been prevalent in the study of Qing rule ever since Farquhar's 1978 essay. Nevertheless, while it is possible to find evidence that seems to support such ideas in the case of the Mongols, as when Saghang Sechen praises the Kangxi emperor for respecting the local traditions of all the people in the empire, it is important to keep in mind Bellah's argument that "multiculturalism is part of the process of assimilation into the dominant culture and thus not in any real sense the expression of cultural pluralism" (2002: 27). For a critique of the Qing's purported multiculturalism, see Bartlett's review of Rawski's *The Last Emperors* (2001: 171–183). In addition, on the Manchu attempt to create a uniform Qing culture based on militarism, see Waley-Cohen 2003.

7. ET: 67v.

8. "While then returning, he encountered Altan, the second son of [Barsubolad] Alag, who came and said, 'Having taken the title of Khan and the Lord's throne, you have pacified the kingdom. Now, there is a petty khan's title, called Hsi-tao qan, "Defender of the Khan's realm," grant this title to me. Let me defend your great state!'" (ET 67v). On Altan Khan's early relationship with the Chakhar Khan, see JTS, 20–27.

9. "To Boshugtu Sechen Jinong, they presented the title 'Cakravartin Sechen Jinong Khan who makes the Golden Wheel Revolve'; to Queen Taigal Jönggen, the title Dara Bodhisattva Nomchi Dalai Sechen Queen Jönggen; to his uncle Manggus Chöökür [the title] Dai Khung Taiji; to his younger brother Öljei [the title of] Bingtü Khung Taiji; to Dashi of the Left Wing [the title of] Üijeng Khung Taiji; to Engke Khoshuuchi [the title of] Khoshuuchi Khung Taiji; the great-grandson of Khutugtai Sechen Khung Taiji of the Right Wing, the son of Batu Khung Taiji, [namely] Saghang Sechen, born in the Ga Dragon Year [1604], at the age of eleven—the princes of the Six Ulus saying amongst themselves that he was the descendant of the man who initiated the Religion and State— via his grandfather [Khutugtai Sechen Khung Taiji], bestowed the title Saghang Sechen Khung Taiji, and at the age of seventeen, inducted him into the ranks of ministers, and solidifying the state, he was greatly beloved. To Manggus Khulachi [the title of] Erdeni Khulachi Khung Taiji . . . in respect of their relative importance, all the other princes, son-in-laws, and ministers, they bestowed titles and ranks one after the other" (ET 86v).

10. "At that time he gathered and assembled the vast, Great Ulus headed by the remaining greater and lesser princes of the Ordos Tümen. And saying, 'When we had emerged from the confusion, we came together,' he gave the title Father Lord to Bodatai

Chöökür, and saying, 'Having befriended us from the outset, he delivered us from the enemy,' he bestowed on Saghang Sechen Khung Taiji the title Erke Sechen Khung Taiji. . . . Also, to the greater and lesser lords and officials and those who had in general given their effort, each was granted [a title] accordingly" (ET: 92r).

11. On this relationship, see for example AQMBD: 109.

12. ET 95r–95v.

13. One such example is found in Saghang Sechen's description of the Kangxi emperor's reign, which in accord with the *ulus/törö* model allowed each *ulus* to keep its own traditions intact. "His son, Engke Amuulang, born in the Ga Horse year [1654], at the age of nine in the Sim Tiger year [1662], ascended the throne and became famed in all directions as the 'Peace and Tranquillity' Khan. In the same year, performing mourning for the sake of his late father he handed down a decree which promulgated mourning to the peoples of whatsoever direction, each according to his own customs, and he completed and brought about by religious and secular custom beneficent deeds for the one who passed on, also in the fashion of whatsoever ulus" (ET 96r).

14. See, for example, the interpretation of Manchu rule in Jagchid and Hyer 1979: 177.

15. Struve 1998: 14.

16. *Üjümücin baraɣun qosiɣun-u jasaɣ wang noyad-un ergümjilegsen bicig,* MS pp. 6–10, CMC no. 11001.

17. Atwood 2000: 129.

18. *Jarliɣ–iyar toɣtaɣaɣsan mongɣol qotong ayimaɣ-un wang güng-üd-ün iledkil sastir,* MS 2:1v, CMC no. 9326.

19. It is also important to note that the idea of distinct *ulus*, or ethno-territories, is not only found in Mongolian sources. In a bilingual Tibetan passport issued by the Panchen Lama in 1714, the "Manchus, Chinese, Ordos, Chakhar, Tümed, Khalkha, Oirads" (Tib. "manju rgya nag ur tu su cha dkar thu mad khal kha o'i rod sogs kyi sa'i char 'khod-pa") are told to respect the rights of the bearer of the document (Schmid 1954: 59–60).

20. *Jarliɣ–iyar toɣtaɣaɣsan mongɣol qotong ayimaɣ-un wang güng-üd-ün iledkil sastir,* MS 2:25v, CMC no. 9326.

21. On Lubsangdanzin's revolt, see Perdue 2005: 243–249.

22. Bulag 2002: 38.

23. After the revolt the Qing court followed the advice of the general Nian Gengyao and divided the Kökenuur Mongols into twenty-nine banners: twenty-one Khoshuud, two Choros, four Torghud, one Khoid, and one Khalkha, each under the direct control of the Manchu amban in Xining (EM 574).

24. Ishihama 1992: 508–513.

25. The creation of a "pan-*ulus*" Mongol nation orchestrated by the Manchu state is perhaps best captured in Giuseppe Castiglione's famous 1775 painting commemorating the return of the Torghuts (Ho and Bronson 2004: 92–93). On this painting and the rituals held for the Mongols at the Wanshu yuan (Garden of Ten Thousand Trees), see R. Yu 2004; and Sommer 2004.

26. This same strategy was also applied in Tibet after the Gurkha war, when Qing

policy shifted toward "the unequivocal subordination of the Tibetan government to the Qing and the assimilation of Tibet into the Qing Empire. . . . On 3 March 1793, Fukkanga memorialized a set of regulations for managing Tibetan affairs, which was revised later in the year before being promulgated in the form of twenty-nine articles. One of the most significant stipulations of the new blueprint for Qing imperial administration was that henceforth officials, such as bka'-blon, were to be chosen jointly by the Dalai Lama and the Qing minister in Tibet" (Sperling 1998: 326, 331). On these policies, see Dabringhaus 1994: 133–238.

27. It is important to note that, unbeknownst to the emperor, the Fifth Dalai Lama was already dead at this time and the regent had assumed power. Although this may certainly have weakened the response to these developments from the Tibetan side, it does not take away from the fact that at this juncture the Kangxi emperor did appropriate this ritual role into the emperorship.

28. On the Qing conquest of the Zunghars and their relations with the Khalkhas, see Perdue 2005: 133–208.

29. Ahmad 1970: 266–267.

30. The "Seven Banners" does not refer to the Qing banner system. The term was originally the Seven Otog; however, in 1655 the Khalkhas accepted Qing terms like "banner" for *otog*, and *zasag* for ruler, though without accepting Qing political structures. Nevertheless, the Seven Otog, or Seven Banners, refers to the group of Khalkhas who had moved north into the area of "Outer Mongolia" in the sixteenth century, while the "Five Banner Khalkha" remained in "Inner Mongolia."

31. *Engke amuyulang-un qorin jiryuduyar on-u dangsa*, MS pp. 10–11.

32. QSL 129:17b, quoted in Ahmad 1970: 258.

33. *Engke amuyulang*, MS pp. 113–114.

34. Ibid., pp. 111–112.

35. On the expanding role of the Qing court in Buddhist affairs and its eventual control of the Buddhist establishment in Tibet (mainly Amdo; central Tibet and Kham remained largely outside Qing control) and Mongolia, see, for example, Sagaster 1967: 86; Moses 1977; Weiers 1988–1989; Martin 1990; Chia 1992: 205–246; Hevia 1993; Dabringhaus 1994, 1997; Bartholomew 1997; Waley-Cohen 1998; Wang 2000.

36. Bawden 1966.

37. Miyawaki 1992: 600–601.

38. Heissig 1961–1962: 566–567.

39. Chiodo 1989–1991: 218.

40. A survey of all the known manuscripts concerning the cult of Chinggis Khan and the relevant publications is found in Solongyod 1999: 15–44.

41. Atwood 1996: 113–123.

42. Skrynnikova 1992/93.

43. BE: 939, quoted in Atwood 2000: 101.

44. BE: 897.

45. Atwood 2000: 129.

46. Cannadine 2001: 101–120.

47. On the "cult of monarchy," or more specifically the awe-inspiring nature of the Qing emperor, see Sperling 1998.

48. Chia has noted that the name given for the annual imperial audience is *chaojin*, which she argues means "pilgrimage to court" (1993: 64).

49. Bulag 2002: 36.

50. "Now to that family of Altan Khan of the Manchus of old there was born Nurhaci Baatur Tayisui. He gathered a multitude at the very outset; through his means and strengths he brought into his power the Three Jürchid of the Water. Next he took the state of Jing Tayisi of the Yekege Chagan Jürchid. After that in the Wu Horse year [1618] he campaigned against China, and when he captured Liaodong, the east province of the Great Ming Emperor, a comet came out of the heavens, and it was a major omen. Vcir Tümei Günding Daiwang Güisi of the Ordos said as follows, 'Oh, this one called Taisui [Ch. Taizu] is a man of great destiny. This star is *suu jali* of a very mighty Khan. Hence he is not like an ordinary man.' In this way the mighty Baatur Taisui was famed in all directions" (ET: 92r).

51. GU: 100.

52. AKMK: 202.

53. Ibid.: 239–240, quoted in Atwood 2000: 99–100.

54. Mostaert 1956b: 253.

55. On the importance of the imperial bestowal of seals and its ritualization of power, see the parallel initiation rites of the Chinese Brotherhoods in DeBernardi 2004: 85.

56. Serruys 1974/5a: 596–597.

57. On this tent and its incorporation into the Chinggis Khan cult, see Chiodo 1992–1993: 100–105; and Andrews 1999.

58. Serruys 1974/5a: 597.

59. Sayinjiryal and Saraldai 1983: 413–470. This chapter has been translated in W. Yu 1989.

60. This was the *Imperially Commissioned Norms and Regulations of the Bureau of Colonial Affairs* (Ch. *Qingding Lifanyuan zeli*). For an edition and study of these laws based on a manuscript housed in the State Library in Ulaanbaatar, see Dylykova 1998.

61. Di Cosmo 1998: 295.

62. Nayiraltu and Altan'orgil 1989: 167–168.

63. CQO: 41–42.

64. Heissig 1959: 168–169.

65. MBOT: 378–379, quoted in Atwood 2000: 98–99.

66. *Yeke yuan ulus-aca jalyamjilaysan mongyol-un surbuljitu noyad-un uysay-a ayimay*, MS pp. 2–4, CMC no. 9140.

67. Sagaster 1992: 150.

68. Since the logic of the Chinese state has recently moved from communism to "market socialism," or perhaps more aptly "national socialism," it is perhaps not surprising that the engagement with the Chinggis Khan cult has also changed. Following the theory of privatization, the PRC government currently wants to sell the Chinggis Khan Mausoleum, the most popular tourist site in Inner Mongolia, to a local Chinese company

called Donglian. "The company plans to demolish the mausoleum to build a larger one, which will be called 'The Second Chinggis Khan Mausoleum,' in order to attract more tourists and generate more profits for the owner, named Hou, a Han-Chinese businessman" (Hyer 2004). On this development and the unrest it has generated among Inner Mongolians, see Brooke 2004.

69. On the issue of Mongol identity, Chinggis Khan and the Chinese state, see Khan 1994; and Bulag 2004: 110.

70. Spiegel 1983: 159–160.

Chapter 4. The Poetics, Rituals and Language of Being Mongol, Buddhist and Qing

1. *Mongγol-un qaγan-u uruγ enedkeg-ün qaγan-aca salaju iregsen ucir anu*, Mong 143 and Mong 146, CMBX, pp. 16–17, and 43.

2. *Mongγol-un qaγan-u uruγ enedkeg-ün qaγan-aca salaju iregsen ucir anu*, MS pp. 2–14, Mong 143.

3. On the source of this episode, see Elliott 2001: 44–47.

4. On the historiographical implications and problems related to mappings of time, see Zerubavel 2003; and on the changes in Mongol conceptualizations of time during the Qing formation, see Elverskog 2005.

5. Comaroff 1994: 304–305.

6. Hastings 1990: 187–190.

7. Damdinsüreng 1982: 920–922.

8. In his study of the text, Kesigtoγtaqu has argued that it was written at the same time as the *White History*, namely, sometime between 1260 and 1330, since both texts have the same geospatial arrangement of the Five-Colored Nations and the Four Subjects (1998: 1–17). However, the dating of both of these texts to the Yuan period is extremely problematic, and both presumably date to the late sixteenth century. Regardless, this manuscript of Chinggis Khan's history is probably the oldest extant Mongol history.

9. Heissig 1966: 9.

10. JTS: 63–64.

11. Huth 1894: 31.

12. Damdinsüren 1979: 39–58.

13. See, for example, the colophons of the 1584 *Altan Gerel* (CMBX: 205–206); Shireetü Güüshi's translations of the *Diamond Sutra* and the twelve-volume *Yum* (Heissig 1959: 44n2, 46n2); the 1708 *Thar-pa Chen-po;* and Shireetü Güüshi's *Uliger-ün Dalai* (Kara 2000: 28–29, 31–33).

14. DeWeese 1994: 443–444.

15. SE: 20–34.

16. Hoog 1983: 38–43. Based on the presentation of the Kashmiri monk Kamalaśrī, the same geneaological progression is also found in Rashiduddin Fazlullah's *History of India (Ta'rikh al-Hind);* see Jahn 1956: 120–127.

17. On this work, see Bareja-Starzynska 1997.

18. Xiao Daheng, in his early-seventeenth-century *Beilü fengsu*, wrote: "The customs

of the barbarians used to be savage and cruel, and for a long time it was impossible to civ-
ilize them. But since they submitted and began to pay tribute, they have conceived a great
regard for the Buddhist faith. Within their tents they constantly adore an image of the
Buddha, and they make him an offering whenever they eat or drink. The rich . . . invite
the lamas to recite prayers, offer incense and bow reverently. All the money they can get
goes for casting statuettes of the Buddha or stupas. Men and women, old and young, always have a rosary in their hands. Some of them make a little box of silver or gold, about
two or three inches in height, into which they put amulets. They carry this box beneath
the left arm, and are never without it, either sitting or lying, sleeping or eating" (English
translation in Bawden 1989: 27–28). On the Mongols' adoption of the Dharma in the pre-
Qing period, see also the Buddhist items in the will of the Khalkha Khan Sholoi, published
by Veit 1983.

19. JTS: 197–198.

20. Pallas 1980: 425.

21. JTS: 60–62.

22. On the continued presence of diverse Buddhist traditions among the post-Yuan
Mongols, see Richardson 1958: 150; Serruys 1962, 1966; Jagchid 1988: 121–127; Sperling
1992; and Coyiji 1996.

23. Ngag-dbang rnam-gyal, *Chos-'byung Ngo-mtshar rgya-mtsho,* quoted in Tuttle
1997: 2.

24. Tuttle 1997: 2–3.

25. JTS: 197.

26. The New Year ritual that is intended to drive out the evil forces for the coming
year was founded by Tsongkhapa and commemorates the miraculous powers that the
Buddha displayed during two weeks of magical contests with a group of heretics (Powers
1995: 190–193). Moreover, on account of this connection with the Gelukpa order, this
ritual has also become a central element in Tibet's protracted civil wars. Shortly after the
Second Dalai Lama (1475–1542) finished his studies in 1498, he was forced to flee Lhasa
as the protector of the Karmapa sect seized control of the city. As a result of this attack the
Gelukpa were denied the ability to perform their most holy ritual, as it was taken over by
the Karmapa. A similar development also occurred during the tenure of the Fourth Dalai
Lama, who also fled Lhasa due to escalating violence, leaving the Karmapa in charge of
the New Year rituals (DMB: 412–413, 1604–1606).

27. Even so, recent scholarship has revealed the continued presence of different Buddhist lineages among the Mongols during the Qing; see Kiripolská 1997 and Charleux
2002.

28. On the creation of Buddhist orthodoxy as part of imperial and state consolidation, see Lewis 1990.

29. On the political role of Gelukpa Buddhism in the seventeenth century, see
Sperling, 2003; and Tsyrempilon 2003.

30. Tuttle, forthcoming.

31. On the often brutal rise to power of the Fifth Dalai Lama, see Yamaguchi 1995
and Sperling 2001. Even though the Great Fifth did eventually wield control over Tibet,

to a large extent the institutionalization of the Dalai Lama and his ritual and political authority was the legacy of the regent Sangyé Gyatso, who wrote twelve major works comprising 3,600 folios on this topic between 1693 and 1701. During the eighteenth century, however, the power of the Dalai Lama fluctuated in tandem with the shifting political winds; see Petech 1950.

32. The Great Fifth was well aware of the possibility of different rulers potentially allying themselves with other Buddhist schools and thereby eclipsing his own power, as was the case with various Mongol princes and their support of the Kagyü. In addition, he was also conscious of the threat to his power presented by the elevation of Tüshiyetü Khan's son as Jebdzundamba Khutugtu. Although later histories present a cordial relation between these two figures, the Dalai Lama and the Jebdzundamba Khutugtu, it is clear that at the time this newly formed Khalkha-centered form of Buddhist rule was a direct threat to Gelukpa power. As Miyawaki has shown, the later histories covering this period expunge all traces of this dispute, creating the linear narrative of Gelukpa authority; yet it can not be ignored that the Jebdzundamba Khutugtu was an incarnation of Taranatha of the Jonang-pa. This was a subsect of the Sakya allied with the Kagyü, which the Great Fifth had brutally suppressed. Likewise the later claim that the Great Fifth bestowed the title "Jebdzundamba" on the Mongol incarnation in 1650, creating an encompassed hierarchy of power, is disproved in the *Qing Shi Lu*, which uses this title already in 1647. Moreover, the bestowal of this rank is not even mentioned in the Great Fifth's autobiography, though he does describe meeting with the Mongol boy (Miyawaki 1992: 600–601). However, the most telling evidence is found in the *Clear Mirror* of Dzaya Pandita Lozang Trinlé, a disciple of the Great Fifth, wherein he describes the Manchu-brokered 1686 peace among the Khalkhas. He notes that Galdan protested to the Qing court the Jebdzundamba's refusal to offer prayers to the Dalai Lama's envoy (Bira 1980: 15), an act that clearly points to competing visions of the authority of the Dalai Lama and the new Khalkha incarnation. Moreover, the Great Fifth also tried to suppress any Buddhist relations with groups other than the Gelukpa. To this end he sent his Khalkha disciple, Dzaya Pandita, back to Khalkha territory with the admonition to crush any rival schools, particularly the Nyingma, which another of the Great Fifth's disciples, Zaya Pandita, was doing among the Oirad.

33. On the history of Neichi Toin, see Heissig 1953a, 1953b, 1954a.

34. DL5: 333.

35. Wilson 1983: 35.

36. *Boyda neyici toyin dalai Manjusri-yin domoy-i todorqai-a geyigülügci cindamani erike*, MS 76r.

37. DL5: 334.

38. *Boyda neyici toyin*, MS 76v–77r.

39. JTS: 136–137.

40. ATL: 641–644. A nearly verbatim version is also found in ANT: 108–111.

41. DL3–4. On the Great Fifth's elevation of the institution of the Dalai Lama in these biographies, see Ishihama 1993.

42. Bawden 1989: 28–29. The episode is in ET: 81v–82r.

43. One can also see this reversal in the visual representations of these relations. Thus,

in the early Mongolian paintings at Mayidari Juu, just west of Hohhot, the Mongol figures are larger and the Tibetan lamas are coming to them. In Tibetan thangkas, on the other hand, such as those of the Great Fifth, the lama is the central figure, to whom the smaller Mongol figures come bearing gifts. See Charleux 1999: 86; and D. Jackson 1996: 204.

44. On the historiography of Ligdan Khan, see Heissig 1979.

45. DeWeese 1994: 164–165.

46. AKMK: 212–213.

47. The identification of Yeke Juu with Kangxi and not Altan Khan did not end with Dharma Güüsi's work of 1739. In a later eighteenth-century history of monasteries in the Hohhot area is the statement, "on account of the antiquity of this temple, it was impossible to establish the year of its founding. During the Degedü-erdemtü [1636–1643] upon the order of the Dayicung [=Dayicing] Emperor . . . the temple was restored and enlarged and given the name Wu-liang: Caylasi ügei" (Serruys 1974–1975b: 228n163). At the end of the nineteenth century, Pozdneyev recorded that the Mongol monks actually living in Yeke Juu Monastery "could not vouch" for the fact that Altan Khan had built it (Pozd-neyev 1977: 37–38). Instead, its history was bound to the Manchu emperors and their bestowal of titles on the monastery.

48. GU 174.

49. On this history, see Heissig 1959: 162–169.

50. Bilig-ün jula, MS 13r.

51. Although the location of Altan Khan's grave is unknown, based on Chinese maps and travel accounts, Serruys has suggested that it may be north of Hohhot (1979a: 102–105). On the importance of dead bodies, their memory and political power, see Kim Haboush 2003.

52. The case of Yemen provides an interesting parallel to this phenomenon. Much as the Mongols sought to reaffirm their identity by means of remythologizing their Buddhist past, the Yemenis also reaffirmed their identity during the Ummayad period by asserting that Islam had come to Yemen before Muhammad. "Yemenis had been the spearhead of Islamic expansion; but during the century of Umayyad rule up to AD 750, and then under the Abassid caliphs, they felt themselves increasingly eclipsed by Arabs of northern origin who came to have more in common with the Byzantines and Persians they had conquered than with their Arabian roots. Yemen's intellectual counterattack produced a great treasure of history and poetry. More important, it created for the Yemenis powerful concepts of their own past. In the tenth century, al-Hamdani, known as the Tongue of Yemen, drew on the works of his predecessors and supplemented them with his own research to produce the massive ten-part genealogical and historical compendium al-Iklil. . . . A large section of the Iklil is devoted to tombs and their occupants. The most notable feature of al-Hamdani's deceased ancients, 'old men dried out upon their beds,' is that they were often buried with an inscription bearing the first half—and sometimes, prophetically, both halves—of the Muslim creed: There is no God but Allah, and Muhammad is the messenger of Allah. The historian, therefore, is demonstrating the existence of Islam in Yemen before Muhammad" (Mackintosh-Smith 2000: 44–45).

53. The date of this work is disputed, but it was probably composed around 1740 (Kämpfe 1983; TH no. 276).

54. GC: 37; see also AE: 74–75.

55. GC: 128. The actual title was Tong Yabghu Qaghan.

56. Reprinted with a preface in Bira 1974: 141–209.

57. Atwood 1992/1993: 19.

58. Whether or not Gombojab's work was influenced by the rising interest in philological studies of the ancient past in the seventeenth and eighteenth centuries (Elman 1984) is unclear.

59. BE: 8.

60. The 1825 *Qad noyad-un aci ür-e-yi delgeregülgci kemekü teüke* even proclaims that the Mongols' mythical ancestor Borte Chino-a was an incarnation of Samantabhadra (MS 2r, CMC no. 9051).

61. ATMG: 57.

62. *Tngri tedkügsen qayan bancin boyda-yi jalaysan tuqai jarliy,* MS 1v–2r.

63. Serruys 1970a: 531.

64. Serruys 1974a: 77

65. Quoted in Hurca 1999: 52.

66. Hastings 1990: 191.

67. On the importance and process of transforming sacred space in order to legitimate new political and social systems, see Eaton 2000: 94–132.

68. See, for example, the history of Chaghan Diyanchi Lama and its description of his relations with the Qing court in the building of monasteries, *Tegüs coytu degedü blam-a cayan diyanci qutuy-tu-yin töröl duradduysan namtar,* MS 13, 22; CMC no. 4760.

69. *Tngri tedkügsen qayan bancin boyda-yi jalaysan tuqai jarliy,* MS 20–21.

70. See, for example, the rituals of mourning mandated for Qing emperors in Mostaert 1961 and Serruys 1977c: 580–581.

71. Miller 1959: 82–84. The development of the cult of Wutai Shan during the Buddhist Qing clearly parallels the initial political Buddhist mandalization of China during the Tang period; see Sen 2003: 76–101.

72. Wakeman 1985: 203.

73. Nima 1989–1991: 221.

74. Brown 1995: 19–20.

75. Atwood 1996: 137.

76. Heissig 1999: 81–84.

77. Although Mergen Gegen's four-volume "Mongolian national liturgy" was published in Beijing (Heissig 1954: no. 162), it appears not to have been in wide circulation or use. It is not found in the major Mongol collections, nor is it found in a list of sutras given to a Beijing monastery in 1786 (CMC no. 10443), nor was it part of the Chakhar monastic library studied by Heissig.

78. Heller 1996: 139.

79. In the traditional Mongol religious view, the south side of the mountain is holy.

80. *Siregetü güüsi corji-yin ijayur-un blam-a Geligjalzan sayin coytu-yin gegegen-u namtar,* MS 22–23; CMC no. 4796.

81. On this process in Japan, see Grapard 1982: 195–221; and in Tibet, see Huber 1999.

82. Hyer and Jagchid 1983: 28.

83. On the Chinese state's historical practice of recognizing and enfeoffing local gods, see Hansen 1990 and Hymes 2002: 181–195.

84. There are two possible dates for this individual, the time of the First Jebdzundamba Khutugtu (1635–1723) or the Fifth Jebdzundamba Khutugtu (b. 1815). The nineteenth century seems more likely, see Bawden 1970: 59.

85. Tatár 1976: 33.

86. Fletcher 1998: 262–268, 354–356.

87. On the idea of "church language" and the history of Buddhist translation, see Nattier 1990.

88. Zieme 1992 and Dunnell 1996. The connection between a vernacular literature and "the nation" can also be found in the modern period, as witnessed in Cambodia; see Keyes 1994: 48.

89. JTS: 65–68.

90. Heissig 1966: 9.

91. CMBX: 205–206.

92. JTS: 210–211. Whether or not this translation was actually prepared is unclear. As noted above, the oldest extant redaction of the Mongolian Kanjur is the so-called Ligdan Khan Kanjur from 1628–1629. At that time six manuscript copies were supposedly prepared, one written in gold (it is now housed in the Library of the Academy of Social Sciences in Hohhot), which may actually be older (Heissig 1998: 158), and five in black ink (one of which is housed at St. Petersburg University [Kasyanenko 1993]). Kollmar-Paulenz has recently argued that this may actually be a different redaction (2002). However, as evidenced in this work and in several colophons (including one that confirms the translation of the Kanjur at this time (Kasyanenko 1993: 158), it is clear that the idea, and possibly even the work of translating the entire Kanjur, was begun and completed at the time of Altan Khan and his descendants (Heissig 1984: 216–220; Uspensky 1997: 113). In fact, it is possible that when Ligdan Khan was engaged in his failed campaign against the Ordos in 1627, he acquired a copy while he was residing in Hohhot (Altan'orgil, Narancoүtu and Altanjiyaү-a 1999: 22), after which he returned east and began the retranslation project of 1628–1629. This included the altering of colophons to erase the evidence of Altan Khan's initial work and the reorganization of the contents. A similar phenomenon also occurred when the Kangxi emperor ordered a Mongolian Kanjur to be prepared in Beijing in 1718–1720.

93. On the extant Mongolian Buddhist literature from the pre-Qing period, see Heissig 1976; and Chiodo 2000.

94. One of the most vocal critics of this process of Tibetanization was the late Qing author Injanashi, who believed that the use of Tibetan by Mongol Buddhists hindered the advancement of the Mongols. In his 1890–1891 "Hypocrisy of the Dharmamasters," he writes: "The speaker of Mongolian who comprehends and grasps [Buddhist] theology in Tibetan is as rare as a star in daylight and a rainbow at night. Yet these lamas developed an arrogance in sneering at those who study [non-Buddhist] books. While these lamas possess the outer appearance of doctrine, they never attained its inner secrets. They [the

lamas] know not even the names and numbers of their Buddhas. . . . What a waste of human intelligence!" (KS: 150).

Chapter 5. The Buddhist Qing and Mongol Localization in the Nineteenth Century

1. On the impact of the Hui rebellions on Ordos, see Sodubilig 1996 and 1998.

2. The history of this land dispute is explained in van Hecken 1960.

3. Serruys 1979b: 220–226.

4. Miles 2004: 34.

5. Heissig 1966: 15. See, for example, the recently discovered nineteenth-century *History of Zasagtu Khan Aimag,* housed at the Central Archives of History of Mongolia, Ochir 2001.

6. ATL: 655.

7. Mostaert 1959: 28.

8. On Gombojab's *Rgya-nags chos-'byung,* see Bira 1970: 32–40; and TH no. 276.

9. On this work see Heissig 1959: 162–170.

10. Gombowangjil was the ruling Grand Duke of East Abaga between 1792 and 1827, and he wrote this history in 1817 (Coyiji 1990: 36–38).

11. *Burqan-u sasin angɤ-a ɤaruɤsan enedkeg töbed mongol-un orod-dur delgeregsen terigüten-ü ayimag,* MS 17, CMC no. 4602; *Sutu boɤda cinggis qaɤan-u üy-e-ece manju-dur aldarsiju angɤ-a qaɤan saɤuɤsan cadig,* MS pp. 34–36, CMC no. 9066.

12. *Erten-ü burqan-u gegen ekilegsen boɤda cinggese boɤda qaɤan-u üyes-ece inaɤsi blam-a gegen boɤda qaɤan üyes-yin ɤandisi-ün tobci megem-e,* MS 4v, CMC no. 4589.

13. "Then although he did not really meet the majesty of the Sakya Panchen, they created the latent karmic bonds [that would reach fruition with Khubilai Khan]" (SE: 43).

14. "Taizu's sixth year, the Blue Tiger Year [1194], at the age of thirty-three, he drove the khan of the Chinese Jin dynasty from the throne, and having gained great power he named the state, Dai Yuan. Also going to the south, he invited one [monk] and took a *sutra* of the good customs of the Chinese Dharma" (SE: 40).

15. The idea that Chinggis Khan met with the Chan monk Haiyün presumably derives from Nianchang's 1323 *Comprehensive Chronicle of Buddhist Patriarchs (Fozu lidai tongzai* T 2036), wherein it is claimed that during the 1214 Mongol campaigns into Shanxi, Haiyun (1202–1257) met with Chinggis Khan. However, this is incorrect. Haiyun actually met Mukhali during the 1219 invasion of Lanzhou, though it is true that upon Mukhali's advice Chinggis Khan subsequenly exempted Chinese Buddhist monks from taxes and corvée. Moreover, Haiyun became a central Buddhist figure among the Mongols in the pre-Yuan period. In 1228, upon the recommendation of Yelü Chucai, he was made abbot of Qingshou Monastery in the capital, and in this capacity he thwarted the Mongols, attempt to purge the clergy through rigorous examinations. In 1237 Chinggis Khan's second empress gave him the title Eminent Scholar, Brilliant Heavenly Guardian of the State. In 1242 Khubilai took the Bodhisattva Vows from Haiyun, and the following year he "baptized" Khubilai's son Zhenjin. Güyüg Khan put him in charge of all Buddhist affairs in north China in 1247, and when the khan died, Haiyun wrote out sixteen copies of a *vinaya*

text in his own blood to protect the empire. Möngke Khan reconfirmed his leading position in 1251, though in 1252 he was replaced by the Tibetan Na mo; whereupon Haiyun continued his teaching and work promoting his Linji school of Buddhism (ISK: 224–242).

16. *Burqan bodisadu-a terigüten qamuγ delekei-yin ejed-ün takiγu takily-a*, MS 6r–7v, CMC no. 3581.

17. On the fox in early tantric Buddhism, see Strickmann 2002: 228–281; and for its importance in Qing culture, see Huntington 2003. On the Mongol worship of the fox, see Serruys 1970a.

18. *töbed kitad mongγol . . . tere γurbaγula nigen eke-ece törögsen ajiγu, Ünegen-ü sang orosiba*, MS 2r, CMC no. 3529. The same passage is found in both Ulaanbaatar *Ünegen-ü sang* manuscripts published by Bawden 1976: 453; however, the Oirat manuscript claims they had the same father (see Bawden 1978: 25).

19. AE: 112–131; BT: 457–472. In his late-nineteenth-century work, the *Rosary of White Lotuses*, Damchø Gyatsho Dharmatala even identifies Altan Khan as an incarnation of Vajrapāṇi (RWL: 219).

20. Jimbadorji also notes that currently China is filled with Christians, although he does not expand on this other religiously identified group (BE 264).

21. This connection is made most evident in the *Jewel Translucent Sutra* wherein, during the 1578 meeting, Altan Khan sends troops out to the East Turkestan Muslims and reminds them of their descent from the Chinggisid line. "Afterwards, [Altan Khan] set out towards Jalaman Mountain for the Oirad Tümen . . . / Üijeng Jaisang, who was immeasurably knowledgable in the ancient stories, customs and legends / Was sent as a messenger to Shah Khan of the White Turbans. When he described the genealogy from Chagatai to the present / [Shah Khan] was greatly pleased and gave as tribute fine western horses and diamonds" (JTS 108–110). In later Mongol histories the Chaghatai lineages of Inner Asia are also included in the narrative of the Mongols.

22. BT: 366.

23. BT: 371–378.

24. On the Buddha's prophecy of decline and its historical and mythic implications, see Nattier 1991.

25. Schubert 1953; Bawden 1984–1985; and Kollmar-Paulenz 1994.

26. Grünwedel 1918; Bernbaum 1980.

27. Heissig 1961: no. 483. There are also four manuscripts of his poetry revolving around Shambhala preserved in the archives of the Inner Mongolia Academy of Social Sciences.

28. *Sambala-yin oron-u teüke orosiba*, MS p. 15, CMC no. 4633: "Now at this time, the 15th of Fall's last month in Daoguang's seventh year [1828], a female red pig year, the 20th [king] Rigdeng Mahabala is sitting on the throne of Shambhala." It is unknown whether this is the first Mongolian translation of this work; nevertheless, it points to a growing reception of the Shambhala legend among the Mongols during this time.

29. *Sambala-yin oron-u teüke orosiba*, MS p. 18, CMC no. 4633.

30. *Sambala-yin oron-u teüke orosiba*, MS pp. 18–19, CMC no. 4633.

31. Rossabi 1988: 200. The actual edict is translated in Cleaves 1992.

32. On the importance of foodways in defining religious, cultural and ethnic boundaries, see Fabre-Vassas 1997; Gillette 2000: 114–166; and Bulag 1998: 194–211. A key marker of differentiation between Chinese and Tibetan Buddhists during the Republican period was also food, especially the question of vegetarianism. See Tuttle 2005.

33. *Sambala-yin oron-u teüke orosiba*, MS p. 19, CMC no. 4633.

34. With Brahmanic sensibilities in mind, the denigration of Muslim foodways is found already in the *Kālacakratantra:* "The barbarians kill camels, horses, and cattle, and briefly cook the flesh with blood. They cook beef and the fluid of the womb with butter and spice, and rice mixed with vegetables, all at once on the fire. Where men eat that with fresh fruit, King Sucandra, where they drink bird eggs, that is the place of demons" (Newman 1995: 288).

35. Even though scholars disagree on the time and place of the *Kālacakratantra*'s initial appearance (between the ninth and eleventh centuries, and in northwest and east India), a central element of the work is the tension between these religious groups. See Orofino 1997; and Newman 1998: 332.

36. Ahmad 1995: 193.

37. At the same time, it is important to keep in mind there is evidence to suggest that Buddhist–Muslim relations were not always antagonistic; see Elverskog 2003. An interesting example of a less confrontational environment between these two groups is found in one of the Khara Khoto documents, which contains both a text of Islamic geomancy and a Tibetan Buddhist treatise; see Kara 2003: 30–34.

38. Newman 1995: 288.

39. Clark 1995.

40. On the Qing incorporation of Xinjiang, see Millward 1998.

41. The lack of resistance may be attributed to the fact that the Qing did not begin fully to incorporate the region until 1821, when Han migration was encouraged. In turn, however, it was after this new policy was instituted that resistance in Xinjiang exploded. To a large extent the Qing therefore lost control of the region during the latter half of the nineteenth century; see Kim Hodong 2004.

42. This history is based on Lipman 1997, and the articles collected in Fletcher 1995.

43. On the development of Sino-Islamic culture, see Ben-Dor Benite 2005.

44. Lipman 1997: 114–115.

45. Since this initial appropriation of Shambhala, Mongols have used the legend in many contexts; and while the constructed enemy in each instance is different, the utilization of the Shambhala myth in forging a new communal identification is the same. The appropriation of Shambhala animated the representation of a larger Buddhist community under threat. Sükhebaatur, the revolutionary hero of twentieth-century Mongolia, wrote a military march to inspire his troops to expel the Chinese and White Russians from Mongolia that stated, "Let us die in this war and be reborn as warriors of the King of Shambhala!" (Bernbaum 1980: 18). Similarly, in Buriatia, visual representations of Shambhala shifted with the times: during the fight against the Red Army, the "barbarians" came from the West, while in the 1940s, as the Buriat communists fought the invading Japanese, in

widely circulated Shambhala posters the barbarians were depicted as coming from the East (Belka 2003: 247–262).

46. Perhaps unsurprisingly, this same concept continued into the Republican period, as attested by Tuttle's investigation of the "human typology" employed in the works of the Ninth Panchen Lama. "By examining how the Panchen Lama deployed terms of human typology I probed whether this modern Chinese discourse influenced the Panchen Lama's thinking. The idea that there were five races as part of China never occurs in the Tibetan texts I have seen. In the Panchen Lama's works, this seems to be the result of the fact that Muslims were never included with the other 'races' (Tibetan, Manchu, Mongol and Chinese) that were associated with Buddhism. As Dai Jitao would argue (see chapter 6), Buddhism was the uniting factor in the eyes of Tibetans such as the Panchen Lama. Thus, even though the lama and his representatives dealt with Muslims, such as those who held power in the Mongolian and Tibetan Affairs Commission or in the regions of Qinghai and Ningxia, they declined to explicitly include this group in any references to racial or ethnic unity. . . . Li Tieh-tseng [even] said that there 'was talk of a Pan-Moslem movement against Buddhist Tibet'" (Tuttle 2005: 143–144, 277).

47. As seen in Injanashi's historical novel *Köke Sudur* of the 1870s, the Mongols continued to see the Muslims as other during the late Qing; however, after the suppression of the Hui uprising the Mongol representation shifted from fear to jealousy. "But then, in this Great Ch'ing Empire, regarding those Moslems who submitted to the empire later than the Mongols did, and who did not contribute to the founding of the dynasty as the Mongols did, care is being taken so as not to let the learned among them be neglected by selecting from among them, according to their schooling, persons to employ in ministerial positions. Why are Mongols alone singled out and excluded from this examination system?" (KS: 63).

48. "Mañjuśrī's Root Tantra" refers to the *Mañjuśrīmulatantra*. In the same way as Roerich has pointed out that Tibetans used this prophecy about Nepal to explain early Tibetan Buddhist history (BA x–xi), the same appears to have occurred in this case as well. However, the Mongol prophecy signals the birth of Chinggis Khan; though unlike Büton's *History of the Dharma* or the fifteenth-century *Blue Annals,* which cite the prophecy in toto (CB 111–121), Gombojab uses only one passage: "there will be different kinds of mlecchas (kla-klo)" (BA 45).

49. SE: 36–37.

50. In his 1859 *Jewel Rosary (Erdeni-yin Erike),* Galdan also confirms that Chinggis Khan was an incarnation of Vajrapāṇi. In addition, he amplifies this connection by asserting that the reason the Mongols are called "Blue Mongols" (*köke mongyol*) is that Chinggis was actually an incarnation of the Blue Vajrapāṇi (CT: 313–315).

51. Bernbaum 1980: 234–236.

52. *Vcirbani-yin qubilyan cinggis qayan aq-a degüü nerün namtar ekilen sambala-yin oron-u bayidal ba / iregedüi cay-dur jibzun blam-a erdeni sasin-u nom-i nomlayu delgen mandayulqu-yin yeke tayalaltu cadig orosiba,* MS p. 21, CMC no. 4651. This same connection is also made in the *Bolor Toli,* quoted in Bawden 1984–1985: 469.

53. van Hecken 1977: 5–14; and Serruys 1977a: 39–55.

54. Appadurai 1990: 1–24.

55. On Mongol social structure, in particular the relations between the noble Taijis and the common Kharachins in Ordos, see Mostaert 1956b: 241–248.

56. There has been much speculation on the origin of this term. It has been hypothesized that Bede is a Mongolian transcription of the Chinese *Beida,* a contraction of *Bei Dada,* "Northern Tatars" (Bira 2002: 200) This name for the northern nomads dates from at least the ninth century (Elliott 2000: 625).

57. The importance of confirming and maintaining the boundaries of these units is reflected in a collection of six letters written between 1793 and 1806, which solely verify the borders of the banner for the Bureau of Colonial Affairs. *Güng Güngsanbambar-un qosiɣun-u nutuɣ-un ügülel.*

58. Serruys 1974/1975a: 582–583.

59. This same narrative is also found in Damchø Gyatsho Dharmatala's Tibetan history of Buddhism written in the 1880s in Inner Mongolia, and may point to an Ordos origin for this work (RWL: 219).

60. A similar phenomenon is found in the early-nineteenth-century Khalkha history of Erdeni Juu, which focuses especially on Abatai Khan, the Khalkha "Buddhist ancestor," and then continues to describe the Khalkha nobility and their relations with the monastery. See Tsendinoi 1999.

61. Serruys 1974/1975a: 600–602.

62. An important work in this regard was Sumba Khambo Ishi-Baljur's short world geography, the 1777 *'Dzam-gling spyi-bshad* (TH no. 320). The Mongol awareness of geography was, however, influenced not only by Tibetan but also Chinese scholarship, as seen in the 1807 translation of a Chinese geography, *Coy tegülder yeke cing ulus-un dotuɣadu ɣajar oron-u kemjiy-a bicig,* CMC no. 9691.

63. See, for example, *Qalɣ-a mongɣol oron-tu angɣ-a burqan-u sasin-u eke-yi oluɣsan ocir-a,* MS CMC no. 4603; *Yeke mongɣol oron-dur degedü nom ɣambar metü ɣaruɣsan yosu-yi nomlaɣsan ilaɣuɣsan sajin erdeni-yi keyigülün üiledügci jula kemegdekü,* MS CMC no. 4611; *Mongɣol-un oron-dur sasin ɣambar metü ɣaruɣsan yosun-a qoyar qaɣad-un üiyes ɣambar metü ɣaruɣsan yosun kiged ilaɣuɣsan-u sasin ger metü arbiduɣsan yosun,* MS CMC no. 4622; *Boɣda jo-bo atisa töbed oron-a jalaraɣsan namtar orosiba,* MS CMC no. 4687; *Boɣda-yin gegegen ten ber qalɣ-a mongɣol-un oron-dur angɣan-a qubilju doturaju olan düri satu üjigsen olangki-yi jirɣaɣulun ayiladduɣsan-u sudur orosiba,* MS CMC no. 4740.

64. On Mongol conceptualizations of space and place, see Humphrey 1995: 135–162.

65. In this regard it is also relevant to note that in modern Mongolian *oron* became the term used for "country."

66. van Hecken 1972: 132–155.

67. Chogchas-un Jirüken is a Mongolian translation of the Tibetan Gzugs-can snying-po, "Heart of Aggregates," which is the Tibetan name for the king of Magadha, Bimbisara, who was converted by the Buddha. During the Buddhist conversion in 1578, the Dalai Lama recognized Khutugtu Sechen Khung-Taiji as being an incarnation of this king and bequeathed him this name as his title. See Mostaert 1957: 551.

68. Serruys 1974/1975a: 605–607.

69. Each banner had two ministers *(tusalayci taiji)*. In Üüshin the northern one worked with the prince at the *yamen* in northern Üüshin, while the southern one had his own seat and headed southern Üüshin. This dual structure enhanced the split between the two different noble families of north and south Üüshin, who had been on very bad terms for decades. See Serruys 1976: 297–306.

70. The "southern dynasty" of Baljur and Ragbajamsan greatly revered their forebears, and the importance to them of the memory of their ancestors is borne out by the fact that Baljur wanted to be buried near his ancestral graves. See Mostaert 1956a: 126.

71. Serruys 1974a: 75, 77, 80, 84.

72. Ibid.: 75–76.

73. Morikawa 2001: 49–56.

74. Mostaert 1934: 67–72.

75. GT: 5.

76. SE: 83–84.

77. Serruys 1985a: 23–24. This representation of Chinggis, Saghang Sechen and Khutugtai Sechen as protective deities is found in a *thangka*-style painting that is used in the contemporary ritual worship of Saghang Sechen and Khutugtai Sechen in Üüshin. See Chiodo 1999: 57.

78. "And as had been prophesied and accordingly written about: the deeds and actions of Khutugtu Sechen Khung Noyan and his descendants, the writing of a ritual text of the fierce deities with Holy Chinggis Khan and his three friends . . . these are all extensively elaborated in the *Shining Mirror*" (SE: 84–85).

79. Mostaert 1957: 544–555. For other texts used in the cult of Saghang Sechen, see Coyidar 1990: 59–60; and Narasun and Öljeyibayar 1986: 188, 202.

80. Chiodo 1999: 58.

81. As Ellen McGill has shown, the Qing was concerned from very earlier on about Mongol movement between banners. "Among the original *(yuanding)* entries in the Lifan yuan section of the *Da Qing huidian shili* are schedules of fines for outer banner Mongols that nomadize across banner borders; those who committed the mistake knowingly were subject to much stricter penalties. In 1662, the Kangxi emperor further specified that Mongols were not to leave their own banners while hunting and reasserted the ban on cross-banner herding. In 1680 the latter was revised to allow Mongol nobles to apply to a Lifan yuan official for permission to pasture in the territory of nearby banners and watchtower stations in the event that the grass in their home banner was not sufficient. The official was to check on the situation of the applicant's banner and if the pasture was found to be flourishing, the noble was to be punished and, the court warned, his requests were likely to be denied in the future. In 1727, the punishments were converted from the confiscation of cattle to a system of fines" ("Qing Quarantine Policy: A Comparison of Inner Mongolia and Taiwan," unpublished paper).

82. Serruys 1974b: 187–189. On the development of banner as a closed political and religious community, see Atwood 2002: 23–32.

83. On the idea of locally bounded Mongol identities during the Qing and their con-

tinuities today, see Bulag 1998: 173–179. Furthermore, on the implications of these identities in relation to intraethnic political strife in Inner Mongolia, see Bulag 2002: 207–244.

84. Mostaert 1957: 543, 565.

85. Coyidar 1990: 60.

86. The term "social cement" is being used in the same way Watson uses it in describing specific social/ritual/performative elements that identify oneself as Chinese versus non-Chinese (1988: 3–19).

87. Robertson 1991: 101.

88. Another piece of evidence that shows the importance, or at least common knowledge, of these cult sites among people of Üüshin, is found in an 1863 law code from Gaikham-shigtu Üüle Monastery in Üüshin (Ch. Ruiyun Si), wherein the monastery's location is described in relation to the burial site of Khung Taiji. "Siralig monastery was built in the area 20 li south of the Khutugtai Sechen Khung-Taiji shrine and 60 li north of Siber Monastery. Its official name is Wonderful Cloud Monastery." *Ordos Üüshin qosiɣun-u ɣayiqamsiɣtai egületü süm-e-yin maɣad temdeglel jici lam-a-nar-un qauli dürim arban jirɣuɣan jüil,* MS p. 1, CMC no. 4872.

89. On the history of the *duguilang* movement, see Atwood 2002: 195–242.

90. Serruys 1977b: 492.

91. Ibid.: 490, 496.

92. Even within Üüshin banner, however, there were other smaller groups who affirmed and ritualized their distinctive identity in other ways, such as the Uygurjin. They performed a ritual toward the standard of their ancestor Mukhali, Chinggis Khan's famous general; see Qasbiligtü 1992: 83–105; and Sagaster 1997.

93. EEET: 164–165.

94. Ibid.:152–158.

95. Ibid.:167–169.

96. On this work, see TH no. 365.

97. Ligeti 1981: 5.

98. *Erten-ü törö gürün-ü ularil ba mongɣol qosiɣun ciɣulɣan-u jigdelel,* MS pp. 20–21, CMC no. 9150.

99. On Inner Mongolian views of "homeland" and the contemporary politics of "delocalization" in the People's Republic of China, see Bulag 1998: 171–183.

100. Kesigbatu, "Sir-a juu-yin maqtaɣal," 143–150.

101. Pozdeneyev 1977: 259.

102. Serruys 1976: 297–299.

103. Serruys 1972/1973: 538–540.

Epilogue

1. Tatsuo 1984: 133.

2. Onon and Pritchatt 1989: 5–16.

3. The issue of the premodern, or solely modern, origins of ethnicity, national con-

sciousness and nationalism is, of course, an enormous debate and has played a large part in the New Qing History (for an overview of these debates, see Millward 2002). And while I do not want to engage directly with these debates, I do, however, believe that modern ethnonational identities are not simply modern phenomena. Rather, they derive from premodern identities that are invariably engaged within and transformed by the forces of modernity and capitalism.

4. The idea that Buddhism was the reason for the Mongols' backwardness can already be found in Injanashi's *Blue History* (*Köke Sudur*) of the 1870s. He notes in the preface that the "decline of our Mongols was the result of too much easy living and pursuing a lofty principle—Buddhism" (KS: 51). In the body of the work, Injanashi continues in this vein, decrying the discord between the lofty philosophical theories of Buddhism and the actual behavior of the monastic community. While this criticism may be a transcultural feature of Buddhism (Chinese Buddhists even composed sutras telling the laity not to criticize the lax behavior of monastics [Overmeyer 1999: 11–13]), among the Mongols Injanashi was not a lone voice. Already in the early eighteenth century, in the commentary to his 1721 Mongolian translation of the *Journey to the West*, Arana was lambasting the incompetence of contemporary Buddhist monks (Atwood 1992/1993:14). A similar critique is also found in the Ordos lama Ishidanjanwangjil's (1854–1907) poem *The Golden Teaching Poem of the Jowo's Majesty (Juu-yin gegen-ü altan suryal bicig),* yet none of these authors goes so far as to reject Buddhism outright.

5. Atwood 1994b: 126–127.

6. Modern secular theory often scapegoats religion, since in accord with Enlightenment ideals religion is solely personal, and if it enters the public sphere, is invariably identified as a political and ideological smokescreen. On the theoretical issue of Enlightenment views on religion and politics, see King 1999: 7–35.

7. The continued prevalence of this view in Mongol scholarship can be seen in two articles recently published in a book coinciding with the "Modern Mongolia: Reclaiming Genghis Khan" exhibit held at the University of Pennsylvania in 2001. Munhtuya Altangerel of the London School of Economics states in her personal historical overview of Mongolia that "when the Manchu Dynasty ruled over greater Mongolia [the] Mongols continuously sought to gain independence. . . . But they could not rid themselves of Manchu oppression for 275 years" (2001: 28–29). Similarly, Nasan Bumaa of the National Museum of Mongolian History asserts that, "Despite the Manchu (Qing) Dynasty's 200-year oppressive rule of Mongolia, my people still retained our language, culture, and traditions" (ibid.: 32).

8. The oversights and failings of Buddhology, as well as the tandem Western "construction" of Buddhism, have been the focus of extensive research. See, for example, the caustic comments and bibliography in Strickmann 1990: 75–76, as well as Almond 1988; Schopen 1991; Faure 1991; Tweed 1992; Silk 1994; Lopez 1995, 1998, 2002; Prothero 1996; Leoshko 2003; and Masuzawa 2005: 121–146.

9. On the continuing debate between these two major theoretical approaches to the study of religion, the phenomenological/theological and modernist/postmodern divide, see the "Essays on 'Religion and Its Study,'" *Journal of the American Academy of Religion* 72 (2004): 141–219.

List of Tibetan Spellings

PHONETIC SPELLING	TIBETAN SPELLING
Amdo	A mdo
Drepung	'Bras spungs
Ganden	Dga' ldan
Gelukpa	Dge lugs pa
Jonangpa	Jo nang pa
Kagyü	Bka' brgyud
Kagyü Taglung	Bka' brgyud stag lung
Khön	'Khon
Kumbum	Sku 'bum
Kungga Nyingpo	Kun-dga' snying po
Kungga Odzer	Kun-dga' 'od zer
Lhasa	Lha sa
Lozang Penden Yeshé	Blo bzang dpal ldan ye shes
Lozang Trinlé	Blo bzang 'phrin las
Ngakwang Kungga Sönam	Nga-dbang kun-dga' bsod nams
Nyingma	Rnying ma
Pakpa Lama	'Phags pa Bla ma
Rölpé Dorjé	Rol pa'i rdo rje
Sakya	Sa skya
Samye	Bsam yas
Sanggyé Gyatso	Sangs rgyas rgya mtsho
Sönam Gyatso	Bsod nams rgya mtsho
Songtsen Gampo	Srong btsan sgam po
Trashi Lhünpo	Bkra shis lhun po
Tsongkhapa	Tsong kha pa
Zhikatsé	Gzhis ka rtse

Chinese Character Glossary

Beijing 北京
Chan 禪
Chengde 承德
chuanguo xi 傳國璽
Daiming 大明
Dayuan 大元
dou'ou 鬥毆
fa tian 法天
guo 國
guoyu 國語
Haiyun 海雲
Hanshu 漢書
Hami 哈密
Hui 回
Jiaqing 嘉慶
Jin 金
jin ren 金人
Kangxi 康熙
Lanzhou 蘭州
li 禮
Li Shiyao 李侍堯
Li Zicheng 李自成
Liao 遼
Liaodong 遼東
Ma Mingxin 馬明新（心）
Mao Zedong 毛澤東
Menggu wu 蒙古巫
Ming 明

Nian Gengyao 年羹堯
Nianchang 念常
Ningxia 寧夏
Qianlong 乾隆
Qingshou 慶壽
Qinshi Huangdi 秦始皇帝
Qing 清
Qinghai 清海
qiren 旗人
Qu Jiusi 瞿九思
Shangdu 上都
Shunzhi 順治
Suiyuan 綏遠
Taiping 太平
Wu Sangui 吳三桂
Wutai Shan 五臺山
Xining 西寧
Xinjiang 新疆
Xiongnu 匈奴
Xuanzang 玄奘
yamen 衙門
Yelü Chucai 耶律楚材
Yongle 永樂
Yongzheng 雍正
Yuan 元
Zhenjin 真金
Zhu Yuanzhang 朱元璋

References

Manuscript Sources

Alasan aɣulan-yin qosiɣun-u qosud wang güng-ner-ün uɣ oboɣ jidkülge-yin casa jisa. CMC no. 9334.

Bilig-ün jula. Inner Mongolia Academy of Social Sciences, cat. no. 22.912 125:1.

Boɣda jo-bo atisa töbed oron-a jalaraɣsan namtar orosiba. CMC no. 4687.

Boɣda neyici toyin dalai manjusri-yin domoɣ-i todorqai-a geyigülügci cindamani erike. Photo reproduction of Beijing blockprint.

Boɣda-yin gegegen ten ber qalɣ-a mongɣol-un oron-dur angɣan-a qubilju doturaju olan düri satu üjigsen olangki-yi jirɣaɣulun ayiladduɣsan-u sudur orosiba. CMC no. 4740.

Burqan bodisadu-a terigüten qamuɣ delekei-yin ejed-ün takiɣu takilɣ-a. CMC no. 3581.

Burqan-u sasin angɣ-a ɣaruɣsan enedkeg töbed mongol-un orod-dur delgeregsen terigüten-ü ayimag. CMC no. 4602.

Coɣ tegülder yeke cing ulus-un dotuɣadu ɣajar oron-u kemjiɣ-a bicig. CMC no. 9691.

Engke amuɣulang-un qorin jirɣuduɣar on-u dangsa. Nr. One Historical Archive, Beijing, no. 51.

Erten-ü burqan-u gegen ekilegsen boɣda cinggese boɣda qaɣan-u üyes-ece inaɣsi blam-a gegen boɣda qaɣan üyes-yin yandisi-ün tobci megem-e. CMC no. 4589.

Erten-ü törö gürün-ü ularil ba mongɣol qosiɣun ciɣulɣan -u jigdelel. CMC no. 9150.

Gegen toli. CMC no. 8340.

Güng Güngsanbambar-un qosiɣun-u nutuɣ-un ügülel. State Library of Mongolia, 548–553/ 96.

Jarliɣ–iɣar toɣtaɣaɣsan mongɣol qotong ayimaɣ-un wang güng-üd-ün iledkil sastir. CMC no. 9326.

Mongɣol-un qaɣan-u uru enedkeg-ün qaɣan-aca salaju iregsen ucir anu. Mong 143, CMBX, pp. 16–17.

Mongol-un oron-dur sasin yambar metü ɣaruɣsan yosun-a qoyar qaɣad-un üiyes yambar metü ɣaruɣsan yosun kiged ilaɣuɣsan-u sasin ger metü arbiduɣsan yosun. CMC no. 4622.

Ordos üüsin qosiɣun-u ɣayiqamsiɣtai egületü süm-e-yin maɣad temdeglel jici lam-a-nar-un qauli dürim arban jirɣuɣan jüil. CMC no. 4872.

Qad noyad-un aci ür-e-yi delgeregülgci kemekü teüke. CMC no. 9051.

Qalɣ-a mongɣol oron-tu angɣ-a burqan-u sasin-u eke-yi oluɣsan ocir-a. CMC no. 4603.

Sambala-yin oron-u teüke orosiba. CMC no. 4633.

Sasin ündüsün süm-e-yin angɣ-a bayiuluɣsan teüke debte. CMC no. 4883.

Siregetü güüsi corji-yin ijaɣur-un blam-a Geligjalzan sayin coɣtu-yin gegegen-u namtar. CMC no. 4796.

Sutu boyda cinggis qayan-u üy-e-ece manju-dur aldarsiju angy-a qayan sayuysan cadig. CMC no. 9066.

Tegüs coytu degedü blam-a cayan diyanci qutuy-tu-yin töröl duradduysan namtar. CMC no. 4760.

Tengri-yin tedkügsen-ü tabiduyar on-u moyai jil-ün yurban sarayin arban-a-aca ekilejü / qosiyun-u dotoraki süsügten noyad qatud tabunang tüsimed jiysatan kiy-a-nar dayasad / kerigten kiged sira qara süsüg-ün egüden-ece süsüglejü ergügsen süsüg ene debter-ün deger-e üiledcü bicikü. CMC no. 10443.

Tngri tedkügsen qayan bancin boyda-yi jalaysan tuqai jarliy. Inner Mongolia Library, no. 03640.

Üjümücin barayun qosiyun-u jasay wang noyad-un ergümjilegsen bicig. CMC no. 11001.
Ünegen-ü sang orosiba. CMC no. 3529.

Vcirbani-yin qubilyan cinggis qayan aq-a degüü nerün namtar ekilen sambala-yin oron-u bayidal ba / iregedüi cay-dur jibzun blam-a erdeni sasin-u nom-i nomlayu delgen mandayulqu-yin yeke tayalaltu cadig orosiba. CMC no. 4651.

Yeke mongyol oron-dur degedü nom yambar metü yaruysan yosu-yi nomlaysan ilayuysan sajin erdeni-yi keyigülün üiledügci jula kemegdekü. CMC no. 4611.

Yeke yuan ulus-aca jalyamjilaysan mongyol-un surbuljitu noyad-un uysay-a ayimay. CMC no. 9140.

Published Sources

Aalto, Pentti. 1961. "Qas Buu Tamaya und Chuan-kuo hsi." In *Studia Sino-Altaica,* ed. Herbert Franke, 12–20. Wiesbaden: Harrassowitz.

Aberle, David. 1953. *Chahar and Dagor Mongol Bureaucratic Administration.* New Haven, CT: Human Relations Area Files.

Ahmad, Zahiruddin. 1970. *Sino-Tibetan Relations in the Seventeenth Century.* Rome: Istituto Italiano per il Medio ed Estremo Oriente.

———. 1995. *A History of Tibet by the Fifth Dalai Lama of Tibet.* Bloomington: Indiana University Press.

Allsen, Thomas T. 1987. *Mongol Imperialism: The Policies of the Grand Qan Möngke in China, Russia, and the Islamic Lands, 1251–1259.* Berkeley: University of California Press.

———. 2001. *Culture and Conquest in Mongol Eurasia.* New York: Cambridge University Press.

Almond, Phillip. 1988. *The British Discovery of Buddhism.* Cambridge: Cambridge University Press.

Altangerel, Munhtuya. 2001. "My Mongolia." In *Modern Mongolia: Reclaiming Genghis Khan,* ed. Paula Sabloff, 1–30. Philadelphia: University of Pennsylvania Museum of Archaeology and Anthropology.

Altan'orgil. 1989. *Kökeqota-yin teüke mongyol surbulji bicig.* 6 vols. Kökeqota: Öbör mongyol-un soyul-un keblel-ün qoriy-a.

Altan'orgil, Narancoytu, and Altanjiyay-a. 1999. "Mongyol qayantu ulus-un qamuy segülci-yin neyislel-Lindan Qaγan-u Caγan Qota." *Öbör Mongγol-un Baγsi-yin Yeke Surγaγuli-yin erdem sinjilegen-ü sedgül* 1: 21–36.

Andrews, Peter A. 1999. "The Shrine Tents of Cinggis Qan at Ejen Qoroγa." In *Antoine Mostaert (1881–1971) C.I.C.M. Missionary and Scholar, Volume One,* ed. Klaus Sagaster, 3–30. Leuven: Ferdinand Verbeist Foundation.

Appadurai, Arjun. 1990. "Disjuncture and Difference in the Global Cultural Economy." *Public Culture* 2, 2: 1–24

Atwill, David G. 2003. "Blinkered Visions: Islamic Identity, Hui Ethnicity, and the Panthay Rebellion in Southwest China, 1856–1873." *The Journal of Asian Studies* 62, 4: 1079–1108.

Atwood, Christopher P. 1992/1993. "The Marvellous Lama in Mongolia: The Phenomenology of a Cultural Borrowing." *Acta Orientalia Academiae Scientiarium Hungaricae* 46, 1: 1–30.

———. 1994a. "National Questions and National Answers in the Chinese Revolution: Or, How Do You Say Minzu in Mongolian?" *Indiana East Asian Working Paper Series on Language and Politics in Modern China* 5: 37–73.

———. 1994b. "Revolutionary Nationalist Mobilization in Inner Mongolia, 1925–1929." Ph.D. diss., Indiana University.

———. 1996. "Buddhism and Popular Ritual in Mongolian Religon: A Re-examination of the Fire Cult." *History of Religion* 36, 2: 112–139.

———. 2000. "'Worshipping Grace': Guilt and Striving in the Mongolian Language of Loyalty." *Late Imperial China* 21: 86–139 .

———. 2002. *Young Mongols and Vigilantes in Inner Mongolia's Interregnum Decades, 1911–1931.* Leiden: Brill.

———. 2004. "Validation by Holiness or Sovereignty: Religious Toleration as Political Theology in the Mongol World Empire of the Thirteenth Century." *The International History Review* 23, 2: 237–256

Banzarov, Dorji. 1981–1982. Trans. J. Nattier and J. R. Krueger. "The Black Faith or Shamanism among the Mongols." *Mongolian Studies* 7: 53–91.

Bareja-Starzynska, Agata. 1997. "The Essentials of Buddhism in the *Ciqula Kereglegci,* a 16th century Mongolian Buddhist Treatise." In *Aspects of Buddhism: Proceedings of the International Seminar on Buddhist Studies, Liw, 25 June 1994.* Warsaw: Oriental Institute.

Bartholomew, Terese Tse. 1997. "Thangkas of the Qianlong Period." In *Tibetan Art: Towards a Definition of Style,* ed. J. C. Singer and Phillip Denwood, 104–117. London: Laurence King Publishing.

Bartlett, Beatrice. 2001. "Review of Evelyn Rawski's *The Last Emperors.*" *Harvard Journal of Asiatic Studies* 61, 1: 171–183.

Baumann, Martin. 2002. "Protective Amulets and Awareness Techniques, or How to Make Sense of Buddhism in the West." In *Westward Dharma: Buddhism beyond Asia,* ed. Charles S. Prebish and Martin Baumann, 51–65. Berkeley: University of California Press.

Bawden, Charles. 1966. "An Event in the Life of the Eighth Jebtsundampa Khutuktu." In *Collectanea Mongolica,* ed. Walther Heissig, 9–19. Wiesbaden: Harrassowitz.

———. 1969a. "A Case of Murder in Eighteenth-Century Mongolia." *Bulletin of the School of Oriental and African Studies* 32, 1: 71–90.

———. 1969b. "The Investigation of a Case of Attempted Murder in Eighteenth-Century Mongolia." *Bulletin of the School of Oriental and African Studies* 32, 2: 571–592.

———. 1969c. "A Juridical Document from Nineteenth Century Mongolia." *Zentralasiatische Studien* 3: 225–256.

———. 1970. "Notes on the Worship of Local Deities in Mongolia." In *Mongolian Studies,* ed. Louis Ligeti, 57–66. Amsterdam: B. R. Grüner.

———. 1976. "The 'Offering the Fox' Again." *Zentralasiatische Studien* 10: 439–473.

———. 1978. "An Oirat Manuscript of the 'Offering the Fox.'" *Zentralasiatische Studien* 12: 7–34.

———. 1984–1985. "The Wish-Prayer for Shambhala Again." *Monumenta Serica* 36: 453–509.

———. 1989. Rpt. of 1968 ed. *The Modern History of Mongolia.* London: Kegan and Paul International.

Belka, Lubos. 2003. "The Myth of Shambhala: Visions, Visualizations, and the Myth's Resurrection in the Twentieth Century in Buryatia." *Archiv Orientální* 71, 3: 247–262.

Bellah, Robert. 2002. "The Protestant Structure of American Culture: Multiculture or Monoculture?" *The Hedgehog Review* 4: 7–28.

Ben-Dor Benite, Zvi. 2005. *The Dao of Muhammad: A Cultural History of Muslims in Late Imperial China.* Cambridge, MA: Harvard East Asian Monographs.

Berger, Patricia. 2003. *Empire of Emptiness: Buddhist Art and Political Authority in Qing China.* Honolulu: University of Hawai'i Press.

Bernbaum, Edwin. 1980. *The Way to Shambhala.* Los Angeles, CA: Jeremy P. Tarcher.

Bira, Sh. 1970. *Mongolian Historical Literature of the XVII–XIX Centuries Written in Tibetan.* Trans. S. Frye. Bloomington, IN: Mongolia Society.

———. 1974. "'Da Tan si yui tszi' Syuan' Tszana v tibetskom perevode Guna Gombozhava." In *Mongol ba Töw Aziin ornuudin tüüxend xolbogdox xoyor xowor surbalj bicig.* Ulaanbaatar: Academy of Sciences.

———. 1999. "Qubilai Qa'an and 'Phags-pa Bla-ma." In *The Mongol Empire and Its Legacy,* ed. Reuven Amitai-Press and David Morgan, 244–249. Boston: Brill.

Bira, Shagdaryn. 2002. *Mongolian Historical Writing from 1200 to 1700.* Trans. John R. Krueger. Bellingham: Center for East Asian Studies, Western Washington University.

Blackburn, Anne. 2001. *Buddhist Learning and Textual Practice in Eighteenth-Century Lankan Monastic Culture.* Princeton, NJ: Princeton University Press.

Brooke, James. 2004. "The Mongolians Are Coming to China! With Heavy Metal!" *New York Times,* November 26, A4.

Brown, Peter. 1995. *Authority and the Sacred: Aspects of Christianization of the Roman World.* Chicago: University of Chicago Press.

Buell, Paul D. 1980. "Kalmyk Tanggaci People: Thoughts on the Mechanics and Impact of Mongol Expansion." *Mongolian Studies* 6: 41–59.

Bulag, Uradyn E. 1998. *Nationalism and Hybridity in Mongolia*. Oxford: Clarendon Press.

———. 2002. *The Mongols at China's Edge: History and the Politics of National Unity*. Lanham: Rowman and Littlefield.

———. 2004. "Inner Mongolia: The Dialectics of Colonization and Ethnicity Building." In *Governing China's Multiethnic Frontiers*, ed. Morris Rossabi, 84–116. Seattle: University of Washington Press.

Bumaa. Nasan. 2001. "The Twentieth Century: From Domination to Democracy." In *Modern Mongolia: Reclaiming Genghis Khan*, ed. Paula Sabloff, 31–60. Philadelphia: University of Pennsylvania Museum of Archaeology and Anthropology.

Cammann, Schuyler. 1949. "The Panchen Lama's Visit to China in 1780: An Episode in Anglo-Tibetan Relations." *Far Eastern Quarterly* 9,1: 3–19.

Cannadine, David. 2001. *Ornamentalism: How the British Saw Their Empire*. New York: Oxford University Press.

Carroll, John M. 2005. *Edge of Empires: Chinese Elites and British Colonials in Hong Kong*. Cambridge, MA: Harvard University Press.

Chan, Hok-lam. 1999. *China and the Mongols: History and Legend under the Yüan and Ming*. Aldershot: Ashgate-Variorum.

Chan, Hok-lam, and W. T. de Bary, eds. 1982. *Yüan Thought: Chinese Thought and Religion under the Mongols*. New York: Columbia University Press.

Charleux, Isabelle. 1998. "Histoire et architecture des temples et monastères lamaïques de Mongolie méridionale." Ph.D. diss., Université de Paris-Sorbonne.

———. 1999. "La peinture des donateurs du temple de Maitreya en Mongolie méridionale." *Arts asiatique* 54: 85–102.

———. 2002. "Padmasambhava's Travel to the North: The Pilgrimage to the Monastery of the Caves and the Old Schools of Tibetan Buddhism in Mongolia." *Central Asiatic Journal* 46, 2: 168–232.

Chayet, Anne. 1984. *Les temples de Jehol et leurs modèles tibétains*. Paris: Éditions Recherche sur les Civilisations.

Chia, Ning. 1992. "The Li-fan Yuan in the Early Ch'ing Dynasty." Ph.D. diss., The Johns Hopkins University.

———. 1993. "The Lifanyuan and the Inner Asian Rituals in Early Qing (1644–1795)." *Late Imperial China* 14, 1: 60–92.

Ching, Leo T. S. 2001. *Becoming Japanese: Colonial Taiwan and the Politics of Identity Formation*. Berkeley: University of California Press.

Chiodo, Elizabeth. 1989–1991. "The Book of the Offerings to the Holy Cinggis Qaγan (Part 1)." *Zentralasiatische Studien* 22: 190–220.

———. 1992–1993. "The Book of the Offerings to the Holy Cinggis Qaγan (Part 2)." *Zentralasiatische Studien* 23: 84–144.

———. 1999. "*Altan γandari*: A Journal on Ordos Culture." In *Antoine Mostaert (1881–1971) C.I.C.M. Missionary and Scholar, Volume One*, ed. Klaus Sagaster, 51–62. Leuven: Ferdinand Verbeist Foundation.

———. 2000. *The Mongolian Manuscripts on Birch Bark from Xarbuxyn Balgas in the Collection of the Mongolian Academy of Sciences*. Wiesbaden: Harrassowitz.

Clark, Larry. 1995. "Buddhist and Muslim Turks at the Millennium." Paper presented at the Colloquium on Pre-Islamic Central Asia, Indiana University, February 16.

Cleaves, F. W. 1949. "The Sino-Mongolian Inscription of 1362 in Memory of Prince Hindu." *Harvard Journal of Asiatic Studies* 12, 1: 1–133.

———. 1952. "The Sino-Mongolian Inscription of 1346." *Harvard Journal of Asiatic Studies* 15, 1: 1–123.

———. 1986. "A Mongolian Rescript of the Fifth Year of Degedü Erdem-tü (1640)." *Harvard Journal of Asiatic Studies* 46, 2: 181–200.

———. 1992. "The Rescript of Qubilai Prohibiting the Slaughtering of Animals by Slitting the Throat." *Journal of Turkish Studies* 16: 67–89.

———. 1995; 1996. "The Mongolian Text of the Tri-Lingual Inscription of 1640. Part I." *Mongolian Studies* 18: 5–48; "Part II: Notes to the Translation." *Mongolian Studies* 19: 1–50.

Cohen, Richard. 2002. "Why Study Indian Buddhism?" In *The Invention of Religion: Rethinking Belief in Politics and History,* ed. Derek R. Peterson and Darren R. Walhof, 19–36. New Brunswick, NJ: Rutgers University Press.

Comaroff, Jean. 1994. "Defying Disenchantment Reflections on Ritual, Power, and History." In *Asian Visions of Authority: Religion and the Modern States of East and Southeast Asia,* ed. C. Keyes, L. Kendall, and H. Hardacre, 301–314. Honolulu: University of Hawai'i Press.

Coyidar. 1990. "Sayang Secen-u saril-un ongyon-u dayily-a takily-a." *Öbör mongγol neyigem-ün sinjileкü uqaγan* 2: 59–60.

Coyiji. 1990. "Altan Erike-yin jokiyaγci Na-ta kemegci ken bui?" *Öbör mongγol neyigemün sinjileкü uqaγan* 3: 36–38.

———. 1996. "Γutugar dalai blam-a aγuljaqu-yin uridaki Altan qaγan ba Töbed-ün burqan-u sasin." *Menggu xue xinxi* 3: 10–26.

———. 1998. *Mongγol-un burqan-u sasin-u teüke. Yeke Mongγol Ulus-un üy-e (1206–1271).* Kökeqota: Öbör mongγol-un arad-un keblel qoriy-a.

Crossley, Pamela K. 1997. *The Manchus.* Cambridge: Blackwell.

———. 1999. *A Translucent Mirror: History and Identity in Qing Imperial Ideology.* Berkeley: University of California Press.

Dabringhaus, Sabine. 1994. *Das Qing-Imperium als Vision und Wirklichkeit: Tibet in Laufbahn und Schriften des Song Yun (1752–1835).* Stuttgart: Steiner.

———. 1997. "Chinese Emperors and Tibetan Monks: Religion as an Instrument of Rule." In *China and Her Neighbours: Borders, Visions of the Other, Foreign Policy 10th to 19th Century China,* ed. Sabine Dabringhaus and Roderich Pitak, 119–134. Wiesbaden: Harrassowitz.

Damdinsüren, Ts. 1979. "Two Mongolian Colophons to the Suvarnaprabhasottama-Sutra." *Acta Orientalia Academiae Scientiarium Hungaricae* 33: 39–58.

Damdinsüreng. 1982. Rpt. of 1957 ed. *Mongγol uran jokiyal-un degeji jaγun bilig.* Hohhot: Nei Menggu Renmin Chubanshe.

Dawson, Christopher, ed. 1955. *The Mongol Mission.* New York: Sheed and Ward.

DeBernardi, Jean. 2004. *Rites of Belonging: Memory, Modernity, and Identity in a Malaysian Chinese Community.* Stanford, CA: Stanford University Press.

de Rachewiltz, Igor. 1972. *Index to the Secret History of the Mongols*. Bloomington: Indiana University Press.

——. 1973. "Some Remarks on the Ideological Foundations of Chinggis Khan's Empire." *Papers on Far Eastern History* 7: 21–36.

——. 1982. "On a Recently Discovered Ms. of Cinggis-Qaɣan's Precepts to His Younger Brothers and Sons." In *Indological and Buddhist Studies*, ed. J. W. de Jong and L. A. Hercus, 427–438. Canberra: Australian National University.

DeWeese, Devin. 1994. *Islamization and Native Religion in the Golden Horde: Baba Tükles and Conversion to Islam in Historical and Epic Tradition*. University Park: Pennsylvania State University Press.

Di Cosmo, Nicola. 1998. "Qing Colonial Administration in Inner Asia." *The International History Review* 20, 2: 287–309.

——. 2002. "Military Aspects of the Manchu Wars against the Caqars." In *Warfare in Inner Asian History (500–1800)*, ed. Nicola Di Cosmo, 337–367. Leiden: Brill.

——. 2003. "Kirghiz Nomads on the Qing Frontier: Tribute, Trade, or Gift Exchange." In *Political Frontiers, Ethnic Boundaries, and Human Geographies in Chinese History*, ed. Nicola Di Cosmo and Don J. Wyatt, 351–372. New York: RoutledgeCurzon.

Di Cosmo, Nicola, and Dalizhabu Bao. 2003. *Manchu–Mongol Relations on the Eve of the Qing Conquest: A Documentary History*. Leiden: Brill.

Dreyfus, George. 1994. "Proto-Nationalism in Tibet." In *Tibetan Studies. Proceedings of the 6th Seminar of the IATS, Fagernes 1992*, ed. Per Kvaerne, 1: 205–218. Oslo: The Institute for Comparative Research in Human Culture.

Dunnell, Ruth. 1992. "The Hsia Origins of the Yüan Institution of Imperial Preceptor." *Asia Major* 5,1: 85–111.

——. 1996. *The Great State of White and High: Buddhism and State Formation in Eleventh-Century Xia*. Honolulu: University of Hawai'i Press.

Durungɣ-a, ed. 1998. *Cinggis Qaɣan-u takil-un sudur orosiba*. Kökeqota: Öbör mongɣol-un arad-un keblel-ün qoriy-a.

Dylykova, S. D. 1998. *Tsaadzhin bichig ("Mongol'skoe ulozhenie") Tsinskoe zakonoda-tel'stvo dlr mongolov 1627–1694 gg*. Moscow.

Eaton, Richard M. 2000. "Temple Desecration and Indo-Muslim States." In *Essays on Islam and Indian History*, 94–132. New York: Oxford University Press.

Ebrey, Patricia B. 1991. *Confucianism and Family Rituals in Imperial China: A Social History of Writing about Rites*. Princeton, NJ: Princeton University Press, 1991.

Elliott, Mark C. 1996. "Manchu (Re)Definitions of the Nation in Early Qing." *Indiana East Asian Working Papers Series on Language and Politics in Modern China* 7: 46–78.

——. 2000."The Limits of Tartary: Manchuria in Imperial and National Geographies." *The Journal of Asian Studies* 59, 3: 603–646.

——. 2001. *The Manchu Way: The Eight Banners and Ethnic Identity in Late Imperial China*. Stanford, CA: Stanford University Press.

——. 2004. "Manchu Historical Consciousness in the Early Qing." In *Temporalities of the Ming–Qing Transition*, ed. Lynn Struve, 31–72. Honolulu: University of Hawai'i Press.

Elman, Benjamin A. 1984. *From Philosophy to Philology: Intellectual and Social Aspects of Change in Late Imperial China.* Cambridge: Council on East Asian Studies.

Elverskog, Johan. 2003. "Islam and Buddhism." *Encyclopedia of Buddhism,* ed. Robert Buswell, Jr., 380–382. New York: Macmillan Reference.

———. 2004. "Things and the Qing: Mongol Culture in the Visual Narrative." *Inner Asia* 6: 137–178.

———. 2005. "Mongolian Time Enters a Qing World." In *Time and Temporality in the Ming–Qing Transition,* ed. Lynn Struve, 142–178. Honolulu: University of Hawai'i Press.

Endicott-West, Elizabeth. 1989. *Mongolian Rule in China: Local Administration in the Yuan Dynasty.* Cambridge, MA: Harvard University Press.

Fabre-Vassas, Claudine. 1997. *The Singular Beast: Jews, Christians, and the Pig.* Trans. Carol Volk. New York: Columbia University Press.

Farquhar, David M. 1960. "The Ch'ing Administration of Mongolia up to the Nineteenth Century." Ph.D. diss., Harvard University.

———. 1968. "The Origins of the Manchus' Mongolian Policy." In *The Chinese World Order,* ed. John K. Fairbank, 198–205. Cambridge, MA: Harvard University Press.

———. 1971. "Mongolian versus Chinese Elements in the Early Manchu State." *Ch'ing-shih wen-t'i* 3: 11–23.

———. 1978. "Emperor as Bodhisattva in the Governance of the Ch'ing Empire." *Harvard Journal of Asiatic Studies* 38, 1: 5–34.

Faure, Bernard. 1991. *The Rhetoric of Immediacy: A Cultural Critique of Chan/Zen Buddhism.* Princeton, NJ: Princeton University Press.

Figes, Orlando. 2002. *Natasha's Dance: A Cultural History of Russia.* New York: Metropolitan Books.

Fisher, Carney. 1988. "Smallpox, Salesman, and Sectarians: Ming–Mongol Relations in the Jiajing Reign (1522–67)." *Ming Studies* 25: 1–23.

Fletcher, Joseph. 1978. "The Heyday of the Ch'ing Order in Mongolia, Sinkiang and Tibet." In *The Cambridge History of China,* ed. Denis Twitchet and John Fairbank, vol. 10, pt. 1, 351–408. New York: Cambridge University Press.

———. 1979–1980. "Turco-Mongolian Monarchic Tradition in the Ottoman Empire." *Harvard Ukranian Studies* 3–4: 236–251.

———. 1995. *Studies on Chinese and Islamic Inner Asia.* Ed. Beatrice Manz. London: Variorum.

Fletcher, Richard. 1998. *The Barbarian Conversion: From Paganism to Christianity.* New York: H. Holt and Co.

Foret, Phillipe. 2000. *Mapping Chengde: The Qing Landscape Enterprise.* Honolulu: University of Hawai'i Press.

Franke, Herbert. 1977. "Additional Remarks on the Mongolian Turfan Fragment TM 92." *The Canada-Mongolia Review* 3, 1: 36.

———. 1978. *From Tribal Chieftain to Universal Emperor and God: The Legitimation of the Yüan Dynasty.* Munich: Verlag der Bayerischen Akademie der Wissenschaften.

———. 1981. "Tibetans in Yüan China." In *China under Mongol Rule,* ed. John Langlois, Jr., 296–328. Princeton, NJ: Princeton University Press.

Geertz, Clifford. 1983. *Local Knowledge: Further Essays in Interpretive Anthropology.* New York: Basic Books.

Geiss, James. 1988. "The Chia-ching reign, 1522–1566." In *The Cambridge History of China,* ed. F. W. Mote, vol. 8, pt. 1, 440–510. New York: Cambridge University Press.

Gillette, Maris Boyd. 2000. *Between Mecca and Beijing: Modernization and Consumption among Urban Chinese Muslims.* Stanford, CA: Stanford University Press.

Gimm, Martin. 2000/1. "Zum mongolischen Mahakala-Kult und zum Beginn der Qing-Dynastie—die Inschrift Shisheng beiji von 1638." *Orient Extremus* 21: 69–105.

Gladney, Dru C. 2004. *Dislocating China: Muslims, Minorities, and other Subaltern Subjects.* Chicago: University of Chicago Press.

Golden, Peter B. 1982. "Imperial Ideology and the Sources of Political Unity amongst the Pre-Cinggisid Nomads of Western Eurasia." *Archivum Eurasiae Medii Aevi* 2: 37–76.

————. 2000. *The King's Dictionary. The Rasulid Hexaglot: Fourteenth Century Vocabularies in Arabic, Persian, Turkic, Greek, Armenian and Mongol.* Leiden: Brill.

Grapard, Alan G. 1982. "Flying Mountains and Walkers of Emptiness: Toward a Definition of Sacred Space in Japanese Religions." *History of Religions* 21: 195–221.

Grünwedel, A. 1918. *Der Weg nach Sambala.* Abhandlung Bayerische Akademie der Wissenschaft 34.

Grupper, Samuel M. 1979. "The Manchu Imperial Cult of the Early Qing Dynasty: Texts and Studies on the Tantric Sanctuary of Mahakala in Mukden." Ph.D. diss., Indiana University.

————. 1984. "Manchu Patronage and Tibetan Buddhism during the First Half of the Ch'ing Dynasty." *The Journal of the Tibet Society* 4: 47–75.

Guy, R. Kent. 2002. "Who Were the Manchus?: A Review Essay." *Journal of Asian Studies* 61, 1: 151–177.

Haenisch, Erich, and Yao Ts'ung-wu (Nach Vorarbeiten von Übersetzt und kommentiert von Peter Olbricht und Elisabeth Pinks. Eingeleitet von Werner Banck). 1980. *Meng-Ta pei-lu und Hei-Ta shih-lüeh. Chinische Gesandtenberichte über die frühen Mongolen 1221 und 1237.* Wiesbaden: Harrassowitz.

Hagiwara Junpei. 1969. "The Political Ideas of Lindan Khan." In *Proceedings of the Third East Asian Altaistic Conference,* ed. Ch'en Chieh-hsien and Sechen Jagchid, 97–128. Taipei.

Hallisey, Charles. 1995. "Roads Taken and Not Taken in the Study of Theravada Buddhism." In *Curators of the Buddha: The Study of Buddhism under Colonialism,* ed. Donald S. Lopez, Jr., 31–62. Chicago: University of Chicago Press.

Hansen, Valerie. 1990. *Changing Gods in Medieval China, 1127–1276.* Princeton, NJ: Princeton University Press.

Hastings, Adrian. 1990. *The Construction of Nationhood: Ethnicity, Religion and Nationalism.* Cambridge: Cambridge University Press, 1990.

Hecken, Joseph van. 1960. "Une dispute entre deux bannières mongoles et le role joué par les missionnaires catholiques." *Monumenta Serica* 19: 276–306.

———. 1972. "Les princes Borjigid des Ordos depuis leur soumission aux mandchoux en 1635 jusqu'à leur disparation en 1951." *Central Asiatic Journal* 16, 2: 132–155.

———. 1977. "Deux documents Mongols concernant les persécutions en Chine en 1900." *The Canada-Mongolia Review* 3, 1: 5–14.

Heissig, Walther. 1953a. "A Mongolian Source to the Lamaist Suppression of Shamanism in the 17th Century." *Anthropos* 48: 1–29, 493–536.

———. 1953b. "Neyici Toyin, Das Leben eines lamaistischen Mönches." *Sinologica* III: 1–44.

———. 1954a. "Neyici Toyin, Das Leben eines lamaistischen Mönches." *Sinologica* IV: 21–38.

———. 1954b. *Die Pekinger lamaistischen Blockdrucke in mongolischer Sprache.* Wiesbaden: Harrassowitz.

———. 1959. *Die Familien-und Kirchengeschichtsschreibung der Mongolen. Teil I: 16.-18. Jahrhundert.* Wiesbaden: Harrassowitz.

———. 1961. *Mongolische Handschriften Blockdrucke Landkarten.* Wiesbaden: Franz Steiner Verlag.

———. 1961–1962. "Eine kleine mongolische Klosterbibliothek aus Tsakhar." *Jahrbuch des Bernischen Historischen Museums in Bern 1961–1962,* 557–590.

———. 1962. *Beiträge zur Übersetzungsgeschichte des mongolischen buddhistischen Kanons.* Göttingen: Vandenhoeck und Ruprecht.

———. 1966. *Die mongolische Steininschrift und Manuskriptfragmente aus Olon süme in der Inneren Mongolei.* Göttingen: Vandenhoeck und Ruprecht.

———. 1976. *Die mongolische Handschriften-Reste aus Olon süme Innere Mongolei (16.–17. Jhdt.).* Wiesbaden: Harrassowitz.

———. 1979. *Die Zeit des letzen mongolischen Groskhans Ligdan (1604–1634).* Opladen: Westdeutscher Verlag.

———. 1980. *The Religions of Mongolia.* Trans. G. Samuel. London: Routledge and Kegan Paul.

———. 1984. "Zur 'Biographe des Altan Khan' der Tümet." *Ural-Altaische Jahrbucher,* Neue Folge 4: 187–221.

———. 1998. "Some Remarks on the Question of the First Translation of the Mongolian Kandjur." In *Essays on Mongolian Studies,* 155–160. Ulaanbaatar: Olon Ulsiin Mongol Sudlaliin Xolboo.

———. 1999. "Problems Arising from Some of Mostaert's Ordos Tales: Additions and Consequences." In *Antoine Mostaert (1881–1971) C.I.C.M. Missionary and Scholar, Volume One,* ed. Klaus Sagaster, 73–84. Leuven: Ferdinand Verbeist Foundation.

Heller, Amy. 1996. "Mongolian Mountain Deities and Local Gods: Examples of Rituals for Their Worship in Tibetan Language." In *Reflections of the Mountain: Essays on the History and Social Meaning of the Mountain Cult in Tibet and the Himalaya,* ed. A. M. Blondeau and Ernst Steinkeller, 133–140. Vienna: Verlag der Österreichischen Akademie der Wissenschaft.

Henss, Michael. 2001a. "The Bodhisattva-Emperor: Tibeto-Chinese Portraits of Sacred and Secular Rule in the Qing Dynasty, Part 1." *Oriental Art* 47, 3: 2–16.

————. 2001b. "The Bodhisattva-Emperor: Tibeto-Chinese Portraits of Sacred and Secular Rule in the Qing Dynasty, Part 2." *Oriental Art* 47, 5: 71–83.

Heuschert, Dorothea. 1998a. *Die Gesetzgebung der Qing für die Mongolean im 17. Jahrhundert anhand des Mongolischen Gesetzbuches aus der Kangxi-Zeit (1662–1722)*. Wiesbaden: Harrassowitz.

————. 1998b. "Legal Pluralism in the Qing Empire: Manchu Legislation for the Mongols." *International History Review* 20, 2: 310–324.

Hevia, James L. 1993. "Emperors, Lamas, and Rituals: Political Implications in Qing Imperial Ceremonies." *Journal of the International Association of Buddhist Studies* 16: 243–278.

————. 1995. *Cherishing Men from Afar: Qing Guest Ritual and the Macartney Embassy of 1793*. Durham, NC: Duke University Press.

————. 2003. *English Lessons: The Pedagogy of Imperialism in Nineteenth-Century China*. Durham, NC: Duke University Press.

Ho, Chuimei, and Bennet Bronson. 2004. *Splendors of China's Forbidden City: The Glorious Reign of Emperor Qianlong*. New York: Merrell Publishers.

Hoog, Constance. 1983. *Prince Jin-gim's Textbook of Tibetan Buddhism*. Leiden: Brill.

Hostetler, Laura. 2001. *Qing Colonial Enterprise: Ethnography and Cartography in Early Modern China*. Chicago: University of Chicago Press.

Huber, Toni. 1999. *The Cult of Pure Crystal Mountain: Popular Pilgrimage and Visionary Landscape in Southeast Tibet*. Oxford: Oxford University Press.

Humphrey, Caroline. 1995. "Chiefly and Shamanist Landscapes in Mongolia." In *The Anthropology of Landscape,* ed. Eric Hirsch and Michael O'Hanlon, 135–162. Oxford: Clarendon Press.

Humphrey, Caroline, and Urgunge Onon. 1996. *Shamans and Elders. Experience, Knowledge, and Power among the Daur Mongols*. Oxford: Oxford University Press.

Huntington, Rania. 2003. *Alien Kind: Foxes and Late Imperial Chinese Narrative*. Cambridge, MA: Harvard University Asia Center.

Hurca, N. 1999. "Attempts to Buddhicise the Cult of Chinggis Khan." *Inner Asia* 1: 45–57.

Huth, Georg. 1894. *Die Inschriften von Tsaghan Baisin. Tibetisch-Mongolischer Text*. Leipzig: F. A. Brockhaus.

Hyer, Eric A. 2004. "Mongols Resist Government's Plan of Privatizing Chinggis Khaan Mausoleum, Police Impose Curfew on College Campuses in Inner Mongolia." *H-Asia*, November 10.

Hyer, Paul, and Sechin Jagchid. 1983. *A Mongolian Living Buddha: Biography of the Kanjurwa Khutugtu*. Albany: SUNY Press.

Hymes, Robert. 2002. *Way and Byway: Taoism, Local Religion, and Models of Divinity in Sung and Modern China*. Berkeley: University of California Press.

Inden, Ronald. 1990. *Imagining India*. New York: Oxford University Press.

Ishihama, Yumiko. 1992. "A Study of the Seals and Titles Conferred by the Dalai Lamas." In *Tibetan Studies: Proceedings of the 5th Seminar of the International Association of Tibetan Studies,* ed. Shoren Ihara and Zuiho Yamaguchi, 501–514. Narita: Naritasan Shinsoji.

————. 1993. "On the Dissemination of the Belief in the Dalai Lamas as a Manifestation of the Bodhisattva Avalokitesvara." *Acta Asiatica* 64: 38–56.

Jackson, David. 1996. *A History of Tibetan Painting: The Great Tibetan Painters and Their Traditions.* Vienna: Verlag der Österreichischen Akademie der Wissenschaften.

Jackson, Peter. 1999. "From Ulus to Khanate: The Making of the Mongol States c. 1220–c. 1290." In *The Mongol Empire and Its Legacy,* ed. R. Amitai-Preiss and D. O. Morgan, 12–37. Leiden: Brill.

Jackson, Peter, and David Morgan. 1990. *The Mission of Friar William of Rubrick. His Journey to the Court of Great Khan Möngke 1253–1255.* London: The Hakluyt Society.

Jagchid, Sechin. 1974. "Mongolian Lamaist Quasi-Feudalism during the Period of Manchu Domination." *Mongolian Studies* 1: 27–54.

————. 1976. "The Manchu Ch'ing Policy Towards Mongolian Religion." In *Tractata Altaica,* ed. Walther Heissig, 301–319. Wiesbaden: Harrassowitz.

————. 1986. "Mongolian–Manchu Intermarriage in the Ch'ing Period." *Zentralasiatische Studien* 19: 68–87

————. 1988. *Essays in Mongolian Studies.* Provo, UT: Brigham Young University.

Jagchid, Sechin, and Paul Hyer. 1979. *Mongolia's Culture and Society.* Boulder, CO: Westview Press.

Jahn, Karl. 1956. "An Indian Legend on the Descent of the Mongols." In *Charisteria orientalia praecipae ad Persiam pertinentia,* 120–127. Prague: Ceskoslovenskae akademie véed.

Janoush, Andreas. 1999. "Emperor as Bodhisattva: The Bodhisattva Ordination and Ritual Assemblies of Emperor Wu of the Liang Dynasty." In *State and Court Ritual in China,* ed. Joseph P. McDermott, 112–149. New York: Cambridge University Press.

Jayawardena, Kumari. 2002. *Nobodies to Somebodies: The Rise of the Colonial Bourgeoisie in Sri Lanka.* New York: Palgrave.

Jensen, Lionel M. 1997. *Manufacturing Confucianism: Chinese Traditions and Universal Civilization.* Durham, NC: Duke University Press.

Kam, Tak-Sing. 2000. "The dGe-lugs-pa Breakthrough: The Uluk Darxan Nangsu Lama's Mission to the Manchus." *Central Asiatic Journal* 44, 2: 161–173.

Kämpfe, Hans-Rainer. 1983. "mGon po skyabs' rGya nag chos 'byung als Quelle des Cindamani-yin erikes." In *Documenta Barbarorum,* ed. K. Sagaster and M. Weiers, 203–209. Wiesbaden: Harrassowitz.

Kapstein, Matthew. 1992. "Remarks on the *Mani bKa'-'bum* and the Cult of Avalokitesvara in Tibet." In *Tibetan Buddhism: Reason and Revelation,* ed. Steven Goodman and Ronald Davidson, 79–93. Albany: SUNY Press.

————. 2000. *The Tibetan Assimilation of Buddhism: Conversion, Contestation and Memory.* New York: Oxford University Press.

Kara, György. 1972. "Une version mongole du *Mani Bka'-'bum:* Le colophon de la traduction Abaga." *Acta Orientalia Hungarica* 27: 19–41.

————. 2000. *The Mongol and Manchu Manuscripts and Blockprints in the Library of the Hungarian Academy of Sciences.* Budapest: Academy of Sciences.

————. 2003. "Mediaeval Mongol Documents from Khara Khoto and East Turkestan in the St. Petersburg Branch of the Institute of Oriental Studies." *Manuscripta Orientalia* 9, 2: 3–40.

Kasyanenko, Zoya K. 1993. *Katalog petersburgskogo rukopis'nogo "Gandjura."* Moscow: Nauka Publishing.

Kesigtoүtaqu. 1998. "Cinggis qaүan-u altan tobci ner-e-tü-yin cadig." In *Cinggis Qaүan-u takil-un sudur orosiba,* ed. Durungү-a, 1–17. Kökeqota: Öbör mongүol-un arad-un keblel-ün qoriy-a.

Keyes, Charles F. 1994. "Communist Revolution and the Buddhist Past in Cambodia." In *Asian Visions of Authority: Religion and the Modern States of East and Southeast Asia,* ed. C. F. Keyes, L. Kendall, and H. Hardacre, 43–74. Honolulu: University of Hawai'i Press.

Khan, Almaz. 1994. "Chinggis Khan: From Imperial Ancestor to Ethnic Hero." In *Cultural Encounters on China's Ethnic Frontiers,* ed. Stevan Harrell, 248–277. Seattle: University of Washington Press.

Khodarkovsky, Michael. 2002. *Russia's Steppe Frontier: The Making of a Colonial Empire, 1500–1800.* Bloomington: Indiana University Press.

Kim Haboush, Jahyun. 2003. "Dead Bodies in the Postwar Discourse of Identity in Seventeenth-Century Korea: Subversion and Literary Production in the Private Sector." *The Journal of Asian Studies* 62, 2: 415–442.

Kim Hodong. 2004. *Holy War in China: The Muslim Rebellion and State in Chinese Central Asia, 1864–1877.* Stanford, CA: Stanford University Press.

King, Richard. 1999. *Orientalism and Religion: Postcolonial Theory, India and "the Mystic East."* New York: Routledge.

Kiripolská, Marta. 1997. "Keüken Qutuүtu, A Robber or a Poet? (A Poem of *Erdeni Keüken Qutuүtu*)." *Zentralasiatische Studien* 27: 99–120.

Kirkland, Russell. 2004. *Taoism: The Enduring Tradition.* New York: Routledge.

Kollmar-Paulenz, Karénina. 1994. "Ein mongolisches Wunschgebet um Wiedergeburt in Sambhala." *Ural-Altaische Jahrbücher* 13: 158–174.

———. 2001. *Erdeni tunumal neretü sudur: Die Biographe des Altan qaүan der Tümed-Mongolen.* Wiesbaden: Harrassowitz.

———. 2002. "The Transmission of the Mongolian Kanjur: A Preliminary Report." In *The Many Canons of Tibetan Buddhism,* ed. Helmut Eimer and David Germano, 151–176. Leiden: Brill.

Krueger, John R. 1969. "Three Oirat-Mongolian Diplomatic Documents of 1691." *Central Asiatic Journal* 12: 286–295.

Lamarre, Thomas. 2000. *Uncovering Heian Japan: An Archaeology of Sensation and Inscription.* Durham, NC: Duke University Press.

Langlois, John D., ed. 1981. *China under Mongol Rule.* Princeton, NJ: Princeton University Press.

Legrand, Jacques. 1976. *L'administration dans la Domination Sino-Mandchoue en Mongolie Qalq-a.* Paris: Institute des hautes études chinoises.

Leoshko, Janice. 2003. *Sacred Traces: British Explorations of Buddhism in South Asia.* Burlington, VT: Ashgate.

Lessing, F. D. 1942. *Yung-ho-kung: An Iconography of the Lamaist Cathedral in Peking.* Stockholm.

Lewis, Mark E. 1990. "The Suppression of the Three Stages Sect: Apocrypha as a Political Issue." In *Chinese Buddhist Apocrypha,* ed. Robert E. Buswell, Jr., 207–238. Honolulu: University of Hawai'i Press.

Ligeti, Louis. 1942. *Catalogue du Kanjur Mongol Imprimé.* Budapest.

———. 1981. *History of Buddhism in Mongolia.* New Delhi.

Li Narangoa. 1998. *Japanische Religionspolitik in der Mongolei 1932–1945: Reformbestrebungen und Dialog zwischen japanischem und mongolischem Buddhismus.* Weisbaden: Harrassowitz.

———. 2003. "Japanese Imperialism and Mongolian Buddhism, 1932–1945." *Critical Asian Studies* 35, 4: 491–514.

Lipman, Jonathan N. 1997. *Familiar Strangers: A History of Muslims in Northwest China.* Seattle: University of Washington Press.

Lopez, Donald S. 1995. "Introduction." In *Curators of the Buddha: The Study of Buddhism under Colonialism,* ed. Donald S. Lopez, 1–29. Chicago: University of Chicago Press.

———. 1998. *Prisoners of Shangri-La: Tibetan Buddhism and the West.* Chicago: University of Chicago Press.

———. 2002. *A Modern Buddhist Bible: Essential Readings from East and West.* Boston: Beacon Press.

Mackintosh-Smith, Tim. 2000. *Yemen: The Unknown Arabia.* New York: The Overlook Press.

Martin, Dan. 1990. "Bonpo Canons and Jesuit Canons: On Sectarian Factors Involved in the Ch'ien-lung Emperor's Second Goldstream Expedition of 1771–1776 Based Primarily on Some Tibetan Sources." *Tibetan Journal* 15: 3–28.

Masuzawa, Tomoko. 2005. *The Invention of World Religions: Or, How European Universalism Was Preserved in the Language of Pluralism.* Chicago: University of Chicago Press.

McRae, John R. 2003. *Seeing through Zen: Encounter, Transformation, and Genealogy in Chinese Chan Buddhism.* Berkeley: University of California Press.

Meyer-Fong, Tobie. 2003. *Building Culture in Early Qing Yangzhou.* Stanford, CA: Stanford University Press.

Miles, Steven B. 2004. "Celebrating the Yu Fan Shrine: Literati Networks and Local Identity in Early Nineteenth-Century Guangzhou." *Late Imperial China* 25, 2: 33–73.

Miller, Robert James. 1959. *Monasteries and Culture Change in Inner Mongolia.* Weisbaden: Harrassowitz.

Millward, James A. 1998. *Beyond the Pass: Economy, Ethnicity, and Empire in Qing Central Asia.* Stanford, CA: Stanford University Press.

———. 2002. "Review of *The Manchu Way.*" *Harvard Journal of Asiatic Studies* 62: 468–478.

———. 2004. "The Qing Formation, the Mongol Legacy, and the 'End of History' in

Early Modern Central Eurasia." In *The Qing Formation in World-Historical Time,* ed. Lynn A. Struve, 92–120. Cambridge, MA: Harvard University Asia Center.

Millward, James, et al. 2004. *New Qing Imperial History: The Making of Inner Asian Empire at Qing Chengde.* New York: RoutledgeCurzon.

Mitchell, Robert, and Nevill Forbes. 1914. *The Chronicle of Novgorod 1016–1471.* London.

Miyawaki, Junko. 1992. "Tibeto-Mongol Relations at the Time of the First Rje btsun dam pa Qutuγtu." In *Tibetan Studies: Proceedings of the 5th Seminar of the International Association of Tibetan Studies, Narita 1989,* ed. Ihara Shoren and Zuiho Yamaguchi, 599–604. Narita: Naritasan Shinsoji.

———. 1997. "The Birth of the Oyirad Khanship." *Central Asiatic Journal* 41: 38–75.

Morikawa, Tetsuo. 2001. "Manuscripts and Manuscript Families of the *Erdeni-yin Tobci.*" *Memoirs of the Toyo Bunko* 59: 49–86.

Moses, Larry. 1977. *The Political Role of Mongolian Buddhism.* Bloomington: Indiana University Press.

Mostaert, Antoine. 1934. "Ordosica." *Bulletin of the Catholic University of Peiping* 9: 67–72.

———. 1956a. *Erdeni-yin Tobci.* Cambridge, MA: Harvard University Press.

———. 1956b. "Matériaux ethnographiques relatifs aux Mongols ordos." *Central Asiatic Journal* 2: 241–294.

———. 1957. "Sur le culte de Saγang Secen et de son bisaieul Qutuγtai Secen chez les Ordos." *Harvard Journal of Asiatic Studies* 20: 534–566.

———. 1959. *Bolor Erike. Mongolian Chronicle.* Cambridge, MA: Harvard University Press.

———. 1961. "Annonce de la mort de l'Empereur Te-tsoung et de l'Impératrice douairière Ts'eu-hi aux Mongols de la bannière d'Otoγ (Ordos)." In *Studia Sino-Altaica,* ed. Herbert Franke, 140–155. Wiesbaden: Harrassowitz.

Mostaert, Antoine, and F. W. Cleaves. 1952. "Trois documents mongols des Archives secrètes vaticanes." *Harvard Journal of Asiatic Studies* 15: 419–506.

———. 1962. *Les Lettres de 1289 et 1305 des ilkhan Arγun et Öljeitü à Philippe le Bel.* Cambridge, MA: Harvard University Press.

Mukherjee, Aditya. 2003. *Imperialism, Nationalism and the Making of the Indian Capitalist Class 1920–1947.* Thousand Oaks, CA: Sage Publications.

Naquin, Susan. 2000. *Peking: Temples and City Life, 1400–1900.* Berkeley: University of California Press.

Narasun, S., and Bu. Öljeyibayar, eds. 1986. *Yeke Juu-yin soyul teüke-yin materiyal, vol. 2.* Dongxiang.

Nattier, Jan. 1990. "Church Language and Vernacular Language in Central Asian Buddhism." *Numen* 37, 2: 195–219.

———. 1991. *Once upon a Future Time: Studies in a Buddhist Prophecy of Decline.* Berkeley, CA: Asian Humanities Press.

Nayiraltu and Altan'orgil, eds. 1989. *Γadaγatu mongγol-un törö-yi jasaqu yabudal-un yamun-u Qauli jüil-ün bicig.* Öbör mongγol-un soyul-un keblel-ün qoriy-a.

Newman, John. 1995. "Eschatology in the Wheel of Time Tantra." In *Buddhism in Practice,* ed. Donald S. Lopez, 284–289. Princeton, NJ: Princeton University Press.

———. 1998. "Islam in the Kalacakra Tantra." *Journal of the International Association of Buddhist Studies* 21, 2: 311–371.

Nima. 1989–1991. "Kürze Darstellung über 'Laicing.'" Trans. Cimeddorji. *Zentralasiatische Studien* 22: 221–243.

Ochir, Ayudain. 2001. "On a Historical Source: Zasagtu Khan aimaɣ-un teüke." *Nomadic: International Institute for the Study of Nomadic Civilization,* p. 4.

O'Donnell, Lynne. 1999. "Mongolia: The Last Frontier Buddhists Are Battling Christians for Market Share in Post-Communist Mongolia." *The Australian,* December 4.

Okada, Hidehiro. 1967. "An Analysis of the Lament of Toɣon Temür." *Zentralasiatische Studien* 1: 55–78.

———. 1972. "Outer Mongolia in the Sixteenth and Seventeenth Century." *Ajia Afurika gengo bunko kenkyu* 5: 69–85.

———. 1984. "The Ordos Jinong in Erdeni-yin Tobci." *Journal of Asian and African Studies* 27: 155–162.

———. 1989. "Dayan Khan in the Battle of Dalan Terigün." In *Gedanke und Wirkung,* ed. W. Heissig and K. Sagaster, 262–270. Wiesbaden: Harrassowitz.

———. 1991. "Origin of the Caqar Mongols." *Mongolian Studies* 14: 155–179.

———. 1992. "The Yüan Seal in the Manchu Hands: The Source of the Ch'ing Legitimacy." In *Altaic Religious Beliefs and Practices,* ed. G. Bethlenfalvy et al. Budapest: Eötvös Loránd University.

———. 1993. "The Mongolian Literary Tradition in Early Manchu Culture." In *Proceedings of the 35th Permanent International Altaistic Conference,* ed. Chieh-hsien Ch'en, 377–386. Taipei: Center for Chinese Studies Materials.

———. 1995. "The *Bilig* Literature in the *Cinggis Qaɣan-u Cadig.*" *Mongolica* 6, 27: 456–471.

Ong, Aihwa. 2003. *Buddha Is Hiding: Refugees, Citizenship, the New America.* Berkeley: University of California Press.

Onon, Urgunge, and Derrick Pritchatt. 1989. *Asia's First Modern Revolution: Mongolia Proclaims Its Independence in 1911.* Leiden: Brill.

Orofino, Giacomella. 1997. "Apropos of Some Foreign Elements in the Kalacakratantra." In *Tibetan Studies: Proceedings of the 7th Seminar of the IATS, Graz, 1995,* ed. H. Krasser et al., 717–724. Vienna: Österreichische Akademie der Wissenschaften, 1997.

Orsi, Robert. 1997. "Everyday Miracles: The Study of Lived Religion." In *Lived Religion in America: Toward a History of Practice,* ed. David D. Hall, 3–21. Princeton, NJ: Princeton University Press.

Orzech, Charles D. 1998. *Politics and Transcendent Wisdom: The Scripture for Humane Kings in the Creation of Chinese Buddhism.* University Park: Pennsylvania State University Press.

Overmeyer, Daniel. 1999. *Precious Volumes: An Introduction to Chinese Sectarian Scriptures from the Sixteenth and Seventeenth Centuries.* Cambridge, MA: Harvard University Asia Center.

Pallas, P. S. 1980. Rpt. of 1776. *Sammlungen historischer Nachrichten über die mongolis-*

chen Völkerschaften. Ed. Siegbert Hummel. Graz: Akademische Druck-u. Verlags-anstalt.

Perdue, Peter C. 2005. *China Marches West: The Qing Conquest of Central Eurasia.* Cambridge, MA: Harvard University Press.

Petech, Luciano. 1950. *China and Tibet in the Early 18th Century.* Leiden: Brill.

———. 1983. "Tibetan Relations with Sung China and with the Mongols." In *China among Equals: The Middle Kingdom and Its Neighbors, 10th–14th Centuries,* ed. Morris Rossabi, 173–201. Berkeley: University of California Press.

———. 1990. *Central Tibet and the Mongols: The Yüan-Sa-skya Period of Tibetan History.* Rome: Istituto Italiano per il Medio Estremo Oriente.

Peterson, Derek R., and Darren R. Walhof. 2002. *The Invention of Religion: Rethinking Belief in Politics and History.* New Brunswick, NJ: Rutgers University Press.

Poppe, Nicholas. 1957. *Mongolian Monuments in the hP'ags-pa Script.* Trans. J. R. Krueger. Wiesbaden: Harrassowitz.

Porter, David. 2001. *Ideographica: The Chinese Cipher in Early Modern Europe.* Stanford, CA: Stanford University Press.

Powers, John. 1995. *Introduction to Tibetan Buddhism.* Ithaca, NY: Snow Lion.

Pozdneyev, A. M. 1977. *Mongolia and the Mongols.* Trans. Alo Raun. Bloomington: Indiana University Press.

Prothero, Stephen. 1996. *The White Buddhist: The Asian Odyssey of Henry Steel Olcott.* Bloomington: Indiana University Press.

Qasbiligtü, C. 1992. "Jingkini bayatur-un oboy-a sitügen-i erkesigülün takiysayar iregsen uyi-yurjin qariyan-u tuqai." *Yeke juu-yin soyul teüke-yin materiyal,* 6: 83–105. Dongxiang.

Ragnubs, Nima Dorjee. 2004. "The Third Panchen Lama's Visit to Chengde." In *New Qing Imperial History: The Making of Inner Asian Empire at Qing Chengde,* ed. James A. Millward et al., 188–198. New York: RoutledgeCurzon.

Ratchnevsky, Paul. 1954. "Die mongolischen Grosskhane und die buddhistische Kirche." In *Asiatica,* ed. J. Schubert and U. Unger, 489–504. Leipzig, 1954.

———. 1970. "Über den mongolischen Kult am Hofe der Grosskhane in China." In *Mongolian Studies,* ed. Louis Ligeti, 417–443. Amsterdam: B. R. Grüner.

Rawski, Evelyn S. 1998. *The Last Emperors: A Social History of Qing Imperial Institutions.* Berkeley: University of California Press.

Richardson, Hugh. 1958. "The Karmapa Sect: A Historical Note." *Journal of the Royal Asiatic Society,* 139–164.

Robertson, Jennifer. 1991. *Native and Newcomer: Making and Remaking a Japanese City.* Berkeley: University of California Press.

Robinson, David. 1999. "Politics, Force, and Ethnicity in Ming China: Mongols and the Abortive Coup of 1461." *Harvard Journal of Asiatic Studies* 59: 79–124.

Rossabi, Morris. 1988. *Khubilai Khan: His Life and Times.* Berkeley: University of California Press.

———. 1995. "Mongolia from Chinggis Khan to Independence." In *Mongolia: The Legacy of Chinggis Khan,* ed. Patricia Berger and Terese Tse Bartholomew, 25–49. New York: Thames and Hudson.

Ruegg, David S. 1991. "Mchod yon, yon mchod and mchodgnas/yon gnas: On the Historiography and Semantics of a Tibetan Religio-social and Religio-political Concept." In *Tibetan History and Language,* ed. Ernst Steinkeller, 441–453. Vienna: Arbeitskreis für Tibetische und Buddhistische Studien Universität Wien.

————. 1995. *Ordre spirituel et ordre temporel dans la pensée bouddhique de l'Inde et du Tibet.* Paris: Collège de France, Publications de l'Institut de civilisation indienne, Série in-8, Fasc. 64, 1995.

————. 1997. "The Preceptor-Donor (*yon mchod*) Relation in Thirteenth Century Tibetan Society and Polity, Its Inner Asian Precursors and Indian Models." In *Tibetan Studies: Proceedings of the 7th Seminar of the International Association of Tibetan Studies, Graz 1995,* ed. H. Krasser et al., 857–872. Vienna: Österreichische Akademie der Wissenschaft.

Sagaster, Klaus. 1967. *Nag Dban blo bzan c'os ldan. Subud Erike, ein Rosenkranz aus Perlen. Die Biographe des 1. Pekinger lCan skya Khutuktu.* Weisbaden: Harrassowitz.

————. 1970. "Die Bittrende des Kilügen Bayatur und der Cinggis-Khan-Kult." In *Mongolian Studies,* ed. Louis Ligeti, 495–505. Amsterdam: B. R. Grüner.

————. 1992. "Ein Ritual aus dem heutigen Cinggis-Heiligtum in Ordos." *Zentralasiatische Studien* 23: 150.

————. 1997. "The 'Real Support' (Jingkini Sitügen) of the Cult of Chinggis Khan." *Mongolica* 6, 27: 627–633.

Sárközi, Alice. 1993. "Mandate of Heaven: Heavenly Support of the Mongol Ruler." In *Altaica Berolinensia,* ed. Barbara Kellner-Heinkele, 215–221. Wiesbaden: Harrassowitz.

Sayinjiryal and Saraldai. 1983. *Altan ordun-u tayily-a.* Beijing: Renmin Chubanshe.

Schmid, Toni. 1954. "A Tibetan Passport from 1714." In *Reports from the Scientific Expedition to the North-Western Provinces of China under the Leadership of Dr. Sven Hedin: Contributions to Ethnography, Linguistics and History of Religion 6,* 59–65. Stockholm: Statens etnografiska museum, 1954.

Schopen, Gregory. 1991. "Archaeology and Protestant Suppositions in the Study of Indian Buddhism." *History of Religions* 31: 1–23.

Schubert, Johannes. 1953. "Das Wunschgebet um Shambhala." *Mittelungen des Instituts für Orientsforschung,* Band 1: 424–473.

Schuh, Dieter. 1976. "Wie ist die Einladung des fünften Karma-pa an den chinesischen Kaiserhof als Fortführung der Tibetpolitik der Mongolen-Khane zu verstehen?" In *Altaica Collecta,* ed. Walther Heissig, 209–244. Wiesbaden: Harrassowitz.

————. 1977. *Erlasse und Sendschreiben mongolischer Herrscher für tibetische Geistliche.* Monumenta Tibetica Historica Abteilung III, Band I. St. Augustin, 1977.

Sen, Sudipta. 2002. "The New Frontiers of Manchu China and the Historiography of Asian Empires." *Journal of Asian Studies* 61, 1: 151–177.

Sen, Tansen. 2003. *Buddhism, Diplomacy, and Trade: The Realignment of Sino-Indian Relations, 600–1400.* Honolulu: University of Hawai'i Press.

Seneviratne, H. L. 1999. *The Work of Kings: The New Buddhism in Sri Lanka.* Chicago: University of Chicago Press.

Serruys, Henry. 1959. *The Mongols in China during the Hung-wu Period (1368–1398)*. Brussels: Institut belge des hautes études chinoises.

———. 1962. "Early Lamaism in Mongolia." *Oriens Extremus* 10: 181–216.

———. 1966. "Additional Note on the Origin of Lamaism in Mongolia." *Oriens Extremus* 13: 165–173.

———. 1967. *Sino-Mongol Relations during the Ming II. The Tribute System and Diplomatic Missions (1400–1600)*. Brussels: Institut belge des hautes études chinoises.

———. 1970a. "A Mongol Prayer to the Spirit of Cinggis-Qan's Flag." In *Mongolian Studies*, ed. Louis Ligeti, 527–535. Amsterdam: B. R. Grüner.

———. 1970b. "Offering of the Fox: A Shamanist Text from Ordos." *Zentralasiatische Studien* 4: 311–325.

———. 1972/1973. "A Socio-political Document from Ordos: The Dürim of Otoɤ from 1923." *Monumenta Serica* 30: 526–621.

———. 1974a. *Kumiss Ceremonies and Horse Races*. Wiesbaden: Harrassowitz.

———. 1974b. "Two Mongolian Documents." *Harvard Journal of Asiatic Studies* 34: 187–189.

———. 1974/1975a. "A Genre of Oral Literature in Mongolia: The Addresses." *Monumenta Serica* 31: 555–613.

———. 1974–1975b. "Two Remarkable Women in Mongolia: The Third Lady Erketü Qatun and Dayicing-Beyiji." *Asia Major* 19, 2: 191–245.

———. 1975. *Sino-Mongol Relations during the Ming III. Trade Relations: The Horse Fairs (1400–1600)*. Brussels: Institut belge des hautes études chinoises.

———. 1976. "A Quarrel among the Noble Families of Üüsin Banner, Ordos." *Central Asiatic Journal* 20: 297–306.

———. 1977a. "Mongol Texts regarding an Anti-Christian Conspiracy in 1903." *Mongolian Studies* 4: 39–55.

———. 1977b. "Documents from Ordos on the 'Revolutionary Circles.' Part I." *Journal of the American Oriental Society* 97, 4: 482–506.

———. 1977c. "Mourning Regulations in Ordos, 1909." *Bulletin of the School of Oriental and African Studies* 40: 580–581.

———. 1979a. "Ongon-u Dabaɤa and other Place Names." *Études mongoles et sibériennes* 10: 91–120.

———. 1979b. "A Question of Land and Landmarks between the Banners of Otoɤ and Üüsin (Ordos), 1904–1906." *Zentralasiatische Studien* 13: 220–226.

———. 1980. "Smallpox in Mongolia during the Ming and Ch'ing Dynasties." *Zentralasiatische Studien* 14, 1: 41–63.

———. 1985a. "An Imperial Restoration in Ordos, 1916–1917." *Études mongoles et sibériennes* 16: 51–59.

———. 1985b. "A Prayer to Cinggis-Qan." *Études mongoles et sibériennes* 16: 17–36.

Sgrol-dkar et al. 1995. *Xizang lishi dangan huicui* [A collection from the historical archives of Tibet]. Beijing: Cultural Relics Publishing House.

Shepard, John R. 1993. *Statecraft and Political Economy on the Taiwan Frontier 1600–1800*. Stanford, CA: Stanford University Press.

Silk, Jonathan. 1994. "The Victorian Creation of Buddhism." *Journal of Indian Philosophy* 22: 171–196.

Skrynnikova, T. D. 1992/1993. "Sülde: The Basic Idea of the Chinggis-khan Cult." *Acta Orientalia Academiai Scientiarum Hungaricae* 46: 51–59.

Smith, Jonathan Z. 1990. *Drudgery Divine: On the Comparison of Early Christianities and the Religions of Late Antiquity.* Chicago: University of Chicago Press.

Smith, Paul Jakov, and Richard von Glahn. 2003. *The Song-Yuan-Ming Transition in Chinese History.* Cambridge, MA: Harvard University Asia Center.

Sodubilig. 1996. "Cing ulus-un jasaɣ-un ɣajar-aca baraɣun qoyitu-yin qotongcud-un bosulɣ-a-yi darungɣuyilaɣsan teyin-ü yeke juu-yin ciɣulɣan-du üjegülügsen nölüge." *Öbör mongɣol-un yeke surɣaɣuli-yin erdem sinjilegen-ü sedkil* 4: 90–100.

———. 1998. "Shan gan huimin qi yi qimen de yike zhao meng [Yeke Juu League during the Hui Rebellion in Shanxi and Gansu]." *Nei Menggu shida bao* 5: 63–68.

Solongɣod, L. Qurcabaɣatur. 1999. *Zum Cinggis-Qaɣan-Kult.* Osaka: National Museum of Ethnology.

Sommer, Deborah. 2004. "The Art and Politics of Painting Qianlong at Chengde." In *New Qing Imperial History: The Making of Inner Asian Empire at Qing Chengde,* ed. James Millward et al., 136–145. New York: RoutledgeCurzon.

Sørensen, Per. 1994. *Tibetan Buddhist Historiography. The Mirror Illuminating the Royal Genealogies. An Annotated Translation of the XIVth Century Tibetan Chronicle: rGyal-rabs gsal-ba'i me-long.* Wiesbaden: Harrassowitz.

Sperling, Elliot. 1987. "Lama to the King of Hsia." *Journal of the Tibet Society* 7: 31–50.

———. 1992. "Notes on References to 'Bri-Gung-pa - Mongol Contact in the Late Sixteenth and Early Seventeenth Centuries." In *Tibetan Studies. Proceedings of the 5th Seminar of the International Association of Tibetan Studies,* ed. Shoren Ihara and Zuiho Yamaguchi, 741–750. Narita: Naritasan Shinshoji.

———. 1994. "Rtsa-mi Lo-tsa-ba Sangs-rgyas grags-pa and the Tangut Background to Early Mongol–Tibetan Relations." In *Tibetan Studies. Proceedings of the 6th Seminar of the International Association of Tibetan Studies, Fagernes 1992,* ed. Per Kvaerne, 801–824. Oslo: The Institute for Comparative Research in Human Culture.

———. 1997. "A Note on the Chi-kya and the two Qi clans in Amdo." In *Les habitants du toit du monde. Études recueilles en homage à Alexander W. Macdonald,* ed. Samten Karmay and Philippe Sagant, 111–124. Nanterre: Societé d'Ethnologie.

———. 1998. "Awe and Submission: A Tibetan Aristocrat at the Court of Qianlong." *International History Review* 20, 2: 325–335.

———. 2001. "'Orientalism' and Aspects of Violence in the Tibetan Tradition." In *Imagining Tibet: Perceptions, Projections, and Fantasies,* ed. Thierry Dodin and Heinz Räther, 317–329. Boston: Wisdom Publications.

———. 2003. "Tibet's Foreign Relations during the Epoch of the Fifth Dalai Lama." In *Lhasa in the Seventeenth Century: The Capital of the Seventeenth Century,* ed. Françoise Pommaret, 119–132. Leiden: Brill.

Spiegel, Gabrielle M. 1983. "The Cult of St. Denis and Capetian Kingship." In *Saints and*

Their Cults: Studies in Religious Sociology, Folklore and History, ed. Stephen Wilson, 141–168. New York: Cambridge University Press.

Strickmann, Michel. 1990. "The Consecration Sutra: A Buddhist Book of Spells." In *Chinese Buddhist Apocrypha,* ed. Robert Buswell, Jr., 75–118. Honolulu: University of Hawai'i Press.

———. 2002. "Tantrists, Foxes, and Shamans." In *Chinese Magical Medicine,* ed. Bernard Faure, 228–281. Stanford, CA: Stanford University Press.

Strong, John S. 1983. *The Legend of King Asoka: A Study and Translation of the Asokavadana.* Princeton, NJ: Princeton University Press.

Struve, Lynn A. 1998. *The Ming–Qing Conflict, 1619–1683. A Historiography and Source Guide.* Ann Arbor, MI: Association for Asian Studies.

———. 2004. "Introduction." In *The Qing Formation in World-Historical Time,* ed. Lynn A. Struve, 1–54. Cambridge, MA: Harvard University Asia Center.

Szerb, János. 1985. "Glosses on the Oeuvre of Bla-ma 'Phags-pa: III. The Patron–Patronized Relationship." In *Soundings in Tibetan Civilization,* ed. Barbara Nimri Aziz and Matthew Kapstein, 165–173. Delhi: Manohar.

Tatár, Magdalena. 1976. "Two Mongolian Texts Concerning the Cult of the Mountains." *Acta Orientalia Academiai Scientiarum Hungaricae* 30, 1: 1–58.

Tatsuo, Nakami. 1984. "A Protest against the Concept of the 'Middle Kingdom': The Mongols and the 1911 Revolution." In *The 1911 Revolution in China: Interpretive Essays,* ed. Eto Shinkichi and Harold Z. Schiffrin, 129–149. Tokyo: University of Tokyo Press.

———. 1996. "New Trends in the Study of Modern Mongolian History: What Effect Have Political and Social Changes Had on Historical Research?" *Acta Asiatica* 76: 12–23.

Teiser, Stephen. 2000. "Perspectives on Readings of the Heart Sutra: The Perfection of Wisdom and the Fear of Buddhism." In *Ways with Words: Writing about Reading Texts from Early China,* ed. Pauline Yu et al., 130–145. Berkeley: University of California Press.

Teng, Emma Jinhua. 2004. *Taiwan's Imagined Geography: Chinese Colonial Travel Writing and Pictures, 1683–1895.* Cambridge, MA: Harvard University Asia Center.

Tsendinoi, A. D. 1999. *Istoriia Erdeni-dzu.* Moscow.

Tsering, Pema. 1978. "rNin ma pa Lamas am Yüan-Kaiserhof." In *Proceedings of the Csoma de Körös Memorial Symposium held at Matrafüred, Hungary 24–30 September 1976,* ed. L. Ligeti, 511–517. Budapest: Akademiao Kiado.

Tsyrempilon, Nikolai. 2003. "Gelugpa and the Qing Empire: A Union of Ideologies." Unpublished paper presented at the Central Eurasian Studies Conference, Indiana University, April 12.

Tucci, Giuseppe. 1949. *Tibetan Painted Scrolls.* 2 vols. Rome: Libreria dello Stato.

Tuttle, Gray. 1997. "Mongolian Incursions and Interactions with Tibetans in Amdo in the Latter Half of the Sixteenth Century." Unpublished paper read at the First International Conference of Amdo Studies, Harvard University.

———. 2005. *Tibetan Buddhists in the Making of Modern China.* New York: Columbia University Press.

———. Forthcoming. "A Tibetan Buddhist Mission to the East: The Fifth Dalai Lama's Journey to Beijing, 1652–1653." In *Tibetan Society and Religion: The Seventeenth and Eighteenth Centuries,* ed. Bryan Cuevas and Kurtis Schaeffer. Leiden: Brill.

Tweed, Thomas A. 1992. *The American Encounter with Buddhism 1844–1912: Victorian Culture and the Limits of Dissent.* Bloomington: Indiana University Press.

Uspensky, V. L. 1997. "The Tibetan Equivalents to the Titles of the Texts in the St. Petersburg Manuscript of the Mongolian Kanjur: A Reconstructed Catalogue." In *Transmission of the Tibetan Canon,* ed. Helmut Eimer, 113–176. Vienna: Verlag der Österreichischen Akademie der Wissenschaften. 1997.

Veer, Peter van der. 2001. *Imperial Encounters: Religion and Modernity in India and Britain.* Princeton, NJ: Princeton University Press.

Veit, Veronika. 1983. "Das Testament des Secen Qan Soloi (1577–1652)." In *Documenta Barbarorum,* ed. K. Sagaster and M. Weiers, 403–411. Wiesbaden: Harrassowitz.

———. 1990. *Die Vier Qane von Qalqa: Ein Beitrag zur Kenntnis der politischen Bedeutung der nordmongolishcen Aristokratie in den Regierungsperioden K'ang-hsi bis Ch'ien-lung (1661–1796) anhand des biographischen handbuchs Iledkil sastir aus dem Jahre 1795.* Weisbaden: Harrassowitz.

———. 1999. "The Ordos Banners according to the Iledkil Sastir of 1795." In *Antoine Mostaert (1881–1971) C.I.C.M. Missionary and Scholar, Volume One,* ed. Klaus Sagaster, 185–204. Leuven: Ferdinand Verbeist Foundation.

Vogelin, Eric. 1940–1941. "Mongol Orders of Submission to European Powers, 1245–1255." *Byzantion* 15: 378–411.

Wakeman, Frederic, Jr. 1985. *The Great Enterprise. The Manchu Reconstruction of Imperial Order in Seventeenth-Century China.* Berkeley: University of California Press.

Waley, Arthur. 1976. *Travels of an Alchemist.* Westport, CT: Greenwood Press.

Waley-Cohen, Joanna. 1998. "Religion, War, and Empire-Building in Eighteenth-Century China." *The International History Review* 20, 2: 336–352.

———. 2002. "Military Ritual and the Qing Empire." In *Warfare in Inner Asian History (500–1800),* ed. Nicola Di Cosmo, 405–444. Leiden: Brill, 2002.

———. 2003. "Changing Spaces of Empire in Eighteenth-Century Qing China." In *Political Frontiers, Ethnic Boundaries, and Human Geographies in Chinese History,* ed. Nicola Di Cosmo and Don J. Wyatt, 324–350. New York: RoutledgeCurzon.

Wang, Xiangyun. 2000. "The Qing Court's Tibet Connection: Lcang skya Rol pa'i rdo rje and the Qianlong Emperor." *Harvard Journal of Asiatic Studies* 60, 1: 125–163.

Wasserstrom, Steven. 1999. *Religion after Religion: Gerschom Scholem, Mircea Eliade, and Henry Corbin at Eranos.* Princeton, NJ: Princeton University Press.

Watson, James L. 1988. "The Structure of Chinese Funerary Rites: Elementary Forms, Ritual Sequence, and the Primary of Performance." In *Death Ritual in Late Imperial and Modern China,* ed. James L. Watson and Evelyn S. Rawski, 3–19. Berkeley: University of California Press.

Weiers, Michael. 1973. "Das Verhältnis des Ligdan Khan zu seinen Völkerschaften." In *Serta Tibeto-Mongolica,* ed. Walther Heissig, 365–376. Wiesbaden: Harrassowitz.

———. 1983. "Der Mandschu-Khortsin Bund von 1626." In *Documenta Barbarorum*, ed. K. Sagaster and M. Weiers, 412–435. Wiesbaden: Harrassowitz.

———. 1987. "Der erste Schriftwechsel zwischen Khalkha und Mandschuren und seine Überlieferung." *Zentralasiatische Studien* 20: 107–139.

———. 1988–1989. "Zum Verhältnis des Ch'ing-Staats zur lamaistischen Kirche an der frühen Yung-Cheng Zeit." *Zentralasiatische Studien* 21: 115–131.

———. 1989–1991. "Mongolenpolitik der Mandschuren und Mandschupolitik der Mongolen zu Beginn der dreissiger Jahre des 17. Jahrhunderts." *Zentralasiatische Studien* 22: 256–275.

———. 1994. "Die historische Dimension des Jade-siegels zur Zeit des mandschuherrschers Hongtaiji." *Zentralasiatische Studien* 24: 119–145.

———. 2000. "Die politische Dimension des Jadessiegels zur Zeit des Mandschuherrschers Hongtaiji." *Zentralasiatische Studien* 30: 103–124.

White, Richard. 1991. *The Middle Ground: Indians, Empires, and Republics in the Great Lakes Region, 1650–1815*. New York: Cambridge University Press.

Wilson, Stephen. 1983. "Introduction." In *Saints and Their Cults: Studies in Religious Sociology, Folklore and History*, ed. Stephen Wilson, 1–53. New York: Cambridge University Press.

Wittfogel, Karl, and Feng Chia-sheng. 1949. *The History of Chinese Society: Liao*. Philadelphia: American Philosophical Society.

Wu Hung. 1995. "Emperor's Masquerade—Costume Portraits of Yongzheng and Qianlong." *Orientations* 27, 7: 25–41.

Wylie, Turrell. 1977. "The First Mongol Conquest of Tibet Re-interpreted." *Harvard Journal of Asiatic Studies* 37: 103–133.

Yamaguchi, Zuiho. 1995. "The Sovereign Power of the Fifth Dalai Lama: sPrul sku gZims-khang-gong-ma and the Removal of Governor Nor-bu." *Memoirs of the Research Department of the Toyo Bunko* 53:1–28.

Yao, Wang. 1994. "The Cult of Mahakala and a Temple in Beijing." *Journal of Chinese Religions* 22: 117–126.

Yao Tao-chung. 1995. "Buddhism and Taoism under the Chin." In *China under Jurchen Rule*, ed. H. C. Tillman and S. H. West, 145–180. Albany: SUNY Press.

Yu, Renqiu. 2004. "Imperial Banquets in the Wanshu yuan." In *New Qing Imperial History: The Making of Inner Asian Empire at Qing Chengde*, ed. James Millward et al., 84–90. New York: RoutledgeCurzon.

Yu, Wonsoo. 1989. "The Five Hundred Shir-a Darqat Families in Ordos: 'People in Eternal Mourning for Chinggis Khan.'" Master's thesis, Indiana University.

Zerubavel, Eviatar. 2003. *Time Maps: Collective Memory and the Social Shape of the Past*. Chicago: University of Chicago Press.

Zieme, Peter. 1992. *Religion und Gessellschaft im Uigurischen Königreich von Qoco*. Opladen: Westdeutscher Verlag.

Zito, Angela. 1997. *Of Body and Brush: Grand Sacrifice as Text/Performance in Eighteenth Century China*. Chicago: University of Chicago Press.

Index

Abaga, 26, 38
Abakhai, 22, 56, 153
Abatai Khan, 23, 33–34, 58, 59, 109,
    203n60
Adai Khan, 52–53
Agwangdorji, Choiji Lama, 122–123
Alashan Mountain Banner, 63–65
Al-Kashgari, 141
Altan Khan, 9, 20, 22–23, 26, 34, 44, 54,
    61; and Buddhism, 44, 55, 93, 109,
    186nn62, 64, 196n47; and Buddhist
    pluralism, 102–104, 107, 111; con-
    version, 96, 101, 107–109, 110–112,
    126, 183n12; descendants of, 57,
    153; and Fourth Dalai Lama, 107;
    Law, 57; reign of, 42, 180n45; state
    of, 23; tomb, 112, 196n51; and
    translation, 124–125
Amarbayaskhulangtu, 61, 78
Amdo, 1, 113, 124, 158, 182n82, 191n35
Aokhan, 25, 28, 29; banner, 37
Appadurai, Arjun, 146
Arana, 206n4
Arbinbayar, 128
Asud, 29
Atwood, Christopher, 71, 80
Ayushi, 124

Baiju, 49
Baljur, 155, 158, 204n70
banner, 24, 29, 31, 38, 66, 72, 83, 92,
    120; bannerman, 6, 24, 34; Forty-
    Nine, 31, 37, 181n51; government,
    204n69; identity, 135, 150–152;
    Kökenuur, 190n23; and local iden-
    tity, 149, 152, 155–159, 162–164;
    Mongol, 24, 31, 152–155; rulers, 82;
    system, 17, 147, 191n30, 204n81;
    and transformation of ulus, 72, 84,
    88

Barsubolod Jinong, 151, 153, 161
Batu Khan, 49
Begtse, 107
Beijing, 1, 2, 51, 64, 74, 76, 81, 89, 91,
    104, 112, 118, 121, 122, 137, 149,
    197n77, 198n92
Beligbadarkhu, 127
Benedict the Pole, Brother, 49
Blue Annals, 113, 202n48
Board of Punishments, 143
Borjigid, 38, 53, 77, 87, 95, 152
Borobalgasu, 127–128, 134
Börte Chino-a, 96, 147
Boshugtu Jinong, 28, 57, 58, 61, 68, 153,
    189n9
Bosnia, 25
Boxer Rebellion, 128, 146
British Empire, 65–66, 80, 188n2
Buddha, 46, 54, 57, 72, 95, 112, 203n67;
    Jowo Sakyamuni, 40; Maitreya, 55
Buddhism, 2, 11, 13, 42, 58, 59, 60, 79,
    112, 173n7, 206n8; Chan, 47, 137;
    Chinese, 136, 206n4; and Chinggis
    Khan, 114–115; Gelukpa, 103, 120,
    122; and history, 109–116, 152–
    155, 162–164; and Islam, 139–142,
    201n37; and language, 123–126,
    198n88; and Mongol *ulus*, 99–101;
    Mongolian, 169–170; and the post-
    Yuan Mongols, 194n22; and Qing
    state, 93–94; and state, 3–5; Tibetan,
    12, 117, 120–123; and vernacular
    literature, 124–126, 198n88; West-
    ern view of, 173n7
Buddhist, 48, 60; "being Buddhist," 7, 12,
    100–102, 110; conversion, 12, 101–
    103, 107; pantheon, 95, 115–116;
    ritual, 114–120, 122
Buddhist explanation, 4, 6–7, 13, 14–16,
    29, 39, 93, 101, 168; origin of, 168;

problems with, 41, 44, 54, 61, 94, 126; and Qing state, 93

Buddhist Qing, 2, 12, 100–101, 134, 135, 168–169; and Dalai Lama, 104–109; and Gelukpa orthodoxy, 116–123; and history, 110–116, 135–139; identity, 89; and Islam, 141–142; and language, 123–126; and Mongolian Buddhism, 120; and rituals, 114–116; and sacred space, 116–120, 138; transethnic, 113, 134–135, 139–146, 152, 163

Buddhist rule, 4–6, 8–9, 11, 15, 16, 17, 48, 93, 101, 126, 183n6; explanation of, 183n6; and local elites, 118–120; and Mongols, 41–43, 46, 54–55; and Qing state, 103–110, 174n13; and the Yuan, 109

Buddhist Studies, 10–13, 168, 176n34, 177n46, 206n8

Bureau of Colonial Affairs, 7, 63, 66, 78, 85–87, 117, 127, 147; and banner borders, 203n57, 204n81. See also *Iledkil Sastir*

Buriats, 201n45

Burkhan Khaldun, 98

Büton, 202n48; *History of the Dharma*, 202n48

Byamba Erke Daiching, 135

Cakravartin, 6, 41, 54, 79, 92

Cambodia, 198n88

Cannadine, David, 65–66, 80

Carpini, Giovanni Plano di, 49, 50

Castiglione, Giuseppe, 190n25

Chagdurjab, 127

Chaghadai, 139

Chaghan Baishing, 96

Chakhar, 16, 28, 68, 100; and cult of Chinggis Khan, 40; khan, 20, 22, 29; *ulus*, 59

Charlemagne, 48

Chengde, 1–2

China, 7, 11, 13, 16, 19, 31, 115, 136, 154; Mongol rule in, 183n7; Western view of, 173n7

Chinese, 18, 134, 135, 137, 182n82; Bud-

dhist canon, 136; colonization, 128, 151, 160, 163, 166, 201n41; and Dalai Lama, 108; törö, 29; *ulus*, 39

Chinggis Khan, 3, 9, 12, 18, 21, 30, 44, 46, 61, 66, 155; *biligs*, 182n75; brothers of, 37; and Buddhist history, 90, 100, 111, 137, 167, 178n49, 199n15; conquest of Jin, 18–19; descendants of, 73, 109, 139; and imperial seal, 31, 92; and Islam, 145; and Kungga Nyingpo, 95, 137; lineage of, 20, 38, 114; and Mongol nobility, 147; policies, 22; seal of, 74; standard (*sülde*) of, 79, 115; as Vajrapani, 202n50. See also cult of Chinggis Khan

Chosgi Odzer, 45

Christianity, 48, 49, 50, 119, 134, 165, 175n15; in China, 200n20; Christians, 3; and nations, 95

Clear Mirror, 58, 113

Clovis, 100

communal identity, 6, 7

communism, 89, 192n68

Confucianism, 3, 48, 51, 173n7, 179n20

Constantine, 100

Croatia, 25

cult of Chinggis Khan, 41; and Buddhism, 114–115; Chinggis Khan Mausoleum, 192n68; and local identity, 157; and political authority, 48–56, 58, 59, 62, 180n32; and PRC, 89, 192n68; and Qing state, 75, 80, 82–89

Dalai Lama, 1–4, 37, 38, 75–78, 91, 101, 107, 110, 203n67; Second, 194n26; Third, 34, 42, 43, 55, 96, 101, 103; Fourth, 47, 107; Fifth, 2, 6, 47–48, 74; Fourteenth, 6; institution of, 195n41. See also Third Dalai Lama; Fifth Dalai Lama

Damchø Gyatsho Dharmatala, 203n59; *Rosary of White Lotuses*, 200n19

Daoism, 48

Darkhads, 85

Dayan Khan, 19, 30, 32, 37, 56, 68, 72; descendants of, 20, 21, 82, 135; and

Khalkha nobility, 135; state of, 19–20, 22, 29, 68, 180n32, 181n51
Dharma, 2, 47, 54, 56, 58, 75, 81–82, 89, 111, 112, 139, 167; critique of, 167; *Golden Wheel with a Thousand Spokes*, 81, 110, 196n47; and Islam, 140–141; and Mongol identity, 137–139; and political authority, 41–44
Dolonuur, 2, 174n10
duguilang, 160–161, 163
Durkheim, Emile, 8
Dzaya Pandita Lozang Trinlé, 195n32

Eight White Tents, 40–41, 48, 52, 58, 81, 87, 186n51, 187n80
elites, 32, 65, 68, 73, 75; transcultural, 70. *See also* Mongol; Mongol nobility
enfeoffment, 122
Erdene Juu, 203n60
Erinchen Sechen Jinong, 40–41, 45, 48, 68, 156, 182n3
ethnicity, 11, 15, 65, 89, 152, 176n38, 178n8, 205n3
Europe, 123
European Union, 15, 34

Fazlullah, Rashiduddin, 50, 193n16
Fifth Dalai Lama, 107, 115, 191n27, 194n31, 195nn41, 43; biographies of Third and Fourth Dalai Lama, 107; *History of Tibet*, 141; and Oirad, 195n32; and other lineages, 195n32; and Shunzhi emperor, 104–107. *See also* Dalai Lama
Five Banner Khalkha, 25, 29, 191n30
Five Treatises, 96
food, 141, 201n32; *halal*, 140, 200n34
France, 48, 89, 100; and Capetian kings, 48, 89

Gaikham-shigtu Üüle Monastery, 205n88
Galdan, 202n50; *Jewel Rosary*, 202n50
Galdan Boshugtu, 64
Galdan Khan, 111
Ganden Monastery, 107

Gelukpa, 1, 3, 74, 101, 157, 167, 168; Buddhist, 100; orthodoxy, 102–109, 116–123, 169; political role, 194n29; and Tibetan language, 123–126; Yellow Teaching/Religion, 61, 102
geography, 152–153, 203n62
God, 14, 18, 46, 50–51, 183n10; decree of, 43; God's blessing, 45, 47, 48, 50, 54, 56–57, 61, 74, 75, 81, 115; highest *(degere Tengri)*, 45, 184n17; will of, 42, 45
Golden Beam Sutra, 125
Golden Horde, 179n19
Golden Summary (Altan tobci, anonymous), 56
Golden Summary of Chinggis Khan, 9, 96
Gombojab, 81, 113, 197n58, 202n48; *Flow of the Ganges*, 81, 111; *History of Buddhism in China*, 112, 136
Gombowangjil, 137, 199n10; *Golden Rosary*, 137
Gonchugjab, 97; *Pearl Rosary*, 97, 99, 137, 145, 157, 158; *Shining Mirror*, 157
Gülüg Khan, 45
Gün Bilig Mergen Jinong, 153, 161
Gurkha war, 190n26
Güüshi Khan, 47, 63–64
Güyüg Khan, 49, 50, 51, 199n15

Haiyun, 137, 199n15
Han dynasty, 112
Heaven. *See* God
Heaven's mandate, 13, 17, 28, 47–48
History of the Yuan, 46, 51, 52
Hohhot, 108, 196n43
Holy Roman Empire, 100
Hong Taiji, 26, 35, 43, 61, 71, 74, 91; and banners, 25; and Buddhism, 75, 188n88; and Buddhist pluralism, 104; and imperial seal, 31; Manchu-Mongol relations, 28–29, 60; view of Buddhism, 118
Hui Muslims, 127, 142, 162

Ibarai Taishi, 22
Iledkil Sastir (Record of the Mongol and

Muslim Nobility), 66, 72, 74. *See also*
Bureau of Colonial Affairs
India, 11, 95, 96, 97; Indian royalty, 90
Injanashi, 198n94; and Buddhism,
198n94, 206n4; and Muslims,
202n47
Inner Mongolia, 2, 6, 10, 19, 37, 96, 151,
163, 167–168, 181n51, 182n82,
192n68
Ishidanjanwangjil, 206n4
Islam, 12, 196n52; and Buddhism, 139–
142, 201n37; Jahriya, 143; Khafiya,
143–144; and Qing state, 142–146;
Salafist, 142; *tajdid,* 142

Jangjia Khutugtu, First, 114; Second, 2
Jebdzundamba Khutugtu, 77, 78, 104,
195n32, 198n84; Eighth, 166
Jewel Translucent Sutra, 9, 52, 58, 62, 99,
102, 107, 112, 125; and Mongol
ulus, 94–96; on Muslims, 200n21;
on political authority, 44–46, 54–
56; and *ulus/törö,* 19
Jigmed-Rigbi-Dorji, 161; *History of Bud-
dhism in Mongolia,* 161
Jimbadorji, 139, 140, 200n20; *Crystal
Mirror,* 139, 145
Jirim League, 119
Jobiltai Khung Taiji, 28
Journey to the West, 113, 206n4
Junggar banner, 155
Jurchen, 14–15, 29, 35, 51, 69; Jin dy-
nasty, 18–19, 35

Kagyü, 104, 195n32; Karmapa, 103,
194n26
Kalacakratantra, 140–141, 200n34; origin of, 200n35
Kangxi emperor, 28, 63–64, 70, 111,
196n47; and cult of Chinggis Khan,
75–79; and Dalai Lama, 77–79; as
Manjusri, 78; and Mongol laws, 85;
and *ulus/törö,* 190n13
Kanjur, 58, 111, 124, 198n92
Kanjurwa Khutugtu, 122
Kapstein, Matthew, 12
karma, 45–46, 61, 109

Kazakhs, 139
Khabatu Khasar, 135, 136
Khalkha, 6, 10, 14, 16, 20, 26, 27, 32, 59,
76–79, 191n30; elite, 75; and fall of
Qing, 166–167; and Jebdzundamba,
104; Mongolia, 72; nobility, 76, 135,
167; relations with Manchus, 75–79;
rulers, 74; state, 33, 37; *ulus,* 33, 35,
58, 78
Kham, 1, 182n82, 191n35
Khanggin banner, 128, 182n3
Kharachin, 28, 61, 73, 135, 136; leader,
30; *otog,* 37; submission to Man-
chus, 135
Khesigbatu, 161, 162, 163; "Praise of Yellow Monastery," 162–163; *Precious
Summary of the Past and Present,* 161
Khorchin, 14–15, 20, 26, 33, 35, 37, 38,
51, 59, 60, 61, 70, 73, 93; banners,
17, 24, 29, 119; elite, 80; leader, 61;
nobility, 14; *otog,* 37; "Three
Deeds," 135; *ulus,* 6, 24, 26, 38
Khoshuud, 73, 74
Khubilai Khan, 3, 51, 74, 93, 101, 109,
111; and Buddhism, 42–44; and
Haiyun, 199n15; and Islam, 140
Khutugtai Sechen Khung Taiji, 43, 54,
68, 107, 154; as incarnation of Bim-
bisara, 203n67; and local identity,
153–155, 159–162; shrine, 160,
205n88; and Üüshin banner, 155–
159
Kileen Baatur, 52, 185n50
Kökenuur, 41, 103, 122; banners,
190n23
Korea, 7, 61, 69
Köten Khan, 46, 48, 111
Kumbum Monastery, 1, 158
Kungga Nyingpo, 12, 44, 95, 137
Kyrgyz, 23

Laikhur Khan, 23
Lama shuo. See Proclamation on Lamas
Latinization, 123
Lhasa, 73, 76, 118, 121, 194n26
Lhundub Bandita, 116
Li Zicheng, 91

Liao dynasty, 14
Ligdan Khan, 27, 28, 43, 59, 68, 95; and
   cult of Chinggis Khan, 87, 187n80;
   failure of, 29, 32, 34, 69, 109; and
   Kanjur, 124; and Sakya, 58, 104;
   White Stupa, 56
Light of Wisdom (Bilig-ün jula), 87, 111,
   136
Lomi, 87; History of the Mongolian
   Borjigid Lineage, 87, 136
Lubsangchoidan, 167
Lubsangchoirag, 158
Lubsangdanzin, 29; Golden Summary,
   107, 135
Lubsangdanzin (Khoshuud), 73

Ma Mingxin, 142
Mahakala statue, 188n88
Mahasammata, 90, 95, 97–98, 149, 167
Manchu: doro (state), 26, 32, 60, 69, 81,
   99, 112, 120; ethnicity, 112; gurun,
   24, 26, 35; oath of allegiance, 29;
   ulus, 27
Manchu emperor, 70, 72, 84, 150; and
   Buddhism, 111; and cult of Chinggis
   Khan, 78–82, 88; and Dharma, 78;
   imperial grace, 70–73, 80–82
Manchus, 20, 60, 69, 135, 138; and banners, 24; and Buddhism, 2, 3–4, 44,
   174n10, 188n88; conversion to Buddhism, 43; and history, 8; Mongol
   relations, 14, 16, 23–27; origin of,
   90–91; use of Buddhism, 44
mandalization, 118, 121–123
Ma-ni Bka'-'bum, 58
Mao Zedong, 6, 93, 94
Mayidari Juu, 195n44
Mecca, 140, 141, 142
Mergen Gegen, 113, 116, 120, 122, 123,
   135, 197n77; Golden Summary, 113,
   135
Mergen Jinong, 46
Ming, 20, 32–33; conquest of Yuan, 19;
   relations with Mongols, 23, 54, 104,
   180n36
modernity, 15, 205n3
Molan Khan, 56

Möngke Khan, 18, 50
Mongol: aristocracy, 85; bannermen, 34;
   banners, 24, 31; civil war, 20, 27,
   30, 34, 38, 59, 105, 109; elite, 66,
   68, 70, 75, 79–81, 117, 119, 124,
   134; histories, 3, 19, 29, 33, 38, 56,
   87, 103, 109, 117, 135, 136,
   179n27; identity, 7, 9–10, 21, 65,
   74, 109; political authority, 17, 38,
   46, 48, 54–58, 65, 76; rule, 47; society, 9, 27, 38, 73, 147, 203n55;
   sources, 2, 4, 7, 9, 20, 32, 70, 74,
   102
Mongol commoners, 134, 147, 159–162,
   165, 203n55
Mongol nobility, 20, 24, 38, 73, 99, 114,
   147, 150, 159–162, 165, 203n55;
   and Buddhism, 118–120; and Mongol ulus, 80–81, 82, 84, 87
Mongol ulus, 17–23, 26, 35, 37, 38, 70,
   79–82, 89, 115–116, 120, 137; and
   Buddhism, 99–101; and commoners, 134, 149, 159–162; and cult of
   Chinggis Khan, 80–85; and elites,
   74–75; and imperial grace, 72–75;
   and localization, 146–147, 162–165;
   and nobility, 134, 150; and Qing
   state, 95–96; and social hierarchy,
   147, 155–162
Mongolian Buddhism, 107, 120, 137,
   169–170
Mongol-Oirad war, 109
Mongols, 3, 21, 24, 27, 31, 59, 70; and
   Buddhism, 101–104, 112–116; and
   Gelukpa, 117–120; and political au-
   thority, 41–48; relations with Man-
   chus, 14, 16, 23–27, 39; and ulus/
   törö, 31–39; view of Manchus, 27–
   30
Mongols-of-the-Qing, 16, 37, 70, 73, 93
Mostaert, Antoine, 82, 156, 158, 159
Muhammad, 140, 141, 196n52
Mukden, 90, 188n88
Mukhali, 199n15, 205n92
Muna Mountain, 19, 52, 138, 185n50
Muslim, 48, 140, 165, 200n21, 202nn46,
   47; Hui, 127; rebellion, 127, 144,

162; ruler of Hami, 23; Turkic, 139. *See also* Islam

Muulikhai Ong, 56

Naiman, 25, 29
Namudai Sechen Khan, 61, 103
Naqshabandi Sufism, 142
Naxi, 108
Neichi Toin, 105–107, 120, 121; *Biography of Neichi Toin*, 106
New Qing History, 10–11, 176n40, 178n8
Ngakwang Kungga Sönam, 46
Nianchang, 47, 199n15
Nicholas II, 166
Norbusangbu, 119
Nurhaci, 14–16, 72; and Buddhism, 104, 188n88; and cult of Chinggis Khan, 81; relations with Mongols, 23, 24, 26, 29, 35, 179n22, 192n50

Ögedei Khan, 18
Oirad, 6, 10, 27, 32, 53, 60, 63, 139; and Buddhism, 195n32; elite, 75; homeland, 138; and Qing, 32; rulers, 74; state, 33
Olon Süme, 96, 125
Ooba Khung Taiji, 14–15, 23
Ööled, 92
Ordos, 23, 25, 34, 40–41, 68, 82, 99, 127, 135, 150, 153, 168; banners, 30, 41; communities, 22; elite, 80; leaders, 25, 56; nobility, 161; political addresses, 83–84, 150–151, 153–156; *ulus*, 32, 40, 153
ornamentalism, 62, 65–66, 72, 76, 83, 99, 100, 117, 122, 153
oron, 152, 203n65
Orsi, Robert, 11
otog, 181n51
Otog banner, 127–133, 168, 182n3
Outer Mongolia, 59, 61, 138, 166–167

Padmasambhava, 113
Pakpa Lama, 41–43, 45, 74, 111; *What Is to Be Known*, 101
Pallas, P. S., 102

Panchen Lama, 158; Second, 145; Sixth, 1–4, 6, 140, 142; Ninth, 202n46; and Muslims, 202n46; and Shambhala, 140, 142, 145
Pelliot, Paul, 49
People's Republic of China, 15, 89, 93–94; and minzu, 89; and *ulus/törö*, 190n19
People's Revolutionary Party of Inner Mongolia, 168
pluralism, 104, 107, 111
Polo, Marco, 52
Potala, 2
Proclamation on Lamas, 3

Qianlong emperor, 1–2, 6, 59, 61, 64, 93, 122; and Buddhism, 1–4; and cult of Chinggis Khan, 86; and Islam, 142–146; literary inquisition, 156; as Manjusri, 115, 118
Qing: rule, 41; Great Qing State, 30; *ulus*, 27, 35
Qing state, 6, 9–10, 12, 27, 32–33, 37, 73, 80, 99, 137, 156, 165; and Buddhism, 104–109, 112, 174n12, 175n16; and colonialism, 178n5; founding of, 92; and Islam, 143–144; and Mongols, 4, 21; technologies of domination, 7–8; and Tibet, 190n26; and Tibetan Buddhism, 120–123
Qinshi Huangdi, 31
qoyar yosu, 43–44, 46, 57, 183nn6, 13
Queen Mandukhai, 19

Ragbajamsan, 155, 204n70
Rashinamjil, 127
Rashipungsug, 59, 60, 82, 113, 121, 136; *Crystal Rosary*, 62, 80, 113; *History of Shireetü Güüshi*, 121
Rasulid Hexaglot, 18
Rinchenkhorlo, 167
Rome, 119
Rubruck, William of, 50

Saghang Sechen, 18, 40, 48, 56, 60, 68, 69, 70, 71, 81; and Buddhist expla-

nation, 29–30; on the Kangxi emperor, 189n6, 190n13; and local identity, 153–155, 159–162; *Precious Summary*, 18, 43, 52, 53, 79, 92–93, 107, 135, 156; and *ulus/törö*, 30–34, 190n13; and Üüshin banner, 155–159
Saint Regimus, 100
Sakya, 44, 58, 74, 104, 106, 195n32
Sakya Pandita, 44, 46, 48, 111
Samdan Sengge, 55
Samye Monastery, 138
Sangye Gyatso, 195n31
Scheut, 127; land dispute, 127–135
seal: bestowal of, 82–85, 192n55; imperial, 91; Jade Jewel, 30–31; and Manchus, 31
Sechen Khan Sholoi, 59, 61, 194n18
Secret History, 18, 96
Sengge Düüreng, 55
Senggerinchen, 4, 146, 161
Setsen Khan, 76–77
Shambhala, 140, 142, 144, 201n45
Shireetü Güüshi, 101; *Diamond Sutra*, 183n13, 193n13; *Üliger-ün dalai*, 193n13; *What Is to Be Known*, 101
Shunzhi emperor, 6, 31, 69, 74, 91; and Fifth Dalai Lama, 104–107
Six Great Ulus, 19–22, 25, 29, 30, 32, 54, 69, 180n32
social hierarchy, 64, 147, 188n2. *See also* ornamentalism
Sönam Gyatso. *See* Dalai Lama: Third; Third Dalai Lama
Song, Southern, 50
Songtsen Gampo, 58, 124
Suiyuan, 128, 163
Sükhebaatur, 201n45
Sumba Khambo, 203n62

Taglung, Kagyü, 102–103
Taiping, 144, 146
Taiwan, 65, 189n3
Tang dynasty, 9, 112, 197n71
Tengri. *See* God
third conversion, 126
Third Dalai Lama, 107; and Ayushi, 124;

and Chinese, 108; and Mongol conversion, 107–108, 111–112. *See also* Dalai Lama
Three Western Ulus, 20–22, 153
Tibet, 87, 93, 96, 97, 103, 113, 115, 121, 154; and Qing state, 191n35
Tibetan language, 117, 121–126
Tibetans, 2, 6, 69, 101, 135, 152, 182n82; and PRC, 94; view of Muslims, 202n46
Toghan Temür Khan, 32–33, 45, 52, 53, 57
törö, 17–19, 22, 30; Daiching, 32; Manchu, 37
Trashi Lhünpo, 2
Tsogtu Taiji, 95, 96, 104
Tsongkhapa, 105, 106, 137, 194n26
Tümed, 20, 25, 28, 34, 61, 73, 81, 93, 94, 99, 153; banner, 161; leader, 28; nobility, 22; Twelve, 25, 37; Ulus, 21, 108
Tümen Jasagtu Khan, 22–23, 43, 68, 69
Turfan, 141
Turk empires, 112–113
Tusalagchi Todai, 158

Üjümüchin, 71, 114
ulus, 17–19, 22, 29–30, 66, 67, 70; and banner, 31, 34, 72, 83, 92
ulus/törö: model, 57, 68, 74, 104, 190n13; system, 24–25, 30, 33–37, 61, 66–70, 72, 73, 81; theory of, 21, 23, 26–27, 31–39, 42, 58, 59, 62, 94, 101
United Nations, 26
Urad banner, 136
Urtukhai Ong, 37, 38, 74
Üüshin banner, 127–128, 153, 182n3; and Buddhism, 162–164; government, 204n69; and social hierarchy, 155–159; worship of ancestors, 204n77
Uygur, 45, 141
Uygurjin, 205n92

Vaisravana, 159

Weber, Max, 8

White History, 51, 54, 186n54, 188n90, 193n8
White Lotus, 102
Wu Sangui, 91
Wutai Shan, 118, 137, 138, 197n71

Xinjiang, 142, 152, 201n41
Xiongnu, 112
Xuanzang, 113

Yangzi, 103
Yeke Juu League, 127, 128, 150, 153, 163; leaders, 86
Yeke Juu Monastery, 111, 196n47
Yellow Temple, 2, 74
Yemen, 142, 196n52

Yongle emperor, 103, 137
Yuan dynasty, 19, 20, 26, 32, 41, 45, 74, 88, 179n23; and Buddhism, 109; emperors, 50; Mongol-Tibet relations, 183n8
Yugoslavia, 25, 26
Yüngshiyebü, 22, 153

Zaya Pandita, 195n32
Zhenjin, 101, 199n15
Zhikatsé, 1
Zhou dynasty, 113
Zhu Yuanzhang, 32–33, 45, 88
Zunghar, 10, 61, 64, 105, 136; Qing conquest, 142, 191; relations with Khalkha, 76; state, 37, 73, 74

About the Author

Johan Elverskog received his M.A. and Ph.D. from Indiana University. His research focuses on the history of Buddhism in Inner Asia, Mongol intellectual history and the cultural history of the Qing dynasty. Among his publications are *Uygur Buddhist Literature* (1997), *The Jewel Translucent Sutra: Altan Khan and the Mongols in the Sixteenth Century* (2003), *The Pearl Rosary* (2006) and numerous journal articles and essays in edited volumes. He is currently an assistant professor in the Department of Religious Studies at Southern Methodist University.